Ports Bishop

ARI BERMAN is a senior contributing writer for *The Nation* and a reporting fellow at the Nation Institute. His writing has also appeared in *The New York Times* and *Rolling Stone,* and he is a frequent commentator on MSNBC and NPR. His first book, *Herding Donkeys: The Fight to Rebuild the Democratic Party and Reshape American Politics*, was published in 2010. He lives in New York City.

ALSO BY ARI BERMAN

Herding Donkeys:
The Fight to Rebuild the Democratic Party
and Reshape American Politics

Additional Praise for *Give Us the Ballot*

"*Give Us the Ballot* makes a powerful case that voting rights are under assault in twenty-first-century America. Current events underscore the book's timeliness . . . [and] Berman buttresses his scathing indictment with extensive documentation." —Wendy Smith, *Los Angeles Times*

"*Give Us the Ballot* explores the struggle over voting rights unleashed by the civil rights revolution, and how it continues to this day. . . . Berman has performed a valuable public service by illuminating this history."
—Eric Foner, *The Nation*

"Comprehensive . . . The value of *Give Us the Ballot* lies in illustrating that the [Voting Rights Act] has never been universally accepted. . . . Ari Berman convincingly shows that the fight for voting rights is far from over."
—Jordan Michael Smith, *The Boston Globe*

"In *Give Us the Ballot*, journalist Ari Berman explores the increasingly sophisticated tricks devised to keep minorities out of the voting booth over the past half century . . . [and] helps us understand why we're still fighting over who gets to exercise this most basic of American rights."
—Rebecca Cohen, *Mother Jones*

"An extremely valuable and terribly timely history of the Voting Rights Act . . . Berman deftly weaves together the politics, the intellectual and legal arguments, the legislative battles, the counterrevolutionary schemes, and the tragic and ironic turns in the story." —Harvey J. Kaye, *The Daily Beast*

"Illuminating . . . *Give Us the Ballot* is a smart compendium of election 'reforms.' Berman removes the facade of intellectual honesty—where voting-rights opponents even bothered to make an argument—and lays bare the many, many ways to game the outcome of an election."
—Scott Porch, *Chicago Tribune*

"Berman's reporting is expertly balanced."
—Walton Muyumba, *The Dallas Morning News*

"The voting rights struggle of the 1960s produced several moments that remain seared in the nation's memory.... Ari Berman tells the story of these stirring moments, and tells it well. But unlike many civil rights chronicles, his account begins rather than ends in the 1960s.... It's an important and absorbing tale."   —Nicholas Stephanopoulos, *The New Rambler*

"*Give Us the Ballot* is a fascinating, if also infuriating, chronicle of the modern era in voting rights—a time when those hard-won rights are suddenly in great jeopardy. Comprehensive, fair-minded and wise, the book tells a haunting story of rights won and rights lost."

—Jeffrey Toobin, author of *The Oath* and *The Nine*

"Ari Berman's *Give Us the Ballot* explains that the VRA's fifty years have seen great gains but also consistent opposition. The specifics may have changed; the campaign to suppress turnout among minorities has not.... Read *Give Us the Ballot*."   —*Richmond Times-Dispatch*

"Incisive ... not just a compelling history, but a cry for help in the recurring struggle to gain what is supposed to be an inalienable right."

—*Kirkus Reviews* (starred review)

"Berman does a superb job of making the history of the right to vote in America not only easily understandable, but riveting.... This is the best kind of popular history—literate, passionate, and persuasive, balancing detail with accessibility."   —*Publishers Weekly* (starred review)

"Ari Berman's *Give Us the Ballot* is a must-read for anyone who cares about the health of American democracy. Written with a deep respect for history, a keen journalistic sensibility, and a visceral passion for fairness, Berman's book takes us on a swift and critical journey through the last fifty years of voting in America.... We have not yet arrived at the healthy democracy the 1965 Voting Rights Act promises is possible, but we have not given up hope. The struggle continues."   —Melissa Harris-Perry

GIVE US THE BALLOT

THE MODERN STRUGGLE FOR

VOTING RIGHTS IN AMERICA

ARI BERMAN

PICADOR FARRAR, STRAUS AND GIROUX NEW YORK

picadorusa.com • picadorbookroom.tumblr.com
twitter.com/picadorusa • facebook.com/picadorusa

Picador® is a U.S. registered trademark and is used by Farrar, Straus and Giroux
under license from Pan Books Limited.

For book club information, please visit facebook.com/picadorbookclub or
e-mail marketing@picadorusa.com.

Designed by Abby Kagan

The Library of Congress has cataloged the Farrar, Straus and Giroux edition as follows:

Berman, Ari.
    Give us the ballot : the modern struggle for voting rights in America / Ari Berman.
        p. cm.
    Includes index.
    ISBN 978-0-374-15827-9 (hardback)
    ISBN 978-0-374-71149-8 (e-book)
        1. Suffrage—United States—History—20th century.   2. Suffrage—United States—
    History—21st century.   3. Minorities—Suffrage—United States.   4. United States—
    Voting Rights Act of 1965.   I. Title.
    JK1846 .B47 2015
    324.6'20973—dc23

                                                                                2015004989

Picador Paperback ISBN 978-1-250-09472-8

Our books may be purchased in bulk for promotional, educational, or business
use. Please contact your local bookseller or the Macmillan Corporate and
Premium Sales Department at 1-800-221-7945, extension 5442, or by
e-mail at MacmillanSpecialMarkets@macmillan.com.

First published by Farrar, Straus and Giroux

First Picador Edition: August 2016

10 9 8 7 6 5 4

For Nora

The vote is the most powerful instrument ever devised
by man for breaking down injustice.

—LYNDON BAINES JOHNSON,
AUGUST 6, 1965

CONTENTS

GIVE US
THE BALLOT

PROLOGUE

Fifty years after he nearly died in the most important march in American civil rights history, Congressman John Lewis returned to Selma, Alabama, on March 7, 2015.

"Hail to the Chief" played as Lewis followed President Barack Obama and former president George W. Bush across Water Avenue in downtown Selma to a podium at the foot of the Edmund Pettus Bridge, named after a former Grand Dragon of the Alabama Ku Klux Klan. One hundred members of Congress, who accompanied Lewis on this civil rights pilgrimage, sat nearby on the blindingly sunny afternoon. A few Democratic senators, including Elizabeth Warren from Massachusetts, held signs that read, VOTING RIGHTS *ARE* CIVIL RIGHTS.

Luci Baines Johnson, the daughter of the former president Lyndon Johnson, sat a few feet away from Peggy Wallace Kennedy, the daughter of the former Alabama governor George Wallace. Their fathers had fought on opposite sides of the battle for civil rights.

Behind the dignitaries, sixty thousand people, some from as far away as South Africa, had converged on Selma to commemorate the fiftieth anniversary of the Bloody Sunday march. It was the largest crowd the small city of twenty thousand had ever seen.

"This city, on the banks of the Alabama River, gave birth to a movement that changed America forever," Lewis said. "Our country will never, ever be the same because of what happened on this bridge." He looked at President Obama. "If someone had told me, when we were crossing this bridge, that one day I would be back here introducing the first African-American president, I would have said you were crazy." The president rose and tightly embraced Lewis. He called the seventy-five-year-old congressman from Georgia "one of my heroes." Then he paid tribute to the Selma marchers.

"There are places and moments in America where this nation's destiny has been decided," the president said. "Selma is such a place. In one afternoon fifty years ago, so much of our turbulent history—the stain of slavery and anguish of civil war, the yoke of segregation and tyranny of Jim Crow, the death of four little girls in Birmingham, and the dream of a Baptist preacher—all that history met on this bridge."

After his speech, the president walked across the Edmund Pettus Bridge hand in hand with Lewis and Amelia Boynton, a one-hundred-three-year-old voting rights activist from Selma who had been beaten unconscious fifty years earlier. The children of Martin Luther King, Jr., marched behind them. The group sang, "Woke up this morning with my mind / Stayed on freedom," as they climbed the bridge. At the top, high above the Alabama River, Lewis grabbed a bullhorn and retold the story of Bloody Sunday.

In 1965, Lewis had walked this same route under far more treacherous conditions. King had called for a march from Selma to Montgomery, the state capital, to protest the death of twenty-six-year-old Jimmie Lee Jackson, who was shot by the police while trying to protect his mother after Alabama state troopers attacked a nighttime civil rights demonstration in Marion, Alabama. Jackson made six dollars a day as a woodcutter and was the youngest deacon in his church. He'd tried unsuccessfully to register to vote five times in Perry County, where only 265 of 5,202 eligible black voters were on the voting rolls. "Jimmie Jackson just wanted to vote," King said at his funeral. "Now we must see that Jimmie Jackson didn't die in vain."

Perry County adjoins Selma, the central front in the civil rights movement's campaign to win the right to vote across the segregated South. The Student Nonviolent Coordinating Committee (SNCC) had been trying to register voters there since 1963. It hadn't gotten very far. When SNCC arrived in Selma, only 156 of the county's 15,000 eligible black citizens were registered to vote. After two years of work, that number had inched up to a mere 335.

On the afternoon of March 7, 1965, Lewis, the twenty-five-year-old chairman of SNCC, threw an orange, an apple, a toothbrush, toothpaste, and two books (Richard Hofstadter's *The American Political Tradition and the Men Who Made It* and *New Seeds of Contemplation*, by the theologian Thomas Merton) into his green army backpack and headed over to Brown Chapel, the redbrick headquarters of Selma's civil rights movement. "We're marching today to dramatize to the nation and to the world," he told reporters outside the church, "that hundreds and thousands of Negro citizens of Alabama, particularly here in the Black Belt area, are denied the right to vote."

Lewis and six hundred marchers came face-to-face with an army of blue-helmeted Alabama state troopers when they reached the Edmund Pettus Bridge. Maj. John Cloud told them to advance no farther. He said they had two minutes to return to their church. Lewis and the others knelt to pray. After one minute and five seconds, the officers put on their gas masks, and, charging into the crowd, brutally clubbed the marchers. Lewis was hit first. When he curled up in the "prayer for protection" position, raising his left hand to shield himself, Lewis was clubbed again by the same state trooper across the left side of his head. He blacked out. "I lost all consciousness," he later said. "I saw death. I really thought I was going to die. I thought it was the last protest."

That evening ABC interrupted its prime-time premiere of *Judgment at Nuremberg* to show fifteen minutes of the horrific footage from Selma to forty-eight million Americans. Many confused viewers thought they were seeing images of Nazi Germany. There had been ample public outrage over atrocities committed against the civil rights movement—when four young girls were killed by a bombing at the Sixteenth Street Baptist Church in Birmingham in 1963 or when three young men were murdered by the Klan in Mississippi during Freedom Summer in 1964—but nothing before had the impact of Bloody Sunday.

Eight days later President Johnson introduced the Voting Rights Act (VRA) before a joint session of Congress. "It is wrong—deadly wrong—to deny any of your fellow Americans the right to vote in this country," the president said in his slow Texan drawl.

One hundred years after the end of the Civil War, the VRA guaranteed the franchise for black Americans and other minority groups and fulfilled the long-overdue promise of the Fifteenth Amendment of 1870, which states that the right to vote "shall not be denied or abridged by the United States or by any State on account of race, color, or previous condition of servitude." The VRA quickly became known as the most important piece of civil rights legislation in the twentieth century and one of the most transformational laws ever passed by Congress.

It suspended literacy tests across the South, authorized the U.S. attorney general to file lawsuits challenging the poll tax, replaced recalcitrant registrars with federal examiners, dispatched federal observers to monitor elections, forced states with the worst histories of voting discrimination to clear electoral changes with the federal government to prevent future discrimination, and laid the foundation for generations of minority elected officials.

The results were almost unimaginable in 1965. In the subsequent decades, the number of black registered voters in the South increased from 31 percent to 73 percent; the number of black elected officials increased from fewer than 500 to 10,500 nationwide; the number of black members of Congress increased from 5 to 44. The four congressional reauthorizations of the VRA lowered the voting age to eighteen, eliminated literacy tests nationwide, and expanded protections for language-minority groups like Hispanics in Texas, Asian-Americans in New York, and Native Americans in Arizona. The VRA became the prime vehicle for expanding voting rights for all Americans.

Because of the law, John Lewis won election to the U.S. House of Representatives, representing Martin Luther King's hometown for nearly three decades. He became known as the "conscience of the Congress."

"When Lyndon Johnson signed the Voting Rights Act," Lewis said, "he helped free and liberate all of us."

Lewis's return to Selma in 2015 should have been a triumphant occasion—a testament to the momentous progress achieved since 1965. Despite the many civil rights victories in the years since Bloody Sunday, however, the mood in Selma was more anxious. As Obama noted in his speech, the VRA, "one of the crowning achievements of our democracy," now stood "weakened, its future subject to political rancor."

The president asked a question that many in Selma had been struggling to answer: "How can that be?"

Two years earlier, Lewis sat inside the Supreme Court, in the first row of spectators, and listened as the justices debated a challenge to Section 5 of the VRA, which he called the "heart and soul" of the law. The case originated in Shelby County, Alabama, just fifty-five miles north of Selma.

Section 5 compelled parts or all of sixteen states where voting discrimination was historically most prevalent, primarily in the South, to have their voting changes approved by the federal government. It was the VRA's most important enforcement provision, the tool that allowed the federal government to ensure that the law did not meet the same cruel fate as Reconstruction, which lasted only twelve years before federal troops pulled out of the South. The genius of the law, Chief Justice Earl Warren wrote in 1966, was to "shift the advantage of time and inertia from the perpetrators of the evil to its victims."

Since 1965 the Justice Department and federal courts had stopped more than three thousand discriminatory voting changes from taking effect under Section 5. Lewis had filed an amicus brief with the Court, noting "the high price many paid for the enactment of the Voting Rights Act and the still higher cost we might yet bear if we prematurely discard one of the most vital tools of our democracy."

The controversial provision had been challenged since its inception. It covered a wide scope of voting changes, from the moving of a polling place to the drawing of lines for nearly every elected office. Once minority voters had registered in large numbers following passage of the law in 1965, Section 5 gave the federal government unique power to preemptively block the "second-generation" voting restrictions frequently employed by white southern legislators to subvert the power of the growing minority vote. "The Act gives a broad interpretation to the right to vote, recognizing that voting includes 'all action necessary to make a vote effective,'" Earl Warren wrote in the landmark 1969 decision *Allen v. State Board of Elections*. That included the right to political representation for long-disenfranchised minority groups.

That decision, opponents of the law argued, gave the VRA a power far beyond what Congress intended when it struck down the literacy tests and related devices that prevented African-Americans from registering to vote. The VRA had become "a tool for guaranteeing minority groups maximum electoral effectiveness," wrote the conservative intellectual Abigail Thernstrom. In her influential 1987 book *Whose Votes Count?*, she dubbed the VRA "an instrument for affirmative action in the electoral sphere."

The question of whether the VRA should simply provide access to the ballot, as Thernstrom believed, or police a much broader scope of the election system, which included encouraging greater representation for African-Americans and other minority groups, as Warren held, was to define the debate over voting rights in the decades after the *Allen* decision. Thernstrom likened the VRA to a "curfew imposed in the wake of the riot." The riot was now over, she argued, and it was time for the federal government to stop telling states how to run their elections.

The Supreme Court had changed radically since the Warren years, moving far to the right. The five conservative justices on the Roberts Court embraced Thernstrom's critique, viewing Section 5 as an antiquated infringement on state sovereignty, treating some states differently from others on the basis of a history of voting discrimination no longer relevant in a country where a black man could be elected president. "The Marshall Plan was very good, too," said Justice Anthony Kennedy, "but times change."

To Justice Antonin Scalia, the overwhelming congressional support for the VRA, most recently in 2006, when Congress reauthorized the act for another twenty-five years by a vote of 390–33 in the House and 98–0 in the Senate, was proof of its unconstitutionality. "Even the name of it is wonderful: The Voting Rights Act," he said facetiously. "Who is going to vote against that in the future?" The hushed courtroom gasped audibly when Scalia attributed support for the law to "a phenomenon that is called perpetuation of racial entitlement."

Lewis couldn't believe what he was hearing. A majority of the Court ignored 250 years of slavery in America, 90 years of Jim Crow, and nearly 50 years of persistent attempts to subvert the VRA. "I was taken aback that it appeared to me that several members of the Court didn't have a sense of the history, what brought us to this point, and not just the legislative history and how it came about," he said after the oral argument. "They seemed to be somewhat indifferent to why people fought so hard and so long to get the act passed in the first place."

It was a day of deep contradictions for Lewis. As he sat in the Supreme Court, a few hundred yards away at the U.S. Capitol, Congress unveiled a new statue of the civil rights leader Rosa Parks, one of Lewis's idols. The six-hundred-pound bronze statue of a sitting Parks rested just south of where Lyndon Johnson had announced the signing of the VRA. The stark contrast illustrated the split personality of American democracy when it came to race and political power: a nation simultaneously founded on liberty and slavery, where racial progress has always been met by equally intense efforts to roll back that progress.

Parks was an invited guest when Johnson signed the VRA on August 6, 1965. Twelve years before famously refusing to move to the back of a segregated bus in Montgomery, she attempted to register to vote. She was denied three times and had to pass a literacy test and pay a poll tax in 1945 just to exercise what should have been her birthright. Parks and King inspired Lewis to join the civil rights movement. The 2006 reauthorization of the VRA by Congress was named after her, the Mississippi civil rights leader Fannie Lou Hamer, and Coretta Scott King.

Four months after Congress honored Parks, the Supreme Court issued a 5–4 opinion, written by Chief Justice John Roberts, invalidating Section 4 of the VRA, the formula that determined which states had to approve their voting changes under Section 5. As a result, no states were now subject to Section 5. The Old Confederacy had been freed from federal oversight.

"In 1965," Roberts wrote, "the States could be divided into those with a recent history of voting tests and low voter registration and turnout and those without those characteristics. Congress based its coverage formula on that distinction. Today the Nation is no longer divided along those lines, yet the Voting Rights Act continues to treat it as if it were."

Lewis watched the news from his Washington office, his two TVs mounted above a bust of LBJ. "I'm in disbelief," he said. "This is a very sad and dark moment for our democracy." The Court, he said, had "put a dagger into the very heart of the Voting Rights Act." It had eviscerated his signature achievement. Forty-eight years after Bloody Sunday, Lewis was once again in the fight of his life.

The Selma march and adoption of the VRA are widely regarded as the climax of the civil rights movement. "Selma was the last act," Lewis wrote in his memoir, *Walking with the Wind*. But the VRA didn't end the debate over voting rights; it started a new one. After all, it took decades of court battles, grassroots organizing efforts, and groundbreaking political campaigns to protect and expand the right to vote in the wake of the VRA. The law profoundly changed American politics: the South flipped from Democrat to Republican, minority voters emerged as a major electoral force, and the courts, the Congress, and the presidency shifted as a consequence.

As the Supreme Court's decision in *Shelby County v. Holder* indicated, the revolution of 1965 spawned an equally committed group of counterrevolutionaries. They did not see Selma as the last act. Since the VRA's passage, they have waged a decades-long campaign to restrict voting rights. They have served in the highest echelons of power and, in recent years, controlled a majority on the Supreme Court. They have set their sights on undoing the accomplishments of the 1960s civil rights movement, including the VRA. The voting rights revolution and counterrevolution have been intertwined.

There have been countless books written about the civil rights movement, but far less attention has been paid to what happened after the dramatic passage of the VRA in 1965 and the turbulent forces it unleashed. This book will tell that story for the first time.

The fight over the right to vote sharply intensified after Barack Obama's election, the pinnacle of the VRA's success. Obama not only won 365 electoral votes in 2008 but he also carried three states of the former Confederacy, where he would not have been able to vote until 1965. After Obama's victory, 395 new voting restrictions were introduced in 49 states from 2011 to 2015. Following the Tea Party's triumph in the 2010 elections, half the states in the country, nearly all of them under Republican control—from Texas to Wisconsin to Pennsylvania—passed laws making it harder to vote. The sudden escalation of efforts to curb voting rights most closely resembled the Redemption period that ended Reconstruction, when every southern state adopted devices like literacy tests and poll taxes to disenfranchise African-American voters.

The new restrictions were subtler than those of the 1890s or 1960s, camouflaging efforts to deter voting with laws that rarely invoked race, introduced with equal fervor in North and South alike. They included requiring proof of citizenship to register to vote, shutting down voter registration drives, curtailing early voting, disenfranchising ex-felons, purging the voter rolls, and mandating government-issued photo IDs to cast a ballot. These moves disproportionately targeted the "coalition of the ascendant"—young people, blacks, Hispanics, women—that propelled Obama to victory in 2008. The NAACP's president, Benjamin Jealous, called these collective efforts "the greatest attacks on voting rights since segregation."

Many of these laws were blocked in court during the 2012 election and helped inspire a backlash among minority voters. For the first time in presidential history, black turnout exceeded white turnout as a percentage in 2012. But the widespread push to restrict voting rights for millions of Americans was not a one-off phenomenon, nor did Obama's reelection silence the debate. As the country continued to change demographically, efforts to restrict the right to vote would become more routine and sophisticated.

The Supreme Court's ruling overturning Section 4 of the VRA, issued eight months after Obama's reelection, underscored the fact that what should be the most settled right in American democracy—the right to vote—remains the most contested. For a country that is famous for exporting democracy across the globe and has branded itself as the shining city on the hill, the United States has a shameful history when it comes to embracing one of its most basic rights at home. In 1787, when the founders ratified the Constitution, only white male property owners could vote in the eleven states of the Union. In 1865, at the end of the Civil War, black men could cast a ballot freely in only five states. Women couldn't vote until 1920.

The remarkably brief Reconstruction period of 1865–1877, when there were twenty-two black members of Congress from the South and six hundred black state legislators, was followed by ninety years of Jim Crow rule. The United States is the only advanced democracy that has ever enfranchised, disenfranchised, and then reenfranchised an entire segment of the population. Despite our many distinctions as a democracy, the enduring debate over who can and cannot participate in it remains a key feature of our national character.

"Our history," the Harvard University historian Alexander Keyssar testified before Congress in 2006, "makes plain that the right to vote can be as fragile as it is fundamental." Half a century after the passage of the VRA, the fragility of the right to vote is all too evident.

1

THE SECOND EMANCIPATION

In December 1964, Lyndon Johnson was in a jubilant mood. He'd just routed Barry Goldwater by twenty-three points, winning 486 electoral votes to Goldwater's 52, the most lopsided victory in U.S. presidential history to date. Five months earlier, on his daughter Luci's seventeenth birthday, he'd signed the Civil Rights Act of 1964, a sweeping law that desegregated schools, restaurants, hotels, parks, and many other public places. When John F. Kennedy's advisers urged LBJ not to push the bill following the assassination, the new president replied, "Well, what the hell's the presidency for?"

Johnson's commitment to civil rights surprised his critics on the left and the right. He was the first southern president since the Civil War. His first vote in the House of Representatives in 1937 came against an anti-lynching law. His first major speech in the Senate was a defense of the filibuster, which had been used so often by southern Democrats to block civil rights legislation. He'd voted against every civil rights bill in Congress from 1937 to 1956. JFK put him on the ticket to win the southern segregationist vote.

Yet LBJ hadn't had a change of heart so much as a change of circumstances and constituency. He was no longer a congressman or senator from Texas, but the president of the United States. He was now free to say what he believed.

Johnson could be crude and manipulative, but he was also unexpectedly compassionate. After graduating from Texas State University–San Marcos, LBJ taught fifth through seventh grades at a segregated Mexican-American school in the south Texas town of Cotulla, where his students showed up barefoot because they were too poor to afford shoes. LBJ cried when he told the story. "It was a genuinely uncontrolled emotion," said Deputy Attorney General Ramsey Clark, a fellow Texan. "It was pretty deep and pretty impressive."

Now Johnson wanted to cement the civil rights revolution by giving African-Americans and other long-disenfranchised minority groups the right to vote, a goal that previous civil rights legislation in 1957, 1960, and 1964 had not accomplished. The ballot, the president believed, would give Mexican-Americans in Cotulla and blacks in Selma the power to change their circumstances. The vote was "the meat in the coconut," he liked to say.

"I want you to undertake the greatest midnight legislative drafting that has happened since Corcoran and Cohen wrote the Holding Company Act," the president instructed the acting attorney general, Nicholas Katzenbach, on December 14, 1964, referring to an obscure New Deal bill in 1935 regulating electric utilities that was written by two senior aides to Franklin Roosevelt. LBJ wanted "a simple, effective method of gettin' 'em registered." He urged Katzenbach and the top lawyers in the Justice Department to "scratch their tails" and "get me some things you'd be proud of, to show your boy, and say, 'Here is what your daddy put through in nineteen sixty-four, -five, -six, -seven.'"

Katzenbach, who'd succeeded Robert Kennedy as the nation's top law enforcement official after Johnson's archrival left to run for the U.S. Senate in New York in the summer of 1964, was not thrilled with the new assignment. He'd spent eight months on Capitol Hill lobbying for the Civil Rights Act, which endured a fifty-seven-day filibuster by southern Democrats, the longest in Senate history. The office of Senate Minority Leader Everett Dirksen of Illinois had practically become his second home. Strong voting rights provisions were stripped from the bill to win congressional support.

"The 1964 Civil Rights Act was exhausting," said Ramsey Clark. "It about expended our goodwill with the Senate and the House. President Johnson insisted we were going to have another round of civil rights legislation, this time on voting . . . There was no enthusiasm in the Justice Department, but Johnson insisted on it."

At the end of December, after consulting with lawyers from the Appeals and Research Section at the DOJ, Katzenbach sent LBJ three options, in order of preference, "to overcome voter apathy and discrimination." Katzenbach's top choice, a constitutional amendment prohibiting states from employing devices like literacy tests and poll taxes that disenfranchised minority voters, "would be the most drastic but probably the most effective of all the alternatives," he wrote. It was also the most "cumbersome," he admitted, because a constitutional amendment needed to be ratified by two-thirds of Congress and three-fourths of states. The second option would be to create a federal commission that would appoint federal officers to register voters for federal elections. The third option would be for the federal government "to assume direct control of registration for voting in both federal and state elections in any area where the percentage of potential Negro registrants actually registered is low."

Civil rights activists favored the last option. "This approach would quickly provide political power to Negroes in proportion to their actual numbers in areas in which they are now disenfranchised," Katzenbach wrote. "On the other hand, its effects on general voter apathy would be relatively minimal . . . Moreover, its constitutionality is more dubious than that of the preceding suggestion."

In his State of the Union address a week later, Johnson vowed to "eliminate every remaining obstacle to the right and the opportunity to vote." Inside the White House, a debate raged among Johnson's inner circle over how and when to push voting rights legislation. "Certainly I have absolutely no problem with the desirability of such legislation, but I do have a problem about the timing and the approach," Lee White, one of LBJ's top advisers on civil rights, wrote to the special assistant Bill Moyers on December 30, 1964. The Civil Rights Act was less than a year old, White argued, and the prospects for passing voting rights legislation did not look particularly favorable. White proposed that 1965 "be a year of test" on civil rights.

Horace Busby, a Johnson aide since 1946 from Texas, was less charitable. "To southern minds and mores," he wrote to White and Moyers, "the proposals of this message would represent a return to Reconstruction."

The mercurial Johnson wanted to keep his legislative options open. Four days after talking with Katzenbach, LBJ met at the White House with Martin Luther King, Jr., who'd been awarded the Nobel Peace Prize that week. King told Johnson that he would soon be launching a voting rights campaign in Selma, where only 2 percent of blacks were registered to vote. He asked the president for his support.

"Martin, you are right about that," Johnson replied. "I'm going to do it eventually, but I can't get voting rights through in this session of Congress." The president's ambitious Great Society agenda took priority. "I need the votes of the southern bloc to get these other things through," Johnson said. "And if I present a voting rights bill, they will block the whole program. So it's just not the wise and the politically expedient thing to do."

King left the meeting dispirited. His voter registration drive in Selma would be aimed as much at the federal government as at the segregated South. "I think we've got to find a way to get this president some power," King told Andrew Young as they departed the White House.

The Alabama senator William Rufus King founded Selma in 1820, naming it after the Ossian poem *The Songs of Selma*, about a town on the high bluffs above a river. "Selma," wrote the historian and LBJ adviser Eric Goldman, "was straight out of a thousand novels about the unreconstructed South, lovely to look at and ugly just beneath the surface." In the 1800s, white planters flocked to the Black Belt, which spanned from Texas to eastern Virginia, to grow cotton in its rich soil, bringing with them many slaves. Selma became a major slave-trading port. The city passed twenty-seven ordinances regulating the behavior of slaves, stipulating, for example, that "any Negro found upon the streets of the city smoking a cigar or pipe or carrying a walking cane must be on conviction punished with 39 lashes."

During the Civil War, Selma manufactured weapons for the Confederacy and was commanded by Gen. Nathan Bedford Forrest, the first Grand Dragon of the Ku Klux Klan. The city was torched during the Battle of Selma in April 1865 and occupied during Reconstruction, when federal troops registered seven hundred thousand emancipated slaves across the South from 1867 to 1868. Following the Civil War, Selma elected numerous black officials, including two congressmen and thirteen state legislators.

Reconstruction prompted a vicious white backlash, which gained traction following the disputed election of 1876, when the Republican Rutherford B. Hayes pulled federal troops out of the South in return for the electoral votes of Florida, South Carolina, and Louisiana. Segregationist whites, known as Redeemers, regained power and quickly targeted black voters, first through violence and fraud and then via devices like literacy and good character tests, poll taxes, and stringent residency requirements. Mississippi became the first state to change its constitution to disenfranchise black voters in 1890. Every other southern state quickly followed. Black voters disappeared seemingly overnight.

"When you pay $1.50 for a poll tax, in Dallas County, I believe you disenfranchise 10 Negroes," Henry Fontaine Reese, a delegate from Selma, argued at Alabama's Constitutional Convention of 1901. "Give us this $1.50 for educational purposes and for the disenfranchisement of a vicious and useless class." Reese represented what Ralph McGill of the *Atlanta Constitution* called "Black Belt thinking," which infected not only Selma but so much of the South. After adoption of the 1901 constitution, the number of black registered votes in Alabama fell from 182,000 to 4,000.

Following the Supreme Court's *Brown v. Board of Education* ruling in 1954 ordering the desegregation of public schools, Selma became the Alabama headquarters of the White Citizens' Council, regarded by civil rights activists as the white-collar Klan, which maintained segregation through political and economic power. The city embodied the southern Democratic policy of massive resistance to civil rights. Its native sons included the Birmingham sheriff, Bull Connor, and the Dallas County sheriff, Jim Clark, who vied for the title of Alabama's most tyrannical segregationist. Clark fashioned himself after Gen. George Patton, carried a cattle prod as a weapon against civil rights activists, and wore a black-and-white pin that read "Never" ("Clark's rejoinder to 'We Shall Overcome,'" wrote *Ramparts* magazine). The Dallas County board of registrars used every device imaginable to keep black voters off the rolls, most notably a literacy test that required them to name all sixty-seven county judges in the state.

Two days after the passage of the Civil Rights Act of 1964, Sheriff Clark arrested four SNCC workers for trying to desegregate the Thirsty Boy drive-in restaurant. Days later Clark arrested John Lewis (his thirty-seventh arrest) and seventy blacks who attempted to register to vote at the Dallas County Courthouse, on one of the two days each month the board of registrars was open. The Circuit Court judge James Hare, who compared blacks with "backward" jungle tribes in his courtroom, issued an injunction banning any meeting of three or more African-Americans in Selma, which effectively ended all civil rights protests.

King had come to Selma to challenge that injunction. "Today marks the beginning of a determined, organized, mobilized campaign to get the right to vote everywhere in Alabama," King told a packed house at Brown Chapel on January 2, 1965, the 102nd anniversary of the Emancipation Proclamation. "If we are refused, we will appeal to Governor George Wallace. If he refuses to listen, we will appeal to the legislature. If they don't listen, we will appeal to the conscience of the Congress in another dramatic march on Washington." He repeated the refrain from his first major speech on voting rights in 1957 at the Lincoln Memorial: "Give us the ballot."

Beginning on January 18, SNCC and King's Southern Christian Leadership Conference (SCLC) teamed up to lead joint voter registration marches to the Dallas County Courthouse, which Clark had guarded like a prison since becoming sheriff in 1955. He'd even moved his family into the county jail next door when the demonstrations began so that he'd be closer to work, where he could spy on the SNCC office across the street from his jailhouse window.

On day one, the six-foot-two, 220-pound Clark, wearing his trademark Eisenhower jacket and military helmet, herded four hundred prospective black voters into an alley behind the courthouse, where they waited all day without ever making it inside to register. When they returned the next day, he arrested sixty-two blacks for unlawful assembly and five more for "criminal provocation." He yanked Amelia Boynton, the stately godmother of Selma's voting rights movement, by the collar of her jacket and threw her into his squad car. The photo appeared on the front page of *The New York Times*.

Clark's crackdown increased pressure on the president to expedite his timetable for voting rights legislation. On February 1, King and five hundred schoolchildren were thrown in jail. "All of us should be concerned with the efforts of our fellow Americans to register to vote in Alabama," Johnson said at a news conference while King sat in his cell.

The turning point in the fight for the right to vote came on February 18, thirty miles from Selma, in the small town of Marion, Coretta Scott King's hometown. Beneath a full orange moon, two hundred blacks held a rare night march from Zion United Methodist Church to the Perry County jail to protest the arrest of the SCLC worker James Orange, who was behind bars for "contributing to the delinquency of minors" after encouraging students to sing freedom songs outside the courthouse.

In a precursor to Bloody Sunday, Alabama state troopers attacked the marchers with nightsticks, sending them fleeing for safety. Jimmie Lee Jackson, his mother, Viola, and his grandfather Cager Lee hid in Mack's Café. Ten state troopers entered and beat Jackson's mother to the ground. When Jackson lunged to protect her, a state trooper shot him point-blank in the stomach. "For the state troopers the action in Marion was like a shot of amphetamine to a speed freak," wrote the civil rights activist Chuck Fager.

In a final indignity, Col. Al Lingo of the Alabama Department of Public Safety served Jackson in the hospital with a warrant for assault and battery with the intent to murder an Alabama state trooper. Jackson died a week later, the "first martyr of the current campaign for the vote," wrote Taylor Branch.

Four thousand people attended two funeral services for Jackson, in Selma and Marion. RACISM KILLED OUR BROTHER, said a large banner on the front of Brown Chapel. Jackson was given a "freedom funeral" in a small tract of woods alongside County Road 183; he was buried in blue denim overalls, a blue denim jumper, white shirt, and necktie—the uniform of the SCLC.

At a mass meeting in Selma, the King aide James Bevel first suggested the idea of marching from Selma to Montgomery to protest Jackson's death at the state capitol. "We are going to bring a voting bill into being in the streets of Selma, Alabama," King vowed.

King met with Johnson in Washington again on March 5, the same day the DOJ's Civil Rights Division finished a rough draft of a voting rights bill. The legislation was based on the last option in Katzenbach's December 1964 memo, a powerful blueprint giving the federal government extensive power over voter registration in the South. Then came Bloody Sunday. "It required the atrocities of Selma," said Senator Paul Douglas of Illinois, "to invoke the Fifteenth Amendment's instructions."

On March 6, 1965, the meeting in the basement of Frazier's Café Society, a popular soul food restaurant in Atlanta, lasted well into the night. Over yams, collard greens, green beans, and corn, a dozen members of the executive committee of SNCC debated whether to march from Selma to Montgomery.

SNCC's executive committee had grown disillusioned with the prospects of changing Selma and doubted the willingness of the federal government to respond to the group's problems. Since 1960 these pioneering young activists had integrated lunch counters in Nashville, desegregated bus travel throughout the Deep South, and organized Freedom Summer in Mississippi. But winning the right to vote, which King called "civil right No. 1," had become their most difficult task. They voted not to march. "We strongly believe that the objectives of the march do not justify the danger and the resources involved," SNCC's leaders wrote to King.

But SNCC's chairman, John Lewis, insisted on marching. "I've been to Selma many times," he said. "I've got arrested with the people there. If they want to march, I'm going to march with them." Lewis, the third of nine kids in a family of impoverished farmers, had grown up only a hundred miles northeast of Selma, outside the small city of Troy. At twenty-five, he'd already been arrested nearly forty times for his civil rights activism, including four times in Selma, and had been badly beaten during Freedom Rides in South Carolina and Montgomery. A devoted adherent to King's gospel of nonviolent resistance, he described his mission as "bringing the Gandhian way into the belly of the Black Belt."

Lewis lacked the eloquence of King, the movie star looks of Julian Bond, or the brash charisma of Stokely Carmichael. He was five feet six, 155 pounds, and spoke with a stutter. But no one doubted his determination and commitment to the cause. "He was fearless, and he didn't mind taking on any danger," said the King aide Andrew Young. He was going to march even if SNCC did not. Shortly after midnight, Lewis hopped into a white Dodge with his friends Bob Mants and Wilson Brown and drove four hours from Selma to Atlanta; he arrived at the SNCC Freedom House at 2021 Eugene Street just before dawn.

At home in Atlanta, King had doubts of his own about the march. The Department of Justice urged him to stay away from Selma because of threats on his life. Since King's SCLC had launched its drive for voting rights in Selma, three thousand civil rights activists, King included, had been arrested, but almost nobody had been registered. "This is Selma, Alabama,"

King wrote in *The New York Times* from his cell in the Dallas County jail on February 5, 1965. "There are more Negroes in jail with me than there are on the voting rolls."

Alabama's governor, George Wallace, who had vowed, "Segregation now, segregation tomorrow, segregation forever," at his inauguration in 1963, made clear his intention to block the march. "I'm not going to have a bunch of niggers walking along a highway in this state as long as I am governor," Wallace said.

On the morning of March 7, King sent Andrew Young to Selma to cancel the march. He caught the 8:00 a.m. flight from Atlanta to Montgomery and sped over to Selma as fast as he could. "The march was a mistake," he said. But it was too late. By the time Young arrived, hundreds of people from Dallas and Perry counties had assembled at Brown Chapel. They were wearing their Sunday best, ready to march.

At 1:45 p.m. Lewis and the King aide Hosea Williams, an idiosyncratic chemist from Savannah, led six hundred local residents in a "Walk for Freedom" from Brown Chapel. They marched in two single-file lines down dusty Sylvan Street, passing a massive foundry that had manufactured weapons for the Confederacy during the Civil War. After a few blocks they turned right on Water Avenue, entering Selma's picturesque business district, and headed for the bridge toward Montgomery, the state capital.

Lewis wore a tan trench coat and a black tie. The streets of downtown Selma were eerily quiet. For once there were no police in sight. "There was no singing, no shouting—just the sound of scuffling feet," Lewis wrote. "There was something holy about it, as if we were walking down a sacred path. It reminded me of Gandhi's march to the sea." Lewis thought the marchers would be arrested but had no idea that the ensuing events would profoundly alter the arc of American history.

As Lewis crossed the muddy Alabama River on Selma's Edmund Pettus Bridge, named after a former Confederate general, he saw "a sea of blue-helmeted, blue-uniformed Alabama state troopers, line after line of them, dozens of battle-ready lawmen stretched from one side of U.S. Highway 80 to the other." Behind them stood Jim Clark's segregationist posse, some of them on horseback, carrying bullwhips and batons wrapped in barbed wire. Reporters gathered on the side of the bridge at Lehmann's Pontiac.

After the Alabama state troopers charged toward Lewis, Clark's posse quickly entered the fray, mimicking the rebel yells of Confederate soldiers while trampling the marchers on horseback. "Tear gas!" someone yelled. The bridge resembled a war zone. The state troopers and Clark's posse chased and beat the fleeing marchers all the way back to Brown Chapel.

Lafayette Surney, a young SNCC worker from Ruleville, Mississippi, filed panicked minute-by-minute reports to SNCC headquarters in Atlanta from a corner pay phone near the bridge. "Police are beating people on the streets," he reported at 3:16 p.m. "Oh, man, they're just picking them up and putting them in ambulances. People are getting hurt bad."

The federal government did nothing to stop the violence. Two Justice Department lawyers watched with horror from the Selma side of the bridge. The FBI agent in charge of Selma had gone fishing that day.

An ambulance supplied by the Medical Committee for Human Rights in New York rescued Lewis and took him back to Brown Chapel. He had no memory of how he escaped from the bridge. "John, speak to the people," the anguished crowd urged him. The bloodied civil rights leader rose to speak. "I don't know how President Johnson can send troops to Vietnam," said the impassioned Lewis, his fractured skull wrapped in a makeshift bandage. "I don't know how he can send troops to the Congo. I don't see how he can send troops to Africa, and he can't send troops to Selma, Alabama. Next time we march, we may have to keep going when we get to Montgomery. We may have to go on to Washington."

He saw double as he spoke from the pulpit. He was soon rushed, along with eighty-three others, to the segregated Good Samaritan Hospital, where "the bitter, acrid smell [of tear gas] filled the room."

In the forty-eight hours following Bloody Sunday there were sympathy marches in eighty American cities, sit-ins at the Justice Department, twenty-four-hour pickets outside the White House, and all-night vigils at Brown Chapel. Hundreds of white ministers heeded King's call and descended on Selma, many demonstrating in the civil rights movement for the first time. Fifteen thousand people marched in Harlem; white sisters from the Nuns of Charity in their black habits linked arms with radical black activists from SNCC. In solidarity Wisconsinites walked fifty-four miles from Beloit to Madison, the same distance as Selma to Montgomery. Olympic medalists ran from New York to Washington along U.S. 1 carrying an unlit freedom torch to deliver to the president.

Lying in his hospital bed in Selma, Lewis received a telegram from Nathan Schwerner, whose twenty-four-year-old son Mickey had been murdered in Mississippi a year earlier, along with the civil rights workers Andrew Goodman and James Chaney. "Thousands of us all over the country are praying for you and your early recovery," Schwerner wrote to Lewis from New York. "To Dr. King and all gallant fighters for human dignity, I want to send my warmest love and assurance that we will continue this great fight wherever discrimination raises its ugly head."

"What the public felt on Monday, in my opinion, was the deepest sense of outrage it has ever felt on the civil rights question," the president's counsel, Harry McPherson, wrote to Johnson.

The president faced intense criticism from Democrats and Republicans. Why hadn't he sent federal marshals to protect the marchers? Where was his promised voting rights bill? The GOP mocked him as "Lyndon Come Lately" on civil rights. LBJ instructed Katzenbach, whom he'd appointed attorney general in late January, to make completion of a voting rights bill "top billing." The former Senate majority leader wanted to see the particulars of the legislation before he spoke publicly about it.

King returned to Selma a day after Bloody Sunday and called for a second march from Selma to Montgomery for the following day. "A man dies when he refuses to stand up for justice," King told the packed congregation at Brown Chapel. "So we're going to stand up right here amid horses. We're going to stand up right here in Alabama amid the billyclubs . . . We're going to stand up amid tear gas. We're going to stand up amid anything they can muster up, letting the world know that we are determined to be free."

Lewis was released from the hospital on the morning of March 9. He was greeted by spontaneous applause when he arrived at Brown Chapel. Governor Wallace had obtained an injunction from a federal court in Montgomery blocking a second march from Selma. Lewis urged King to defy it; King had never done that before. "The march is legitimate, injunction or no injunction," Lewis said. "Whatever we do depends on what the people want to do."

The president leaned heavily for advice on Katzenbach, the youngest member of his cabinet. The forty-three-year-old lawyer, known for his rumpled suits and dry humor, had impeccable credentials: boarding school at Phillips Exeter Academy, college at Princeton, law school at Yale. His middle name, deBelleville, came from a forebear who was Napoleon's brother's doctor. John Doar, the assistant attorney general for civil rights, had been his roommate at Princeton. The journalist Victor Navasky called them the "Ivy League Gentlemen" of the Justice Department.

But Katzenbach was also no stranger to a crisis. He'd been shot down over the Mediterranean as an army pilot during World War II and twice escaped from Italian prison camps before finishing college by reading books supplied by the Red Cross at a prisoner of war camp near Munich. He was most famous inside the administration for squaring off against George Wallace when the Alabama governor tried to block the integration of the University of Alabama in 1963 by standing in the doorway of Foster Auditorium. *Life* magazine called him "a calm enforcer," with "the best poker face in the Johnson administration."

Katzenbach woke King at 5:00 a.m. to ask him to cancel the march, which the Justice Department feared could lead to another episode of violence. King refused. "I would rather die on the highways of Alabama," he told the congregation at Brown Chapel, "than make a butchery of my conscience." Katzenbach dispatched Doar, a lanky, no-nonsense Wisconsinite well liked by civil rights activists, to monitor events on the ground.

Doar had grown up in New Richmond, Wisconsin, in a family of Lincoln Republicans. He'd been with the Civil Rights Division since 1960 and had handled some of the federal government's most sensitive assignments in the South. He'd escorted James Meredith to integrate the University of Mississippi amid a frenzied white mob. He'd prosecuted the killers of Goodman, Chaney, and Schwerner in Philadelphia, Mississippi. No one worked harder than the gruff and demanding Doar. "He was a straight arrow if there ever was one," said Ramsey Clark. "He was like Sergeant Friday: 'Just the facts, ma'am.'"

That afternoon King and two thousand demonstrators, black and white, representing all religions, left Brown Chapel and once again headed for the Edmund Pettus Bridge. Lewis, who stayed behind to heal, described the scene as "very, very tense." The left-wing magazine *Ramparts* dubbed it the "charge of the Bible Brigade." The marchers locked arms and sang "We Shall Overcome" as they crossed the bridge, facing off with the Alabama state troopers for a second time.

Katzenbach rolled up his sleeves and chain-smoked cigarettes in his mammoth walnut-paneled Washington office, as two hundred young activists held a sit-in in the corridor outside. He listened to dispatches from Doar over a squawk box hooked into two telephone lines while examining a large map of Selma borrowed from the Agriculture Department. "They were allowed to go over the bridge," Doar reported from the Justice Department's third-floor office in Selma's federal building, overlooking the bridge. "Dr. King is there, and several elderly ladies. They're over the bridge. They have halted . . .

"King is walking back this way," Doar said. "He's asking the marchers to turn back." Afraid of violating the federal injunction, King had knelt in prayer, then asked the marchers to return to Brown Chapel. "King has turned around," Katzenbach told Bill Moyers at the White House. "It looks very good. More like the March on Washington than anything. They're going back to the church. John Doar feels this will take away a lot of the bad taste of the brutality on Sunday. It looks O.K. for the moment."

But following the march, events took another tragic turn. James Reeb, a white Unitarian minister from Boston, and two friends walked the wrong route back from dinner and passed the Silver Moon Café, a notorious white supremacist hangout. They were assaulted by four white hoodlums, one of whom smashed Reeb on the temple with a club before the others jumped on him. Customers inside the Silver Moon could see the fight, but no one went outside to stop it. The thirty-eight-year-old father of four, who directed a low-income housing project for the American Friends Service Committee in the black ghetto of Roxbury, Massachusetts, where he sent his children to a predominantly black school, was rushed to a hospital in Birmingham in critical condition.

Johnson received the news at Camp David, where he was huddling with Secretary of Defense Robert McNamara and Secretary of State Dean Rusk to discuss Vietnam. "How many Jim Reebs is it going to take before those people understand the intensity of this movement?" he wondered.

Reeb died in Birmingham the next day, the second martyr of Selma. Lewis held a moment of silence for his "fallen brother" at Brown Chapel. Students from Howard staged a sit-in at the White House. The picketers grew outside, marching back and forth along Pennsylvania Avenue, chanting at LBJ: "Just you wait for '68." The death of a white man in Selma shocked the country and increased pressure on Johnson to act swiftly.

The president spent four hours on Friday meeting with two delegations of religious and civil rights leaders. Sending federal marshals to Selma, Johnson argued, would alienate the moderate whites whose support the White House needed to pass a voting rights bill. The Episcopal bishop Paul Moore, Jr., of New York asked the president why it had taken so long for legislation to reach Congress. "Two reasons," Johnson replied. "First, it's got to pass. We can't risk defeat or dilution by filibuster on this one. This bill has got to go up there clean, simple and powerful. Second, we don't want the law declared unconstitutional. This can't be just a two-line bill, as somebody suggested. The wherefores and therefores are insurance against that."

On Friday evening Johnson received word that George Wallace had requested a meeting in Washington, which the president hoped to use to his advantage. They met the next morning, as chants of "Freedom now, freedom now" blanketed the White House. For three hours the president lectured Wallace on civil rights, sitting close and never averting his gaze. Johnson's six-foot-four-inch frame towered over the five-foot-seven-inch governor.

"You can't stop a fever by putting an ice pack on your head," Johnson said to Wallace. "You've got to get to the cause of the fever." If Wallace wanted to end all demonstrations, Johnson told him, he should issue an immediate declaration for "universal suffrage in the State of Alabama and the United States of America." The Alabama governor left the White House in a tizzy. "If I hadn't left when I did, he'd have me coming out for civil rights," Wallace joked to friends afterward.

On Saturday morning a finished voting rights bill finally reached the president's desk. Johnson went directly from the meeting with Wallace to a hastily arranged press conference in the Rose Garden, where he spoke publicly for the first time since Bloody Sunday. "The events of last Sunday cannot and will not be repeated, but the demonstrations in Selma have a much larger meaning," the president said. "They are a protest against a deep and very unjust flaw in American democracy itself. Ninety-five years ago our Constitution was amended to require that no American be denied the right to vote because of race, or color. Almost a century later, Americans are kept from voting simply because they are Negroes. Therefore, this Monday, I will send to Congress a request for legislation to carry out the amendment of the Constitution. Wherever there is discrimination, this law will strike down all restrictions used to deny the right to vote."

A bill to guarantee all Americans the right to vote free of discrimination, once and for all, would be announced Monday night. "The Attorney General can draft, and Congress can pass a law," Johnson said, "but only the President can use his office as a great moral instrument."

"Mistuh Speak-ah!" shouted the House doorkeeper William "Fish Bait" Miller of Pascagoula, Mississippi. "The Prez-dent of the Yoo-nited States." LBJ entered the Capitol chamber at 9:00 p.m. on March 15 to deliver one of the most important speeches of his presidency, addressing a joint session of Congress for the first time since Harry Truman had called on the body to break a railroad strike in 1946.

Johnson rubbed his nose, looked down at his text, and began in a methodical Texan drawl. "At times history and fate meet at a single time in a single place to shape a turning point in man's unending search for freedom," he said. "So it was at Lexington and Concord. So it was a century ago at Appomattox. So it was last week in Selma, Alabama."

Seventy million Americans—more than a third of the total U.S. population—tuned in. LBJ underlined important words on his reading copy for emphasis: <u>Lexington</u>, <u>Concord</u>, <u>Appomattox</u>, <u>Selma</u>. "I could feel the tension in the chamber," LBJ later wrote. "I could hear the emotion in the echoes of my words. I tried to speed it up a little."

The first applause in the hushed chamber didn't come until after he'd spoken for four minutes, when the president quoted a verse from Matthew 16:26: "For with a country as with a person, 'What is a man profited, if he shall gain the whole world, and lose his own soul?'"

The speech, drafted in less than twelve hours by the former Kennedy speechwriter Richard Goodwin, brilliantly framed the cause of voting rights not as an issue of black versus white but as right versus wrong. Despite the country's tortured racial history, the president argued that denying the right to vote undermined the ideals of liberty and freedom that made America exceptional. "Many of the issues of civil rights are very complex and most difficult. But about this there can and should be no argument. Every American citizen must have an equal right to vote," the president said to a fourth round of applause.

Events in Selma ensured that 1965 would not be like 1957, 1960, or 1964, when Congress had stalled or watered down previous civil rights bills. "This time, on this issue, there must be no delay, or no hesitation and or no compromise with our purpose," the president said to his first standing ovation. The applause lasted a minute before Emanuel Celler, the chairman of the House Judiciary Committee, jumped to his feet. The rest of the chamber soon followed, minus the absent Mississippi and Virginia delegations, who'd boycotted the speech.

"What happened in Selma is part of a far larger movement which reaches into every section and State of America," the president said. "It is the effort of American Negroes to secure for themselves the full blessings of American life. Their cause must be our cause too. Because it is not just Negroes, but really it is all of us, who must overcome the crippling legacy of bigotry and injustice."

The president paused. He thought about the picket lines in Birmingham, the sit-ins in Greensboro, the marches in Selma. Then he leaned forward, scrunched his eyes, and uttered the four most transcendent words of his presidency: "And . . . we . . . shall . . . overcome."

The words shocked friends and foes alike. "I almost fell out of my chair when the president spoke," wrote Katzenbach.

Lewis watched the address with King and his aides in Selma, squeezed into the living room of the local dentist Sullivan Jackson. MLK's confidants saw the civil rights leader cry for the first time in his life. Andrew Young thought about how three months earlier LBJ had told King that a voting rights bill would not be possible in 1965. "We were all teary eyed," Young said. "It was moving from complete rejection to complete acceptance. I didn't believe in ninety days he would be making a 'We Shall Overcome' speech."

"That speech was the most meaningful speech that any American president has given in modern times on the whole question of civil rights," Lewis said. "To hear Lyndon Johnson say, 'And we shall overcome,' it was beautiful."

The president ended the address by telling the story of his time as a teacher in Cotulla, describing how his students "were poor and they came to class without breakfast, hungry." He remembered "the pain of prejudice" in their eyes. "I never thought then, in 1928, that I would be standing here in 1965. It never even occurred to me in my fondest dreams that I might have the chance to help the sons and daughters of those students and to help people like them all over this country," the president said. "But now I do have that chance—and I'll let you in on a secret—I mean to use it," he said forcefully, to a thirty-fifth round of applause and second standing ovation.

The speech lasted forty-five minutes and twenty seconds, with eight minutes and forty seconds of applause. The president exited to another standing ovation, blowing two kisses to his wife and elder daughter in the ladies' balcony. He'd just delivered the greatest speech of his presidency, which King called "the most moving, eloquent, unequivocal and passionate plea for human rights ever made by any president." The White House titled the address "The American Promise." Civil rights activists, for decades to come, would call it the We Shall Overcome speech.

The White House switchboard was jammed to capacity with enthusiastic responses. At a midnight dinner with Goodwin and the legislative aide Larry O'Brien, Johnson read aloud the blue telegrams as they arrived. "Mr. President, you made me feel ten feet tall as an American citizen but you were a good twenty feet taller than I," wrote Albert Herling, the managing editor of ABC News.

Not everyone was so enthusiastic. *The Atlanta Journal* agreed with the substance but found the address "too long, too tedious, too melodramatic." Many southern newspapers and politicians condemned it. The *Richmond Times-Dispatch* said LBJ had exploited the "near-hysteria generated by events in Selma." George Wallace accused the president of singing "the song of the Communist street marchers and their poor dupes."

But that was a minority opinion. A Gallup Poll showed Johnson with the highest approval rating ever by a president on the issue of civil rights. Four out of five Americans, including a majority of white southerners, supported the voting rights bill. Bloody Sunday "was a considerable force for movement, legislatively," said O'Brien, LBJ's liaison to Capitol Hill. "You can understand a march; you can see some cop belting some poor black guy. That has a greater impact than citing a lot of statistics."

"We will make it from Selma to Montgomery," King told Lewis when the speech was over, "and the Voting Rights Act will be passed."

Two days after LBJ's speech, Judge Frank Johnson authorized the march from Selma to Montgomery. The first march, on Bloody Sunday, Johnson wrote, "involved nothing more than a peaceful effort on the part of Negro citizens to exercise a classic constitutional right; that is, the right to assemble peaceably and to petition one's government for the redress of grievances."

King announced Johnson's order over a bullhorn to a cheering throng of supporters during a news conference in Montgomery, where just a day earlier police on horseback had attacked a civil rights demonstration downtown. Wallace refused to provide protection for the "so-called march from Selma," so LBJ federalized 1,863 Alabama national guardsmen to police the route, along with 1,000 U.S. Army troops, 100 FBI men, and 100 federal marshals. Katzenbach sent Clark and Doar to lead the DOJ's efforts. They encountered a city, once the most oppressive in the South, now "hovering between festivity and chaos," *The New York Times* reported.

At 12:47 p.m. on March 21, two weeks after Bloody Sunday, thirty-two hundred marchers embarked on a third attempt from Selma. In the front row, wearing pink-and-white leis donated by a minister from Hawaii, stood Lewis, the Episcopal Church deacon Phyllis Edwards of San Francisco, the SCLC vice president Ralph Abernathy, King, UN undersecretary and fellow Nobel Peace Prize winner Ralph Bunche, Rabbi Abraham Joshua Heschel, and the Reverend Fred Shuttlesworth of Birmingham. "When we get to Montgomery, we are going to go up to Governor Wallace's door and say, 'George, it's all over now,' " joked Abernathy. " 'We've got the ballot!' "

Next to Lewis marched Cager Lee, the eighty-three-year-old grandfather of Jimmie Lee Jackson, in a fedora and heavy wool coat. "He had to die for something," Lee said. "And thank God it was for this." Lee's father had been a slave, sold from Bedford, Virginia, to the Alabama Black Belt. Jimmie Jackson's middle name, Lee, came from the owner of his great-grandfather's slave. "How could you ever think a day like this would come?" Lee said. He marched a few miles each day with tears in his eyes, repeating to himself, "Just got to tramp some more."

The procession of rabbis, priests, nuns, ministers, lawyers, doctors, farmers, and housewives marched 7.3 miles the first day to the east end of Selma, where they pitched four large tents in a farmer's field. On day two, after 11 miles, they exited Dallas County and entered Lowndes County, where not a single black voter had been registered until the week before. "We are not afraid," the marchers sang as they crossed the county line. When Jefferson

Davis Highway narrowed to two lanes, the number of marchers was reduced to three hundred, on Judge Johnson's orders.

White supremacists did their best to intimidate the marchers. A massive billboard in Selma showed King at an alleged "Communist training
school." The Alabama legislature passed a resolution alleging that there
had been "evidence of much fornication" in the tents, as lurid stories of
interracial orgies circulated among conservative segregationists. "The sex
orgies in the streets and churches were worse then [sic] in the days of
ancient Rome," said Jim Clark. To which Lewis replied: "All these segregationists can think of is fornication, and that is why there are so many
different shades of Negroes."

Scarier plots were alleged. The FBI notified agents that twelve hundred
adult white males with past felony convictions for racist offenses had driven
to the Selma/Montgomery area with rifles in their car. "It was like a magnet
for racial hatred," Ramsey Clark said. He drove back and forth between
Selma and Montgomery, looking behind trees, checking out barns.

On day five, as the marchers entered Montgomery, the crowd swelled
to twenty-five thousand. Despite having suffered a concussion on Bloody
Sunday, Lewis walked the entire fifty-four-mile route. It was like a second
March on Washington, with the civil rights leaders Bayard Rustin, A. Philip
Randolph, Roy Wilkins, James Farmer, Lewis, and King reunited in Montgomery. All the struggles of the civil rights movement—the bus boycott in
Montgomery, the sit-ins in Greensboro and Nashville, the Freedom Rides
through the Deep South, the March on Washington, the desegregation of
Birmingham, the Mississippi Freedom Summer, Bloody Sunday—culminated
in the triumphant walk from Selma to Montgomery. "The march was like
a holy crusade," said Lewis. "You felt like you were participating in something so mighty, it was bigger than any of us."

They marched down the wide lanes of Dexter Avenue, past the church
where King had preached from 1954 to 1960, toward the Greek Revival
Alabama state capitol, where Jefferson Davis had taken the oath as the first
Confederate president. They came within seventy-five yards of the governor's office, where Wallace could be seen peeking through his Venetian
blinds, muttering, "That's quite a crowd."

"We have walked on meandering highways and rested our bodies on rocky byways," said King on the steps of the capitol. "They told us we wouldn't get here. And there were those who said that we would get here only over their dead bodies, but all the world today knows that we are here and that we are standing before the forces of power in the state of Alabama, saying, 'We ain't goin' let nobody turn us around.'"

When King finished, the huge crowd locked arms and sang "We Shall Overcome" one last time. Selma to Montgomery was the last great march of the 1960s civil rights movement. "There was never a march like this one before and there hasn't been once since," Lewis said.

Emanuel Celler, a seventy-seven-year-old Democrat from Brooklyn, began hearings on the Voting Rights Act (VRA) in Subcommittee Number 5 of the House Judiciary Committee three days after Johnson's speech, convening morning and night. "The climate of public opinion throughout the Nation has so changed[,] because of the Alabama outrages, as to make assured passage of this solid bill—a bill that would have been inconceivable a year ago," Celler said in his opening statement.

The legislation had been drafted by a small group of lawyers in the Appeals and Research Section of the Justice Department, under the supervision of Harold Greene, who had escaped Nazi Germany in 1938 and earned his law degree through night classes at George Washington University. Solicitor General Archibald Cox, a brilliant lawyer from Harvard, and his top aide, Louis Claiborne, contributed important revisions.

The most important feature of the law eliminated literacy tests and other disenfranchising devices in states where less than 50 percent of eligible voters had registered or cast ballots in the 1964 presidential election, which covered Alabama, Georgia, Louisiana, Mississippi, South Carolina, Virginia, and thirty-four counties in North Carolina, along with Alaska; Apache County, Arizona; Elmore County, Idaho; and Aroostook County, Maine. This formula, though imperfect, captured the key southern states where the bulk of black voters were disenfranchised.

"We knew where the problems were—what states had to be covered—but you just couldn't name the states in the legislation," said Howard Glickstein, who as a young lawyer in the Appeals and Research Section helped draft the bill. "So we kept fooling around, trying to find a formula. Eventually the idea of basing it on registration and voting turnout came up."

In addition, to guard against future discrimination, the legislation compelled those states and jurisdictions with the worst histories of voting discrimination to clear any subsequent voting changes with a three-judge federal district court in Washington or the attorney general. It authorized the attorney general to send federal examiners to register voters in counties with well-documented records of using discriminatory voting tests or from which the AG received twenty-five complaints from local residents. It dispatched federal observers to monitor elections for compliance. And it applied to all elections—local, state, and federal.

Katzenbach testified first on behalf of the VRA. The previous civil rights acts of 1957, 1960, and 1964 had failed, he explained, by relying on obstructionist southern courts to adjudicate voting rights cases on a lengthy case-by-case basis. The DOJ had filed seventy-one voting rights lawsuits since 1961, but only 31 percent of eligible black citizens were registered to vote in seven southern states. From 1958 to 1964 the number of African-Americans registered rose by only 2 percent in Mississippi and 5 percent in Alabama. "The lesson is plain," said Katzenbach. "The three present statutes have had only minimal effect. They have been too slow."

Selma was a perfect case study. It took thirteen months before the DOJ's first case against the Dallas County Board of Registrars, filed in April 1961, went to trial. The court found evidence of past discrimination but alleged that the current board of registrars was not discriminating against African-Americans, even though prospective black voters were forced to spell words like "emolument" or explain complicated excerpts of the Alabama Constitution to the registrar's satisfaction.

Two and a half years after the original suit was filed, the court of appeals reversed the district court but refused to order that the board of registrars treat blacks the same as whites, who almost never had to pass a literacy test. Even after a federal judge struck down Dallas County's stringent literacy test in early 1965, the board of registrars still failed three-fourths of black applicants.

Frustrated voting rights lawyers in the 1960s liked to tell a joke encapsulating their experiences:

A black college professor who is fluent in multiple languages walks into a county registrar's office in the Deep South. The registrar hands him a paper in Chinese and says, "OK, that's your literacy test. Can you read that?"

"Oh, I can read that real good," the professor replies.

"Oh, yeah?" the registrar responds. "What does it say?"

"Ain't no black people votin' in this county this year."

Justice Department lawyers spent an average of twenty-eight months on each case, reviewing up to thirty-six thousand pages of voter registration records, only to be rebuffed by local courts or ignored by local registrars. "What is necessary, what is essential, is a new approach, an approach which goes beyond the tortuous, often-ineffective pace of litigation," Katzenbach testified. "What is required is a systematic, automatic method to deal with discriminatory tests, with discriminatory testers, and with discriminatory threats." By immediately outlawing devices like literacy tests, transferring voter registration authority to the federal government when necessary, and applying federal standards to state elections, the VRA would succeed where previous laws had failed.

A series of southern congressmen, state attorneys general, and local officials testified against the bill. "If the president's law is passed, the South will disappear from the civilized world just as surely and certainly as Haiti did in 1804," predicted W. B. Hicks, the executive secretary of the Virginia-based Liberty Lobby, a spin-off of the right-wing John Birch Society.

When the Senate Judiciary Committee began hearings on March 23, the North Carolina senator Sam Ervin, who fancied himself the country's leading constitutional scholar, quizzed the attorney general for three days about technicalities of the law. He then invited a score of renowned segregationist local officials to publicly denounce it.

"Have you ever seen a more drastic proposal to vest more arbitrary power in public officials than that one?" Ervin asked Leander Perez, the notoriously hard-line political boss of Louisiana's Plaquemines Parish, where only ninety-six of two thousand eligible blacks were registered to vote.

"I said it was worse than the Thaddeus Stevens legislation during Reconstruction, sir, and it is," Perez responded. "It is the most nefarious—it is inconceivable that Americans would do that to Americans." He described the VRA as a Communist plot for the Black Belt, which the Republican senator Everett Dirksen of Illinois called "about as stupid a statement as has ever been uttered in this hearing."

Other opponents criticized the VRA's formula, which they noted covered six Deep South states and parts of North Carolina but not Arkansas,

Florida, Tennessee, or Texas. The Republican congressman Bo Callaway of Georgia sarcastically suggested that the DOJ should instead have chosen "all states which have an average altitude of 100 to 900 feet, an average yearly temperature of 68 degrees to 77 degrees at 7 a.m., average humidity of 80 to 87%, and a coastline of 50 to 400 miles. With this formula we encompass all the Southern states attacked by H.R. 6400, but have the added advantage of including all of North Carolina and excluding Alaska."

Such criticism had little impact on the law's prospects in Congress, especially as prominent opponents of previous civil rights bills, like the Louisiana senator Russell Long, the Senate's second most powerful Democrat, voiced their early support for the VRA. "Congress has attempted on a number of occasions to implement the 15th Amendment but has failed in its efforts due to dilatory and evasive action by certain state and local officials and in some instances by outright defiance of the law," Long testified. "Mr. Chairman, it is way past time when our patience must come to an end. Freedom demands that legislative action be taken now to remove effectively all racial barriers to the right to vote."

The murder of the white Detroit housewife Viola Liuzzo, a thirty-nine-year-old mother of five gunned down on Route 80 by Alabama Klansmen after she had attended the Selma to Montgomery march, had further solidified support for the legislation. She was the third martyr of the Selma protests.

The Mississippi senator James Eastland, the cigar-chomping chairman of the Senate Judiciary Committee, was renowned for killing 121 of 122 civil rights bills in his committee since 1953. Only 161 of 13,524 African-Americans in his hometown of Sunflower County were registered to vote. He said of the VRA, "I am opposed to every word and every line in [it]." But the Senate voted, 67–13, on March 18 to limit debate in Eastland's committee to three weeks, eliminating his ability to stonewall the bill.

The legislation passed the Senate, 73–19, on May 25 and the House, 333–85, on July 9. A dispute over the poll tax temporarily held up final passage. Liberals wanted to automatically ban the tax, as with literacy tests, but Katzenbach preferred to fight it through litigation, which he thought would soon succeed before the Supreme Court. Katzenbach secured an endorsement from King in late July for a compromise that authorized the attorney general to file suits against the poll tax in select southern states, which ended the logjam. The legislation passed largely as introduced five months earlier, unscathed by southern opposition.

The VRA's overwhelming passage resulted from a number of converging factors: the clear denial of black voting rights in the South under Jim Crow; profound public outrage about the violence in Selma; a disciplined and compelling civil rights movement; the most liberal Congress since the New Deal; a Republican Party filled with northern moderates, many of them senior figures; and a president in LBJ who specialized in steering complex legislation through the Congress.

When both houses of Congress reached agreement on final legislation, Dirksen invited LBJ over to his office for a "good, stiff bourbon" after the president complained that "I can't even drink Sanka [at the White House], I just have to drink this damned old root beer." One of his signature achievements at hand, LBJ happily returned to his old stomping grounds.

On the morning of August 6, 1965, the day he signed the VRA, Johnson invited John Lewis of SNCC and James Farmer of the Congress of Racial Equality (CORE) to the Oval Office for a chat. Lewis got there early and talked with the president for fifteen minutes before Farmer arrived. Lewis had met the president a few times at the White House in meetings with other civil rights leaders, but this was their first one-on-one conversation.

They both were poor country boys who had grown up with no electricity or running water. Johnson came from the hardscrabble Texas Hill Country; Lewis, from the impoverished Alabama Black Belt. Stylistically, however, they couldn't have been more different. LBJ was loud and profane; Lewis, quiet and devout. The White House was the last place Lewis had ever expected to visit after growing up in Troy.

He had been raised on a hundred-acre farm bought for three hundred dollars in cash, "every penny my father had to his name," he said. They grew cotton, corn, and peanuts. Lewis read via smoky kerosene lamps and used the Sears, Roebucks catalog for toilet paper in the outhouse. He was a serious, studious child, who liked to preach to his family's chickens, baptizing the birds in empty syrup cans filled with water.

Lewis became taken with the civil rights movement when he first heard King preach on WMRA radio out of Montgomery at the beginning of 1955, when he was a sophomore in high school. "The Montgomery bus boycott changed my life more than any other event before or since," he wrote. He followed the news every day on the radio or in the newspapers. Lewis gave his first sermon five days before his sixteenth birthday, in 1956. *The Montgomery Advertiser* called him the "boy preacher" of Pike County.

Lewis wanted to integrate local Troy State University, but his parents wouldn't let him, so he attended American Baptist College in Nashville instead. His roommate, Bernard Lafayette, was the first SNCC worker sent to Selma. Lewis became one of a groundbreaking group of students who desegregated Nashville's lunch counters in 1960, under the tutelage of the theologian James Lawson, a devotee of Gandhi. "I was like a soldier in a nonviolent army," Lewis said.

Since Bloody Sunday, Lewis had become more closely identified with the cause of voting rights than any other civil rights leader besides King. Perhaps that was why Johnson invited him to the White House on that historic day. Lewis sat upright on a couch; Johnson sprawled on a lounge chair. "Now John, you've got to go back and get all those folks registered," the president told him. "You've got to go back and get those boys by the balls. Just like a bull gets on top of a cow. You've got to get 'em by the balls and you've got to squeeze, squeeze till they hurt." A shocked Lewis could barely get a word in.

After meeting with Lewis and Farmer, Johnson called his eighteen-year-old daughter Luci, who was on "daddy duty" that day. She usually met him in the East Room for presidential receptions. That day the president told her to meet him in the Diplomatic Room, because they were heading to the U.S. Capitol.

"Daddy, why are we going to the Capitol?" she asked her father.

"Luci Baines, we have to go to the Capitol," Johnson said to his daughter. "It's the only place to go. As a result of this great legislation becoming the law of the land, there will be many men and women who will not be returning to these hallowed halls because of the decision they have made to support it. And because of this great legislation that I will be signing into law, there will be many men and women who will have an opportunity to come to the halls of Congress who could have never have come otherwise."

They arrived at the Capitol Rotunda at noon for the nationally televised announcement. To Johnson's right was a statue of Abraham Lincoln; to his left, a bust of the Great Emancipator; behind his podium, John Trumbull's massive painting of the surrender of Cornwallis by the British army in Yorktown, Virginia, in 1781, the last battle of the Revolutionary War. "Today is a triumph for freedom as huge as any victory that has ever been won on any battlefield," the president said.

After his twenty-minute speech, Johnson headed to the ornate President's Room near the Senate chamber, where he signed the bill at a wooden desk from the 1860s that he'd used as Senate majority leader. He sat beneath a giant chandelier in the room where Lincoln had signed the precursor to the Emancipation Proclamation 104 years earlier. Members of Congress congratulated Johnson as they walked past his desk: "a great, great speech," "a magnificent presentation." He used fifty pens to sign the law, giving the first one to Vice President Hubert Humphrey, the second to Dirksen, the third to the New York senator Robert Kennedy.

After handing pens to congressional leaders, Johnson got up and gave one to King, who was standing next to Rosa Parks. The leaders of the civil rights movement looked on with triumph, including Lewis, the only veteran of Bloody Sunday who made it to Washington that day.

"C'mon around here," Johnson told Lewis, handing him a pen from his desk. Lewis later framed the pen and hung it in his living room, along with a copy of the bill. He called the VRA's signing "a high point in modern America, probably the nation's finest hour in terms of civil rights."

Johnson's own feelings were more complex. After signing the Civil Rights Act of 1964, he'd famously remarked to Bill Moyers: "I think we just delivered the South to the Republican Party for a long time to come." Upon signing the VRA, Johnson "felt a great sense of victory on one side and a great sense of fear on the other," his daughter Luci remembered. The president knew that the legislation, more than any previous civil rights bill, would fundamentally transform American democracy, unleashing deep changes in American politics that would be well beyond his control. "It would be written in the history books," Luci Baines Johnson said. "But now the history had to be made."

2

THE SECOND RECONSTRUCTION

Two days after LBJ signed the VRA, John Lewis took the president's salty words to heart ("get those boys by the balls") and traveled to racially fraught Americus, Georgia, where he was arrested, again, for protesting the existence of two separate voter registration lines—one for blacks, one for whites. After Attorney General Katzenbach threatened to send federal examiners to the county to register black voters, local officials hired two African-American women as the first black county registrars. They registered 1,230 black voters in the week following the VRA's signing, tripling the number on the rolls.

The Justice Department wasted no time in implementing the new law. After years of frustrating, often fruitless investigations, they finally had the power to eradicate voting discrimination across the South. On August 5, a day before LBJ signed the VRA, John Doar sent his colleagues the ambitious schedule for the week. His instructions:

The Voting Rights bill will be signed Friday at noon.
One poll tax suit must be on a plane for Mississippi Friday night.
A form letter with two enclosures: (1) the Voting Rights Act of 1965 and (2) the Civil Service Commission regulations enclosed—must be mailed

to the registrars in Louisiana, Mississippi, Alabama, Georgia, South Carolina, Virginia and parts of North Carolina by Saturday night.

Justification memos for the designation of examiners in particular counties must be prepared for the Attorney General by Sunday night. These justification memos are very, very important and must be done with the utmost care by the lawyers and with the most up-to-date information contained therein.

On Monday night additional regulations will be published in the Federal Register. These regulations have been prepared by the Divisions and the Civil Service Commission.

On Tuesday the examiners will begin to operate offices within the selected counties and we will have teams of lawyers in the area to assist them.

Additional things to be done: Memo of instructions to the FBI and supplemental instructions advising the FBI of all steps taken to implement the bill.

It was imperative, given the high stakes of the law, that the rollout go as smoothly as possible. "Doing everything so quickly sent a signal that there would be no temporizing with the new law," said Doar's first assistant, Stephen Pollak. "On every front, it was important to be out of the box right away because that was the best way to foster voluntary compliance."

Signing up the South's 2.5 million unregistered black voters took priority. In June, Pollak had drawn up a list of forty-nine first-tier counties and twenty backups with histories of voting discrimination where federal examiners could be sent to register black voters. Katzenbach settled on nine counties for starters—four in Alabama, three in Louisiana, two in Mississippi—hotbeds of segregationist resistance where only 2 to 10 percent of blacks were registered compared with 65 to 100 percent of whites. The attorney general wanted to start small, considering the political sensitivity of the assignment, and give other counties the chance to comply before sending more examiners in.

"The decision to appoint examiners will be taken where it is clear that past denials of the right to vote justify it or where present compliance with federal law, including the Voting Rights Act, is insufficient to assure prompt registration of all eligible citizens," Katzenbach wrote to every county registrar in the covered states. "The primary responsibility for registration remains with state and county officials. The Voting Rights Act of 1965 is designed to permit registration to remain a local matter so long as all citizens are registered fairly, promptly and in accordance with the law."

To those counties selected for federal examiners, Katzenbach wrote to local officials: "I hereby certify that in my judgment the appointment of examiners is necessary to enforce the guarantees of the Fifteenth Amendment to the Constitution of the United States." On August 4, one hundred employees from the U.S. Civil Service Commission arrived at the Justice Department for a three-day orientation. They watched the signing of the VRA on closed-circuit TV and took a crash course in Voting Rights 101 from Doar. These career civil servants, who were in charge of vetting government employees, had been tapped as federal examiners. They would now be on the front lines of democratizing the South. It was a thrilling and, at times, terrifying assignment for these obscure government bureaucrats. "I never dreamed we would get involved in anything like this," one of the officials said.

Timothy Mullis, a World War II vet from Palm Beach County, Florida, who worked as an investigator in the commission's Atlanta office, was put in charge of registering voters in Selma, one of the VRA's most important tasks. His relaxed disposition earned him the nickname Beau Bachelor. On August 9, Mullis flew to Selma, checked into the Holiday Inn, and headed over to the Beaux Arts federal building across from the Dallas County Courthouse, where his team of examiners would begin registering voters the next day, down the hall from the office of the Justice Department. He carried a thick manual with six chapters of instructions for the examiners. "Why are we here?" it asked. "Congress decided it is necessary to ensure that persons could qualify to vote without discrimination because of race."

The examiners set up registration offices in county government buildings, local post offices, or makeshift trailers if they couldn't find any other space. In Selma, Mullis ate breakfast at the Holiday Inn and lunch and dinner at the officers' mess at Craig Air Force Base. The examiners, all native southerners, knew better than to expect the customary southern hospitality from local whites. "This morning, in some counties, federal agents, lineal descendants of the Reconstruction corrupters, will be at work showing illiterates where to make their marks," *The Montgomery Advertiser* editorialized.

Mullis, who was white, oversaw a dozen examiners in Selma, including

four black federal workers from Selma, Tuskegee, and Atlanta. It was a segregationist's worst nightmare: blacks registering other blacks in the Deep
South. "You couldn't have found anywhere a better group of men to do
that kind of work," Mullis said. "It was almost like they were made for the
job . . . Everybody was motivated. And everybody realized the eyes of the
nation were upon them. And here they were in Selma listing eligible voters.
It was kind of a thrill . . . They felt like they were doing something bigger
than themselves."

On August 10, Ardies Mauldin, a nurse, and her husband, Thomas, a
deliveryman for a wholesale grocery company, rose early and headed for
the federal building to register to vote. Their seventeen-year-old son, Charles,
had marched behind Lewis during Bloody Sunday and inspired them to
become active in the civil rights movement. "When things were going along
smooth, I didn't think much about it," Ardies Mauldin said. "But when
they started running horses over people, then I got mad."

The fifty-two-year-old Mauldin had tried to register twice in recent
months, first at the Dallas County Courthouse and then through a federal
court in Mobile, but had been rejected both times. Now she was determined
to take advantage of the new VRA. The Mauldins walked up fifty-two
steps to the third-floor examiners' office, passing a sign that read NOTICE:
IT IS A FEDERAL CRIME TO DEPRIVE, OR ATTEMPT TO DEPRIVE, ANY PER-
SON OF ANY RIGHTS SECURED BY THE VOTING RIGHTS ACT OF 1965.

Instead of giving Mauldin a complicated literacy test designed for her to
fail, Mullis's team asked her eleven simple questions, to get her basic bio-
graphical data and determine whether she had ever been convicted of a
crime or confined to a mental institution. Within ten minutes she was
given a small white square voting certificate with a unique number. Mauldin's said "1." She was the first voter registered under the VRA. Fittingly, it
happened in Selma. "It didn't take but a few minutes," she said. "I don't
know why it couldn't have been like that in the first place." Thurgood Marshall, the first African-American Supreme Court justice, later gave LBJ a
gold-plated replica of her voting certificate as a farewell memento.

As Mauldin exited the federal building, the line of prospective black
voters stretched down the stairs, into the lobby, out the door, and around
the block. "These people, when they came in our office, they were grate-

ful," Mullis said. "'Praise the Lord!' 'I'm here at last!' 'I've made it!' 'I'm gonna vote!'"

Sheriff Clark watched the scene from the courthouse, where local officials could no longer prevent black voters from registering to vote. The entire structure of white supremacy in Selma, which he'd so fervently worked to maintain for over a decade, was quickly crumbling before his eyes. "The whole thing's so ridiculous I haven't gotten over it yet," Clark said. "In fact, I'm nauseated." To which Tom Wicker of *The New York Times* replied, "He is going to be a desperately sick man before long."

On day one examiners registered 1,114 black voters in nine counties, including 107 in Selma, increasing the number of black voters by nearly two-thirds. "The turnout far exceeded expectations," said a spokesman for the Civil Service Commission. Katzenbach more than doubled the number of federal examiners, from eighteen to thirty-eight, because of high demand. "I want to get everybody registered every place I can," the president told him. "Your presence don't hurt a damn bit, it helps."

The examiners registered 1,733 voters on day two, easily surpassing in two days the 1,764 black voters who had been registered in the nine counties before the VRA took effect. By the close of business on Friday, 7,000 black voters had been registered, four times as many as were previously on the rolls. That number jumped to 20,000 by August 21, when the Civil Service Commission's president, John Macy, briefed LBJ at his ranch in the Texas Hill Country. "It was clear," *The New York Times* wrote, "that something revolutionary was happening in the Deep South."

Katzenbach slowly and deliberately expanded the number of counties with federal examiners. "Our whole philosophy had always been to try to make southern officials obey the law, not do the job for them," he wrote. "In a sense federal registrars were like federal troops; using them meant we had failed to get southern registrars, like southern sheriffs, to obey the law."

When the examiners arrived in Marion, Alabama, Jimmie Lee Jackson's hometown, on August 18, his grandfather Cager Lee went down to their office and registered to vote for the first time in his life. He proudly held up his voting certificate for photographers to capture. The number of black voters in Perry County rose from 265 to 2,460 in the next six weeks.

"60,000 Register in 3 Dixie States," the front page of the *Chicago De-*

fender reported on August 26. In just two weeks, fifty federal examiners in 13 counties had registered 27,385 black voters, while local officials in 251 counties in Alabama, Georgia, Louisiana, and Mississippi added 32,000 African-Americans to the rolls. That included John Lewis's parents, Willie Mae and Eddie, who finally registered at the Pike County Courthouse in Troy. "My mother became a crusader," Lewis said. "She had reservations about my involvement in the movement, but after the Voting Rights Act was passed into law, she thought everyone should become registered and vote." The Lewises voted in every presidential election from 1968 on.

It was hard to overstate the impact of deploying federal voter registration officials to the South for the first time since Reconstruction. Before six examiners from San Antonio, Oklahoma City, Fort Worth, Little Rock, and Dallas arrived in Clinton, Louisiana, the county seat of East Feliciana Parish, thirty miles northeast of Baton Rouge, only 182 of 6,081 voting-age African-Americans were registered. The parish registrar was an Exalted Cyclops of the KKK. The district attorney had personally purged nearly every black voter from the rolls. From January 1, 1964, to June 30, 1965, 277 blacks had applied for registration and 223 had been rejected.

In Clinton, the examiners set up shop in the top floor of the two-story Kline Building across from the courthouse downtown, in a small, dusty room with a rickety old air conditioner. Chris Weatherspoon, a sixty-three-year-old farmer from nearby Wilson, who grew cotton, corn, peas, and potatoes on fifteen acres, was the first person in line on August 10.

He'd tried to register five times with the parish registrar, Henry Earl Palmer, who had hung a poster behind his desk depicting Martin Luther King as a Communist. "Chris, you missed just one word on the test," Palmer would tell Weatherspoon each time he took the literacy test.

But the arrival of the examiners brought a drastic change. "Would you like to register, sir?" Weatherspoon was asked by an examiner when he entered the office. He sat in a folding chair across from a row of desks and put his hat in his lap. "I was praying to the Lord that this time would come," Weatherspoon said.

Over fifteen hundred black voters registered in East Feliciana Parish during the first week, ten times as many as were previously on the rolls. Within three weeks, over twenty-one hundred would register. "We've been occupied by the feds," complained District Attorney Richard Kilbourne.

"And now the Feds are fixing it so the Negroes can take over." In a sign of the parish's changing politics, Kilbourne maintained that he had "a good many colored friends, but I expect I would have to make some effort to get their vote."

"I imagine this will result in some big changes," said Sheriff Arch Doughty on the courthouse lawn. "But maybe it will be all right, as long as they leave our schools and little malt shops alone, and don't marry our daughters."

After failing legislatively, southern segregationists turned to the courts to block the VRA. On Wednesday, August 11, the New Orleans parish registrar, Albert P. Gallinghouse, filed the first lawsuit challenging the constitutionality of the VRA, claiming that the Twenty-fourth Amendment, which prohibits the poll tax for federal elections, gave states the power to set qualifications for state and local elections. A week later George Wallace obtained from local probate judges an injunction preventing examiners in six counties, including Dallas County, from adding voters to the rolls. Mississippi soon followed suit, signaling that more legal challenges would follow. "This is the kickoff," said the Mississippi attorney general, Joe Patterson.

On October 19, Sidney Provensal, the lawyer for Leander Perez, the notoriously racist political boss of the Louisiana delta, convened a meeting at the Hotel Washington "to fight the constitutional battle against the VRA in every way." The attendees included the South's leading segregationists: the North Carolina senator Sam Ervin; assistant attorneys general from Louisiana, Mississippi, and Virginia; and representatives of Governor Wallace, the South Carolina governor Robert McNair, and the Mississippi senator James Eastland. Senator Ervin "remarked that bad laws often get through legislative mills, and that, under our system, bad legislation must be contested and defeated in the courts," Wallace's lawyer, Frank Mizell, reported.

At the time of the meeting, 110,000 black voters had been registered under the VRA in the first two months: 54,000 through local officials and 56,000 by federal examiners in twenty counties. The South Carolina delegation announced its state's intention to challenge the constitutionality of the VRA before the Supreme Court, inviting the rest of the southern states to join the suit as amici curiae. Three days later South Carolina filed its challenge, alleging that the law "arbitrarily, unconstitutionally and unlawfully" restricted the state's right to "exercise her sovereign power to

prescribe fair and reasonable qualifications for registration of her electorate and the conduct of her elections." The Supreme Court, for only the fifteenth time in its history, decided to hear the case directly, with no prior
appeal from the lower courts.

South Carolina prided itself on being first when it came to southern
resistance. It was the home of the Great Nullifier, John Calhoun, the vice
president under John Quincy Adams, who published a highly influential
manifesto in 1828 arguing that states had a duty to reject federal laws they
deemed unconstitutional. South Carolina was the first state to leave the
Union and the first to fire shots at Fort Sumter during the Civil War. Its
governor in 1948, Strom Thurmond, an ardent segregationist, was the first
high-profile Democrat to leave the party over the issue of civil rights when
he ran for president on the States' Rights Democratic Party ticket after
Harry Truman desegregated the army.

The Supreme Court began oral arguments in *South Carolina v. Katzenbach* on January 17, 1966, Katzenbach's forty-fourth birthday. By that time
240,000 black voters had been added to the rolls in the seven southern
states covered by the law. The arguments lasted seven hours, over the course
of two days, the fourth-longest trial in Supreme Court history. Alabama,
Georgia, Louisiana, Mississippi, and Virginia joined South Carolina's challenge. Eighteen northern states filed briefs siding with the federal government. The verdict, said Chief Justice Earl Warren, would have "wide and
profound implications in the life of our nation."

The law's opponents made three principal arguments against the VRA.
Number one: contrary to conventional wisdom and documented record, literacy tests were not discriminatory. "Because we have a lot of illiterates, and
because we keep them from voting, we are accused of discrimination," argued the South Carolina counsel, David Robinson, a boyish lawyer from
Columbia. Virginia's assistant attorney general, R. D. McIlwaine III, who
would argue against interracial marriage in the landmark 1967 case *Lov-
ing v. Virginia*, called his state's literacy test "the most non-discriminatory
literacy test that could possibly be imagined."

Number two: events in Selma had forced Congress to rush to judgment.
"Congress was deliberating under the pressure and influence of people who
were threatening revolution and rebellion in the streets," argued the Georgia deputy assistant attorney general, E. Freeman Leverett. "I would hope

that as long as this court sits, that Congress cannot, to appease a mob in the streets, invoke an unconstitutional means to achieve a constitutional end."

Number three: states, not the federal government, had the right to set voting qualifications. "I don't think Congress ever intended that the right to regulate elections would be taken away from the various legislatures," argued the Louisiana attorney general, Jack P. F. Gremillion. "Let me tell you somethin' about this court . . . You've done a good job on these here constitutional cases, like a falcon covering a hawk. I want you to keep on doing a good job. This court is going to find that Congress cannot take over the judiciary."

Day one wasn't exactly the birthday present Katzenbach was hoping for. He sat quietly in the courtroom next to Doar and Solicitor General Thurgood Marshall, who had argued the landmark *Brown v. Board of Education* case twelve years earlier, taking notes for four hours while opponents of the VRA slammed the "drastic and despotic legislation." Katzenbach, wearing the traditional patrician Supreme Court attire—black cutaway coat with long tails, striped trousers, and striped tie—rose on day two to defend the administration. The AG was both defendant and defense counsel for the federal government.

His hands and voice were shaking as he began. He'd never argued a case as big as this one. Katzenbach steadied himself, speaking calmly and deliberately. "The position of the United States Government in this case can be very simply stated," he told the packed courtroom. "Section 2 of the 15th Amendment gives to Congress the right to enforce Section 1 by 'appropriate legislation.' We contend this act was appropriate legislation. It is well adapted, and it operates fairly and reasonably to achieve an objective which is within the power of Congress to achieve."

The VRA was a response not to "a mob on the street," as opponents claimed, but to ninety years of disregard for the Fifteenth Amendment, which culminated in Bloody Sunday, Katzenbach argued. "Public sentiment was outraged. The whole nation looked to Congress to find a workable solution, a solution that would establish the integrity and viability of the 15th Amendment and, even more importantly, the integrity and viability of our basic democratic institutions."

On March 7, 1966, the first anniversary of Bloody Sunday, the Supreme Court upheld the constitutionality of the VRA by a vote of 8–1. "After enduring nearly a century of widespread resistance to the Fifteenth Amendment, Congress has marshaled an array of potent weapons against the evil, with authority in the Attorney General to employ them effectively," wrote Chief Justice Warren. "We here hold that the portions of the Voting Rights Act properly before us are a valid means for carrying out the commands of the Fifteenth Amendment. Hopefully, millions of non-white Americans will now be able to participate for the first time on an equal basis in the government under which they live."

In the lone dissent, Justice Hugo Black of Alabama objected to Section 5 of the act, known as preclearance, which compelled states with the worst histories of voting discrimination to clear their voting changes with the federal government. "The requirement that States come to Washington to have their laws judged is reminiscent of the deeply resented practices used by the English crown in dealing with the American colonies," he wrote. Black's dissent received almost no attention at the time but became increasingly influential in the years to follow.

The VRA had easily survived its first major challenge. The 302,000 African-Americans who had registered under the law in the past year would have their rights protected, and millions more would get an opportunity to exercise their most fundamental right. "What the court has now said is that this Congressional power extends far enough to do the job effectively," wrote *The Washington Post*. "The broad sweep of the Court's opinion will be a milepost of great significance on the road toward achievement of equal rights."

Three weeks later, in a case argued by Thurgood Marshall, the Supreme Court struck down the poll tax in Virginia by a vote of 6–3, signaling the demise of the tax across the South. "The right to vote," wrote Justice William Douglas, "is too precious, too fundamental, to be burdened or conditioned."

The VRA was off to a very good start, but opponents of the law weren't done fighting.

With the constitutional challenges behind them, the Department of Justice began preparing for the first elections under the VRA. Registering voters was one thing; holding free and fair elections in the Deep South was quite another. Less than a year after the VRA's passage, black candidates had a chance to run for office, and win, for the first time since Reconstruction.

The first major test would be in Alabama, the birthplace of the VRA.

"The division's most important project in the immediate future is the coming Alabama primary elections on May 3rd and May 30th," Doar wrote to his colleagues in March 1966. "We intend to use these elections as a pilot project for programming and accomplishing effective enforcement of the Voting Rights Act of 1965 . . . Efforts to date will be meaningless if Negroes, in fact, are not able to vote and have their votes properly counted at all elections in the South between now, November 1968 and thereafter."

The number of black registered voters in Alabama had increased from 113,000 before the VRA to 235,000 by the time of the 1966 Democratic primaries. Nearly half of blacks in Alabama were now registered, and they constituted 16 percent of the state's electorate. Fifty-two black candidates qualified to run for office; they included Fred Gray, Rosa Parks's lawyer during the Montgomery bus boycott, and the Reverend Obie Scott, Jr., King's brother-in-law.

The DOJ set up field offices in Birmingham, Montgomery, and Selma to monitor the Alabama elections and sent attorneys to twenty-one high-risk counties. The Civil Service Commission dispatched 375 workers as federal observers to seven counties with the worst records of voting discrimination, including Dallas County. Katzenbach sent letters to 4,000 election officials urging them to comply with the law. If there was foul play, the department was going to find it.

Everyone in the state followed two marquee matchups. In Selma the public safety director, Wilson Baker, squared off against Jim Clark for sheriff. Statewide, Richmond Flowers, the state's moderate attorney general, was running for governor against George Wallace's wife, Lurleen, who had entered the race because Alabama law prevented her husband from seeking a third consecutive term.

The whole world was paying attention to the Alabama elections. King barnstormed the Black Belt in advance of the primary, driving eighty miles per hour from stop to stop on his typically frenzied schedule. "I was in Paris not long ago and people were still asking me, 'How about Jim Clark?'" King said when he returned to Brown Chapel. He urged the congregation to "nonviolently retire [Clark] forever and evermore." The number of registered black voters in Selma had surged from 1,516 before the VRA to 10,186, fast approaching the 12,000 registered whites. "Selma wrote the Voting Rights Act," King said. "Now we have to help ourselves."

A week earlier Baker had spoken at Brown Chapel and picked up the endorsement of the Dallas County Voters League, Selma's leading black civil rights group. Baker had been trained at the University of Alabama and had earned the grudging respect of civil rights workers during the 1965 demonstrations. "I'm a segregationist," he said bluntly, "but if I was a nigger I'd be doing just what they're doing." He pledged at Brown Chapel: "Nobody, Negro or White, will ever have to have to hang his head because he voted for me."

Clark, meanwhile, had removed his "Never" pin in favor of the more subtle slogan "For law and order." His main piece of campaign literature, however, was a booklet from the John Birch Society alleging that the Communist plan to subvert the U.S. government would begin in Selma with his defeat.

A debate broke out within the civil rights movement over whom to support. SNCC, now under the militant leadership of Stokely Carmichael, urged blacks to vote only for black candidates. "We'd rather see Jim Clark elected than Wilson Baker, because Baker would give the Democratic Party a respectability it doesn't deserve," Carmichael said. "To ask Negroes to get in the Democratic Party is like asking Jews to join the Nazi Party." SNCC had started its own political party in neighboring Lowndes County, the Lowndes County Freedom Organization, with the emblem of a black panther.

King and the SCLC, meanwhile, called for a "unified Negro vote" and backed moderate white candidates like Baker and Flowers. "Baker wasn't our liberator, but he was a hell of a lot better than Clark, and without us, he would lose," wrote the Selma civil rights attorney J. L. Chestnut. Most blacks in Selma agreed.

Election Day was a momentous occasion for African-Americans in Alabama. Cager Lee woke up well before dawn on May 3, "just a little excited" about voting in his first election in eighty-three years. He arrived at the Perry County Courthouse four hours before polls opened at 8:00 a.m. with a big toothless smile across his weathered face. "I just wanted to make sure I finally [made it here]," he said. He was accompanied by his daughter Viola, Jimmie Lee Jackson's mother, who thought about her son as she voted for the first time. There were black candidates running for state legislator, sheriff, county commissioner, and tax collector in Perry County, and federal observers on hand to make sure the balloting went smoothly.

In Selma, Ardies and Thomas Mauldin joined hundreds of black voters at the polls, in a line that stretched six blocks from the courthouse down-town to the black neighborhood around Brown Chapel. "I'm going to vote just as far against Jim Clark as I can anybody in this world," said Mary Reese, an elderly black Selmian. "I been waiting him out for a long time. A LONG time." Doar drove by and remarked, "There are more people in that line than there were registered Negro voters when I first came to Selma."

People showed up from all over Dallas County to vote. A fifty-two-year-old tenant farmer from rural Carlowville walked sixteen miles to cast a ballot. "Man, this is the second emancipation," he said. "I ain't never voted before, but the Lord willing, I sure mean to vote this time." Doar headed out to the tiny town of Orville, eighteen miles from Selma, which had scarcely more than a general store, and watched five hundred of the seven hundred registered blacks patiently fill out their ballots at four polling places.

There was a massive turnout across the state. Eighty percent of regis-tered blacks voted; half of them had not even been registered the year be-fore. Over seventeen thousand people voted in Selma, a huge increase over the sixty-five hundred who had cast ballots in prior elections. Dallas County had an extremely long paper ballot, listing seventy-three candi-dates for twenty-four positions. Results were very slow to come in.

The sheriff's race was neck and neck. First Clark was up, then Baker as results were tallied late from Selma's black neighborhoods. As his lead slipped away, Clark, once again wearing a gold-plated "Never" pin for Elec-tion Day, grew increasingly angry, yelling at reporters on the courthouse steps. In the wee hours of the morning, replacement clerks were sent in to count the rest of the ballots, which Justice Department lawyers carefully monitored. The preliminary count showed Baker defeating Clark with enough votes to avoid a runoff.

But the next day, Clark appeared before the Dallas County Democratic Executive Committee, which was controlled by segregationist hard-liners, and persuaded them not to accept six boxes of ballots from black wards in Selma that overwhelmingly favored Baker. Of the eighteen hundred disputed ballots, more than sixteen hundred were for Baker. Without those votes, Baker would have to face Clark in a runoff. "The boxes were so in-fected with irregularities as to make it impossible to determine which were proper and valid ballots and which were not," said the Democratic chair-man, Alston Keith. *The Washington Post* called it a "ballot box coup."

Late on May 4, Doar called the DOJ attorney Brian Landsberg in Montgomery and told him to get to Selma as fast as he could. Landsberg and the attorney Lou Kauder worked all night at the federal building drafting a complaint against the Dallas County Democratic Executive Committee. Every few hours they'd awaken their supervisor, John Douglas, who was sleeping on the floor, for comments. He'd mutter a few words, then go back to sleep. By the morning the legal complaint was done.

Doar sent the DOJ attorney George Rayborn on the first flight to Mobile to file the complaint with Judge Daniel Thomas in Alabama's Southern District Court. Unfortunately, Thomas was out of town and could not be located. So Doar drove to Montgomery and cornered Judge Frank Johnson, who had approved the Selma to Montgomery march and was playing golf at Maxwell Air Force Base. The judge stepped away from the links, issued a restraining order against the Democratic Executive Committee, and ordered a trial for May 16.

Wallace's best lawyer, Frank Mizell, defended Sheriff Clark. Mizell, who called himself "Alabama's Segregation Leader," was counsel to the Alabama Sovereignty Commission, which Wallace had formed to resist federal civil rights laws by methods that included spying on citizens participating in the civil rights movement and funding White Citizens' Councils. Mizell claimed that the sixteen hundred "nigger ballots" had been "stuffed" by black poll workers and faulted the "arrogance" of the Justice Department in bringing the suit.

That drew a heated response from Doar, who jumped to his feet in the Selma courtroom. "It is not a case of arrogance on the part of those 1,600 voters, not arrogance on the part of the United States, not arrogance on the part of the Justice Department," he said. "It is the arrogance of those people who happen to control 23 votes on the Dallas County Executive Committee."

The trial had ramifications far beyond Selma. "The right to vote is the foundation of this country," Doar said in his closing argument. "If it can be swept away by an arbitrary, wholesale action of this Committee, it doesn't mean very much."

Judge Thomas, back from his vacation, sided with the Justice Department. "The Court listened to testimony concerning alleged defects in the six boxes for almost two days," he wrote. "The Court did not hear at that time any evidence which would indicate that votes were bought or sold, that boxes were stuffed, or that there was any misconduct on the part of polling officials or voters which could be construed as even approaching fraud."

Clark's ballot box coup had failed. After a decade of terrorizing blacks in Selma, he was out of a job. "To get rid of Sheriff Clark with Wilson Baker showed the value of the act," said the DOJ attorney Brian Landsberg. "It brought about real change in the lives of people; it brought about real change in the power balance."

Elsewhere in Alabama, the results were more mixed for black voters. Twenty-three of fifty-two black candidates advanced to a runoff, but none won an outright majority. Only five black candidates prevailed in the May 31 runoff: a coroner in Sumter County, a school board member in Greene County, a tax collector, a county commissioner, and a sheriff in Macon County.

Lucius Amerson, a thirty-two-year-old postman who had been a paratrooper in the Korean War, became the first black sheriff in the South since Reconstruction. His hometown had been the site of the infamous Tuskegee gerrymander in 1957, when a white legislator redrew the predominantly black town's boundaries to exclude all but twelve blacks but none of the whites. "I didn't know if I could win, but it was a matter of trying as hard as I could," Amerson said. "There was a lot of apathy among the Negroes in the community. They didn't know what would happen if a Negro got elected sheriff, and of course some felt that a Negro just possibly could not do the job or that he would not get the cooperation from the white element."

These modest black achievements were overshadowed by Lurleen Wallace's landslide victory; the governor's wife defeated opponent Richmond Flowers by over 250,000 votes. While federal examiners were signing up black voters amid much hoopla, George Wallace quietly engineered a skillful countermobilization drive of his own. "This voting bill is not going to affect Alabama the way many people think," said an official in the governor's office. "What it is going to accomplish is the biggest registration of whites in our history."

In January 1966, Wallace sent a red, white, and blue pamphlet to all the white public school students in the state, encouraging their parents to "register and vote for Freedom's Sake." The 200,000 people who had written letters to the governor also received responses from his State Sovereignty

Commission urging them to register. As a result, Wallace signed up 110,000 new white voters in the nine months preceding the primary, nearly matching the number of black registrants.

Flowers played right into Wallace's hands by campaigning extensively in black neighborhoods and touting endorsements from civil rights leaders like King. "Dr. King's endorsement hung over the Attorney General's neck like an albatross for all segregationists to see," wrote Jack Nelson of the *Los Angeles Times*. Despite the VRA's early accomplishments, the conservative white vote remained a formidable force in southern politics. White Alabamians, who still made up 84 percent of the state's electorate, had a very different response to the civil rights protests from the rest of the country. "It was at Selma a year ago that Wallace really won Tuesday's election," the pollster Samuel Lubell concluded.

On June 4, 1966, James Meredith, the first black student at the University of Mississippi, left the Peabody Hotel in Memphis wearing a pith helmet and carrying an ivory-tipped African cane and began to walk 220 miles to his destination, the Mississippi capital, Jackson. He called it the March Against Fear.

Why was Meredith marching? There were now 130,000 black registered voters in Mississippi, up from 30,000 in 1964 (when only 6.7 percent of eligible blacks were registered), but there were still 450,000 unregistered blacks. Federal examiners were signing up voters in a third of the counties in Mississippi, more than in any other state, but there were still no examiners in the thirty counties where less than 25 percent of the population had registered. Eighty percent of black Mississippians lived below the poverty line, and only 2 percent attended integrated schools. A year after the passage of the VRA, "Jim Crow was still the rule rather than the exception," wrote John Dittmer in *Local People: The Struggle for Civil Rights in Mississippi*.

Meredith urged black onlookers along the highway to "register and vote. And if you have any trouble, just let me know. I'll be on the highway for several days. We'll get some federal registrars in here. We're going to make the president do what he said he was going to do or show that he was lying." He made it twelve miles to the Tennessee line on his first day and fourteen miles into Mississippi on day two, until a voice cried out from the woods near Hernando, "I only want James Meredith." Aubrey James

Norvell, an unemployed hardware clerk from Memphis, hit Meredith with seventy pellets of buckshot, leaving him writhing in pain on U.S. 51. The shooting was the seventeenth incident of violence in connection with registration and voting in the South since the Voting Rights Act went into effect, the Southern Regional Council reported.

To civil rights activists, Mississippi was synonymous with bloodshed. The lynching of Emmett Till, the assassination of Medgar Evers, the murders of Goodman, Chaney, and Schwerner. "Just to mention Mississippi, to cross the state line from Alabama and go there, it just created all types of problems in my own mind," said John Lewis. "It seemed like when you just drove over the state line, something happened to the air, to the environment. It was a psychological thing . . . Alabama is bad; Alabama is hell. But to go to Mississippi at the time was worse than hell."

White segregationists resisted the VRA and other civil rights laws more fiercely in Mississippi than anywhere else in the South. When federal examiners arrived in Leflore County, where only 281 of 13,567 blacks were registered beforehand, a sign announcing their arrival was torn into pieces by Byron De La Beckwith, a Klansman twice acquitted of murdering Evers (he wouldn't be convicted until 1994). In January 1966, fourteen Klansmen firebombed the Hattiesburg home of the NAACP leader Vernon Dahmer. The epigraph on his tombstone read, "If you don't vote, you don't count."

The continued attacks exasperated and radicalized civil rights activists. Following Meredith's shooting, civil rights leaders called for federal examiners to be sent to all six hundred counties in the Deep South. (Examiners had been registering voters in forty-two counties.) "Only thus will ballots instead of buckshot become the voice of the South," wrote King, Carmichael, and Floyd McKissick of CORE. They continued the walk in Meredith's stead, hoping to replicate the Selma to Montgomery march in Mississippi.

The next day voters headed to the polls in the 1966 Mississippi congressional primaries. Five black candidates were running for office under the banner of the Mississippi Freedom Democratic Party (MFDP), which had been established in 1964 to challenge the segregated Democratic Party. Clifton Whitley, a thirty-two-year-old minister from Holly Springs who ran a catfish cooperative, challenged the powerful Senate Judiciary Committee chairman, James Eastland. "It is time," Whitley said, "for all Mississippians to protest the lawless character of our state, and to do something to bring about a condition of law and order in our state that is free of racial characteristics."

But scared away from the polls by the Meredith shooting, only a quarter of registered black Mississippians voted. MFDP candidates were routed by margins ranging from four to one to twenty-five to one. There was one bright spot, however. Whitley had defeated Eastland in two majority-black western Mississippi counties along the Mississippi River, Claiborne and Jefferson. In Claiborne, the number of black registered voters had surged from 0.7 percent to 78 percent after federal examiners arrived. That alone terrified Mississippi segregationists. After Jim Clark's defeat in Selma, they weren't taking any chances.

The next day the all-white Mississippi legislature revived a proposal to consolidate counties in the state. Previously a county could be consolidated only if a majority of voters approved the change. But under the new amendment, two-thirds of the legislature could make the decision for the county instead. The state senator P. M. Watkins of Claiborne County revived the county consolidation proposal. Consolidation would be desirable "if voter registration percentages get out of balance," editorialized *The Daily Times Leader* of West Point, Mississippi.

As a result of the legislative change, the two counties Whitley had won, Claiborne and Jefferson, would be consolidated with larger white counties, effectively ensuring that black candidates would not be elected to office. "All they are trying to do is avoid a few Negro votes," said the state senator E. K. Collins of Laurel, Mississippi. "I am tired of whispering around a tree about it. Let's come out in the open and say it."

The consolidation amendment was one of thirteen voting changes passed by the Mississippi legislature in a special session in 1966 to nullify the emerging black vote. "In 1966," wrote Frank Parker in *Black Votes Count: Political Empowerment in Mississippi After 1965*, "the state legislature gerrymandered the congressional district lines to prevent the election of a black member of Congress; denied black voters representation in the state legislature by creating large, multi-member state legislative districts in which black voting strength was diluted; authorized counties to switch to at-large elections for members of the county boards of supervisors and county school boards to prevent the election of black candidates; abolished elections for county school superintendents in numerous counties; and increased the qualifying requirements for independent candidates to prevent black independents from qualifying to run for office."

One of the new laws stipulated that Mississippi Freedom Democratic Party candidates now had to submit ten times as many signatures as before to qualify for office, could not use signatures from illiterate voters, had to certify the signatures as valid with white county clerks, and could not run in the general election as independent candidates if they voted in the Democratic primary, which prevented Whitley from running against Eastland again in November 1966.

Another legal change allowed counties to hold a referendum on whether school superintendents should be elected or appointed, except in eleven counties where the legislature ordered they be appointed. This included Claiborne and Jefferson counties. "The only common element is that Negroes happen to be in the majority in 9 of 11 of the counties," said Elliott Lichtman, an attorney with the Lawyers' Committee for Civil Rights Under Law in Jackson.

Mississippi also changed its method of elections for offices like state legislature, county boards of supervisors, and school boards. Instead of electing candidates from districts, where black voters could elect their preferred candidates in neighborhoods where they were a numerical majority, majority-white counties with substantial black populations instead held elections on a countywide basis, known as at-large elections. In Hinds County, which included the city of Jackson, there were enough black voters to elect four black house members and two black senators to the state legislature. But under the at-large method of elections, whites in Hinds County, who constituted 60 percent of voters, could guarantee that all fifteen representatives were white.

These kinds of electoral manipulations weren't unique to Mississippi. All across the South, once blacks began registering in large numbers, white politicians changed the rules of the game to protect their own power. The "great upsurge in voter registration, voting, and other forms of political participation by Negroes in the South" had been met with "many new barriers to full and equal political participation," wrote the U.S. Commission on Civil Rights. "The shift was from preventing blacks from voting to preventing blacks from winning or deciding elections," said Armand Derfner of the Lawyers' Constitutional Defense Committee (LCDC) in Jackson.

As a consequence, black candidates in the Deep South won only ten elected offices in the November 1966 elections, far short of initial expectations. In addition, Republicans capitalized on growing opposition to Lyndon Johnson's policies at home and abroad, picking up forty-seven seats in the House, including thirteen from the South, and three in the Senate. Support for the VRA among white southerners eroded quickly. Massive black rioting in Watts, Los Angeles, five days after the passage of the VRA, contributed to a white countermobilization in the North and the South, which helped elect archconservative governors like Ronald Reagan in California and Lester Maddox in Georgia. Maddox was best known for arming his friends with ax handles and waving a pistol at three black Georgia Tech students who asked to be seated at his Atlanta restaurant, the Pickrick, following the passage of the Civil Rights Act of 1964. *The New York Times Magazine* called his surprise victory "the nation's most dramatic example of the white backlash against racial change, and a triumph of small-town, segregationist resentments."

When LBJ sent another civil rights bill to Congress in 1966, calling for fair housing, the protection of civil rights workers, and integrated juries, it was filibustered in the Senate. A year after the passage of the VRA, the mood of the country had changed dramatically. "It would have been hard to pass the Emancipation Proclamation in the atmosphere prevailing this summer," wrote the Johnson aide Harry McPherson.

Armand Derfner first arrived in Mississippi as a twenty-seven-year-old civil rights lawyer in 1965. He'd been through a lot in his young life. His family, Polish Jews, escaped the Holocaust by traveling to Paris on forged Swedish passports. They made it out of France just hours before Hitler invaded, on Derfner's second birthday, taking a train to Spain and then Portugal before boarding a Greek ship for New York.

But nothing quite prepared him for Mississippi. He took his passport and arranged for a letter of credit from his bank before he left from New York. "It was like a foreign country to me," he said. His dog was poisoned. His car was shot at. He was arrested in the middle of a court proceeding by an angry judge and jailed for contempt of court.

There were three civil rights law firms in Jackson at the time: Derfner's

LCDC, which had been set up by the ACLU, the Lawyers' Committee for Civil Rights Under Law, and the NAACP Legal Defense Fund (LDF). Each had a little storefront on Farish Street, the city's bustling black business district, fortified with brick and thick glass to minimize damage in case of a bombing. Judge Harold Cox of the Southern District of Mississippi dismissively referred to them as the Farish Street Crowd.

Clifton Whitley and two other plaintiffs, J. C. Fairley, of the Hattiesburg NAACP, and Charles Bunton, a civil rights activist from Claiborne County, retained Derfner and Elliott Lichtman of the Lawyers' Committee as legal counsel. They challenged three legislative changes passed by the Mississippi legislature in 1966: the qualifying requirements for independent candidates, the appointment of school superintendents, and the switch to at-large elections for county supervisors. The lawsuits alleged that the voting changes violated Section 5 of the VRA because Mississippi had not submitted them for federal review.

In October 1967, a month before statewide elections in Mississippi, a three-judge district court ruled against the plaintiffs. Section 5, the court declared, applied only to voter registration rules and did not cover voting changes that prevented candidates from running for or winning elected office. The civil rights activists appealed to the Supreme Court.

In 1967, 120 black candidates ran for office in Mississippi. One candidate, the schoolteacher Robert Clark, used the legislature's voting changes to his unexpected advantage. Clark was born in Holmes County, in the impoverished delta, on a farm purchased by his great-grandfather, a newly freed slave. His county was the fifth poorest in the nation, with the distinction of giving Barry Goldwater the highest percentage of the vote in the 1964 presidential election (96.6 percent) of anywhere in the United States. Only twenty black voters were registered as of 1960.

Clark's parents had saved enough money for him to attend Jackson State University sixty miles away. Inspired by *Brown v. Board of Education*, he earned a master's in education at Michigan State University. He returned to Mississippi to teach high school in Holmes County and applied for a five-hundred-thousand-dollar training program for adult education through the Department of Public Welfare.

The grant needed the support of the county superintendent for education, who refused to sign on. So Clark asked if he could petition the board of education instead. "Yes, you can meet with the board, but don't bring no big crowd up here, now," the superintendent said.

When Clark met with the board, it told him, "When the superintendent asks for an adult education program, we will have one."

"You mean that if the superintendent asks for a program that you will have one in the county?" Clark asked.

"Yes, that's right," the board replied.

"Well, next year you will have an adult education program in Holmes County, because I am hereby announcing my candidacy for superintendent, right now," Clark replied.

Two representatives from Holmes County promptly introduced legislation in 1966 requiring that the superintendent of schools be appointed instead of elected in Holmes County. So Clark decided to run for the state legislature instead, against J. P. Love, the longtime chairman of the house Education Committee. By that time the number of black registered voters in Holmes County had skyrocketed from twenty to sixty-three hundred, over two-thirds signed up by federal examiners. Clark won the election by 116 votes, becoming the first black member of the Mississippi legislature since 1894.

But his challenges didn't end there. Love contested the result on the basis of alleged "election irregularities." When that failed, seventeen of the twenty-two winning black candidates in 1967, including Clark, had trouble securing the insurance bonds needed to assume office. The Mississippi elections showed the impact of the legislature's voting changes in 1966. Other than Clark, the rest of the winners were mostly elected to minor positions like constable, chancery clerk, and justice of the peace. "The 1966 election laws contributed heavily to the outcome of many races," wrote John Dittmer. "Counties that changed to at-large voting elected no black supervisors, and all seven blacks running for the legislature in multimember districts also lost." Nearly as many black candidates were disqualified from running because of the new rules for independent candidates as ultimately won.

The Supreme Court decided to hear the challenges to the Mississippi election laws on October 15–16, 1968, three weeks before the presidential election. The three cases were consolidated with a fourth case from Virginia, concerning whether the state could assist illiterates with casting a ballot. The four cases became known as *Allen v. State Board of Elections*.

The case raised a number of important questions: Could a private plaintiff bring a lawsuit under the VRA? Did a covered state like Mississippi have to have all of its voting changes, no matter how minor, approved by the federal government? Did Section 5 of the VRA protect the ability of citizens not only to register to vote but also to exercise political power more broadly? The latter question, in particular, was to determine the impact of the VRA for years to come.

Up until the argument, Section 5 had received scant attention from the states or the federal government. The Justice Department had received only 251 submissions of voting changes since 1965, 90 percent from Georgia and none from Alabama, Louisiana, and Mississippi, where federal examiners had registered the bulk of voters. "I don't think that suing to enjoin voting changes not submitted for preclearance was really on the agenda of the department then," said Stephen Pollak, who had replaced John Doar as assistant attorney general for civil rights in 1967. "At the time, systemically, the department was concerned with implementing the act and had very limited person power." The Justice Department's top priorities were overseeing the registration of black voters and making sure elections were held fairly, not reviewing the voting changes of southern states.

A day before oral arguments, Derfner went to get a haircut. When he came back, his wife told him, "Not good enough. You have to do it again." So he got a second one. He was thirty years old and terribly nervous about arguing his first case before the High Court. "We could have lost the case on any number of grounds before we got to the merits," he said.

Like *Katzenbach v. South Carolina*, the oral arguments lasted two days. Day one concerned Virginia; day two, Mississippi. Derfner spoke first on behalf of Clifton Whitley. "The question in these three consolidated cases from the Southern District of Mississippi," he said, "is how much room Congress intended to leave when it passed the Voting Rights Act of 1965 to allow the Southern states covered by the Voting Rights Act to continue evading the guarantees of the Fifteenth Amendment."

His answer: not much. "We believe that what Congress sought to do in 1965 was to ensure that they would not have to pass a Voting Rights Act of

1966 because they knew that on each occasion, when they had passed legislation before that, the states that they were aiming at had then come up with another new provision that had not been covered by the Act . . . And so, we think that Section 5 was passed very broadly in order to cover everything possible that could be covered under the Fifteenth Amendment."

Elliott Lichtman, twenty-nine, argued for the plaintiffs Bunton and Fairley. "Our position is that, given the rather strong possibility that there might have been a discriminatory motive, this is just the kind of statute Congress wanted submitted to the Attorney General for his scrutiny," he argued. "Our position is that Section 5 was intended to cover any new statute which relates to the effectiveness of the right to vote."

Pollak, the assistant attorney general for civil rights, argued for the government in support of the plaintiffs. "I believe the facts of these cases bear witness to the prophetic vision of the Congress in enacting the Voting Rights Act," he said. "It was concerned, as the reports of the committees and the debates indicate, that once the barriers to registration were struck down, the states covered by the Voting Rights Act might resort, as they had resorted through the previous 100 years, to other statutes to preclude effective votes by Negroes."

The Mississippi assistant attorney general, William Allain, who was to serve as governor from 1984 to 1988, represented the defense. He knew Derfner socially and used to ask him playfully, "What do you hear lately from your bosses in Moscow?" Allain kept a sign outside the Mississippi attorney general's office that said, CIVIL WRONGS DIVISION.

The VRA regulated only voter registration and nothing beyond that, Allain argued. "We say this Court cannot command nor direct the State of Mississippi to do something which is beyond the scope of the Act itself," he said.

The dueling interpretations of the VRA had ramifications far beyond Mississippi. After failing to strike down the VRA as unconstitutional in 1966, southern states sought to severely limit the impact of the law. If the VRA applied only to voter registration, as Mississippi maintained, it would become largely irrelevant once black voters registered in significant numbers. But if the law covered a wide variety of voting changes—and states like Mississippi had to obtain federal approval for those changes—then the act would become much more powerful and far-reaching.

The Supreme Court strongly disagreed with Mississippi's argument. On March 3, 1969, Chief Justice Earl Warren issued an unexpectedly sweeping 7–2 decision that left no doubt about Section 5's power to regulate all voting changes, no matter how small or seemingly innocuous. "The Voting Rights Act was aimed at the subtle, as well as the obvious, state regulations which have the effect of denying citizens their right to vote because of their race," Warren wrote. "The right to vote can be affected by a dilution of voting power, as well as by an absolute prohibition on casting a ballot."

As in the *Katzenbach* decision, Justice Black of Alabama dissented vigorously. "This is reminiscent of old Reconstruction days, when soldiers controlled the South and when those States were compelled to make reports to military commanders of what they did," he wrote.

It received little attention at the time, but the *Allen* decision became one of the most important of the many landmark cases decided by the Warren Court. Overnight the VRA had wiped out nearly a century of voting discrimination in 1965. Since then a million blacks had registered to vote in the South, and the number of black elected officials had increased more than fivefold. Now, the Court said, the federal government had a mandate to block the more cunning "second-generation" voting barriers that had emerged after the law's passage, to ensure that long-disenfranchised minority groups could not just register to vote but could run for office and win.

Following the *Allen* ruling, Mississippi finally submitted the three disputed voting changes for federal approval. The Justice Department rejected all three, in its first Section 5 objection in the state.

"If it had not been for *Allen*," Derfner said, "the Voting Rights Act wouldn't have meant a fraction of what it's come to mean."

On December 11–14, 1968, two hundred black officeholders, including Lucius Amerson of Alabama and Robert Clark of Mississippi, attended the first Southwide Conference of Black Elected Officials at the stately Dinkler Plaza Hotel in downtown Atlanta. "Four years ago," said Attorney General Ramsey Clark, "we could have held this meeting in the telephone booth in the lobby and not interfered with anyone who wanted to make a phone call."

Lyndon Johnson did not attend the proceedings, though he did send a telegram. But a month later, at his final press conference, the outgoing president was asked, "What, sir, do you regard as your greatest accomplishment?"

The Voting Rights Act, Johnson replied. "I believe if everyone has the right to vote that they can take care of their own problems pretty well," the president said. "As you can see, when they are electing Southern sheriffs, Southern mayors, and Southern judges, the Negroes have been emancipated a great deal. It is going to correct injustice of decades and centuries. I think it is going to make it possible for this government to endure, not half slave and half free, but united."

Yet a new administration in Washington would soon enter office with a very different view of the country.

3

THE SOUTHERN STRATEGY

It was a coincidence oft noted in the history books. Five days after LBJ signed the VRA, deadly riots broke out in the Los Angeles neighborhood of Watts after police stopped a black man accused of drunk driving and a confrontation ensued. The violence between August 11 and August 16, 1965, left thirty-four people dead, one thousand injured, four thousand arrested, one thousand buildings destroyed, and forty million dollars in damages. It was "the most violent civil disturbance since the New York City draft riots of 1863," wrote the historian Rick Perlstein.

The riots were front-page news across the country, covered in the most sensationalized tones. The cover of *Life* showed a black youth carrying a table and chair out of a burning home. The magazine sent nine correspondents to cover the story and ran eleven pages of color photos in its August 27, 1965, edition, with captions like " 'Get Whitey!' The War Cry That Terrorized Los Angeles," and "In a Roaring Inferno 'Burn Baby Burn.' "

"All through the South whites began locking their doors more carefully and laying in extra supplies of ammunition for their hunting rifles," reported the civil rights activist Chuck Fager in Selma. "Watts was more than two thousand miles away, but some of the Black Belt whites' most terrifying nightmares were being played out in color on their own living room television screens."

Watts signaled the end of the "We Shall Overcome" phase of the civil rights struggle. Nine months later, during an all-night meeting in Atlanta, John Lewis was ousted as chairman of SNCC by Stokely Carmichael, a provocative and charismatic twenty-four-year-old immigrant from Trinidad who grew up in the Bronx. Carmichael styled himself the spokesman for angry black youth in places like Watts, who felt ignored by the southern-focused, church-based civil rights movement of the early 1960s and didn't see quick material benefits from the much-heralded civil rights laws.

"Some old SNCC veterans still respected him," Stanley Wise, SNCC's new executive director, said of Lewis. "But a lot of the new ones didn't have that feeling. The old day of love was gone." The militants had dislodged the moderates.

In his first move as SNCC chairman, Carmichael withdrew the organization from the White House Conference on Civil Rights in June 1966. A week later, during James Meredith's March Against Fear in Mississippi, Carmichael introduced the chant of "Black power" during a tense standoff with police in Canton, Mississippi. "That night in Canton, I felt like the uninvited guest," Lewis said. Black power, berets, and Frantz Fanon's revolutionary book *The Wretched of the Earth* replaced "Freedom Now," denim overalls, and the autobiography of Mahatma Gandhi as SNCC staples. White civil rights activists would be expelled from SNCC by the end of the year, and the word "nonviolent" subsequently deleted from its name. "The fires of frustration and discontent were burning, without a doubt," Lewis said.

He resigned from SNCC shortly after the Meredith march, delivering a blistering rebuke to Carmichael's black power philosophy. "No good can come of it," Lewis told Jack Nelson of the *Los Angeles Times*. "I agree with Dr. King that racism is implied in the slogan. And what is scaring the hell out of the people going to do for the Negroes in the long run?"

Lewis took a long train ride from Atlanta to New York, where he had accepted a job reviewing grant proposals for the liberal Field Foundation. He lived outside the South for the first time in his life. "It was lonesome, leaving the movement," he said. "I felt somewhat lost." He rented a small apartment in Chelsea, on Twenty-first Street between Eighth and Ninth avenues, where he hung a black-and-white photo by Danny Lyon of segregated drinking fountains at the county courthouse in Albany, Georgia, a giant electric cooler for whites alongside a tiny spigot marked "Colored." Lewis desperately missed home. "I wanted to come back South," he said. "Every chance I got, on a weekend or when I could afford it, I would come back."

At night, over cans of Rheingold beer, Lewis exchanged long letters with his friend Julian Bond, SNCC's former communications director, who represented the new wave of young black elected officials down South. Bond won election to the Georgia House of Representatives from Atlanta in November 1965, at twenty-five, but the legislature refused to seat him after Bond said he agreed with a SNCC statement denouncing the war in Vietnam. "The hostility from white legislators," Bond said, "was nearly absolute."

Bond told Lewis what was happening in the South. Lewis urged Bond not to stop fighting. Bond won two more elections before the Supreme Court unanimously ordered the legislature to seat him in December 1966. His travails illustrated the difficulties encountered by black politicians in the South, even after they were elected.

Lewis watched helplessly in New York during the summer of 1966 as black rioting spread from Watts to forty American cities, including sleepy midwestern towns like Omaha and Des Moines. "Our nation is moving toward two societies, one black, one white—separate and unequal," the National Advisory Commission on Civil Disorders concluded. Southern conservatives took a different view, blaming the civil rights movement for domestic unrest. "The more laws that are passed in this nation on the national, state, and local levels, the more rioting and looting we have," said the North Carolina senator Sam Ervin.

Lewis returned to Atlanta after a year to do community organizing work for the Southern Regional Council, which funded liberal causes in the South. When President Johnson announced he would not seek reelection because of the unpopularity of the Vietnam War, Lewis joined the insurgent presidential campaign of Robert Kennedy, who he believed was the only politician in America who could unite the fractured nation, especially blacks and whites.

He was with Kennedy in the black slums of Indianapolis when they received the news that Martin Luther King, Jr., had been assassinated on April 4, 1968. Kennedy broke the news to the shocked crowd during an evening rally, delivering one of his finest impromptu speeches. "I'm sorry, John," Kennedy told Lewis. "You've lost a leader. We've lost a leader."

Riots erupted in 110 American cities following King's death, as even neighborhoods in the nation's capital burned to the ground. "We lost Dr. King, but we still have Bobby Kennedy," Lewis said to himself, trying to lessen the blow from the death of his mentor. After attending King's funeral in Atlanta, he flew first to Oregon and then to California for the Kennedy campaign, courting black and Hispanic voters alongside Cesar Chavez of the United Farm Workers. "John, you let me down today, you sent more Mexican-Americans to turn out to vote than Negroes," Kennedy joked when the returns showed him narrowly defeating Eugene McCarthy in California.

Lewis watched Kennedy's victory speech in the candidate's suite at the Ambassador Hotel, alongside the Kennedy family and the civil rights activist Charles Evers, whose brother Medgar had been assassinated in Mississippi hours after JFK's first civil rights speech in 1963. Then came another shocking tragedy, when Sirhan Sirhan shot Kennedy in the head minutes after he left the podium. Lewis dropped to the floor in tears. He couldn't stop crying. Two months after King's assassination, Kennedy was now gone. His trip back to Atlanta was "the loneliest, longest flight of my life."

The violence reached the Democratic convention in August 1968, when Chicago police assaulted antiwar demonstrators with billy clubs and tear gas. The scene in Grant Park reminded Lewis of Birmingham and Selma. The first presidential election he voted in would be a heartbreaking one. "In 1968," wrote Andrew Young, "it seemed that everything that could go wrong did go wrong."

In the spring of 1966, Harry Dent, the chairman of the South Carolina Republican Party, visited Richard Nixon in his twenty-fourth-floor law office at 20 Broad Street in lower Manhattan. He asked the former vice president to headline a 950-person, hundred-dollar-a-plate Republican dinner in Columbia. Dent had made his name in politics as a top aide to the South Carolina senator Strom Thurmond, one of the country's foremost opponents of civil rights and a new power broker in the Republican Party. Nixon accepted, well aware that the road to the GOP presidential nomination and the White House in 1968 would travel through Dixie.

The fundraiser turned out well, and on his way back to the airport Nixon bluntly told Dent, "I'm running for the presidency." But he worried about splitting the southern vote with George Wallace, who was preparing to launch a third-party presidential bid in 1968. The Dallas County sheriff,

Jim Clark, and other segregationist leaders had begun planning Wallace's campaign immediately after Lurleen Wallace's election as Alabama governor in 1966. If Wallace carried most of the South, Nixon told Dent, he would be "unable to win enough votes in the rest of the country to gain a clear majority."

Dent told Nixon, "Thurmond was the only Southern leader in the GOP who could rally Southerners to a Republican banner." Nixon had already begun courting South Carolina's sixty-four-year-old junior senator, telling the press in Columbia, "Strom is no racist. Strom is a man of courage and integrity." Nixon charmed Dent, whose family's beloved wire-haired terrier had been run over by a car that night, by sending him a new dog, which Dent named Richard Nixon.

It was a remarkable about-face for Nixon, one that illustrated the sudden transformation of the Republican Party.

In 1964, four years after Nixon had narrowly lost the presidency to JFK, the Arizona senator Barry Goldwater won the Republican nomination for president thanks to a conservative insurgency led by white southerners. Southern delegates to the GOP convention in San Francisco dubbed their hotel Fort Sumter. Goldwater had supported civil rights legislation in 1957 and 1960 but changed his tune when President Kennedy aligned with the civil rights movement. "We're not going to get the Negro vote as a bloc in 1964 and 1968, so we ought to go hunting where the ducks are," he told a gathering of Republican state party chairmen in Atlanta in 1961.

Goldwater had been one of only six Republicans in the Senate to vote against the Civil Rights Act of 1964. His nomination, for the first time, "publicly defined the Republican Party as anti–civil rights," wrote Thomas and Mary Edsall in *Chain Reaction: The Impact of Race, Rights, and Taxes on American Politics.*

In September 1964, Thurmond endorsed Goldwater in a dramatic televised announcement played throughout the South. "The party of our fathers is dead," he said, wearing a gold elephant pin while sitting in front of a giant photo of Goldwater. "Those who took its name are engaged in another Reconstruction." Democrats had "become the party of minority groups, power-hungry union leaders, political bosses and big businessmen looking for government contracts and favors." Thurmond's abandonment of the Democratic Party had "enormous significance," wrote the *National*

Review, "one of those by-products of the Goldwater candidacy that will ripple through the political history of this country for many years to come."

Thurmond had long been at the vanguard of southern Democratic opposition to civil rights. In 1948, after Harry Truman desegregated the military and created the President's Committee on Civil Rights, Thurmond, then governor of South Carolina, walked out of the Democratic convention in Philadelphia and ran for president on the Dixiecrat ticket. Upon accepting the nomination of the States' Rights Democratic Party in Birmingham, he declared, "I wanna tell you, ladies and gentlemen, that there's not enough troops in the army to force the Southern people to break down segregation and admit the Nigra race into our theaters, into our swimming pools, into our homes, and into our churches." That November, Thurmond won four southern states: Alabama, Louisiana, South Carolina, and Mississippi.

Eight years later, Thurmond organized the "Southern Manifesto"—signed by over one hundred members of Congress—which called for a policy of massive resistance toward *Brown v. Board of Education*. The next year he staged the longest filibuster in Senate history, lasting twenty-four hours and eighteen minutes, against the Civil Rights Act of 1957. The first civil rights bill passed by Congress since Reconstruction, it established the Civil Rights Division of the Department of Justice. "Do not be deceived by the statements that the main purpose of this bill is to protect the voting rights of Negro citizens," he warned his Senate colleagues, munching on cold steak and pumpernickel bread during his marathon speech. "The real purpose is to arm the federal courts with a vicious weapon to enforce race mixing."

Thurmond was one of only two GOP senators—John Tower of Texas was the other—to vote against the Civil Rights Act of 1964 and the VRA. He called the VRA "the most patently unconstitutional piece of legislation approved by the Congress since Reconstruction days." On the Senate floor, he denounced the civil rights movement as "nothing more nor less than a war against society—in short, an insurrection."

Thurmond campaigned energetically for Goldwater across the South. "Goldwater and Thurmond were like the golddust twins," wrote Dent. Thurmond put Dent in charge of southern operations for Goldwater. Dent was like a son to Thurmond. After growing up in the small central South Carolina town of St. Matthews, in a county named after the Great Nullifier, John Calhoun, Dent had joined Thurmond's staff as a driver in 1950, while a student at Presbyterian College, and became his top aide at twenty-seven, the youngest administrative assistant in the U.S. Senate. The red-haired, teetotaling Southern Baptist deacon was only interested in religion and politics (unlike Thurmond, who, at twenty-two, had fathered a secret daughter with his family's sixteen-year-old black maid).

Dent's commitment to the church didn't stop him from perfecting the dark art of southern politics, using practically any means necessary to achieve victory. One Republican ad in the South, criticizing LBJ's civil rights bill, featured a picture of a disheveled white woman in a dress and high heels, who had been "seized and beaten by a Negro mob" at a traffic stop. The bold lettering at the bottom said: "Barry Goldwater, For States' Rights! For the South!" Despite LBJ's landslide victory in 1964, Goldwater carried five southern states, and Thurmond emerged as the poster child for Dixie Republicanism. The realignment of the South, which LBJ had forecast in 1964, was close at hand.

Following the election, Goldwater conservatives took control of GOP state parties across the South, including in South Carolina, where Dent became the GOP chair. "The party of Lincoln has become the party of the white man in much of Dixie," wrote the *Los Angeles Times*. The South Carolina GOP convention in March 1966 took place beneath a huge Confederate flag, with no blacks in attendance. "We don't see anything we can do this year to pick up the Negro vote," Dent said. "President Johnson has it in his pocket." So Dent, to use Goldwater's phrase, went hunting where the ducks were.

Nixon was not the obvious choice of the ascendant Goldwater/Thurmond wing of the Republican Party. He'd supported strong civil rights bills as Eisenhower's vice president and issued a statement with New York's governor, Nelson Rockefeller, in 1960 stating: "Our program for civil rights must assure aggressive action to remove the remaining vestiges of segregation or discrimination in all areas of national life—voting and housing, schools and jobs." Nixon had supported the Civil Rights Act and the VRA, criticizing LBJ for not having introduced a voting bill sooner in 1965. He warned that the GOP "must not compromise its strong position on civil rights for the purpose of gaining votes in Southern states."

But Nixon's principles were notoriously flexible. He sensed an opportunity to attract conservative white voters as the country turned away from the civil rights movement and newly registered black voters flocked to the Democratic Party after 1965. When Nixon traveled across the country in 1966 for Republican candidates, logging 127,000 miles during forty visits—half of them in the South—he inveighed against "riots, violence in the streets and mob rule" and "extremists of both races." After speaking at another event for the South Carolina GOP in the fall of 1966, Nixon told his aide Pat Buchanan, "This is the future of this Party, right here in the South."

Nixon's conversion was the reverse of Johnson's. He was now denouncing civil rights efforts that he previously supported. "The newest of the new Nixons," wrote Andrew Kopkind of *The New Republic*, "seems to be materializing in the Goldwater image."

In 1968, Dent allied with the GOP chairmen Clarke Reed of Mississippi and Bill Muffin of Florida to make sure the South had major influence over the GOP presidential nominating process. They called themselves the Greenville Group because their meetings took place in Reed's kitchen in Greenville. They wanted the major candidates—Nixon, Ronald Reagan, Nelson Rockefeller—to "come a-callin', dressed up in their best bib and tucker," Dent said.

Nixon met the southern chairmen on May 31, 1968, in Atlanta, welcomed at the airport with a huge banner: DIXIELAND IS NIXONLAND. It was his first campaign swing through the South in 1968 and a critical meeting for Nixon; the southern states constituted half of the votes needed to win the GOP nomination at the convention. "I was doing serious courting and hard counting," Nixon said.

He met with a dozen party chairmen over two days at the Marriott; Dent invited Thurmond to Atlanta on day two. "They tell me you are the only man who can defeat Wallace," Nixon told Thurmond. "Will you help us?" In return for Thurmond's support, Nixon pledged to appoint "strict constructionists" to the Supreme Court, not like the judges who had desegregated the schools and upheld the VRA, and to no longer treat the South as "a whipping boy" on civil rights. He promised, in essence, to reverse the civil rights revolution that Johnson had advanced and that he had earlier supported.

"Nixon," said Dent, "affirmed what people in the South wanted to hear." Three weeks later Thurmond endorsed Nixon, saying he had the best stance on civil rights of the GOP candidates and "offers America the best hope of recovering from domestic lawlessness . . . and a power grasping Supreme Court."

Before the GOP convention in Miami, Thurmond sent a telegram to every southern delegate. "Richard Nixon's position is sound on law and order, Vietnam, the Supreme Court, military superiority, fiscal sanity, and decentralization of power," it said. "He is best for unity and victory in 1968. Our country needs him, and he needs our support in Miami. See you at the convention."

Once in Miami, Thurmond became, in Dent's words, "the chief of the Nixon fire brigade." He and Dent met with scores of southern delegates, starring in the Strom and Harry Show. "Harry would sell Strom as the statesman who had put his long career on the line for Southern Republicanism, and Strom would sell Nixon as a winner whom we could trust," said the Thurmond aide Fred Buzhardt.

At Thurmond's urging, Nixon met with every southern state delegation over tumblers of whiskey at his eighteenth-floor suite at the Hilton Plaza. He said he would appoint only conservative judges to the bench, would pick a vice presidential nominee who would not offend the South, and wouldn't capitulate to "satisfy some professional civil rights group." Nixon said he had no problem with southerners using "non-discriminatory" literacy tests and would amend the VRA so that it no longer singled out southern states. Nixon's promises and Thurmond's relentless lobbying—he patrolled the convention floor with a megaphone before the final vote—kept southern delegates from defecting to Reagan and preempted support for Wallace.

Only 3.5 percent of the delegates to the GOP convention were black. The Massachusetts senator Edward Brooke was the only prominent black speaker. In the air-conditioned halls of the Miami Beach Convention Center, it was as if the civil rights movement had never happened. "He's prostituted himself to get the Southern vote," said the baseball star Jackie Robinson, who had supported Nixon in 1960.

The Democratic convention in 1968 had twice as many black delegates and seated integrated delegations from states like Mississippi and Georgia. The segregationist Georgia governor, Lester Maddox, walked out in protest of Julian Bond's Georgia contingent, denouncing the Democrats as the party of "looting, burning, killing and draft-card burning."

Nixon's plan worked; he was nominated on the first ballot. Thurmond accompanied Nixon to the podium when he gave his acceptance speech and stood onstage as orange balloons fell from the rafters. The columnists Rowland Evans and Robert Novak called it "truly Strom Thurmond's convention." The Democratic nominee, Hubert Humphrey, dubbed the GOP ticket "the Nixiecrats."

In the general election, Nixon refined Goldwater's southern strategy. Unlike Goldwater, who "ran as a racist candidate," Nixon said, the 1968 GOP nominee campaigned on racial themes without explicitly mentioning race. "Law and order" replaced "states' rights." Pledging to weaken the enforcement of civil rights laws replaced outright opposition to them. Nixon "always couched his views in such a way that a citizen could avoid admitting to himself that he was attracted by a racist appeal," said his top aide, John Ehrlichman.

Even Wallace had learned the new code words of American politics. "I don't talk about race or segregation anymore," he said in September 1968. "We're talking about law and order, and local control of schools, not those other things." His campaign was drawing huge crowds in the North— seventy thousand at Boston Common, twenty thousand at Madison Square Garden, fifteen thousand in Detroit, twelve thousand in San Francisco. Wallace's increasing popularity intensified Nixon's courtship of the white southern vote. "I think the ideas expressed by George Wallace are the ideas a great many Republicans espouse," said Nixon's southern campaign director, the Georgia congressman Bo Callaway.

Dent did for Nixon what he'd done for Goldwater, running the southern-focused Thurmond Speaks for Nixon-Agnew Committee out of his law office at the Palmetto State Life Building in Columbia. The committee was structured independently, but Nixon's campaign manager, John Mitchell, cleared all decisions, subject to Thurmond's veto. Dent flew to New York weekly to brief the campaign. Thurmond's committee blanketed the South, dragging down Wallace's numbers from Memphis to Miami.

TV commercials featured the country music star Stuart Hamblen singing a tune about white southerners chasing a rabbit named George Wallace down a hole while the enemy of the South, Hubert Humphrey, moved into the White House. Posters were put up declaring: "Senator Thurmond denied the Republican nomination to the liberal Gov. Rockefeller . . . Help strengthen Strom Thurmond's position in the new Republican administration with a rousing endorsement of Richard Nixon on Nov. 5." Red, white, and blue "Help Strom Elect Nixon" bumper stickers were distributed throughout the South at every Thurmond campaign stop.

Nixon premised his own campaign almost entirely on winning the white backlash vote. There were almost no images of blacks in his ads, except to show them rioting. One ad featured a militant snare drum and discordant piano chords alongside disturbing images of domestic unrest. "The first civil right of every American is to be free from domestic violence," said the narrator, followed by the ominous slogan "This time, vote like your whole world depended on it." Two weeks before the election, Nixon cut an ad aimed specifically at southern whites. "I pledge to you we will return law and order in this country," he said.

The battle between Nixon and Wallace in the South eclipsed the burgeoning black vote, which was lukewarm for Humphrey, who'd been a stalwart backer of civil rights but was damaged irreparably by supporting the Vietnam War. "The fact is that the Southern Negro has the franchise but no choice," said Vernon Jordan of the Voter Education Project. Nine hundred thousand black voters had registered in the South since the VRA, but over a million white voters had too, limiting the impact of the black vote. On Election Day, black turnout was up 7 percent compared with 1964, and Nixon received just 12 percent of black ballots, compared with 32 percent in 1960. But the sizable black vote was not enough to offset white defections from the Democratic Party, which the southern scholars Earl and Merle Black called "The Great White Switch."

Nixon won 301 electoral votes to 191 for Humphrey and 46 for Wallace. Nixon and Wallace together carried every state in the South except for Texas. Nixon narrowly defeated Wallace in the eleven states of the Confederacy, 34.7 percent to 34.3 percent. On Election Day Thurmond sprinted across South Carolina, which went for Nixon by six points, before flying to New York for the campaign's victory party. "Strom, you did a fabulous job!" Nixon told him.

Dent was awarded a prominent job in the White House, as the political adviser in charge of all things southern. R. W. Apple of *The New York Times* called his appointment "a small quid for a big quo." The overseer of Nixon's southern strategy, his campaign manager, John Mitchell, became attorney general. *Time* dubbed the new administration "Uncle Strom's Cabin."

On August 6, 1970, key parts of the VRA were set to expire. These included provisions giving the federal government the power to approve voting changes from select southern states, dispatch federal examiners to register voters, and send federal observers to monitor elections. "The fact that you had federal interference with state elections and an automatic review provision—those provisions were pretty extreme," said Ben Zelenko, counsel to the House Judiciary Committee chairman, Emanuel Celler. "So the tradeoff was to make them temporary." President Johnson had told Celler in 1965: "I don't want to have to go through what we went through in '64 to get voting rights passed."

In his last State of the Union address in January 1969, Johnson called for the temporary provisions of the VRA to be renewed for another five years. The Democratic and Republican leaders of the House Judiciary Committee, Celler of New York and Bill McCulloch of Ohio, promptly introduced legislation in Congress and scheduled hearings for May and June 1969. "When I voted for the Voting Rights Act of 1965, I hoped that five years would be ample time," said McCulloch at the start of the hearings in Room 2141 of the Rayburn Office Building, where the VRA had originated. "But resistance to the program has been more subtle and more effective than I thought possible. A whole arsenal of racist weapons has been perfected."

The number of black registered voters had doubled in the seven southern states covered under Section 5, and the number of black elected officials had increased from sixty-five to four hundred across the South. But there were still no black members of Congress or statewide officials from the southern states, and the black voter registration rate lagged twenty-four points behind whites. Jurisdictions throughout the South had changed their electoral procedures, making it harder for black candidates to run for and win elected office. "The history of the Voting Rights Act has shown that 350 years of oppression cannot be eradicated in 5 years," McCulloch said.

Meanwhile, Nixon's southern supporters, to whom he in large part owed his presidency, were itching to get out from under the law. "John, this is extremely important to us," Nixon's southern campaign director, Bo Callaway, wrote to Attorney General Mitchell. "I believe most Southerners would feel that the Nixon administration broke a strong commitment to the South if it allowed an extension of the present bill."

In March 1969, two months after Nixon's inauguration, the chairmen of the GOP state parties in the South held a strategy session at the Sheraton-Carlton Hotel two blocks from the White House. Nixon sent his southern emissary, Harry Dent, to greet them. Dent's old friend from the Greenville Group, Clarke Reed of Mississippi, urged the Nixon administration to draft a voting rights bill for "the nation as a whole without regional discrimination." Dent assured the group that the new administration, unlike the previous one, shared their concerns. "The Voting Rights Act looks like it's coming along pretty good," Dent said, "so that the monkey will be off the backs of the South."

Nixon's southern strategy had followed him to the White House. "As to the whole Southern strategy that Harry S. Dent Sr. and others put together in 1968," the RNC chairman Lee Atwater later admitted, "opposition to the Voting Rights Act would have been a central part of keeping the South."

That would become clear three months later, when Mitchell introduced Nixon's new plan for the VRA on Capitol Hill. Nicknamed the Heavyweight by the president, Mitchell was "dour, taciturn, formidably efficient . . . with all the human graces of the Sheriff of Nottingham," according to *Time*. The press called him "Mr. Southern Strategy." He was widely considered the most conservative member of the administration and took a very different approach to the attorney general job from his predecessors Ramsey Clark and Nick Katzenbach. "I think this is an institution for law enforcement, not social improvement," Mitchell said.

He'd canceled five appearances before Subcommittee No. 5 of the House Judiciary Committee before finally appearing in June 1969. Nixon's bill, the first civil rights legislation sent to Congress by the president, radically altered the VRA by extending the law to the entire country and eliminating Section 5 of the act, whose powers the Supreme Court had significantly expanded three months earlier in *Allen v. State Board of Elections*.

"I cannot support what amounts to regional legislation," Mitchell told the committee, echoing Nixon's campaign promise to Thurmond in 1968.

Mitchell admitted that nationwide application of the VRA would cripple enforcement of the law. "With the entire nation covered, it would be impossible for the Civil Rights Division of the Department of Justice to screen every voting change in every county in the nation," he said. Removing Section 5 would restore the status quo before 1965, when discriminatory voting laws could be blocked only after lengthy litigation in the courts. "In contrast to the 1965 act, our proposal leaves the decision to the court, where it belongs," Mitchell said. "It properly places the burden of proof on the government and not the states."

The leaders of the Judiciary Committee were incredulous. Applying the act nationwide, Celler argued, "is like saying because you have a flood in Mississippi you have to build a dam in Idaho." McCulloch, the courtly conservative from central Ohio, was even more blunt. "The administration creates a remedy for which there is no wrong and leaves grievous wrongs without adequate remedy," he said. "I ask you, my friends and my colleagues, what kind of civil rights or a human rights bill is that? That is not the kind of civil rights legislation that gives hope to black America."

Theodore Hesburgh, the president of Notre Dame, whom Nixon had installed as head of the Civil Rights Commission, told Mitchell: "Your proposed alternative would turn back the clock to 1957, relying on the slow process of litigation to try to keep up with rapidly enacted changes in the laws . . . It is an open invitation to those states which denied the vote to minority citizens in the past to resume doing so in the future, through insertion of disingenuous technicalities and changes in their election laws."

Forty civil rights activists from Alabama, led by Sallie Mae Hadnott of Prattville, one county over from Selma, staged a sit-in at Mitchell's office to protest the administration's civil rights policy. The columnists Evans and Novak called Nixon's proposal "by far the most ominous break with civil rights that the administration had yet attempted."

Mitchell's plan, said Celler, would turn the VRA "into smoke and ashes."

On November 5, 1968, four black farmers—Harry Means, Frenchie Burton, Vassie Knott, and Levi Morrow—went to the polls in Greene County, Alabama, seventy miles northwest of Selma. They were running for county commission, along with two black candidates for the school board, J. A. Posey and Robert Hines, on the ticket of the National Democratic Party of

Alabama (NDPA), which had been founded to challenge the segregated Alabama Democratic Party.

Before the VRA, only three hundred of five thousand eligible black voters were registered in Greene County, one of the smallest and poorest counties in the state. Blacks needed a white man to vouch for them in order to get on the rolls, and no white man had done so in Greene County since the 1950s. By 1968, however, thanks to the help of federal registrars stationed in a trailer outside the Greene County Courthouse in Eutaw, four thousand blacks had registered in the county and black candidates were on the verge of taking control of the county commission and school board. Whereas whites had outnumbered blacks eightfold on the rolls before the VRA, blacks now outnumbered whites by two to one.

But when the NDPA candidates arrived at the polls, they were shocked to find their names missing from the ballot. Seventeen local NDPA candidates won in Alabama on November 5, but none would be able to take office in Greene County.

A year earlier Alabama had passed a law requiring independent candidates to qualify for the ballot by March 1, eight months before the general election. But the NDPA candidates weren't nominated until May 1968, after they had lost in the Democratic primaries, so the Alabama secretary of state, Mabel Amos, disqualified them from running that fall. The case was immediately appealed to the Supreme Court, with the renowned civil rights lawyer Charles Morgan, Jr., director of the ACLU's Atlanta office, representing the NDPA candidates. On October 18, 1968, the Supreme Court unanimously ruled that the candidates be placed on the ballot. Black leaders like Julian Bond and Coretta Scott King urged black voters to vote for the eagle party, referring to the NDPA symbol.

On Election Night the NDPA's president, John Cashin, a well-to-do dentist from Huntsville, called the Greene County probate judge, Dennis Herndon, the top election official, to find out what happened.

"My Greene County chairman tells me that our candidates aren't on the ballot," Cashin told Herndon.

"That's right, they sure aren't," Herndon responded.

"But the US Supreme Court ordered them on the ballot," Cashin said.

"Well, I've got a copy of that order, too, and in my opinion they are not legally qualified," Herndon replied. (He later claimed that he had never received the Supreme Court's notice.) He'd left the candidates off the ballot rather than serve in an integrated government.

Ten days after the election, Morgan filed suit to void the results and hold Herndon in contempt of court. The case, *Hadnott v. Amos*, was argued a day after Nixon's inauguration. It concerned, Morgan said, "the theft of the right to vote." The opinion came down on March 25, three weeks after *Allen v. State Board of Elections*, one of the last delivered before Chief Justice Earl Warren retired.

The Court ruled, 6–2, that the Alabama law, which was similar to the restrictions on independent candidates in Mississippi challenged by Clifton Whitley in the *Allen* case, was unlawful because it had not been submitted to the federal government under Section 5. The Court ordered new elections for July and instructed a district court in Montgomery to examine whether to hold Herndon in contempt. It was the first time the Supreme Court had ordered new elections because of a violation under the VRA. The lead plaintiff was Sallie Mae Hadnott, who led the sit-in at Attorney General Mitchell's office.

On July 29, 1969, with federal observers from the Justice Department on the scene to prevent foul play, new elections were held. The SCLC leaders Ralph Abernathy and Hosea Williams were also on hand to assist black voters, holding sixteen get-out-the-vote rallies at black churches in the last week of the campaign. The six NDPA candidates were finally elected, and Greene County became the first Deep South county since Reconstruction where blacks controlled the county government and school board. "We are going to replicate this throughout the Black Belt," said Abernathy, King's successor at the SCLC.

At the inauguration ceremony, two thousand jubilant blacks swarmed the streets of tiny Eutaw outside the two-story stucco courthouse, raising their right fists and chanting, "Soul power." The Indiana senator Birch Bayh flew down from Washington, calling the results "a victory for justice." Abernathy led the crowds toward the segregated pool, where they broke down the locks and jumped in. "The pool is integrated now," he said triumphantly on the sweltering August day, savoring the first of many changes that would come to Greene County.

"The provisions of the 1965 Voting Rights Act made these results possible," said John T. Nixon, the Justice Department lawyer who'd been assigned

to Greene County since 1965. Three months after the election, Nixon resigned from the Civil Rights Division in protest.

"At the present time," he said, "there is no leadership in civil rights
enforcement coming from the White House, the attorney general's office or
[the assistant attorney general for civil rights] Jerris Leonard's office." The
gains in Greene County, Nixon told Congress, were at risk of being wiped
away by the administration's VRA proposal.

Two hundred miles west of Greene County, in the clay hills between Vicks-
burg and Natchez in southwestern Mississippi, Charles Evers placed his
hand on the Bible and took the oath of office as the new mayor of Fayette,
becoming the first black mayor of a biracial Mississippi town since Reconstruction. Just six years earlier, Evers's younger brother, Medgar, the field
secretary for the Mississippi NAACP, had been gunned down outside his
Jackson home with a bundle of "Jim Crow Must Go" T-shirts in his arms.

Charles, a gregarious nightclub owner, moved back to Mississippi from
Chicago after Medgar's death and took his brother's job, on the front lines
of Mississippi's civil rights struggle. Medgar's widow, Myrlie Evers, stood
nearby at his inauguration. A four-foot statue of her husband would be unveiled that day, next to the town's Confederate memorial. "We've come a
long way, ain't we?" Evers said. He had run on the slogan "Don't vote for a
black man. Or a white man. Just a good man."

Before 1965 there had been only one black voter in Fayette's Jefferson
County. Now Evers and a slate of a dozen black aldermen and election officers had taken over city government, just as in Greene County. The number
of black registered voters in Mississippi had soared from 30,000 to 236,000
in four years. Evers called the VRA "the greatest deterrent to racial discrimination we have ever had."

Over a thousand well-wishers, almost as many people as lived in the
town itself, braved the hundred-degree heat and descended on Fayette for
the inauguration. The dignitaries included Shirley McLaine, Julian Bond,
and a newly married John Lewis. The former DOJ lawyers Ramsey Clark
and John Doar, who'd investigated Medgar Evers's killing, stood at the rear
of the crowd. LBJ sent a congratulatory telegram. "Oh my, this is some
black power," said the Mississippi NAACP president, Aaron Henry.

Fayette was poor and rural, and there wasn't much left when the cotton farming became mechanized. "We got no jobs," Evers said. "We're seventy-five percent of that town, and sixty-five percent of us blacks are on welfare. Twenty percent are unemployed. The average level of education is less than the fifth grade. The average income is under a thousand dollars. There is not a single playground or swimming pool in town. It's not just the black folks who don't have these things. Nobody does. There are shack houses and no sewers. This is what white America has done to us. But we twelve blacks are going to make it better for blacks and whites."

Despite victory in Fayette, black political power was still the exception in Mississippi rather than the rule. Of the 200 blacks who ran for office in 50 towns in the municipal elections of 1969, only 24 were elected, half of them in Fayette. The state had 1 black mayor out of 270, 1 black legislator out of 174, no black sheriffs, and no black statewide officials. The progress made was shaky at best. If the VRA wasn't extended, Evers said, "we're through."

On Capitol Hill, during the hearings of the Senate Judiciary Committee's Subcommittee on Constitutional Rights, Thurmond endorsed Nixon's voting rights bill. "I have stated before that I do not favor the invasion of the federal government into those areas that are properly within the jurisdiction of the states," he said, "and for that reason I favor no extension of the present so-called Voting Rights Act, but if legislation in this area is to exist, then I would rather have the kind of proposal favored by the Nixon administration."

"To be honest with you, senator," responded Clarence Mitchell, the NAACP's top lobbyist in Washington, "it is clear that this is being done by the Nixon administration as the means of saying to you, because you left the Democratic Party and are in the Republican Party, that we are going to do things the way Senator Thurmond wants them done."

"Do you ascribe an ulterior motive to the Nixon administration in advocating that this bill apply nationwide to all states and all people alike rather than to a continuation of a punitive measure that applies to only a few states?" an incredulous Thurmond asked Mitchell.

"First I would say the measure is not punitive," Mitchell said. "It is a proper measure. It is legally correct. I would say that regardless of whether the Nixon administration has an ulterior motive or not, a disastrous result would follow if this Voting Rights Act were to expire."

"Do you have knowledge of any people who have been denied the right to register and vote?" Thurmond responded. "We will have them investigated. We would like to know. If those things had been corrected—do you want to continually charge a state and a people with any alleged injustice that occurred many years ago? Why don't you commend them for any improvements they make?"

"We could fill this room with the record of the discrimination in the state of South Carolina," Mitchell told Thurmond. "South Carolina has fought us all the way, and they have been very worthy opponents. It has been a good fight. But now that it appears we have won we don't want to have a situation develop where the White House gives back to South Carolina all the rights to discriminate that we have succeeded in wresting from them."

"We are not asking the White House to give us back anything," Thurmond said. "We are asking that South Carolina be given the same treatment as Indiana, New York, Washington, D.C., and every other state . . . We are not on the same basis now simply because my state voted for Goldwater in 1964 and the other states voted for Goldwater . . . This act is nothing more than a device created to inflict political punishment upon one section of the country."

Joseph Rauh, the longtime counsel for the Leadership Conference on Civil Rights, jumped in. "What sets apart the states that are covered was not Goldwater," Rauh told Thurmond. "What sets them apart was the long record of violations of law that you had for years, really from the Civil War to 1964."

In South Carolina the number of black registered voters had increased from 37 to 51 percent since 1965 but still lagged thirty points behind white registration. Only 28 percent of blacks were registered in Thurmond's home of Edgefield County, compared with 96 percent of whites—statistics that convinced many in Congress of the VRA's ongoing necessity.

The House acted first. In July 1969 the House Judiciary Committee overwhelmingly approved a clean five-year extension of the VRA and disregarded Nixon's bill. But Nixon's plan was resurrected in the House Rules Committee by the chairman, William Colmer of Mississippi, a longtime segregationist who had sponsored the "Southern Manifesto" with Thurmond. He called the VRA a "civil wrong bill." The Rules Committee approved both the Celler-McCulloch bill and Nixon's.

Then, in a stunning turn of events on the night of December 12, 1969, the House passed Nixon's bill, 208–203. Civil rights supporters, who had been on the floor of the House to celebrate, instead mourned the VRA's most significant defeat. "It looks like the Klan was on the floor of Congress voting to lynch the Negro at the polls," Clarence Mitchell said. The *New York Times* columnist Russell Baker satirically wrote that Thurmond would next ask Nixon to support a bill "repealing the 1960's."

But the bipartisan voting rights coalition in the Senate, led by Hugh Scott of Pennsylvania, who had followed Everett Dirksen as Senate GOP leader, struck back. Scott was born in Fredericksburg, Virginia, on an estate owned by George Washington, and his grandfather had fought in the Confederate army. But since moving to Philadelphia to practice law and winning election to Congress in 1941, representing a state with the third-highest number of blacks in the country, Scott had been a staunch supporter of civil rights.

He immediately introduced compromise legislation, which banned literacy tests nationwide, as Nixon wanted, but retained Section 5, so that states in the South still had to submit their voting changes for federal approval. Scott ordered the Senate Judiciary Committee, led by the Mississippi senator James Eastland, to clear a bill by March 1. Thurmond was the only Republican on the Judiciary Committee to oppose Scott's bill.

In March 1969, northern Democrats and Republicans defeated southern attempts to weaken the bill. The southern senators refrained from filibustering, afraid that it would hurt Nixon's bid to put a conservative southerner on the Supreme Court. (The Senate still ended up blocking the nominations of Clement Haynsworth of South Carolina and G. Harrold Carswell of Florida, rejecting a key part of Nixon's southern strategy.) At the last hour, the Massachusetts senator Ted Kennedy slipped in an amendment granting eighteen-year-olds the right to vote in state and federal elections. "I believe the time has come to lower the voting age in the United States, and thereby to bring American youth into the mainstream of our political process," Kennedy said. If they were old enough to fight in Vietnam, he argued, they were old enough to vote.

The Senate approved the Scott-Kennedy bill by a vote of 64–12. The House concurred, 272 to 132, in June, two months before the VRA was set to expire. The young crowd in the packed House gallery roared with approval.

The new bill had emerged stronger than the 1965 one, preserving not only the key features of the original but enfranchising eleven million eighteen- to twenty-one-year-olds, banning literacy tests in fourteen nonsouthern states, and eliminating burdensome residency requirements to no more than thirty days before an election. The VRA had become not just a law benefitting black Americans but a vehicle to expand voting rights for all Americans, supported by a strong bipartisan consensus in Congress.

The only remaining obstacle was Nixon's veto pen. He believed Kennedy's eighteen-year-old amendment was "unconstitutional" and knew that the continuation of Section 5 would anger his southern supporters. Nixon's aides hotly debated what he should do. "A veto of the anti-South discriminatory provisions of the Voting Rights section would help solidify your support in Dixie," William Timmons, the assistant for legislative affairs, wrote to the president.

Attorneys in the Civil Rights Division unanimously urged Nixon to support the VRA extension, as did his more liberal aides. "To veto the Voting Rights Act would be taken as a gross and gratuitous slap in the face of black America; it would offend and outrage not only the blacks, but also millions of others who identify, in greater or lesser degree, with black aspirations," wrote the speechwriter Ray Price. "We should bear very clearly in mind that whatever their views on other black claims—housing, jobs, schools, etc.—the right to vote is one thing that practically all Americans agree on. Therefore, appear[ing] to be aligning ourselves with the Thurmonds and the Eastlands on this one, we invite the label of blatant racism."

In May 1970, four students had been killed by national guardsmen at Kent State University and two students had been shot by police at Jackson State College during antiwar protests. Against this violent backdrop, the adviser Leonard Garment added, "I cannot emphasize how harmful [a veto] would be. It could produce the most bitter reaction from blacks, youth, and others, since the President took office."

"Am concerned re volatile situation," Nixon wrote to aides. He decided to sign the bill to keep the "goddamn country" from "blowing up." At the signing ceremony at the Rose Garden on June 23, 1970, Nixon deleted every reference to the South to placate his southern backers but nonetheless hailed the advent of black political power. "In the five years since its enactment, close to 1 million Negroes have been registered to vote for the first time and more than 400 Negro officials have been elected to local offices," the president said. "These are more than election statistics; they are dramatic evidence that the American system works. They stand as an answer to those who claim that there is no recourse except to the streets."

Thurmond was furious. He accused the president of breaking his campaign promise not to sign "regional" legislation by agreeing to the "unconstitutional" and "unjust" bill. The party of Lincoln had defeated the party of Thurmond—for now.

Big changes kept coming to Greene County. In November 1970, blacks took over every major elective post. The thirty-one-year-old NAACP leader Thomas Gilmore, a graduate of Selma University who had been Dr. King's "man in Greene County," defeated Sheriff William Lee, a former football star at the University of Alabama whose family had held the office for generations. Gilmore's uncle, William McKinley Branch, who had been fired from his job as a public school teacher for registering black voters in the early 1960s, ousted Judge Herndon as the county's probate judge and most powerful official. Sheriff Gilmore proclaimed Greene County "the black capital of the United States."

Shortly after the election, a three-judge district court in Montgomery (which included Judge Frank Johnson, who had authorized the Selma to Montgomery march in 1965) found Herndon in contempt of court for deliberately leaving the black NDPA candidates off the ballot in 1968. He was instructed to pay a $5,452 fine to the candidates, the first such contempt order under the VRA. "This court don't do no fooling around," said the sixty-seven-year-old county commissioner Frenchie Burton, one of the six men Herndon had tried to keep from office.

Elsewhere in Alabama, George Wallace was in the fight of his life, struggling to reclaim the governor's mansion from his wife's successor, Albert Brewer. Brewer defeated Wallace by twelve thousand votes in the 1970 Democratic primary by forging a biracial coalition of moderate whites and newly enfranchised blacks, whose numbers had nearly tripled in five years. "Three hundred thousand nigger votes is mighty hard to overcome," Wallace told factory workers in Gadsden.

Because neither candidate won a majority, the race went to a runoff, where Wallace unleashed his most racist campaign yet, ripping into the "bloc vote" (the new code word for black voters) and Brewer's "spotted alliance." A Selma-based Wallace committee, run by Jim Clark and his White Citizens' Council friends, ran newspaper ads showing a young blond girl on the beach surrounded by seven grinning black boys. "This Could Be Alabama Four Years from Now!" the caption read. "Blacks Vow to Take Over Alabama!"

Another Wallace radio ad featured a police siren, with two cars pulling up to the side of a road. "Suppose your wife is driving home at 11 o'clock at night," said the somber narrator. "She is stopped by a highway patrolman. He turns out to be black. Think about it . . . Elect George Wallace."

Alabama voter registration offices, which were usually open only a few days a month, suddenly kept extended hours, as cars bearing Wallace bumper stickers shuttled unregistered whites to the local registrar. More than fifty thousand new voters, nearly all of them white, registered between the primary and the runoff. Wallace won the runoff by thirty-four thousand votes. "The principal factor that moved Wallace from a deficit of nearly twelve thousand against Brewer on May 5 to a commanding majority in the space of four weeks clearly was his hammering away at Brewer's black voter support in the first primary," wrote Ted Pearson of *The Birmingham News*.

"It was nigger, nigger, nigger, all over again," a disgusted Brewer said afterward. "I hoped race would not be an issue in this campaign, but it boils down to a hate and smear issue. And if that's what it takes to win, the cost is too high." At the start of the 1970s, despite notable black victories in places like Fayette and Greene County, the New South still looked plenty old.

Nixon's southern strategy had suffered a major blow with the reauthorization of the VRA, but it was far from dead. The Nixon Justice Department was among the most politicized in history, and it was impossible to tell where politics ended and policy began. Attorney General Mitchell had tapped as his assistant the twenty-nine-year-old wunderkind Kevin Phillips, whose book *The Emerging Republican Majority* became the bible for the administration's political strategy.

Phillips viewed the South, along with the heartland, "as the pillar of a national conservative party." The countermobilization of white voters in response to black political advances was essential for the GOP, Phillips said, because "white Democrats will desert their party in droves the minute it becomes a black party." When Jack Veneman, the undersecretary of health, education, and welfare, complained about the Nixon administration's sluggish school desegregation policy, the White House counsel John Ehrlichman told him: "The blacks aren't where our votes are."

The *National Review* publisher William Rusher said Phillips's book "will do for conservative Republicanism what 'Uncle Tom's Cabin' did for the cause of abolitionism." Because of its controversial subject matter, Dent urged Nixon to "follow Phillips['s] plan" but "disavow it publicly." Nixon read the book over Christmas and told his chief of staff, H. R. Haldeman, in early 1970: "Use Phillips as an analyst—study his strategy—don't think in terms of old-line ethnics, go for Poles, Italians, Irish, must learn to understand Silent Majority . . . don't go for Jews and blacks." He wrote to Haldeman that when it came to civil rights "nothing more done in South beyond law requires."

Mitchell installed Jerris Leonard, the head of Wisconsin's borrowing agency, as assistant attorney general for civil rights. Like Mitchell, Leonard had little practical experience with civil rights policy. He was no John Doar. "Jerris Leonard was something of a joke as head of the Civil Rights Division," said the Nixon counsel John Dean. "He was a lightweight. You didn't have to spend much time with him to realize that."

Dent kept close tabs on Leonard and took an active role in the DOJ. "We all knew Harry," said Jim Turner, the deputy assistant attorney general for civil rights. "I know Jerry Leonard talked to him a lot." When Leonard and Dent collaborated on legislation—codrafting Nixon's VRA bill, for example—the end result usually bore Dent's imprimatur. "Since I have been in this division and heading it, I have done my very best to lean over backwards to give the benefit of the doubt to Southern states and Southern communities," Leonard wrote to the Alabama Republican congressman Jack Edwards.

Tensions quickly developed within the Civil Rights Division, whose lawyers rebelled against the southern strategy. After Leonard, with Dent's pressure, overruled his staff and slowed down the pace of school desegregation in Mississippi, sixty-five of seventy-four attorneys in the division sent a letter to their bosses opposing the decision that leaked to the press. "It was a very rocky road for a while," said Turner. "We lost a lot of lawyers."

Another revolt soon followed the VRA's reauthorization, when DOJ lawyers protested the administration's lax implementation of the law.

It was no secret in Mississippi that Charles Evers, the "black Moses," was planning to run for governor in 1971. The number of blacks registered in Mississippi had skyrocketed from 6 to 60 percent since 1965. (The number of white voters had also increased significantly, from 70 to 91 percent.) No black man had run for governor in Mississippi since Reconstruction, but Evers recruited 110 black candidates to campaign alongside him, challenging every elective office in the state. "These Are *Your* Candidates," said posters distributed across black communities in Mississippi. "Support Them. Work for Them. Vote for Them."

Under Mississippi election law, a third-party candidate, like Evers, could win with a plurality of the vote. "In our present state, that is a very dangerous situation," said the state representative Irby Turner of the majority-black Humphreys County. Turner and other white members of the Mississippi legislature introduced legislation to abolish party primaries and require a majority vote to win, so that black candidates wouldn't get elected if the white vote split.

Mississippi's governor, Paul Johnson, vetoed the open primary law in 1966, but the legislature resurrected it after Evers narrowly lost a special election for Congress in 1968. The legislation became known as the "Charles Evers bill" and passed in the spring of 1970, over the protest of Representative Robert Clark, who remained the sole black member of the legislature. The Mississippi attorney general, A. F. Summer, submitted it to the Justice Department for federal approval.

Civil Rights Division lawyers, along with black candidates like Evers and voting rights lawyers like Armand Derfner, strongly urged Leonard to block the law. "I believe the history of the Mississippi Open Primary Law is inextricably intertwined with efforts to maintain white only office holders and therefore is objectionable," Turner wrote to Leonard.

The department had sixty days to register an objection. On the last review day, Turner learned that Leonard had recommended to Mitchell that he approve the law. He felt betrayed. Gerald Jones, the chief of the Civil Rights Division's new Voting and Public Accommodations Section, one of only a few black lawyers in the department, angrily told Leonard that he didn't see any reason to have a Civil Rights Division if the open primary law wasn't blocked.

"The politics were on at that point and the attorney general was not going to object and the assistant attorney general didn't want to recommend that," said Richard Bourne, a trial attorney in the twelve-member voting section. "So the assistant attorney general came up with this half-assed argument that he didn't have to take a position, which was just absurd."

Leonard wrote to Summer, the Mississippi attorney general, saying that because he could not conclude that the law was discriminatory, the open primary law could go into effect. "The position the department took was outrageous," Bourne said. "There was nothing in the VRA that authorized it . . . There's no question that we had a deep sense that the southern strategy was weakening our hand in terms of our ability to deal straightforwardly with the people we were supposed to be controlling—that is, the southern states that had to report to us."

Evers, with the help of the Lawyers' Committee for Civil Rights Under Law, appealed the DOJ's decision to a three-judge court in Jackson, which was no friend of civil rights. But in a surprisingly scathing opinion on April 27, 1970, the Mississippi court blocked the open primary law. Mississippi's "humiliation in bringing the law to Washington for bureaucratic approval," the court wrote, was exacerbated by "an obtuse, patronizing failure by federal government officials to discharge the duties Congress placed upon them."

Despite the court's rebuke, Leonard had begun drafting new guidelines for Section 5 that followed the DOJ's convoluted decision-making process in the open primary case; if the attorney general could not definitively conclude whether a law was discriminatory, the law would be approved. The burden of proof was transferred from the states to the federal government. "I have told the Congress on repeated occasions that their legislation places an impossible burden on the attorney general's office," Mitchell said. "We do not, of course, have the capacity that the courts have to undertake an evidentiary hearing to get at the factors involved."

Shortly after the open primary fiasco, the department considered another controversial plan from Mississippi requiring the reregistration of voters in connection with county redistricting plans for the 1971 elections. A third of Mississippi's counties—constituting 40 percent of the state's black voters—wanted every registered voter to register again. "All the work that we've done since the Voting Rights Act of 1965 is going down the drain," said Evers. "There's no way in hell we're going to be able to reregister all the folks that we've got registered."

John Lewis, after taking a fact-finding trip to Mississippi in April 1971, concurred with Evers. Lewis had recently become head of the Voter Education Project (VEP), the South's leading voting rights group, which funded local registration drives, trained black candidates, and studied the impact of the VRA. "The re-registration process currently being conducted in over 20 counties violates the letter and spirit of the 1965 and 1970 Voting Rights Act," Lewis wrote to Mitchell. "It seems clear that the intent of this action, and certainly the effect, is to roll back the advances which black Mississippians have made in their efforts to obtain the right to vote during recent years."

But once again, the Nixon administration failed to block a controversial voting change from Mississippi. Mitchell had been "unable to reach the conclusion that the projected effect would be to deprive Negro voters of rights under the Voting Rights Act," he wrote to Summer. "It is a palpable fraud," the Los Angeles Times wrote of the reregistration proposal, "and the Department of Justice is a collaborator in the deception." Lewis called on the DOJ to send federal examiners to every county where reregistration took place, but Mitchell dispatched them to only three.

The U.S. Commission on Civil Rights, a widely respected watchdog agency, accused the administration of "de facto repeal of . . . Section 5." Fourteen GOP senators, led by Hugh Scott, urged Mitchell and Leonard to reverse their interpretation of Section 5, which the senators found "difficult to comprehend." The newly formed Civil Rights Oversight Subcommittee of the House Judiciary Committee held hearings investigating the administration's enforcement of the VRA. "The Attorney General is attempting to accomplish by administrative action in 1971 what he failed to accomplish in 1970 by legislative action," said the chairman, Don Edwards, Democrat of California. "I was here when we enacted the Voting Rights Act, and I can assure you this kind of enforcement we didn't have in mind at all."

Facing strong pressure from Congress and a revolt from Civil Rights Division lawyers, the administration reversed its position on the Section 5 guidelines, which were released in September 1971. The states, not the federal government, needed to show that a voting change was not discriminatory in order to get it approved. The department also secured written assurances from Mississippi election officials that prior registrations would be accepted at the polls in 1971. The new guidelines "calmed things down quite a bit and increased vastly the number of submissions," Turner said.

The department set up a special unit within the voting section to work exclusively on Section 5 cases, which became the bulk of the voting section's work. Also in 1971, in a case originating out of Canton, Mississippi, brought by the voting rights lawyer Armand Derfner, the Supreme Court ruled, 8–1, in *Perkins v. Matthews* that moving the location of polling places, annexing new territory to change the electoral population, or modifying how candidates were elected all fell under the purview of Section 5, further broadening the statute. "After that, things really started changing," Derfner said.

The work of the voting section shifted from making sure people could register and vote freely to stopping election changes that denied minority voters political representation. The VRA's scope and impact increased dramatically as a result. "When I first got to the department in 1968, we monitored elections to make sure they weren't stolen on Election Day," said Bourne. "After a while we stopped doing that. Our focus became Section 5. We knew after the *Allen* decision and the 1970 census that we were going to be very busy."

The number of voting changes submitted by states under Section 5 grew from 110 in 1970 to 333 in 1971 to 1,359 in 1972, and the number of DOJ objections rose from 3 to 14 to 71. "We got a million submissions," said Karl Shurtliff, a trial attorney in the Section 5 unit. "Every time you objected to one, a more sophisticated response came in. It was a cat and mouse game. There was a great deal of effort put forward by the southern states to screw over black voters and candidates. They didn't want to give up easily, nor did they."

In late June 1971, days before the July 1 deadline for reregistration, John Lewis and Julian Bond launched a frenetic voter mobilization tour across Mississippi, speaking at thirty-nine stops in twenty-five counties in six days to twenty thousand blacks, urging them to register and vote in the upcoming election. "Our trip was an attempt to conquer the fear that black citizens have," Lewis said. "We had to demonstrate to the people of Mississippi that they were not alone in their struggle."

Posters for the Voter Education Project showed Lewis and Bond surrounded by a crowd of everyday blacks wearing Afros and Kangols. "Let the Voice of Our People Be Heard!" they declared. "Register and Vote!"

Lewis and Bond made for an odd couple. Lewis, the veteran organizer, was intense and quiet, wearing frumpy suits and a scraggly mustache and sideburns. Bond, the star politician, was dashing and wry, always sporting fashionable suits and a perfectly coiffed Afro. "Back then Julian was like a boy wonder," Lewis said. "All the young women were attracted to him."

They were Mr. Endurance and Mr. Cool. Bond's father had been a university professor; Lewis's, a farmer. But the two friends from SNCC were nearly inseparable. "They complemented each other," said the VEP's communications director, Archie Allen. "John was the southern black everyman. Julian was the articulate politician. Both were equally recognized by people in the field because of their history."

Unlike in years past, Lewis and Bond were treated like dignitaries instead of outside agitators in Mississippi. They were greeted warmly by the sheriff in Canton, where five years earlier police had tear-gassed civil rights activists, including Lewis, outside the courthouse steps during the Meredith march, and were given a police escort in Greenville. It was a far cry from a decade ago, when Lewis had been locked up in the state's notorious Parchman prison for forty-five days after the Freedom Rides stopped in Jackson.

"I had no idea that in 10 years black people would be challenging just about the entire state," Lewis said. Movement friends like Fannie Lou Hamer of Ruleville and Aaron Henry of Clarksdale were running for the state legislature alongside Evers for governor. "The closed society had begun to open its doors to the knock of the black ballot," Lewis said.

Their stops included civil rights battlegrounds like Belzoni, where fifteen years earlier George Lee, the first black to register in Humphreys County, was shot to death in his car after leading a group of blacks to register at the county courthouse. As Lewis and Bond spoke during an evening rally at a small black church, Belzoni's mayor, Henry H. Gantz, a well-dressed middle-aged white man, unexpectedly burst through the door and walked down the center of the aisle. In the past, Gantz might've arrested everyone in the church for unlawful assembly. Instead, he clasped Bond and Lewis by the hand and told them: "Welcome to Belzoni. You two are doing wonderful work. You're fighting bigotry and injustice. You're a credit to your race."

"He didn't come down to the church to hear us speak," an amused Bond said to the stunned crowd afterward. "He came down to be seen hearing us speak. He likes being mayor of Belzoni. He wants to go on being mayor of Belzoni. The reason he came to that church was that the black people have a weapon. It's not a two-by-four; it's not a gun or a brick. This weapon is the vote. You go down to the mayor's office and hit him with a two-by-four, and he'll remember it the next day. But if you hit him with the vote, he'll remember it for the rest of his natural-born life."

"There's one thing about white southerners—they can count," Lewis said. "When blacks got registered, they knew they had to reach out to them."

But while white candidates now wanted blacks to vote for them, most white voters in Mississippi still didn't want blacks to represent them. In November 1971, 52 black candidates, twice as many as during the last state-wide election in 1967, were elected, but 259 of 309 black candidates lost: they included 28 of 29 for state legislature, 14 of 14 for sheriff, 10 of 10 for chancery clerk, 10 of 10 for county school superintendent, and 67 of 74 for county board of supervisors. Evers won only 22 percent of the gubernatorial vote.

There were numerous reasons for the lopsided defeat. Blacks reported widespread economic intimidation from the white power structure; applicants who applied for loans in some counties were told to "go see Charles Evers." Black election workers were not allowed to monitor the polls in many places on Election Day, despite the presence of a thousand federal observers from the Civil Service Commission. Uncertainty over reregistration persuaded some blacks, convinced they wouldn't be allowed to vote, to stay home. Evers's well-publicized bid for governor, which included statewide television ads—a first for a black candidate in Mississippi—prompted a large white countermobilization. Half of registered black voters turned out, compared with 75 percent of whites.

"The strategy of mounting a highly publicized, comprehensive assault on white power in order to mobilize black voters backfired seriously," wrote the political scientist Lester Salamon of Vanderbilt University. "Instead of mobilizing black voters, the strategy's main effect was to mobilize white anxieties."

Explained one white banker: "All my land and everything I own is in this county and same goes for my neighbors. If the blacks take control, we're finished. Now you don't expect us just to stand by and see that happen, do you?"

That same year Lewis testified before Congress during hearings on enforcement of the VRA. He described a South of "two extremes," where "hope and optimism" mingled with "a climate of despair." Black political power was flourishing in places like Greene County and Fayette, but conservative whites still prevailed throughout states like Alabama and Mississippi. It was not at all clear which direction the South would go. "In 1971, the weight of the federal government was not felt in the affirmative enforcement of the 1965 Voting Rights Act," Lewis said. "Black elected officials and voters in 1972 must be on guard against attempts to dilute the power and influence of the black vote."

Andrew Young never would have been elected to Congress if it hadn't been for the VRA. In 1970, at the urging of his close friends Lewis and Bond, Young had run for Georgia's Fifth Congressional District against the incumbent Republican, Fletcher Thompson. He'd lost by fifteen points, winning all of the black votes but none of the white ones.

Young was planning to run again in 1972, especially because Thompson had decided to run for Senate, when the Georgia legislature drew new districts for Congress and the statehouse. The legislature, which was 95 percent white, split the city of Atlanta, which was 52 percent black, into three districts where whites had a clear majority. The new maps "hack up Atlanta worse than Vietnam is divided," wrote a columnist for *The Atlanta Constitution*. The Fifth District plan took out the historically black west side of the city, the hub of the civil rights movement, and put in the conservative white part of Fulton County. It was drawn to facilitate the election of "a white, moderate, Democratic Congressman," said Representative G. D. Adams of Atlanta.

The new lines excluded Young's brick ranch house at 177 Chicamauga Place by one block. No one thought it was a coincidence. "There was no question in my mind that it was deliberate," Young said. He called the plan "a clear case of racial gerrymandering." The Justice Department blocked the map under Section 5 because it discriminated against minority voters.

So the legislature drew a new district that added Atlanta's black west side, along with a liberal white pocket of the city near Emory University, increasing the black voting-age population from 32 to 38 percent. The new map didn't guarantee Young's victory, but it gave him a chance.

Young had long-standing ties to the civil rights movement. His wife, Jean, had grown up in Perry County, Alabama, Jimmie Lee Jackson's hometown, and had been childhood friends with Coretta Scott King. Coretta introduced Young to her future husband, and he soon became one of King's most trusted aides at the SCLC, known for his diplomacy. "King was the spear thrower and Andy came behind and put it all together," Bond said. "He could be the man on the tightrope and he never slipped."

He needed to walk that tightrope in 1972, courting black voters without alienating moderate whites. "The reason I ran was that we felt we had been moving the South forward, and then all of a sudden Nixon comes in with his southern strategy, trying to repolarize the South," Young said. "Atlanta, in the meantime, had launched this campaign back in the sixties called 'The City Too Busy to Hate.' Atlanta did not want to be Little Rock or Birmingham." Young wanted to prove that a liberal black man who had been a top organizer in the civil rights movement could be elected from a majority-white district in the Deep South—no easy feat.

The forty-year-old Young assembled what he called a "New South Coalition: black votes, liberal votes, white labor votes." His campaign slogans, "Think Young" and "Atlanta's Got Young Ideas," emphasized his image as a fresh face on the political scene. He'd already established credibility with Atlanta's white leadership by heading the city's Community Relations Committee in 1970. Despite his national profile, Young focused on bread-and-butter issues of concern to the city, like improving public education and sustainable urban development. He was the rare candidate who would get an envelope of hundred-dollar bills from an executive at Coca-Cola and a brown paper bag full of twenties from the numbers guys on Auburn Avenue.

In his second bid for Congress, Young faced off against the state representative Rodney Cook, a moderate Republican from Atlanta who was considered the most politically successful Republican in the city's history. The Nixon White House made Cook's election a top priority for its 1972 southern strategy. Dent traveled to Atlanta carrying a telegram announcing Nixon's support for Cook. "Rodney will have an 'in' with the president,"

Dent told reporters. "There is no question about that." Cook was one of only two Georgia Republicans to travel in Nixon's motorcade when the president appeared before 250,000 supporters during a campaign stop in downtown Atlanta.

Cook relentlessly tried to connect Young to the Democratic presidential nominee, George McGovern, who Georgians joked couldn't carry the state if Robert E. Lee was his running mate. Despite his moderate reputation, Cook made Young's race a major issue in the campaign. He ran a newspaper ad denouncing Young's support for integrated busing, showing a photo of his face next to a grainy one of his opponent, with the caption "What's the Difference? . . . Plenty." A Cook campaign letter to white voters claimed that Young would build low-cost black housing in white neighborhoods, stating, "Cook opposes the concept of disrupting single family neighborhoods with the low-cost public housing programs of racial integration. Young embraces the concept."

The VRA saved Young's campaign again at a pivotal moment. Many polling places had changed in the district because of redistricting, and twice as many black precincts were relocated, compared with white ones. An astounding sixty of sixty-two predominantly black neighborhoods had new polling places, which confused voters. Public housing projects were divided into three or four different precincts, and neighborhoods split between highways and railroad tracks, which made voting even more inconvenient for black voters. Residents weren't notified until only a few weeks before the August Democratic primary.

Young's campaign lawyers challenged the Fulton County Board of Elections' decision, alleging that it was the type of discriminatory voting change outlawed under Section 5. The campaign focused on eighteen black precincts with the most egregious obstacles to the ballot box. A federal court ruled in Young's favor, giving a critical boost to his effort to court black voters.

The campaign made a Herculean effort to increase black turnout. Every black registered voter received at least three communications from Young's campaign, by phone, letter, or door to door. Young spoke at three or four black churches every Sunday. He was out every morning at six during the last month of the campaign, greeting prospective voters at bus stops on their way to work. The campaign organized a large volunteer network to drive voters from thirty-two major transportation hubs to the polls. A voter reg-istration drive by nonpartisan organizations like the VEP and NAACP added twenty thousand new black voters to the rolls.

Election Day, November 7, dawned cold and rainy, but "for the first time, black voting was actually higher for Congress than for President," wrote the Young strategists Stuart Eizenstat and William Barutio. Young de-feated Cook by ten points. He won 98 percent of the black vote and 26 percent of the white vote. Nixon carried the Fifth District by 3,443 votes, winning a landslide 75 percent of the vote in Georgia against McGovern, but Young prevailed by 8,000 votes. "I lost Old South voters and picked up New South voters," he said.

Young achieved many firsts. He became the first black member of Congress from the South since North Carolina's George White in 1901 and Georgia's first black congressman since Jefferson Long in 1870. He was one of the first black House members to represent a majority-white district and the first whose election was directly attributable to the VRA. "Andy's vic-tory," said Lewis, "dramatizes the point that when blacks put up good, at-tractive candidates who are committed to biracial government they can draw support from all segments of society."

Young's election represented a critical turning point in the history of voting rights and the politics of the South. The protections of the VRA gave Young the opportunity to successfully run for office, and his victory showed that a high-profile black candidate in the South could prevail with white crossover support.

Atlanta wasn't the only place where history was being made in 1972. In Selma, five black candidates were elected to the city council; they were led by Frederick Douglas Reese, the longtime head of the Dallas County Voters League, which had organized countless marches to the county courthouse during the voting rights campaign of 1965. He was to become chairman of the city streets committee, the second most powerful figure in city govern-ment. "Even white people had to go through him if they wanted a stop sign," wrote the lawyer J. L. Chestnut.

Integrated government had come at long last to the center of segrega-tionist resistance in the Deep South. "People have got more rights, more priv-ileges, than they have ever had before," said Selma's Ardies Mauldin, the first black voter registered under the VRA. "They look more like citizens now."

In Texas, the thirty-six-year-old state senator Barbara Jordan from Houston joined Young as the second black member of Congress since Reconstruction and the first black congresswoman from the South. In 1972, 271 new black candidates were elected, the highest single-year total in a century. The number of black officeholders in the South rose from 72 in 1965 to 1,114. The same year that Nixon carried every state except for Massachusetts against McGovern also turned out to be a historic moment for black politics in the South.

In 1965, King had predicted this would happen. "I think within the next 8 or 10 years, we will see new and marvelous developments in this area," he said after meeting with LBJ the day before the president signed the VRA. "And I think we will see a great rise in the percentage of Negroes represented in government, both local and national."

The civil rights activists of the sixties had become the politicians of the seventies. "By the mid-1970s the civil rights movement—the 'death' of which had been widely reported in the late 1960s—had moved off the streets and into the voting booths, and thereby into city halls, state legislative chambers, and finally the halls of Congress," wrote Jack Bass and Walter De Vries in *The Transformation of Southern Politics*. Lewis called it "the peaceful revolution."

4

HANDS THAT PICK COTTON

In the spring of 1961, following the sit-ins and Freedom Rides, Bobby Kennedy hosted a group of young civil rights activists from SNCC and CORE at the Justice Department. He urged them to focus on voter registration instead of direct-action protests. The activists refused to call off the street demonstrations but agreed to incorporate voting drives into their work. "There was no separation between action and voter registration," John Lewis wrote.

King endorsed the effort, calling the vote "the central front" of the civil rights struggle. The Kennedys lined up funding from major liberal foundations like Field and Ford to create the Voter Education Project (VEP) of the Southern Regional Council. Its first director, Wiley Branton, was an Arkansas civil rights lawyer best known for desegregating the Little Rock public schools in 1957.

From 1962 to 1964 the VEP registered 688,000 black voters in the South, more than had registered in the previous decade. When Branton left to become a special assistant to Attorney General Katzenbach in the Johnson administration, Vernon Jordan, the field director of the Georgia NAACP, became the VEP's new executive director following passage of the VRA. Katzenbach called the VEP's relaunch in 1966 "an undertaking so wise in its concept, so great in its need, and so large in its promise."

Jordan ran the organization for four years, during which time a million black voters were registered in the South, before leaving for New York to head the National Urban League. Leslie Dunbar, the head of the Southern Regional Council, recruited Lewis as Jordan's replacement. "It gave me an opportunity to reconnect with people and organizations that I had seen emerge in the sixties," Lewis said. "I saw it as a continuation of the civil rights struggle."

After the deaths of King and Kennedy, Lewis had gone "into a funk," he said. "After a while I had what I call an executive session with myself, and I said I must not become dead or hostile, I must keep the faith, and I got back out there." The VEP was the perfect landing spot for Lewis. "John was known as Mr. Voter Registration throughout the South," said his communications director, Archie Allen. "We were exploiting, in a good way, his history and role with SNCC."

Lewis recruited old friends from the movement—like Allen, who was from Nashville, and the field director Sherrill Marcus, from Birmingham—to work on his small staff. "The South was changing," he said. "You no longer had the overt racist governors. It was the beginning of what some called the New South. You no longer had people, to a significant degree, trying to harass those who wanted to register to vote. But people were not encouraging people to register to vote. So we had to do that."

From his fourth-floor office at 52 Fairlie Street in downtown Atlanta, in the redbrick Birmingham Railroad building, Lewis oversaw a flourishing of black political power in the 1970s, when "a new era of moderation" suddenly defined Southern politics.

"The Voter Education Project was made to order as the next step in the voting rights movement," said his friend Andrew Young. "VEP was ready to move."

Two months after visiting Mississippi in 1971, Lewis and Bond arrived in Louisiana for a three-day tour of the state, focusing on fifteen parishes where seventy thousand unregistered blacks lived. The civil rights struggle in Louisiana had received a fraction of the coverage of Alabama or Mississippi, even though segregation there had been just as ironclad.

In 1962, only 150,000 blacks, 31 percent of eligible voters, were registered in Louisiana. Nine years later that figure had doubled, but there were still 200,000 unregistered blacks scattered across the state's forty-eight parishes. At stop twenty-six, on August 5, 1971, Lewis and Bond visited Tensas Parish in northeastern Louisiana, on the Mississippi border, the last parish to allow blacks to register to vote, where only 15 had been on the rolls in 1964. "Register and Vote!" said a poster advertising the event, featuring black-and-white photos of Lewis and Bond. "Old Enough to Fight—Old Enough to Vote. Hear the Voice of Your People!"

The midday crowd in the tiny town of Waterproof, population nine hundred, packed into the Good Samaritan Hall, a rickety one-room schoolhouse. Despite its name, Waterproof flooded frequently. During the great flood of 1912, small steamships navigated through the streets. The town had been physically relocated three times. Cotton was the major crop, and most blacks lived in dire poverty, making less than forty dollars a week. There was no sewer system in the black neighborhoods and few paved roads.

Though blacks totaled 60 percent of the population in Waterproof, they made up only 46 percent of registered voters and held only two elected seats, councilman and Democratic committeeman. "Mr. Bond and Mr. Lewis are going to find that here in Waterproof, for the blacks and the whites, it's still yesterday," said Harold Turner, a thirty-four-year-old teacher and Grambling State University graduate who served as the town's lone black councilman.

Inside the Good Samaritan Hall, Lewis, wearing a suit and black polka-dot tie despite the sweltering heat, told the enthusiastic crowd: "We come to Louisiana because we believe in the ballot and we believe that the vote can be a mighty weapon for change.

"When an oppressed people make up their minds to be free, nothing can stop them," he said to cheers. He told the audience that "the day of tea and cookie relations is over." It was Lewis's phrase for when blacks and whites got together to discuss race relations in a place like Waterproof and the "whites drink all of the tea and the blacks eat all of the cookies and when it's all over the whites say, 'If all the colored people were like you we wouldn't mind being with them.'"

Lewis's mission at the VEP was to get black citizens in forlorn places like Waterproof to exercise the political power they now had. It wasn't enough to "wear an Afro and say 'right on,'" he said. "You've got to organize."

Black organizing in Waterproof began in 1969, with a two-thousand-dollar grant from the VEP to the Progressive Civil League of Tensas Parish, run by Ples E. Bell, "a real go-getter," according to a VEP memo, who had served as an army first lieutenant before becoming a teacher in the nearby town of St. Joseph. In the prior election, in 1967, only 34 percent of blacks were registered, and not a single black ran for office in Tensas Parish. But Bell immediately began signing up new voters at such a pace—registering 310 in ten days—that the white registrar closed his office to process the "paper work."

"Unquestionably, the Tensas Parish project is the best I have seen in a long time—rural or urban," wrote the VEP field director Weldon Rougeau. "There has been an awakening in Tensas, something beautiful, something signifying a rebirth of courage." Eight hundred black voters were registered as a result of the VEP grant, bringing the number of black registrants near parity with whites.

In the 1970 election, hopeful blacks contested all five city council seats in Waterproof. But fewer than half of eligible blacks voted, and only Turner was elected. Whites told their black employees, most of them maids or farmworkers, that "there is no use wasting time voting," and they would lose their food stamps if they did. The town's only doctor, a white man, told his black patients he would leave Waterproof if blacks took over city government. Fear and intimidation led to voter apathy. "Our problem is that we have people who don't know black politics can bring real change to their lives," Turner said.

But in the year following Lewis and Bond's visit, five blacks were elected in Waterproof, taking offices ranging from police juror to school board to justice of the peace.

"It was these poor indigenous people that came out," Lewis said of his visit. "So by going there, I think we gave them a sense of hope and optimism."

When Lewis returned in the summer of 1975, four years after his speech at Good Samaritan Hall, blacks had taken over Waterproof's city government, with Turner as mayor alongside five black city councilmen and a black chief of police. "It was so moving," Lewis said. "I saw the results of our work and investment." It was precisely this type of "continued, unglamorous, day-to-day work," Lewis said, that would determine "the future political health of the South."

On August 6, 1975, the temporary provisions of the VRA were once again set to expire. Eight months earlier, a broad array of civil rights leaders gathered at Ebenezer Baptist Church in Atlanta on King's forty-sixth birthday to call for the VRA's renewal. "It is a must that the Act be extended," Lewis said, "for it is the lifeblood of the civil rights movement."

Since 1965 the number of black elected officials in the South had increased 2,000 percent, from 72 to 1,588, and black registration in the South had grown from 2.2 million to 3.4 million. The gap between white and black registration had shrunk from 44 percent in 1962 to 11 percent. There were 95 black state legislators in the Old Confederacy, compared with 0 when the VEP first launched. The number of Section 5 submissions from southern states had also increased by 2,000 percent, from 255 from 1966 to 1970 (7 percent of total changes) to 5,337 from 1971 to 1975 (93 percent of changes).

But black politicians, for all their gains, still held only 2 percent of the region's 79,000 elected positions, and 2.5 million blacks remained unregistered. Blacks controlled a majority of seats in the county governments of only 6 of the South's 101 majority-black counties, and there were 362 majority-black towns and cities without a single black elected official.

Once black citizens registered in large numbers, states shifted to diluting the minority vote. Every state covered under Section 5 submitted a redistricting plan for its state legislature after the 1970 census. "For each state, either a court has found all or part of the redistricting plan discriminatory, or the Department of Justice has objected to it under Section 5 of the Voting Rights Act," reported the U.S. Commission on Civil Rights, which supported a ten-year extension of the VRA. Since the Section 5 guidelines had been instituted in 1971, the DOJ had objected to fifty-eight different redistricting plans; drawing new district lines or changing the electoral system to prevent blacks from winning office had become the most common means by which southern states tried to limit minority representation. During the previous four years, the DOJ issued 163 objections to 300 discriminatory voting changes.

On March 7, 1975, four days after Lewis testified before Congress in favor of the VRA's renewal, the VEP held a massive march in Selma to commemorate the tenth anniversary of Bloody Sunday. Under a clear sky and brisk wind, five thousand people from across Alabama marched across the Edmund Pettus Bridge in the biggest voting rights demonstration in the

South since the Selma to Montgomery march, led by Lewis, Coretta Scott King, and the Selma city councilman Fred Reese.

Interracial government had brought big changes to Selma. Col. Al Lingo of the Alabama state troopers was dead, Jim Clark was selling insurance in North Carolina, and Mayor Joe Smitherman, instead of trying to block the march, took part in the festivities. "We've come a long way," Reese said. "Whites who couldn't tip their hats have learned to do it. People who couldn't say 'Mister or Miss' to a black have learned to say it mighty fine. We've got black policemen, black secretaries, and we can use the public restrooms. The word 'nigger' is almost out of existence."

Before the march, the civil rights activists rallied at Brown Chapel. "We used to sing, 'before I'd be a slave I'd be buried in my grave,'" said the Reverend L. L. Anderson. "But I'm here to tell you, before I see the Voting Rights Act go out of existence, I'll not only be buried in my grave, I'll go to hell first." The crowd in the packed church jumped to their feet and roared with approval.

Unlike in 1970, when Nixon tried to gut the VRA, his successor, Gerald Ford, announced his support for a clean five-year extension. The debate in 1975 wasn't over whether the VRA would be renewed, but for whom.

In February 1975, Modesto Rodriguez, a thirty-three-year-old farmer from Pearsall, Texas, traveled 1,650 miles to Washington to testify before Congress. Rodriguez wanted Congress to amend the VRA to cover Texas and Spanish-speaking citizens across the Southwest, who had become America's "forgotten minority."

"I want to tell you what Chicanos have to go through in the town where I live," Rodriguez said. "Democracy does not come easily and we are asking for your help in this matter."

Rodriguez grew watermelons, peanuts, wheat, maize, and corn on his family's ranch. He had the bulky frame and dark complexion of someone who spent a lot of time in the fields. "He was an everyman to Hispanic politicians. In some ways he was very sophisticated; in some ways he was very simple," said George Korbel, a lawyer for the Mexican American Legal Defense and Educational Fund (MALDEF) in San Antonio, who arranged for Rodriguez to testify. "When I told him we were going to Washington, he thought he was going to Washington State."

Pearsall, the county seat of Frio County, was a poor, sleepy town of fifty-six hundred, with one main road surrounded by farmland, an hour southwest of San Antonio and thirty miles north of Cotulla, where LBJ once taught. The stories Rodriguez described to Congress weren't so different from the ones LBJ told his friends about discrimination against Hispanics in South Texas. They weren't so different from the extensive testimony Congress heard in 1965 about voting discrimination toward blacks in the Deep South.

Rodriguez was the local chairman of the La Raza Unida Party ("The United People's Party"), a Chicano nationalist third party hatched in a graduate political science seminar in 1967 at St. Mary's College in San Antonio. It was modeled after black independent efforts like the Mississippi Freedom Democratic Party. "Our political lives have been controlled by whites who do not represent our interests and who exploit us not only politically but also economically," he told the Subcommittee on Civil and Constitutional Rights of the House Judiciary Committee.

Before becoming active in politics, Rodriguez took out a loan with the local bank to make improvements on his farm. After he joined La Raza Unida, the bank called and told him he had ninety days to find refinancing. He spent two years calling around, but no bank would lend him the money. Rodriguez learned that A. R. Galloway of the Security State Bank had urged other banks not to lend to him. When Rodriguez finally found a local rancher willing to lend him the money, he confronted Galloway at his bank. Galloway tried to persuade the rancher, in front of Rodriguez, not to help Modesto with the loan. He did the same to Rodriguez's friend Francisco Lopez, who hauled crops to the market in his three trucks. "If you are going to help Chicano political organizations," Galloway told Lopez, "get Chicano political organizations to finance you."

When economic intimidation didn't work, the Anglo power structure, which made up a quarter of Frio County but controlled nearly every influential position, turned to politics. In 1973, Paul Morales, La Raza Unida's candidate for mayor of Pearsall, narrowly defeated the Anglo candidate Buddy White by sixty-five votes. After the election, the county judge subpoenaed two hundred Chicano voters, but no whites, for alleged election irregularities and threw out a hundred votes that were marked with an "X" instead of a signature by illiterate voters. Morales was removed from office and lost his construction business after whites boycotted it. Sixteen Chicano voters, under pressure from the county, pleaded guilty to election law violations.

The subpoenas had a chilling effect on Chicano political participation. Turnout dropped significantly in the next election. "Now when I try to get people to register to vote, they say 'Go to hell, Modesto,'" Rodriguez said. "'We don't want any part of politics.'" For good measure, the county moved the only polling place from the predominantly Chicano west side of Pearsall back to the heavily Anglo east side. They also annexed surrounding white neighborhoods to dilute Chicano voting strength and shortened the hours of the election so that it would be harder for farmworkers to get to the polls before or after work.

As a result of economic and political intimidation, fewer than half of Chicanos were registered to vote in Frio County, compared with two-thirds of Anglos. Illiteracy and poverty were major obstacles to the ballot box. A third of all Mexican-Americans in Texas lived below the poverty line, double the rate for Anglos. The average Mexican-American child attended only seven years of school, and half of Chicano children dropped out before graduating from high school. Texas printed its election materials only in English, which served as a de facto literacy test for Chicanos, and provided little assistance to Spanish-speaking voters. Rodriguez estimated that 60 percent of Spanish-speaking citizens in Frio County couldn't read English, and 30 percent couldn't speak it. "For Chicanos it was made easier to get to a war zone than to a voting booth," he said.

Gerrymandering also kept Chicano political power at bay. Chicanos made up 75 percent of Frio County's population but held only one of four county commission seats. That's because, in 1973, the all-white county commission redrew its lines to put 97 percent of Mexican-Americans in one district, so that Anglos would safely control the other three.

"There has been a great failure on the part of the state of Texas to protect the voting rights of the Chicano electorate," Rodriguez told Congress. "For the protection of our voting rights we are now relying on the Congress and more specifically on this subcommittee to act to extend federal protection of the right to vote to the nine million Spanish-speaking citizens of this country."

Rodriguez's harrowing testimony riveted the committee members. "You have made a very impressive case and we thank you very much for coming all the way here and submitting to us this very valuable testimony," said the subcommittee's chairman, Don Edwards.

"Thank you, Mr. Rodriguez," seconded Congressman Herman Badillo of New York City. "I thank you for having brought this testimony to this subcommittee so we can see the full extent of the denial or abridgment of the right to vote of especially the Spanish-speaking people in Texas."

The problems Rodriguez described weren't specific to Frio County or Texas. Nationally, only 44 percent of Spanish-surnamed citizens were registered in 1972, compared with 68 percent of blacks and 73 percent of whites. Only 38 percent voted in the 1972 election, compared with 54 percent of blacks and 65 percent of whites.

Mexican-Americans in Texas made up 16 percent of registered voters but held just 2.5 percent of elected positions; the numbers were even worse in California, where Latinos constituted 12 percent of registered voters but only 0.7 percent of elected offices. Los Angeles had 1 million Mexican-American residents, over a quarter of the city's population, but not a single one served on the city council or in the state legislature. East L.A., where 225,000 Mexican-Americans lived, had been divided into seven state house districts, five senatorial districts, and four congressional districts, so that the Mexican-American population did not exceed 20 percent in any of them.

The House members Badillo of the Bronx, Ed Roybal of Los Angeles, and Barbara Jordan of Houston introduced legislation to rectify this situation. Their bill required bilingual election materials to be printed in areas where language minorities—defined as persons of Spanish heritage, American Indians, Asian-Americans, and Alaskan natives—made up more than 5 percent of the voting-age population. It also forced those same jurisdictions to have their election changes approved by the federal government if less than 50 percent of eligible voters had registered or voted as of the 1972 election, which had the important distinction of covering Texas under Section 5. (Many believed that Texas had not been covered in 1965 on LBJ's orders.)

Jordan became the national face for broadening the VRA. "Nearly all the forms of discriminatory voting practices suffered by blacks in the South are being suffered by Mexican-Americans in the Southwest," she said.

Jordan had arrived in Congress in 1972 as the first black woman elected from the South. "Jordan has been a First and an Only for so long that the words seem like part of her name to Texas newspaper readers," wrote Molly Ivins in *The Washington Post*. She grew up in Houston's working-class Fifth Ward, the youngest daughter of a Baptist preacher and warehouse delivery-man, and attended Texas Southern University at sixteen and then Boston University Law School, where she was the only woman in her class.

Despite her impressive intellect and considerable savvy, Jordan didn't have an easy path to politics. She lost her first two races for the Texas House of Representatives, in 1962 and 1964, because the seat was elected at large and Houston's white majority wouldn't vote for a black candidate. "My political career was not assisted through passage of the Voting Rights Act," Jordan testified before the House. "I know firsthand the difficulty minorities have in participating in the political process as equals. The same discriminatory practices which moved the Congress to pass the Voting Rights Act in 1965, and renew it in 1970, are practiced in Texas today."

Only in 1966, following the Supreme Court's "one person, one vote" ruling in *Reynolds v. Sims*, did the legislature draw a single-member district for the Texas senate that Jordan could win. She quickly became chummy with the state's old boys' club and, while serving on the state senate's Redistricting Committee, drew a new majority-black congressional seat for herself. "She proved that black is beautiful before we knew what it meant," LBJ said. Her critics dismissively called her a "a black LBJ."

Jordan came to national prominence two years after arriving in Congress, when the House Judiciary Committee held nationally televised hearings on the impeachment of Richard Nixon. "My faith in the Constitution is whole, it is complete, it is total," she said on the evening of June 25, 1974. "And I am not going to sit here and be an idle spectator to the diminution, the subversion, the destruction, of the Constitution."

"If the Voting Rights Act could have protected you four years earlier," Congressman Caldwell Butler of Virginia told Jordan at the VRA hearings in 1975, "by this time you would probably be president of the United States."

Jordan's friend Andrew Young, the first African-American to serve on the House Rules Committee, also testified before the Judiciary Committee in 1975. "Extension of the Voting Rights Act is a matter of political life or death for me," he said. He showed the civil rights subcommittee clips of the documentary *King: A Filmed Record*. "When we started to walk from Selma to Montgomery, I had no idea I would be walking into Congress within ten years," he said. Without the VRA, Young told his colleagues, "I would not be here today." He backed Jordan's legislation to broaden the VRA. "The same kind of things that happened to us in 1965," he said, "are happening to people of Spanish origin."

Jordan also received support from John Lewis, who had been directing VEP grants to black and Hispanic voter registration organizations in Texas since 1972. "It would be a mockery of the whole Voting Rights Act effort during the past 10 years if we leave the Voting Rights Act as it is and not cover the other minorities in this country," he testified.

But not everyone applauded Jordan's stance. The entire Texas delegation, with the exception of Representative Bob Krueger of New Braunfels, opposed covering the state. And powerful figures within the civil rights movement, led by Clarence Mitchell, the chief lobbyist for the NAACP, worried that expanding the act would jeopardize its extension. "Let me put it this way," Mitchell told *The Washington Post*. "If you've got something that is working, you want to be very sure you don't improve it out of existence."

The crafty Mitchell, who was known as the 101st senator because of his power on Capitol Hill, had already visited Ford at the White House and secured a pledge for a simple five-year extension of the 1970 act. He'd also "limited" the scope of an important report on the VRA by the U.S. Commission on Civil Rights, so that it didn't study voting problems in the Southwest.

"At that point, Mexican-Americans were just not as visible on the national stage in any of the civil rights groups," said Patricia Villareal, a lawyer from San Antonio who helped draft the 1975 VRA amendments for Congressman Edwards. "So there was a lot of feeling among the more senior black leadership that Mexican-Americans were newcomers. They thought, 'What are you doing fooling around with our act?'"

The testimony of Chicano activists like Rodriguez, combined with Jordan's relentless lobbying of her black colleagues, persuaded Congress to expand the VRA. "The involvement of Congresswoman Jordan made a tremendous difference," Villareal said. "She took a very hard stance that it needed to be done."

———

On July 20, 1975, three lawyers from the Department of Justice traveled to Pearsall to meet with Rodriguez. They asked him to recruit other Chicanos who could testify about voting discrimination if and when the DOJ sued Frio County.

After the lawyers left for San Antonio, Rodriguez went to the Buenos Aires bar to look for witnesses. At 10:50 p.m., when he and ten friends were drinking beer and playing pool, a half dozen police officers and officials from the Texas Alcoholic Beverage Commission raided the bar. They ordered everyone outside and arrested Rodriguez's friend Daniel Carbajal. Rodriguez asked for Carbajal's keys so he could drive his car home. When he inquired what the charges against Carbajal were, an officer called Rodriguez a smart-ass.

Rick Dennis of the Texas Alcoholic Beverage Commission came up from behind Rodriguez and struck him hard on the back of the head with a heavy flashlight. Dennis and four other officers kicked and beat Rodriguez to the ground and threw him into the squad car. He was charged with public intoxication, interfering with an officer, resisting arrest, and assault on a police officer.

When his sister, Modesta, arrived at the Frio County jail, the front steps were covered with Modesto's blood. She called George Korbel of MALDEF and asked what she should do.

"Jesus Christ," Korbel said, "take him to a hospital."

"We can't take him to a hospital," she said. "They will kill him at the hospital."

Unconscious and incoherent, Rodriguez was airlifted to a hospital in San Antonio, where he spent twenty-four hours recovering. He suffered a punctured eardrum and permanent hearing loss in his left ear. (The state later conceded damages; a judge awarded Rodriguez ten thousand dollars for "pain, suffering, humiliation and injury to his reputation.")

"We always felt like the officers were ordered to do it," said the MALDEF lawyer Al Kauffman, who worked in Frio County. "The word was out that Modesto was looking for people to work on the Voting Rights Act."

If anyone had doubts about the scope of discrimination against Mexican-Americans in places like South Texas, Rodriguez's beating put them to rest.

———

The House overwhelmingly passed a ten-year extension of the VRA, adopting Barbara Jordan's new protections for language minorities, 341 to 70, on June 5, 1975, despite complaints from Representative Robert McClory, Republican of Illinois, that it would encourage "multilingualism" in the nation. Hugh Scott, Birch Bayh, and Philip Hart introduced similar legislation in the Senate. It was expected to pass easily until President Ford, in a bid to court southern delegates at the 1976 GOP convention, resurrected Nixon's southern strategy by pledging to nationalize the VRA, as Nixon had tried to do in 1969 and 1970.

The Senate blocked Ford's last-minute attempt to weaken the law, defeating the amendment introduced by the Mississippi senator John Stennis, 48 to 38. The West Virginia senator Robert Byrd negotiated a compromise that extended the act for seven years, instead of ten, but left the House bill otherwise intact. As in 1970, what the New York Republican senator Jacob Javits called a "heavy consensus" for the VRA prevailed. The Senate bill passed, 77 to 12, on July 25. Only 6 southern Democrats and 6 southern and western Republicans, including Strom Thurmond, voted against it.

Exactly ten years after LBJ signed the VRA in 1965, President Ford signed the 1975 amendments in the Rose Garden. Lewis attended the ceremony, just as he had in 1965. "The right to vote is at the very foundation of our American system," Ford said. "There must be no question whatsoever about the right of each eligible American to participate in our electoral process."

Barbara Jordan stood over the president's left shoulder as he signed the bill. She asked him to give her an autographed copy of the index cards he read from during his speech. "That was my first big legislative victory and I wanted a memento," she said.

In addition to the states covered in 1965, the new act required 513 jurisdictions in 30 states to hold bilingual elections and 276 additional counties to approve voting changes under Section 5—all of Texas, along with 14 counties in Arizona; Kings and Merced counties in California; El Paso County, Colorado; Hardee, Hillsborough, and Monroe counties in Florida; and Bronx and Kings counties in New York. The VRA had already empowered black Americans and expanded the franchise to eighteen-year-olds. Now it covered the country's fourth-largest state and extended vital protections to new groups like Hispanics in the Southwest, Native Americans in Arizona, and Asian-Americans in New York City.

The new VRA made an immediate difference. Within months of the law taking effect, the DOJ stopped a massive voter purge in Texas. The number of Mexican-Americans holding county and municipal offices in Texas increased from 353 to 559 in the decade after the 1975 amendments. All across the state, from San Antonio to Frio County, the federal government and civil rights groups sued to force hundreds of county commissions, city councils, and school boards to adopt fair districts that didn't deny representation to Mexican-Americans. Hispanic political power flourished beyond Texas, with the number of Hispanic members of Congress from the Southwest rising from 1 in 1975 to 9 by 1985. City councils in America's three largest cities—New York, Chicago, and Los Angeles—became integrated because of the VRA.

Who voted for the bill was as impressive as what it did. Southern Democrats in the House supported it by two to one, 52 to 26, the first time in the twentieth century that a majority of southern congressmen backed civil rights legislation. (Southern Republicans in the House voted, 17 to 10, against it, illustrating the reversal of the parties in the South on civil rights.) "The 1974 class of southern Democrats voted 12–1 in support of the Voting Rights Act extension," wrote Jack Bass and Walter De Vries, "and the 1972 class of southern Democrats voted 10–2 for the measure."

"It has helped to emancipate and liberate all of us, black and white," said Representative John Buchanan of Birmingham. "We in Alabama believe in the right to vote for our citizens," echoed Representative Walter Flowers from Selma. "The South has rejoined the Union," said Representative Gillis Long of Louisiana.

In a speech before black mayors, Andrew Young summed up the change in southern politics: "It used to be Southern politics was just 'nigger' politics, who could 'outnigger' the other—then you registered 10 to 15 percent in the community and folk would start saying 'Nigra,' and then you get 35 to 40 percent registered and it's amazing how quick they learned how to say 'Nee-grow,' and now that we've got 50, 60, 70 percent of the black votes registered in the South, everybody's proud to be associated with their black brothers and sisters."

In 1954, as segregationist White Citizens' Councils were springing up all over the South in response to *Brown v. Board of Education*, the chief of police and a Baptist minister in Plains, Georgia, visited Jimmy Carter at his peanut warehouse and urged him to join the local council. Carter refused. The men returned a few days later and told Carter he was the only white man in Plains who hadn't joined. That didn't change his mind. The men returned a third time with some of Carter's customers, who threatened to boycott his peanut farming business if he didn't join. If he couldn't afford the five-dollar dues, they would lend it to him. "I've got $5," Carter responded. "And I'd flush it down the toilet before I'd give it to you."

Carter grew up in the segregated South, but in his tiny hometown in rural southwestern Georgia, three hundred whites lived alongside four hundred blacks. When he became chairman of the local school board in 1961, Carter voted to integrate the schools and admit blacks to the Plains Baptist Church. His mom, Lillian, whom he called "the most liberal person in the state of Georgia," had her car vandalized when she ran the local LBJ campaign office and his son Chip was beaten up at school for wearing an LBJ button in 1964. "In Sumter County you could literally get killed for saying the kind of things Jimmy did," Andrew Young said.

When Carter ran for governor in 1970, however, as a little-known forty-six-year-old peanut farmer and state senator, he courted the same working-class white voters who'd pulled the lever for Lester "Ax Handle" Maddox in 1966 and said he'd invite George Wallace to speak at the Georgia statehouse. He'd be just another second-rate Wallace, many thought, like so many governors before him in the South.

But in his inaugural address in 1971, Carter revealed his progressive views on race. "I say to you quite frankly that the time for racial discrimination is over," he told the people of Georgia. "No poor, rural, weak, or black person should ever have to bear the additional burden of being deprived of the opportunity of an education, a job, or simple justice."

As governor, Carter increased the number of blacks in prominent government positions from three to fifty-three, established a biracial commission to deal with racial problems, and hung an official portrait of Martin Luther King at the state capitol alongside the segregationist ghosts of Georgia's past. At the unveiling, he locked arms with King's wife, Coretta, and sang "We Shall Overcome." Because federal examiners had spent little time in Georgia—a concession to LBJ's mentor, the Georgia senator Richard

Russell—Carter deputized every high school principal in the state to register voters.

Along with Carter, moderate whites were elected to the governorships of Florida (Reuben Askew), Arkansas (Dale Bumpers), and South Carolina (John West) in 1970, and Louisiana (Edwin Edwards) and Mississippi (William Waller) in 1971. "In 1970 there was a whole group of governors elected, none of whom were identified as racist or inclined toward any substantial degree of additional segregation than their opponents," Carter said. "In the election of major figures around the country at the local level, we've seen a substantial trend toward the election of candidates who are either black themselves or who openly profess to believe in the equal treatment of black and white citizens."

"White politicians no longer have to project racism to win elections," explained Andrew Young. "The black vote has set the white politician free to be a better person."

Carter quickly became the poster child for the ascendant "New South." *Time* put his face on the cover in front of the states of the Confederacy, with the headline DIXIE WHISTLES A DIFFERENT TUNE.

Black leaders cheered the changing political climate. "I saw the 1970 election as the emergence of a new South, because you had Carter elected governor in Georgia, Reuben Askew in Florida, and Dale Bumpers in Arkansas," said Young. "All of a sudden the Old South was gone and there were three new faces. So the next stage for me was that one of these three faces had to replace Wallace as the face of the South."

In the 1976 Democratic primary for president, the two faces of the South squared off in the pivotal Florida primary. Carter, who'd won a surprise victory in the Iowa caucus, had been anointed leader of the Democrats' anti-Wallace effort. Bond and Young endorsed him in advance of the Florida primary, the candidates' first major test in the South. "Wallace pulled the whole Democratic Party to the right," Young said. "To get the country moving again, Wallaceism had to be stopped in the South where it started. The defeat of George Wallace may end up being the defeat of overt political racism in America."

The Alabama governor had carried the Sunshine State in the 1972 Democratic primaries and, despite suffering paralysis after being shot five times on the campaign trail in Maryland in May 1972, remained a formidable opponent, especially in the South. He'd moderated his image after his brazenly racist 1970 gubernatorial campaign, crowning a black homecoming queen at the University of Alabama and delivering state aid to black communities. In his 1974 reelection campaign he'd been endorsed by black politicians like Sheriff John Hulett of Lowndes County and Judge William McKinley Branch of Greene County, winning 25 percent of the black vote. NEW BLACK SUPPORT HELPED WALLACE WIN, reported the *Los Angeles Times* on May 9, 1974, an inconceivable headline in 1965.

But many black voters would understandably never forgive Wallace for his segregationist past. "[Carter's] effort to defeat George C. Wallace became symbolic," Lewis said. "David against Goliath. He has projected himself as something good and decent coming out of the South." In contrast with Wallace, who appealed to conservative voters in the Florida Panhandle and attacked Carter for hanging a portrait of King in the Georgia capitol, Carter campaigned extensively in black churches and beauty shops, calling the VRA "the best thing that ever happened to the South."

"It's a matter of who best represents the South," Carter said. "Is it George Wallace or is it people like myself and Askew and Bumpers and West?" On March 9, Florida voters chose the New South over the Old. Carter defeated Wallace, 35 percent to 31 percent, winning 72 percent of Florida's black vote and strong majorities among racially moderate whites. Two weeks later Carter crushed Wallace in North Carolina, another state the Alabama governor carried in 1972, by twenty points, winning 90 percent of the black vote. Wallace was finished, and Carter was well on his way to becoming the Democratic nominee.

On July 12, 1976, Barbara Jordan became the first African-American politician to deliver the keynote speech at the Democratic convention, eight years before Jesse Jackson and twenty-eight years before a young Illinois state senator named Barack Obama would take the same stage. She entered Madison Square Garden to an extended standing ovation, with black and white delegates applauding for over two minutes.

"It was one hundred and forty-four years ago that members of the Democratic Party first met in convention to select a presidential candidate," said Jordan, wearing a bright pistachio green blouse and matching collarless jacket. "But there is something different about tonight. There is something special about tonight. What is different? What is special? I, Barbara Jordan, am a keynote speaker." A big smile flashed on her face, to loud and sustained cheers. "I feel that, notwithstanding the past, that my presence here is one additional bit of evidence that the American Dream need not forever be deferred."

Jordan's speech and Carter's nomination symbolized the transformation of the Democratic Party. They were nominating a southerner, but there would be no Confederate flags or renditions of "Dixie" in New York. Young was one of three Democrats chosen to nominate Carter. "I'm ready to lay down the burden of race," he said. "And Jimmy Carter comes from a part of the country that, whether you know it or not, has done just that."

After endorsing Carter in Florida, Young traveled to forty-one states on his behalf, preaching that "a New South really does exist." "Young's endorsement of Carter was like an endorsement from the movement," Archie Allen said. The Georgia congressman became Carter's closest black confidant. "I knew Jimmy when he was governor, but not well," he said. "When I really got to know him, I found that he had great understanding and sympathy for blacks and poor people, something very important to me."

As red, white, and blue balloons fell from the rafters celebrating Carter's nomination, Aaron Henry, the longtime head of the Mississippi NAACP, hugged Ross Barnett, Jr., the son of Mississippi's virulently segregationist governor from 1960 to 1964, who had walked out of the 1960 Democratic convention protesting civil rights. Just twelve years earlier, LBJ had refused to seat the integrated Mississippi Freedom Democratic Party delegation at the Democratic convention in Atlantic City. Now the 1976 Mississippi delegation was split evenly between blacks and whites.

"Is this the New South?" a delegate asked Henry.

"Just ask Ross Barnett Jr.," Henry responded with a grin.

"That's right! That's right!" Barnett shouted.

Martin Luther King, Sr., delivered the benediction at the convention's closing ceremony. "I have had many trials and tribulations, many ups and downs," said the seventy-seven-year-old preacher. "But I ain't gonna let nobody keep me down. I'm going on and see what's at the end." He told the delegates, "If you don't have a forgiving heart, get on your knees." In true movement fashion, they responded by singing "We Shall Overcome."

Carter's convention felt less like a political rally and more like a baptism for national redemption.

Every governor in the South designated July 1976 "Voter Registration Month," urging all unregistered persons to register and vote in the bicentennial year. "The goal for which MLK gave his life and the goal for which Andrew Young and John Lewis were beaten and imprisoned can be realized," Carter told fifteen hundred guests at a VEP fundraising dinner in Atlanta. "If I'm elected President, I want to put John Lewis out of business." He promised to introduce a plan to automatically register every U.S. citizen eighteen and older, which he said would "transform, in a beneficial way, the politics of our country."

The dinner raised sixty thousand dollars for the VEP. "It was our best fundraising dinner ever," Lewis said. The 1976 election promised to be the organization's most ambitious effort yet.

The VEP funded eighty-seven local voter registration projects, and Lewis visited all eleven southern states alongside Coretta Scott King and the Reverend Joseph Lowery of the SCLC, signing up thousands in southern towns like Anniston, Alabama, and Florence, South Carolina. The VEP plastered thousands of posters across the South that read, "Hands That Pick Cotton . . . Now Can Pick Our Public Officials," which became the mantra of civil rights activists in 1976.

The VEP commissioned the Hollywood producer Norman Lear to direct a series of TV and radio spots featuring celebrities like Muhammad Ali and characters from hit sitcoms like *All in the Family, Maude,* and *Chico and the Man.* Ali, at his training camp in upstate New York, called the vote "the great equalizer." In another ad, Archie Bunker heatedly debated candidates with his hippie son-in-law, Michael Stivic. "You know why I'm voting?" Bunker said. "Because he is!"

In addition, the VEP joined the National Coalition on Black Voter Participation's "Operation Big Vote," which targeted black voters in thirty-six cities in thirteen states. *The New York Times* called it the "biggest voter registration and get-out-the-vote campaign since the civil rights movement."

To court black voters, Carter hired nineteen black staffers and appointed Ben Brown, the chairman of the Georgia Legislative Black Caucus, as his deputy campaign manager. "We are going all out for the votes of blacks and other minorities in the general election, just as we did in the primaries," Brown said. The Republican nominee, Gerald Ford, made little effort to attract black voters, which his campaign manager, James Baker, assumed "would be 10 percent [for Republicans], regardless."

Carter campaigned heavily in black strongholds like Watts, telling audiences: "I could not stand here today as a candidate for president of the United States had it not been for Martin Luther King Jr." In his second-to-last rally before the election, Carter appeared before fifty thousand in downtown Los Angeles, with Coretta Scott King and Barbara Jordan by his side.

Not since Bobby Kennedy had a white candidate for president attracted such significant black support. "I would urge my brothers and sisters to regard Tuesday, November 2, as a 'day of liberation' and to vote as if our lives and future depend on it," John Lewis said. "They do."

Election Night was a nail-biter. Carter did well in the Northeast and the Midwest, but Ford dominated the West. As Tuesday rolled into Wednesday, the winner had yet to be decided.

In the wee hours of Wednesday morning, all eyes were on Mississippi's seven electoral votes, which would be enough to put Carter over the top. "I heard that it may depend on how Mississippi went, and I thought 'Lord have mercy,'" Young said. At 3:30 a.m., NBC called the Magnolia State for Carter. He'd won by 11,537 votes. The state that voted 87 percent for Goldwater in 1964 had just sealed the election for a product of the Deep South who had closely aligned himself with the civil rights movement.

Carter owed his election to black ballots, not just in Mississippi, where a third of his total came from black voters, but across the South. He'd carried every southern state except Virginia, winning only 45 percent of the southern white vote but 95 percent of the black vote. "What made a key difference for the Carter-Mondale ticket was the record turnout of black voters in Dixie," wrote none other than Harry Dent, who had been advising the Ford campaign. "They saved Carter in the South, and the South won the election for Carter."

"The black vote in the South on November 2, 1976, was the largest and most decisive exercise of minority political power in this century," concurred a VEP analysis. The southern black electorate had increased from one and a half million when the VEP started in 1962 to four million by 1976, and the number of black officials had grown from seventy-two to two thousand. "Fifteen years of tedious and non-glamorous activities produced dramatic, visible and immediate results."

Nationally, Carter lost the white vote, 48 percent to 51 percent, but he won roughly 92 percent of the 6.6 million black votes, according to Washington's Joint Center for Political Studies. Black ballots also gave him the margin of victory in northern states like Maryland, Missouri, Pennsylvania, and Ohio, and black and Hispanic voters put Carter over the top in Texas, a victory made possible by the 1975 amendments to the VRA.

Sitting in his living room in Atlanta, Lewis cried when Carter was elected. "Those tears weren't about me," he wrote. "They were about the fact that the hands that picked cotton had now picked a president."

Newly enfranchised voters like Ardies and Thomas Mauldin in Selma and Modesto Rodriguez in Frio County had made the difference. "The Voting Rights Act and the efforts of so many indigenous groups all across the South created the climate for someone like Jimmy Carter to become the Democratic nominee and be elected president," Lewis said.

The election of 1876 ended the First Reconstruction. The election of 1976 solidified the promise of the second one. In the early-morning hours of November 3, 1976, Lewis thought about his mentor, Dr. King, and how they had sat together in Selma to watch LBJ announce the VRA. "I wish—Lord, how I wish—Martin were alive today," he said. "He would be very, very happy. Through it all, the lunch counter sit-ins, the bus strike, the marches and everything, the bottom line was voting."

5

THE COUNTERREVOLUTION

John Lewis spent the week of June 13–20, 1964, in Oxford, Ohio, helping to train hundreds of college-age volunteers who were heading to Mississippi for Freedom Summer. A bulletin in the lobby of the training headquarters at the Western College for Women underscored the danger of the assignment: "Before you leave Oxford, write your Congressmen asking them to act to insure your safety. Contact should be established with them before you reach Mississippi."

Among those present were Mickey Schwerner, twenty-four, a graduate student in social work at Columbia University; Andrew Goodman, twenty, an anthropology major at Queens College; and James Chaney, twenty-one, a volunteer with CORE from Meridian, Mississippi. Chaney, Goodman, and Schwerner left the training early to investigate a fire at Mount Zion Methodist Church near Philadelphia, Mississippi, forty miles from Chaney's hometown. He and Schwerner had spoken there over Memorial Day, urging local blacks to start a Freedom School and register to vote.

On the night of June 21, while attending a relative's funeral in Alabama, Lewis received a call that the three civil rights workers were missing. They'd been arrested on the way to the church, had been taken to the Neshoba County jail in Philadelphia, and hadn't been heard from since. The Freedom

Summer project hadn't even started yet—half the trainees were still in Ohio—and already three workers had disappeared.

Lewis caught the first flight to Mississippi and immediately began searching for the bodies when he and a small group of SNCC workers arrived in Philadelphia, a town of 8,000 in rural central Mississippi, two hundred miles west of Selma. They scoured the flat, scrubby landscape where Schwerner's charred blue station wagon had been found, clearing through brush and digging through dirt. "It was so dangerous," Lewis said. "It was so ill advised." It was hardly a secret that the White Citizens' Council and the Klan controlled Neshoba County. Not a single African-American, out of a black population of 2,565, had been allowed to register to vote.

Forty-four days after the disappearance, the bodies of Chaney, Goodman, and Schwerner were found in an earthen dam that the owner, Olen Burrage, bragged could hold a hundred civil rights workers. The church fire had been set by Klansmen to lure the civil rights activists to Neshoba County, where they were arrested and abducted according to plan. They'd killed Goodman and Schwerner, both white, with single shots, then mutilated Chaney, who was African-American, beyond recognition. It was the first interracial lynching in U.S. history.

The bodies were discovered just a few miles from the site of the Neshoba County Fair, one of the state's preeminent social and political gatherings, known as "Mississippi's giant house party." The fair had begun in 1889, a year before the Mississippi Constitutional Convention ratified the Mississippi Plan that disenfranchised nearly every one of the state's black voters through the poll tax and literacy test. The first major politician to speak at the fair in the early 1900s was Governor James K. Vardaman, the "Great White Chief," who once said, "If it is necessary every Negro in the state will be lynched; it will be done to maintain white supremacy."

Since then, the Neshoba County Fair had been a hotbed of resistance to desegregation and a required stop for any politician hoping to win higher office in the state. In August 1964, despite the discovery of Chaney's, Goodman's, and Schwerner's remains just days earlier, the fair proceeded as planned. The invited speakers included George Wallace, Barry Goldwater, Jr., and the state's staunchly segregationist governor, Ross Barnett. The only blacks at the fair were there to clean the cabins.

On August 3, 1980, nearly sixteen years to the day when the bodies of Chaney, Goodman, and Schwerner were discovered, Ronald Reagan kicked off his general election campaign for president at the Neshoba County Fair. He spoke at the grandstand of the red clay horse track, surrounded by six hundred cabins with names like the Fox Den and Ye Old King's Castle, colorfully decorated in pastels and often flying Confederate flags.

Reagan, the first presidential candidate to ever speak at the fair, received a thunderous welcome from the nearly all-white audience. "We want Reagan!" the crowd of ten thousand chanted. The year before, the Mississippi Republican chairman, Michael Retzer, told the Republican National Committee (RNC) that the fair would be a good place to court "George Wallace–inclined voters."

"I believe in states' rights," Reagan told the crowd. "I believe in people doing as much as they can for themselves at the community level and at the private level. And I believe that we've distorted the balance of our government today by giving powers that were never intended in the Constitution to that federal establishment. And if I do get the job I'm looking for, I'm going to devote myself to trying to reorder those priorities and to restore to the states and local communities those functions which properly belong there."

The phrase "states' rights," which had long been the rallying cry of southern segregationists, had not been part of the candidate's usual stump speech, nor had reporters heard him use it before on the campaign trail in 1980. *The Clarion-Ledger* of Jackson and *The New York Times* noted Reagan's words at the top of their coverage. (At a Reagan rally in Jackson on the eve of the election, Strom Thurmond was to say, far less subtly: "We want that federal government to keep their filthy hands off the rights of the states.")

Jimmy Carter responded to Reagan's speech at the Ebenezer Baptist Church in Atlanta, where King once preached. "You've seen in this campaign," he said, "the stirrings of hate and the rebirth of code words like 'states' rights' in a speech in Mississippi."

Reagan's talk of states' rights might have gone unnoticed had it not been said in a place like Neshoba County, by a candidate who had opposed every major civil rights law of the 1960s, including the Civil Rights Act of 1964, the Voting Rights Act of 1965, and the Fair Housing Act of 1968.

Reagan was a westerner who thought like a southerner on civil rights issues. "You can't guarantee someone's freedom by imposing on someone
else's," he explained.

When it came to voting rights, Reagan believed "the Constitution very
specifically relegates control of voter registration to local government." He
sympathized with the goals of the VRA but found its "vindictive, selective
application" to certain southern states "unconstitutional." The Deep South
states had made the same argument before the Supreme Court when they
unsuccessfully challenged the constitutionality of the VRA in 1966. Reagan told a biographer during the 1980 campaign that the law had been
"humiliating to the South."

When Andrew Young, who had served as Carter's ambassador to the
United Nations from 1977 to 1979, first heard Reagan's speech, he remembered his visit to Neshoba County after Chaney, Goodman, and Schwerner disappeared. "The thought of Philadelphia, Miss., always sends chills
up my spine," Young wrote in *The Washington Post*. "I'm obsessed with a
chilling question: what 'states rights' would candidate Reagan revive? . . .
Traditionally, these code words have been the electoral language of Wallace, Goldwater and the Nixon southern strategy. So one must ask: Is Reagan saying that he intends to do everything he can to turn the clock back to
the Mississippi justice of 1964? Do the powers of state and local governments include the right to end the voting rights of black citizens?"

"For a presidential candidate to kick off his campaign there, that was
heartbreaking," John Lewis said. "It was a direct slap in the face of the movement and all of the progress that we were trying to make."

Ronald Reagan had come of age politically as a Goldwater Republican.
He frequently introduced Goldwater on the campaign trail in 1964 and
usually stole the show, prompting voters to ask, "Which one is the candidate?" A week before the presidential election, Reagan delivered a prime-
time address for the Goldwater campaign on national TV, which catapulted
the actor turned politician to national prominence and became known
as the Speech.

He ran as the heir to Goldwater in 1968 and 1976, positioning himself
as the conservative alternative to Nixon and Ford. Time and time again, in
places like Neshoba County, he'd turned to white southerners for support.

Clarke Reed, the chairman of the Mississippi Republican Party, told Reagan at a rally in the state: "We've loved you for a long time. Nowhere else in this country are you better understood and respected." Reagan responded: "If there's a Southern strategy, I'm part of it."

In 1980, Reagan broadened and nationalized the southern strategy pioneered by Goldwater in 1964 and refined by Nixon in 1968. He skillfully combined the small-government conservatism of Goldwater with the anti-government populism of Wallace.

As Reagan explained in a 1977 speech to the American Conservative Union, the Republican Party could appeal to its base through lower taxes and less government regulation while adding new support from groups like white working-class Democrats by embracing "the so-called social issues— law and order, abortion, busing [and] quota systems."

If the 1964 election had been a mandate for LBJ and his support for civil rights, then the 1980 election was a mandate for Ronald Reagan and his conservative counterrevolution. In sixteen years, with practically the same platform, the Republican Party had gone from losing forty-four states in 1964 to winning forty-four states in 1980.

When Reagan said he wanted to "get the government off the backs of our people," that philosophy applied to civil rights as much as anything else. His speech in Neshoba County was a prelude to the heated fights of the next eight years.

"What the Administration is trying to do," said Althea Simmons, the Washington, D.C., director of the NAACP, "is not just put civil rights on the back burner, but take it off the stove completely."

In an ironic twist, Reagan lifted his civil rights ideology from the civil rights movement.

Thurgood Marshall's favorite quote came from Justice John Marshall Harlan's lone dissent in *Plessy v. Ferguson*. "Our Constitution is color-blind and neither knows nor tolerates classes among citizens," Harlan wrote in response to the Supreme Court's 7–1 decision in 1896 upholding "separate but equal" state segregation laws. "In respect of civil rights, all citizens are equal before the law."

Harlan took the phrase from Albion Tourgee, the lawyer for thirty-year-old Homer Plessy, a black man of Creole heritage arrested in 1892 for sitting in the "white" car of the East Louisiana Railroad. "Justice is pictured blind and her daughter, the Law, ought at least to be color-blind," Tourgee wrote in his brief.

Harlan's line became Marshall's "Bible," said the lawyer Constance Baker Motley, who worked with Marshall for many years at the NAACP Legal Defense Fund. "During his most depressed moments . . . Marshall would read aloud passages from Harlan's amazing dissent . . . It became our basic creed." Marshall utilized Harlan's color-blind appeal to great effect in *Brown v. Board of Education*, when the Court finally overturned *Plessy*.

Color blindness became a prominent organizing principle of the 1950s and 1960s civil rights movement, expressed most eloquently by Martin Luther King in his "I Have a Dream" speech when he talked about his hope that "my four little children will one day live in a nation where they will not be judged by the color of their skin but by the content of their character."

But King also knew that color blindness could be adopted by critics of civil rights to block efforts to dismantle the legacy of discrimination by opposing any consideration of race in public policy. "Whenever this issue of compensatory or preferential treatment for the Negro is raised, some of our friends recoil in horror," King wrote in his 1964 book *Why We Can't Wait*. "The Negro should be granted equality, they agree; but he should ask nothing more. On the surface, this appears reasonable, but it is not realistic. For it is obvious that if a man is entering the starting line in a race 300 years after another man, he first would have to perform some impossible feat in order to catch up with his fellow runner."

Lyndon Johnson expanded on King's theme during his commencement address at Howard University in June 1965, which became one of his most famous civil rights speeches. "You do not take a person who, for years, has been hobbled by chains and liberate him, bring him up to the starting line of a race and then say, 'You are free to compete with all the others,' and still justly believe that you have been completely fair," Johnson said. "Thus it is not enough just to open the gates of opportunity. All our citizens must have the ability to walk through those gates. This is the next and the more profound stage of the battle for civil rights. We seek not just freedom but opportunity. We seek not just legal equity but human ability, not just equality as a right and a theory but equality as a fact and equality as a result."

The new phase of the civil rights struggle described by Johnson attracted critics on the right and, most notably, the left who believed that the civil rights movement had abandoned its color-blind ideal by moving from "equality as a fact" to "equality as a result." The most high-profile early liberal critic of racial preferences was the University of California–Berkeley sociologist Nathan Glazer. "There was a clash between two ideals," Glazer said. "One was the ideal of meritocracy, the other was the ideal of representative inclusion."

Glazer was straight out of academic central casting, with tortoiseshell glasses, a shock of gray hair, and a high-pitched New York City accent. He was raised in East Harlem and the East Bronx by left-wing Russian Jews and attended City College in the early 1940s alongside the noted intellectuals Irving Kristol, Daniel Bell, and Irving Howe. They spent their days in the gothic Alcove No. 1 above the school's cafeteria, hotly debating between "the anti-Stalinist left and the Stalinist left," Kristol joked.

Glazer considered himself "a man of the left" when he started teaching at UC Berkeley, but student demonstrations pushed him to the right. By 1964, in the pages of *Commentary*, he had written an essay entitled "Negroes and Jews: The New Challenge to Pluralism," which lamented "the shift of Negro demands from abstract equality to group consideration, from color-blind to color-conscious."

In 1965, his friends Kristol and Bell founded *The Public Interest*, a small yet influential quarterly journal based in New York that Glazer wrote for regularly. In 1972, Kristol signed a "Democrats for Nixon" letter in *The New York Times* that marked the beginning of the neoconservative movement. Glazer moved to Harvard in 1969 and took over as coeditor of *The Public Interest* after Bell, a fellow Harvard sociologist, left out of frustration with the magazine's increasing conservatism.

In 1975, Glazer published *Affirmative Discrimination*, the first book-length critique of affirmative action in employment, education, and housing, which quickly became the definitive word on the subject in conservative circles. He helped pioneer the view that by the 1970s the federal remedies for discrimination—busing, quotas, timetables for integration—were as bad as the original crime of segregation. The subscribers to this ideology included Reagan. Color blindness had shifted from a liberal ideal to a conservative one.

Glazer's central thesis held that the Civil Rights Act of 1964 had been perverted far beyond its original aim. "In 1964 we declared that no account should be taken of race, color, national origin or religion in the spheres of voting, jobs and education (in 1968, we added housing)," Glazer wrote. "Yet no sooner had we made this national assertion than we entered into an unexpected enterprise of recording the color, race, and national origin of every individual in every significant sphere of his life. Having placed into law the dissenting opinion of *Plessy v. Ferguson* that our Constitution is color-blind, we entered into a period of color and group-consciousness with a vengeance."

By the late 1970s, leading conservative law professors like Antonin Scalia of the University of Chicago had embraced Glazer's critique. Scalia wrote a biting commentary on Justice Harry Blackmun's famous line in a 1978 California affirmative action case that "in order to get beyond racism, we must first take account of race," which Scalia labeled "The Disease as Cure" in an influential essay in the *Washington University Law Review*. "Every panel needs an anti-hero, and I fill that role on this one," Scalia wrote. "I have grave doubts about the wisdom of where we are going in affirmative action, and in equal protection generally. I frankly find this area an embarrassment to teach."

Blacks, Scalia maintained, should be treated no differently from the Irish, Italians, Jews, or Poles who were discriminated against by the Anglo-Saxon majority when they arrived in the United States. "The affirmative action system now in place," he wrote, "is based upon concepts of racial indebtedness and racial entitlement rather than individual worth and individual need; that is to say . . . It is racist."

In the spring of 1978, Glazer went to lunch in Cambridge with Abigail Thernstrom, who had completed a Ph.D. in government at Harvard and was married to the Harvard historian Stephan Thernstrom. Glazer told Thernstrom, who had a fourteen-year-old daughter, to "stop taking care of the kids and get to work."

Thernstrom and Glazer had much in common. Like Glazer, she was a red-diaper baby, raised in the Hudson Valley hamlet of Croton-on-Hudson on the left-wing estate Finney Farm, where the radical journalist John Reed (played by Warren Beatty in the movie *Reds*) kept a cottage. Her parents were Stalinists who "never made a dime," and Thernstrom grew up in an integrated "cocoon in which race didn't matter," she said.

She attended Barnard and then Harvard, where she met her husband at a lecture by the left-wing investigative journalist I. F. Stone. Stephan was a member of Harvard's New Left club, and both Thernstroms were strong supporters of the civil rights movement. They protested outside Woolworth's in Cambridge during the sit-ins and planned to travel south with SNCC in 1964 before Abigail became pregnant with her daughter Melanie.

Over lunch, Glazer urged Thernstrom to "become the world's greatest authority on some one little topic." That summer, after reading a Supreme Court opinion about a controversial redistricting case concerning Hasidic Jews in Brooklyn, she discovered the topic of voting rights.

The 1970 reauthorization of the VRA added three counties in New York City—Kings (Brooklyn), New York (Manhattan), and Bronx—under Section 5 of the VRA because they used a literacy test and voter turnout was below 50 percent in the 1968 election. When New York submitted its redistricting plan for the state legislature following the 1970 census, the Department of Justice urged the adoption of two legislative districts in the Williamsburg area of Brooklyn with a minority population of roughly 65 percent, which would be sufficient to elect minority representatives. To accommodate the black and Puerto Rican voters in the area, the state divided the neighborhood's thirty thousand Hasidic voters into two senate districts and two assembly districts. The Hasidim sued, arguing that the Fourteenth and Fifteenth Amendments forbade the consideration of race in redistricting.

The federal government backed New York. "You cannot do redistricting without having racial considerations in mind, unless you are willing to forget about the Voting Rights Act of 1965," argued the Nixon solicitor general Robert Bork. The Supreme Court concurred, in a 7–1 opinion. "Compliance with the Act in reapportionment cases will often necessitate the use of racial considerations in drawing district lines," wrote Justice Byron White in March 1977, "and the Constitution does not prevent a state subject to the Act from deliberately creating or preserving black majorities in particular districts in order to ensure that its reapportionment plan complies with Section 5."

Thernstrom strongly disagreed with the opinion. She viewed the redistricting plan as an obvious racial gerrymander—a dangerous form of affirmative action in electoral politics—and an illustration of how the Supreme Court's prevailing interpretation of the VRA had "clearly lost its way." When she next saw Glazer, Thernstrom said she wanted to write on the topic for *The Public Interest*, which he encouraged her to do. "I was pushing people to make the case," he said.

Thernstrom described Glazer as "the single most important intellectual influence in my life." In an essay in the spring 1979 issue of *The Public Interest*, "The Odd Evolution of the Voting Rights Act," Thernstrom argued, like Glazer on the Civil Rights Act, that a once-noble law had produced negative unintended consequences when the focus shifted from registration to representation.

"Immediate and massive registration was precisely the purpose of the legislation, but today the simplicity of that aim has been largely forgotten," Thernstrom wrote. "The Voting Rights Act . . . ushered in a dual revolution; not only were the names of two million blacks added to the registration rolls, but the definition of enfranchisement changed. The right to vote came to mean the right to equal electoral result and maximum political effectiveness."

To supporters of the VRA, the "odd evolution" Thernstrom described was perfectly logical. After blacks and other minorities registered to vote in large numbers, the next step would be for them to secure political representation and for the VRA to protect against the second generation of barriers to minority political power. "The Act gives a broad interpretation to the right to vote, recognizing that voting includes 'all action necessary to make a vote effective,'" Earl Warren famously wrote in *Allen v. State Board of Elections*. "The right to vote can be affected by a dilution of voting power, as well as by an absolute prohibition on casting a ballot."

Thernstrom viewed the *Allen* decision as the precise moment when the scope of the VRA became "definitively altered." The expansion of the act, particularly Section 5, violated the original intent of Congress and betrayed the color-blind ideal the VRA was meant to advance. "He is envisioning color-coordinated politics—the color of the candidate unfailingly matching the color of his constituency," she wrote of Warren. "And he is asserting the right of a minority racial bloc to equal access to the political process. *Allen* set the tone for all future Voting Rights Act litigation. It permanently blurred the distinction between disenfranchisement and dilution, and between equality of political opportunity and equality of electoral result."

Thernstrom had an acerbic edge to her writing that made her a natural polemicist. Under her telling of the VRA, she was the true integrationist and the Warren Court, Justice Department bureaucrats, and voting rights activists were no better than the segregationists they were indicting. Her argument wasn't so different from those advanced unsuccessfully by Mississippi in the *Allen* case in 1969 and by southern politicians trying to protect majority-white districts, but Thernstrom's essay drew wide attention, especially for an obscure journal article, partly because of who she was and partly because of when it was published. The article won her a prestigious grant from the Twentieth Century Fund to write a book critiquing the VRA.

"The Reagan era was a godsend for her," said the Harvard sociologist Orlando Patterson, who knew Thernstrom from Cambridge. As a Harvard-educated former liberal who initially supported the civil rights movement but would soon lead the intellectual crusade against the VRA, she became the foremost neoconservative of the voting rights counterrevolution, with the perfect pedigree for the role. The arguments she made catalyzed and foreshadowed the voting rights debates of the 1980s.

"The battle of the Voting Rights Act," Glazer said, "became an issue of representation."

Thernstrom's arguments about the VRA played out in real time in Mobile, Alabama.

In 1925, thirty years before Rosa Parks declined to move to the back of a bus in Montgomery, John LeFlore, a twenty-five-year-old postal worker in Mobile, refused to give up his seat on a segregated streetcar to a white man. A scuffle ensued, and both men were arrested. The white man was promptly released while LeFlore remained in jail. The experience persuaded LeFlore to start a Mobile chapter of the NAACP, which he considered "a duty to [his] race."

Fifty years later, LeFlore visited the law office of his friend Vernon Crawford, Mobile's foremost black civil rights lawyer, and asked him to file a lawsuit challenging the structure of the city's governing commission and school board. Despite blacks' constituting a third of the port city's population, no black had ever been elected to a position of prominence in Mobile,

largely because since 1911 city council and school board members had been
elected citywide, rather than from specific districts. That meant no black
candidate could be elected without substantial white support, which had
never been forthcoming, and given the city's racially polarized voting, no
white candidate with substantial black support had a realistic chance of
winning office, either. Blacks were completely shut out from influence in
Alabama's third-largest city.

In 1974, LeFlore had been elected to the Alabama House of Representatives, representing the black section of Mobile. That would have been impossible under the city's at-large system. At-large elections were the primary
impediment to black representation not just in Mobile but nationwide, especially across the South. In 1978, the U.S. Commission on Civil Rights
surveyed twenty-nine municipalities in the South that had black majorities
and populations of more than twenty-five hundred but no black elected officials. Seventy-five percent of them used at-large elections. "At-large election
systems appear to have a severe negative effect," the commission found, "and
they are extensively used."

When jurisdictions switched from at-large to district elections, as LeFlore
advocated in Mobile, minority representation increased dramatically. "In
Texas during the period 1970 to 1978, 29 at-large or multimember systems
were changed voluntarily or through litigation to single-member districts or
mixed plans," reported the commission. "Immediately prior to these changes,
the 29 systems elected 9 blacks and 8 Hispanics to office. Immediately after
the respective changes, 26 blacks and 24 Hispanics were elected."

The catalyst for these changes had been the Supreme Court's 1973 decision *White v. Regester*, which struck down at-large elections for the Texas
legislature in Dallas and San Antonio. The Court found that despite a large
minority population in each county, few minority candidates had been
elected, through no fault of their own. The Court's decision signaled that
at-large elections could be struck down as discriminatory when "the totality
of circumstances"—a history of past discrimination, the continuation of
present-day discrimination, structural barriers to political power—gave minorities less of an opportunity than whites to elect their preferred candidates.

Three young white civil rights lawyers who had attended University
of Alabama Law School together—Larry Menefee, James Blacksher, and
Edward Still—took charge of the Mobile suit. LeFlore's friend Wiley Bolden,

a World War I veteran and insurance agent who had cofounded the Mobile NAACP, became the lead plaintiff. They charged that Mobile's government violated the Fourteenth Amendment, the Fifteenth Amendment, and Section 2 of the VRA, a little-used provision of the VRA whose language mirrored the Fifteenth Amendment.

Unlike Section 5, which covered only select southern states, on a temporary basis, and gave the federal government the power to preemptively block discriminatory voting changes filed after 1965, Section 2 applied nationwide, on a permanent basis; put the burden of proof on plaintiffs to show that a voting change was discriminatory; and could be used to challenge electoral structures adopted before 1965, as was the case with many at-large systems. After *White v. Regester*, vote dilution lawsuits began to be filed across the South, with Mobile being the highest-profile example.

In July 1976, the U.S. District Court judge Virgil Pittman, whom LBJ had appointed to the bench in 1966, convened a six-day trial in *Bolden v. City of Mobile* with thirty-seven witnesses. He personally toured the city with lawyers from both sides. That October he issued a sweeping opinion striking down at-large elections for the city commission in favor of a mayor-council structure, with nine single-member council districts, similar to recent plans adopted by Birmingham and Montgomery.

Mobile, Pittman found, continued to be separate and unequal in nearly every facet of life, including housing, schools, jobs, and politics. White neighborhoods had paved roads, wide sidewalks, and proper drainage, but black ones did not. The Mobile Fire Department had hired only 15 black employees out of 435. The public schools were 45 percent black, but the school board was all white. No black candidate had ever been elected at large. "Practically all active candidates for public office testified it is highly unlikely that anytime in the foreseeable future, under the at-large system, that a black can be elected against a white," Pittman concluded.

Black Mobilians and voting rights lawyers celebrated the decision, filing new vote dilution suits challenging at-large elections in cities like Little Rock and Selma. Most white Mobilians were incredulous. The Mobile *Press-Register* denounced the judge for transforming the city into "Pittmanville," by acting as "judge-jury-legislator-executive." The newly formed Constitutional Crisis Committee, an offshoot of the White Citizens' Council, ran a full-page ad in the newspaper calling for Pittman's impeachment and arrest.

While the suit was on appeal, the United Klans of America marched through downtown.

The Fifth Circuit Court of Appeals affirmed Pittman's ruling, which Mobile appealed to the Supreme Court. The U.S. government sided with the black plaintiffs. Jim Blacksher, trying his first voting rights case, received counsel from Armand Derfner, who had argued *Allen v. State Board of Elections.* "He kept telling me, 'Just keep saying *White v. Regester,*'" Blacksher recalled.

The case had to be argued twice, in March 1979 and in October 1979, because Justice Blackmun was ill the first time and the eight justices deadlocked in his absence. The debate in *Bolden* revealed a fundamental divide about how much protection the Reconstruction amendments and the VRA provided for minority voters and whether the right to vote stopped at the ballot box or extended to the halls of power.

"The election system in operation in Mobile strikes at the very heart and purpose of the Fifteenth Amendment," Blacksher argued in his brief. "In form blacks are able to mark and cast ballots, but in substance they are disenfranchised." The city of Mobile, echoing Thernstrom's critique, responded that the creation of majority-black districts amounted to "affirmative action" and would lead to "proportional representation by race as . . . a constitutional requirement."

The Court had changed significantly since the *Allen* decision. Nixon had appointed four justices—Chief Justice Warren Burger and Justices Lewis Powell, William Rehnquist, and Harry Blackmun—shifting a previously liberal court to the center-right. In a 6–3 decision on April 22, 1980, the Court sided with Mobile. "Racially discriminatory motivation is a necessary ingredient of a Fifteenth Amendment violation," wrote Justice Potter Stewart, an Eisenhower appointee. "The Amendment does not entail the right to have Negro candidates elected, but prohibits only purposefully discriminatory denial or abridgment by government of the freedom to vote 'on account of race, color, or previous condition of servitude.'"

Thurgood Marshall, the lone African-American on the Court, drafted a furious thirty-five-page dissent, twice as long as Stewart's opinion, and was joined by Justices William Brennan and Byron White. "A plurality of the Court concludes that, in the absence of proof of intentional discrimination by the State, the right to vote provides the politically powerless with nothing more than the right to cast meaningless ballots," Marshall wrote. "An interpretation of the Fifteenth Amendment limiting its prohibitions to the outright denial of the ballot would convert the words of the Amendment into language illusory in symbol, and hollow in substance."

Blacksher felt the blood rush from his face when Menefee walked into his office and told him the verdict. The decision represented the most significant setback for the VRA since 1965. Every civil rights lawyer knew that intentional discrimination, which had never before been required under the VRA, was virtually impossible to prove. "It was clearly viewed as an effort by conservatives to slow civil rights enforcement," Menefee said. Thernstrom, in contrast, praised the Court's new intent test as "principled, simple, and tight."

At an impassioned mass meeting in Mobile days after the decision, the state representative James Buskey, who assumed LeFlore's seat after the latter's death in 1976, exclaimed: "An act of war has been declared on black people!" Blacksher called the verdict "the biggest step backwards in civil rights to come from the Nixon court." He worried that minority voters would be "trapped in a tragic historical Catch-22. Their votes will continue to be submerged by an election system in whose adoption they had no voice, while the Supreme Court's demand for proof of invidious intent prevents them from attacking it in court."

Vote dilution lawsuits immediately came to a halt. The Department of Justice shelved half a dozen suits against at-large elections, including two in Selma's Dallas County challenging the county commission and school board. Cities like Baton Rouge, Hattiesburg, and Little Rock, which had been put on notice, no longer had to worry about an integrated government. In the first eight months of 1980, fewer than ten new cases were filed in federal courts challenging discriminatory election systems, compared with sixty the year before. When Mobile's school board reconvened in May 1980, the white chairman, as his first order of business, dismissed the two black members who had been elected from single-member districts.

In two years, the temporary provisions of the VRA were set to expire. Ronald Reagan, who had long been hostile to voting rights, would soon take office. "If most people had not yet started thinking ahead to the fate of the Voting Rights Act of 1982," wrote Armand Derfner, "the Mobile decision was a loud alarm."

In late 1980, Derfner, who had moved to Charleston, South Carolina, in 1974, told a friend he was temporarily relocating to Washington to work on the reauthorization of the VRA. "There's been an election, you know?" his friend responded.

The prospects for the VRA's reauthorization in late 1980 and early 1981 looked grim. In addition to Reagan's landslide election, Republicans took control of the Senate for the first time since 1954, picking up twelve seats. Strom Thurmond replaced Ted Kennedy as chairman of the Senate Judiciary Committee, about as dramatic a reversal as one could find, and quickly reiterated his long-held view that Section 5 should apply to all fifty states, a deceptive way to cripple enforcement of the law. President Reagan shared Thurmond's position.

Senator Orrin Hatch, an ultraconservative Republican from Utah, became the new chairman of the Senate Judiciary Committee's Subcommittee on the Constitution, which had jurisdiction over the VRA reauthorization. In December 1980, Hatch had successfully filibustered the last major civil rights bill considered by Congress, the Fair Housing Act of 1980, by requiring that plaintiffs show intentional discrimination to prove a violation, as the Supreme Court had done with Section 2 in Mobile.

"Nineteen eighty," said Ralph Neas, executive director of the Leadership Conference on Civil Rights (LCCR), "was probably the worst period for civil rights in a long, long time."

On April 7, 1981, at a press conference in the Senate Rules Committee, Ted Kennedy, the GOP senator Charles "Mac" Mathias of Maryland, and the House Judiciary chairman, Peter Rodino—the main sponsors of the VRA's 1975 reauthorization—unveiled legislation extending the temporary provisions of the VRA for ten years and reversing the Mobile decision by requiring plaintiffs to prove only the effects of voting discrimination under Section 2, not the intent. Each of these goals looked difficult on its own and appeared nearly impossible when put together. Some members of the civil rights coalition worried that adding an amendment to Section 2 would sink the entire bill.

At the LCCR's town house office in Dupont Circle, veteran civil rights litigators like Derfner and lobbyists like Neas prepared for a protracted battle. "If we have to take Reagan on, there's nothing better than the right to vote," said the group's counsel, Joe Rauh, who'd been intimately involved in every major piece of civil rights legislation.

The LCCR had been founded in 1950 by A. Philip Randolph of the Brotherhood of Sleeping Car Porters, Roy Wilkins of the NAACP, and Arnold Aronson of the Jewish Council for Public Affairs. It had since grown to a coalition of 165 national organizations representing blacks, Hispanics, Asian-Americans, unions, women, senior citizens, disabled persons, and religious groups. Every member of the coalition made the VRA reauthorization its top legislative priority for 1981–1982. It became the "litmus test" for how members of Congress were judged on civil rights.

Neas, the LCCR's executive director, described himself as zero for four when it came to his civil rights background; he was white, Republican, male, and Catholic. But he'd spent eight years working for the Republican Edward Brooke of Massachusetts, the only black senator from 1967 to 1979, acquiring intimate knowledge of Capitol Hill. The VRA reauthorization became the defining test of whether the civil rights movement could tame Reagan and preserve the bipartisan civil rights consensus forged in Congress in the 1960s. "If we couldn't win on the Voting Rights Act, which had been compared to motherhood, apple pie, the Constitution and baseball, we probably couldn't win on anything," Neas said.

The reauthorization effort began in the House, where Democrats still retained a fifty-two-seat majority. A resounding vote for the VRA in the House would put pressure on the Senate and Reagan administration. On June 12, 1981, the House Judiciary Committee's Subcommittee on Civil and Constitutional Rights, which had begun hearings on the VRA the previous month, arrived in Montgomery, the birthplace of the civil rights movement, for a crucial field hearing. The gathering took place at the federal courthouse downtown, where Judge Frank Johnson had authorized the march from Selma to Montgomery.

Three congressmen made the trip: the subcommittee's chairman, Don Edwards; Representative Harold Washington of Illinois, who would soon become the first black mayor of Chicago; and the ranking Republican on the subcommittee, Henry Hyde of Cicero, Illinois. Hyde was best known for supporting a constitutional amendment to ban abortion. In the House, he'd introduced legislation to eliminate Section 5 of the VRA. "My view is that the handful of Southern States have been in the penalty box for nearly 17 years; they have improved their voting rights records, and hence ought to be treated like every other jurisdiction in the land," Hyde explained.

Maggie Bozeman, a fifty-year-old second-grade teacher from the small rural western town of Aliceville, Alabama, traveled 150 miles to testify before the committee. Bozeman was the NAACP president of Pickens County, which was over 40 percent black but where blacks held no countywide office.

Bozeman was well known in Alabama civil rights circles as feisty and unafraid. "She changed the weather in the room when she walked in," said Lani Guinier, a young lawyer with the NAACP Legal Defense Fund. "She was like a tornado."

Bozeman testified that voter registration hours in Alabama were limited from 9:00 a.m. to 4:00 p.m., when few working people could make it, and the county had not hired any deputy registrars despite the state's recommendation. In Pickens County, instead of voting by secret ballot behind curtains, "we have open house voting," Bozeman told the committee. "In most polling places there is no privacy whatsoever. I mean whatsoever. For example, if I vote at the armory, I must go there and go to the table which has the letter B. I and all the other voters whose name end in B must mark our ballots in the presence of others using the same table."

Bozeman was monitored and photographed by the deputy sheriff when she assisted elderly and illiterate voters at the polls. In the 1980 election, law enforcement officials visited the homes of every black family that requested absentee ballots in Pickens County to make sure they were out of town. Bozeman herself was indicted on charges of voter fraud for helping newly registered black voters fill out their absentee ballots. (An all-white jury sentenced her to four years in jail before a judge threw out the conviction.)

"Just being a voter in Pickens County is a wearying experience," she told the committee. "Sometimes I feel like giving up, but I keep going on. Indeed, the thing that keeps me going on is to know that I can call upon the Justice Department for relief if need be. If Congress takes the Voting Rights Act protection from us in Pickens County in the state of Alabama, we voters in rural Alabama may as well start whistling Dixie."

Hyde listened "with great interest and concern" to Bozeman's testimony. Her descriptions of voting in Pickens County were "outrageous, absolutely outrageous," he said. "These are very serious charges and facts."

"Is it really true that finally when in Pickens County black people come to vote that there are law enforcement officers standing by?" Edwards asked.

"It is true, sir," Bozeman responded.

The conversation continued:

Edwards: "This is not before 1965? This is now?"

Bozeman: "This is now, in the 1980 election."

Hyde: "Taking pictures is outrageous. That is nonsense."

Bozeman: "It happens."

Hyde: "You ought to charge them a fee for having them take your picture . . . Would you repeat something? You don't have a secret ballot in Pickens County? You vote on a table in front of everybody?"

Bozeman: "Yes. Open house. Just like here now."

Hyde: "Does that still go on?"

Bozeman: "1980."

Hyde: "Everybody sees how you vote?"

Bozeman: "Yes."

Hyde: "No booths, no curtains, nothing like that?"

Bozeman: "In one precinct where there was the Justice Department . . . they had little curtains in Aliceville, but in other parts of the county, still open house in 1980."

At the end of the exchange, Hyde admitted that "I think preclearance is important. More and more I am inclined to think we must retain preclearance." He scrapped his plan to eliminate Section 5 and instead offered an amendment making it easier for jurisdictions with clean records to bail out from the statute, which the House adopted in modified form. "You're being dishonest if you don't change your mind after hearing the facts," he explained. "I was wrong and now I want to be right."

The conversion of Hyde, one of the most conservative members of the House, marked a critical turning point in the VRA reauthorization debate. Neas described it as the "first major breakthrough in the legislative process" and the "first indication that we have a chance to win this battle."

The hearings, spanning eighteen days and including over a hundred witnesses, had worked as planned. "We wanted to put a human face on the

VRA," Neas said. The *Congressional Record* also established a clear need for the law. There had been more Section 5 objections in six southern states from 1975 to 1980 (382) than from 1965 to 1974 (257). The number of black registered voters in those states had doubled since 1965, but there remained a twenty-three-point gap between black and white registered voters. Nationwide, the number of black elected officials had skyrocketed from 1,000 in 1970 to 5,000 by 1980—including black mayors in Los Angeles, Atlanta, Birmingham, and New Orleans—but that still represented less than 1 percent of total officeholders.

A week after the hearings ended in July, Hyde sent a note to Reagan urging him to support the VRA reauthorization. "If you move quickly, you may be able to broaden your constituency by eliminating a fear which plagues the black community most: that the time will soon return when they [are] literally unable to vote, or in the alternative, made to feel that they have no meaningful impact whatsoever on their destiny," Hyde wrote.

On July 31, the House Judiciary Committee passed a bipartisan bill extending the VRA's temporary provisions for ten years and amending Section 2 by a vote of 23–1. In early October, it cleared the House, 389–24, by far the largest margin in the VRA's legislative history. "It was just like old times," said the subcommittee chairman Edwards. "We creamed 'em."

Despite the president's prior opposition to the VRA, the Reagan administration refrained from taking a position during the House proceedings. That June, Reagan had asked Attorney General William French Smith to undertake a three-month study of the law and submit his recommendations by October. "I am sensitive to the controversy which has attached itself to some of the act's provisions, in particular those provisions which impose burdens unequally upon different parts of the nation," Reagan wrote. "But I am sensitive also to the fact that the spirit of the act marks this nation's commitment to full equality for all Americans, regardless of race, color or national origin." For the first time in the VRA's legislative history, no one from the White House testified before the House.

"They weren't awake in the House," Derfner said of the law's opponents. "The Reagan administration had just come in. The ideologues weren't geared up yet."

No one expected that to be the case when the House bill reached the desk of Strom Thurmond and the Republican Senate.

On November 6, 1981, the *Los Angeles Times* published a bombshell A1 story: "Reagan to Extend Voting Act: Reportedly Will OK It in Virtually Any Form."

"President Reagan, apparently trying to send a positive signal to blacks, is expected to announce today that he will sign a 10-year extension of the landmark 1965 Voting Rights Act—in virtually any form that Congress sends it to him," wrote the reporter, George Skelton. "Administration sources told the *Times* Thursday night that the president, after considering the issue for several months, basically has sided against conservative advisors in the Justice Department who had advocated trying to roll back key features of the act."

The prominent Republicans lobbying for Reagan to support a strong VRA bill included Harry Dent, the former architect of Nixon's 1968 southern strategy, who had quit politics to become a Baptist preacher. "When I look back, my biggest regret now is anything I did that stood in the way of the rights of black people," Dent said. "Or any people." He told Reagan that the South had "learned to live with" the VRA, and so should he. "The whole question is kind of passé in the South," Dent said. "But the question of voting rights is not passé for black people."

William Bradford Reynolds, the newly confirmed assistant attorney general for civil rights, read the article to his blindsided boss, Attorney General Smith. A month earlier, Smith had sent Reagan his confidential twenty-one-page assessment of the VRA, which urged the president to oppose any bill—like the House version—that overrode the Supreme Court's requirement for intentional discrimination in Section 2 cases.

"If Reagan endorses the bill the way it is written, it will mean proportional representation," Reynolds told Smith. "This president cannot do that. If Ronald Reagan endorses this bill, it will be contrary to everything he said he believed in during the campaign."

Smith, who had been Reagan's personal lawyer for fifteen years and a key member of his kitchen cabinet, angrily called the White House and said, "I want to see the president. I'm coming over. Clear the decks." On the ride from the Justice Department to the White House, Smith and Reynolds discussed what they would tell the president: "You campaigned against quotas. But this bill will mean that lines [will] be drawn to promote proportional representation by race."

The White House had summoned reporters for a briefing on the administration's position. But neither Reagan nor the attorney general appeared as planned. Instead, the White House released a seven-paragraph statement specifying that Reagan would sign a ten-year extension of the current law or a "modified" version of the House bill. "I believe that the act should retain the 'intent' test under existing law, rather than changing to a new and untested 'effects' standard," the president's statement said. Reagan had capitulated to Smith and Reynolds.

"The die was cast," said Neas. "The decision was made to go with Reynolds and that crowd at the Department of Justice. That's when the Reagan administration basically said, 'Smith and Reynolds are determining our civil rights policy.'" The Civil Rights Division of the DOJ became ground zero for the administration's counterrevolution in civil rights.

In January 1981, the Heritage Foundation, the leading conservative think tank in Washington, had released "Mandate for Leadership: Policy Management in a Conservative Administration," a three-thousand-page blueprint for the new administration. It became required reading in Reagan's Washington. "Civil Rights is one of the two most radicalized elements of the Justice Department," the report said. "In the past, attorneys in this division have used the threat of widescale resignations to intimidate conservative administrations into moderating their anti–affirmative action policies. This cannot be allowed to happen again. The Assistant Attorney General for Civil Rights must be someone who is willing to 'take the heat' for policies intended to reverse the use of discrimination to end discrimination. He must understand from the beginning that he may be forced to resign."

That man was Reynolds, the key architect of the Reagan administration's civil rights policies. Little was known about Reynolds when he took the job. He had spent three years in the Nixon solicitor general's office under Erwin Griswold, the former dean of Harvard Law School and a well-respected moderate Republican, who had recommended Reynolds to Smith. When administration officials couldn't find an African-American for the position with sufficiently conservative views, they chose Reynolds. "I don't think he has very broad experience in civil rights matters," Griswold said. "But then stop and think about it for a moment: do you think they are going to appoint someone with extensive civil rights experience to head that division?"

Those who predicted that the forty-year-old Reynolds, who specialized in airlines and utilities litigation, would be a Rockefeller Republican be-cause of his relationship with Griswold and his patrician background (his ancestors arrived on the *Mayflower*, and his mother was a du Pont) were sadly mistaken. Reynolds subscribed to Thernstrom's brand of hard-line color-blind conservatism. "Color-blindness will be the mainstay of the civil rights policy of the Reagan administration," he wrote to the head of the U.S. Commission on Civil Rights. Reynolds believed that "government-imposed discrimination" had created "a kind of racial spoils system in America" fa-voring historically disadvantaged minorities over whites, an argument that no head of the Civil Rights Division had ever made before.

Reynolds viewed his job as simply upholding the original color-blind ideals of the civil rights movement, which the civil rights activists of the 1970s had abandoned. "Before, you didn't have the programs that were de-signed to focus on color," Reynolds said. "In the 1950s, for example, which all of us recognized was as wrong as you could get, you didn't have a quota program or an affirmative action program or a voting rights program. During that era, the cry for color blindness was to try to wake people up to the fact that everything was color-coded . . . When you get to the 1980s, the problem was that the solution to discrimination became to color-code."

Others were more skeptical of the motives for the Reagan administra-tion's full-throated embrace of color blindness. "It did make me somewhat uncomfortable," Nathan Glazer admitted. "There were at least two elements in the Republican appeal to color blindness: one was the appeal to the South; the other was the appeal to racism, no question about it."

Regardless of the motive, during Reynolds's tenure, under the banner of color blindness, ending busing became more important than desegregating schools, dismantling quotas became more important than integrating the workforce or academia, and preventing proportional representation became more important than achieving a multiracial government. "It was something of a mantra," Reynolds's deputy Chuck Cooper, a conservative Alabamian and former clerk for Justice William Rehnquist, said of color blindness. "It was at the root of the Reagan Justice Department's enforce-ment philosophy."

Seemingly overnight, the priorities for the Civil Rights Division shifted dramatically. "There was never, in any of the cases I had handled up to that point, a question of 'Well, what's the effect on the white community?'" said

Gerry Hebert, a blunt-spoken Irish-American lawyer from Massachusetts who served as deputy director of litigation in the Civil Rights Division's voting section. "The fact was that you had blacks in the Deep South that had been lynched, disenfranchised, and marginalized, and then for people to come in and say, 'What's the effect on the white community?' that was unheard of."

Reynolds's predecessor, Drew Days, had been a civil rights lawyer with the NAACP Legal Defense Fund for eight years before becoming the first black assistant attorney general for civil rights under Carter. "The whole philosophy of Drew Days in the Carter administration was top-level support for active enforcement of the Voting Rights Act," Hebert said. "Drew Days came from a civil rights background, was interested in enforcing civil rights across the board, and wasn't shy or coy about it. None of those things were present with Brad Reynolds."

The contrast between Days and Reynolds epitomized the change from Carter to Reagan on civil rights. "There will never be any attempt while I am president to weaken the great civil rights acts that have passed in the years gone by," Carter said when he became president. Carter appointed the first black division head at the DOJ (Days), the first black woman cabinet member (Patricia Harris), and the first black UN ambassador (Young). John Lewis helped direct antipoverty efforts for the administration. Carter named more blacks, Hispanics, and women to the federal judiciary than all previous administrations combined. For the first time in history, disciples of the civil rights movement played a role in enforcing the nation's civil rights laws.

Career lawyers at the Civil Rights Division, who'd compiled a near-impeccable legal record since the 1960s and had worked tirelessly to integrate all aspects of American life, viewed Reynolds as a catastrophic threat to the bipartisan mandate for their work. "We had a period from the end of Nixon to the end of Carter that was hard to top," said Jim Turner, who had been with the division since 1965. "Civil rights enforcement was pretty much left to the professionals. Then Reagan came in, and that all started to change."

When the VRA debate began in the Senate in early 1982, the Justice Department focused all its ammunition on preserving the *Mobile v. Bolden* decision. Limiting civil rights enforcement to individual cases of inten-

tional discrimination, rather than broad protection for previously marginalized and disenfranchised groups, had emerged as a top conservative
priority. "No 'pattern of discrimination case' may be filed *unless there is
clear proof of an intent to discriminate*," the Heritage Foundation recommended in January 1981. Simply examining the effects of discrimination in
civil rights cases "couldn't be squared with the ideal of color blindness,"
Cooper said.

The House debate on the VRA had largely centered on the continued
need for Section 5, which Reynolds and other administration officials opposed but recognized as a hopeless battle. "Since there seems to be virtually
no likelihood that Congress will seriously entertain proposed legislation to
repeal the special provisions of the Voting Rights Act, we are not pursuing
this alternative as a viable option for serious consideration," Reynolds wrote
to Smith on August 16, 1981. He instead proposed for Sections 2 and 5 a
"single standard" requiring proof of intentional discrimination. "We should,
at the very least, strive to maintain for Section 2 the 'purpose' standard announced in *City of Mobile v. Bolden*," he wrote.

The Dallas *Times Herald* ran a cartoon mocking the administration's
position. "We don't oppose the extension of the Voting Rights Act . . . but
we think the test of discrimination should be intent not effect," a fictional
Smith said at a press conference. "Won't that cripple enforcement of the Act?"
a reporter asked. "That is not our intent," Smith responded.

To make the case against Section 2, Smith and Reynolds turned to a
twenty-six-year-old special assistant to the attorney general named John
Glover Roberts.

Roberts was born in Buffalo but grew up in Long Beach, Indiana, an
affluent, all-white, heavily Republican enclave on Lake Michigan, where his
father worked as an electrical engineer for Bethlehem Steel. Roberts attended the private Notre Dame Catholic School and then La Lumiere, a prestigious all-boys prep school in the tranquil woods of northern Indiana, far
away from the antiwar and civil rights unrest of the 1960s.

After high school, Roberts became a "Harvard Harvard." He studied
history as an undergraduate, writing his thesis on British liberalism in the
early twentieth century, and graduated in three years. His classmates included precocious young conservatives like the antitax crusader Grover
Norquist and the future Michigan senator Spencer Abraham. Roberts

then enrolled at Harvard Law School, where he became editor of the law review. Morton Horwitz, a professor of American legal history at Harvard, remembered him as "a conservative looking for a conservative ideology in American history."

Roberts found that ideology in Washington, beginning in the chambers of Justice Rehnquist, whom Roberts clerked for from July 1980 to August 1981. Rehnquist, known as the Lone Ranger when he joined the Court in 1971 because of his conservative views, proudly displayed a Lone Ranger figurine on his desk. "In the 1970s and 1980s, Rehnquist was in a class of his own," said Neas. "He was the lone vote or one of two votes against a civil rights consensus."

Rehnquist's cramped twenty-by-fifteen-foot office functioned as a federalist society before there was an official Federalist Society, the closest place to the center of an emerging conservative legal movement. He was an old-school states' rights conservative long after it was fashionable, unafraid of taking deeply unpopular positions when it came to issues like civil rights.

In 1952, as a twenty-eight-year-old clerk to Justice Robert Jackson, Rehnquist had written an explosive memo as the Court prepared to hear the first round of arguments in *Brown v. Board of Education*. "I realize that it is an unpopular and unhumanitarian position, for which I have been excoriated by 'liberal' colleagues, but I think *Plessy v. Ferguson* was right and should be re-affirmed," Rehnquist wrote.

A year later he urged Jackson to uphold an all-white primary for a Texas Democratic club. "It is about time the Court faced the fact that the white people of the South do not like the colored people," Rehnquist wrote. "The Constitution restrains them from effecting this dislike through state action but it most assuredly did not appoint the Court as a sociological watchdog to rear up every time private discrimination raises its admittedly ugly head." On both occasions, Jackson—and the Court—disagreed.

After picking up undergraduate, graduate, and law degrees from Stanford and clerking for Jackson, Rehnquist moved to Arizona, where Goldwater's brand of libertarian conservatism was on the rise. Rehnquist urged Goldwater to oppose the Civil Rights Act, on the ground that the federal government couldn't tell private property owners what to do, and wrote a major speech for him during the 1964 campaign defending the vote.

"It has been well-said that the Constitution is color-blind," Goldwater remarked at the Conrad Hilton in Chicago. "And so it is just as wrong to compel children to attend certain schools for the sake of so-called integration as for the sake of segregation . . . Our aim, as I understand it, is neither to establish a segregated society nor to establish an integrated society. It is to preserve a free society."

Rehnquist's opposition to civil rights laws on federalism grounds and the rebranding of that opposition as principled color blindness became a staple of the Reagan administration's position on civil rights. "Color blindness became a mechanism for maintaining the old regime in a respectable way," said the Harvard law professor Randall Kennedy.

During his nomination to the Supreme Court in 1971, Rehnquist's political activities in Arizona attracted controversy in Washington. From 1960 to 1964 Rehnquist directed "ballot security" operations for the Maricopa County Republican Party in Phoenix, known as "Operation Eagle Eye," which was designed to challenge the eligibility of Democratic voters at the polls. Civil rights activists with the NAACP in Arizona testified that Rehnquist had personally administered literacy tests to black and Hispanic voters at Democratic precincts in Phoenix, questioning their qualifications by asking them to read portions of the Constitution.

"Over the years, there has been only one area of civil rights legislation where conservatives, liberals and even some of the Deep South members of the Senate and House could reach agreement," Clarence Mitchell and Joe Rauh wrote in *The Washington Post*. "That is the right to vote. Thus, because of his personal and organizational involvement in denying Negroes the right to vote in Arizona, Mr. Rehnquist is out of step even with many segregationists who welcome voting by colored Americans." Rehnquist denied the allegations and was confirmed, 68–26.

His views on voting rights did not moderate when he joined the Supreme Court. He backed the Court's plurality decision in *Mobile v. Bolden*. That same day, when the Court upheld a challenge to the constitutionality of Section 5 from the city of Rome, Georgia, Rehnquist dissented. Rome was nearly a quarter black but had no black officials. The city had undertaken sixty annexations from 1964 to 1975 to add white residents, which diluted the black vote, and had not submitted the changes to the DOJ despite being covered under Section 5. When the DOJ learned of the annexations, it objected to thirteen of them. Rome appealed to the Supreme Court, arguing that Section 5 prohibited only instances of intentional discrimination, which the DOJ had not alleged.

Unlike in the *Mobile* case, the Court, in a 6–3 decision written by Justice Marshall, disagreed that Section 5 required a finding of purposeful discrimination, because Congress intended the statute as an extraordinary remedy for persistent and intractable voting discrimination in select states. "The Act does not exceed Congress' power to enforce the Fifteenth Amendment," Marshall wrote.

"[I] disagree with the Court's decision permitting Congress to straitjacket the city of Rome in this manner," Rehnquist replied. "The enforcement provisions of the Civil War Amendments were not premised on the notion that Congress could empower a later generation of blacks to 'get even' for wrongs inflicted on their forebears . . . To permit congressional power to prohibit the conduct challenged in this case requires state and local governments to cede far more of their powers to the Federal Government than the Civil War Amendments ever envisioned."

The Rome dissent epitomized Rehnquist's approach to civil rights cases. "Rehnquist has a constitutional program for the nation: he wants to free the states from the restrictions of the national Constitution, particularly those emanating from the Civil War Amendments and the Bill of Rights," Owen Fiss and Charles Krauthammer wrote in *The New Republic*. They described his philosophy as "a return to the antebellum Constitution"—the period when blacks were enslaved.

Roberts arrived in Rehnquist's chambers three months after the *Mobile* and *Rome* opinions. He called Rehnquist "the boss" and became his star clerk. "John Roberts is proving to be an absolutely first-rate law clerk," Rehnquist wrote to Roberts's previous employer, Judge Henry Friendly of the Second Circuit Court of Appeals. They had similar roots: Roberts was from Indiana; Rehnquist, from Wisconsin. "The initial meeting left a strong impression on me," Roberts wrote. "Justice Rehnquist was friendly and unpretentious. He wore scuffed Hush Puppy shoes. That was my first lesson. Clothes do not make the man. The Justice sported long sideburns and Buddy Holly glasses long after they were fashionable. And he wore loud ties that I am confident were never fashionable."

Rehnquist's conservative legal beliefs had a far greater influence on Roberts than his outdated fashion. Paul Smith, a prominent civil rights lawyer who clerked at the time for Justice Powell, had known Roberts in college and clerked alongside him at the Second Circuit before they arrived in D.C. "He was very conservative," Smith remembered. "Very funny. Very argumentative." They debated cases over lunch in the Supreme Court cafeteria. "He was definitely in sync with Rehnquist," Smith said. "John was not a believer in the courts giving rights to minorities and the downtrodden. That was the basic Rehnquist philosophy."

Among Rehnquist's three clerks, Roberts stood out. "The other clerks were conservative but didn't have the ideological edge that John did," Smith said. "Rehnquist reinforced John's preexisting philosophies." Clerking for Rehnquist became Roberts's entrée to the Reagan DOJ. The Lone Ranger's radical views were quickly embraced as the consensus among the department's new arrivals.

The DOJ became the nerve center of the Reagan revolution, the most intellectually vibrant and ideologically conservative agency of the federal government. Roberts's peers would soon be the future leaders of the conservative legal movement, from his boss, Kenneth Starr, the counselor to Attorney General Smith, to influential young lawyers like Chuck Cooper, Michael Carvin, Roger Clegg, and Bruce Fein, who would profoundly change the direction of the law.

"We all came in with a great disdain for Earl Warren," said Fein, a thirty-four-year-old assistant to Deputy Attorney General Edward Schmults. He likened the camaraderie among the young deputies to Shakespeare's famous St. Crispin's Day speech in *Henry V*: "We few, we happy few, we band of brothers."

"This is an exciting time to be at the Justice Department," Roberts wrote to Friendly. "So much that has been taken for granted for so long is being seriously reconsidered."

Civil rights policy became one of Roberts's primary responsibilities when he arrived as a special assistant to Smith in the fall of 1981, with voting rights the largest part of his portfolio. He led the charge against the House VRA bill, writing upwards of twenty-five memos opposing an effects test for Section 2; drafting talking points, speeches, and op-eds for Smith and Reynolds; preparing administration officials for their testimony before the Senate; attending weekly strategy sessions; and working closely with like-minded senators on Capitol Hill. He was asked to be "a bit of a pro-vocateur, a gadfly," said Theodore Olson, the assistant attorney general for legal counsel.

On December 22, 1981, a month before the Senate began hearings on the VRA, Roberts sent an extensive memo titled "Why Section 2 of the Voting Rights Act Should Be Retained Unchanged," to Smith for circulation to senators and their staffs.

"The House-passed version of Section 2 would in essence establish a 'right' in racial and language minorities to electoral representation proportional to their population in the community," Roberts wrote. "Incorporation of an effects test in Section 2 would establish essentially a quota system for electoral politics . . . Violations of Section 2 should not be made too easy to prove, since they provide a basis for the most intrusive interference imaginable by federal courts into state and local processes."

A week earlier Senators Kennedy and Mathias had lined up sixty-one Senate cosponsors for the House bill, forty Democrats and twenty-one Republicans, enough to overcome a Republican filibuster. "They must not have read the bill," a shocked Thurmond told NPR's Nina Totenberg when she broke the news to him.

The Senate announcement was a clarion call for Roberts. "Brad Reynolds has expressed some reservations about circulating any written statement on this question to the Hill, for fear that the statement would end up in the press and be subject to attack," he wrote to Smith. "My own view is that something must be done to educate the Senators on the seriousness of this problem."

In memo after memo, Roberts recast the House version of Section 2 as yet another misguided form of affirmative action. "An effects test would eventually lead to a quota system in all areas, since only when effects are mathematically proportionate would the test be satisfied," Roberts wrote to Starr on January 5, 1982. "I do not believe this to be the aim of our civil rights laws, or the intent of Congress or the Framers, and therefore do not embrace the effects test."

On January 26, when Smith met with Reagan at the White House to discuss the VRA, Roberts told him: "This meeting presents an opportunity to solidify the Administration's position once and for all, to head off any retrenchment efforts, and to enlist the active support of the White House personnel for our position. I recommend taking a very positive and aggressive stance." He urged the attorney general to tell the president: "An effects test for Section 2 could also lead to a quota system in electoral politics, as the President himself recognized . . . Just as we oppose quotas in employment and education, so too we oppose them in elections."

Roberts expressed confidence that his position would prevail. "Do not be fooled by the House vote or the 61 Senate sponsors of the House bill into believing that the President cannot win on this issue," he wrote to Smith. "Once the senators are educated on the differences between the President's position and the House bill, and the serious dangers in the House bill, solid support will emerge for the President's position."

The next day, when Smith testified before the Senate, he echoed Roberts's argument about Section 2, saying: "I think that if carried to its logical conclusion, proportional representation or, put another way, quotas, would be the end result."

Opposition to an effects test became an obsession for Roberts. After Smith's testimony, he drafted hard-hitting op-eds for Smith and Reynolds in *The New York Times* and *The Washington Post* restating the quota argument. "The frequent writings in this area by our adversaries have gone unanswered for too long," he told Reynolds.

The *Times* responded with an incensed editorial. "The Reagan Administration is stepping up its opposition to a strengthened Voting Rights Act by playing on fears of racial quotas," the paper wrote. "By talking so anxiously about quotas at this point, the Administration unnecessarily inflames the debate over voting rights renewal."

Roberts distributed his ghostwritten op-eds and talking points, along with a *Wall Street Journal* editorial against the House bill, to senators and their staffs. Reynolds restated Roberts's argument when he testified before the Senate on the last day of hearings. "An 'effects' test under amended Section 2 would likely lead to the widespread restructuring by federal courts of electoral procedures and systems at all levels of Government—from the U.S. House of Representatives to local school boards—on no more than a finding that the election system is not designed to avoid disproportionate election results," Reynolds said. "The change in Section 2 would change that fundamental right to a right to have certain election results rather than simply the right to cast your vote free of racial discrimination."

Roberts had a remarkable level of clout among the top officials in the

Justice Department for a twentysomething special assistant. "John had a lot of influence, not only in his memos," said Reynolds. "We sat down and talked about it a lot."

Roberts's positions put him sharply at odds with the career lawyers in the Civil Rights Division, who unanimously supported an effects test for Section 2 and personally knew how difficult it was to prove intentional discrimination. "We hardly agreed on anything," said Jim Turner, who twice argued the *Mobile v. Bolden* case before the Supreme Court. "He would decide against the Civil Rights Division lawyers' approach at the drop of a hat."

The split over the VRA led to open warfare within the division. "It was Brad Reynolds, Chuck Cooper, and John Roberts that were constantly pushing back," said Gerry Hebert. "John seemed like he always had it in for the Voting Rights Act. I remember him being a zealot when it came to having fundamental suspicions about the Voting Rights Act's utility."

Roberts wasn't the only one enjoying newfound influence in Reagan's Washington. The administration had embraced Abigail Thernstrom's critique of the VRA, and she had struck up a close friendship with Hatch and his chief counsel, Stephen Markman. Markman called Derfner and said he'd like to open the first day of Senate hearings with Thernstrom and Derfner as the first two witnesses.

Derfner couldn't believe it. Hatch wanted a seasoned voting rights lawyer with twenty years of experience to debate a little-known academic who'd published one major article on the VRA in an obscure journal. Ironically, Thernstrom benefited from a form of ideological affirmative action that elevated previously liberal critics of civil rights as prominent conservative spokespersons.

Thernstrom ultimately declined to testify, for fear of upsetting the liberal voting rights lawyers she needed to interview for her book (although she had published a *Washington Post* op-ed in August 1981 critiquing the VRA despite vowing to stay neutral), but Hatch called scores of neoconservative law and public policy professors, like Michael Levin of the City University of New York and James Blumstein of Vanderbilt University, to testify against the House bill in her stead. "Those who have been long-time supporters of the Voting Rights Act," said John Bunzel of Stanford's Hoover Institution, are "in retreat because we are troubled by the efforts of some of the sponsors of a new extension to redefine in a major way the meaning and direction of 'equal electoral opportunity' by creating an artificial mix of race and politics."

On an overcast, sticky afternoon on June 1981, Jesse Jackson led two thousand civil rights supporters on a four-hour march from Strom Thurmond High School, home of the Fighting Rebels, to the Edgefield County town square, where a statue of Thurmond stood outside the courthouse. They marched two abreast on Highway 23 through the peach fields of western South Carolina along the Savannah River, singing "Ain't Gonna Let Strom Thurmond Turn Me Around" as they passed the stately white house where Thurmond had grown up.

"To blacks in Edgefield County, the Voting Rights Act has been an Indian treaty," said Jackson, who had grown up a hundred miles away in Greenville. "Everybody signed it, but nobody follows it."

It was the largest march of black people in Edgefield County since 1881, when five thousand black residents fled for Arkansas after the end of Reconstruction in the greatest single exodus in South Carolina history. Accompanying Jackson at the head of the line was Tom McCain, a professor of mathematics at Payne College with a Ph.D. in education administration from Ohio State University. In 1974, McCain asked Laughlin McDonald of the ACLU's voting rights project in Atlanta, who was from Winnsboro, South Carolina, to challenge the at-large structure of the Edgefield County town council, which had long been controlled by five white men. McDonald retained Derfner as his cocounsel.

Though Edgefield was 44 percent black, as in Mobile, no black had ever been elected to the county council. McCain, who attended segregated schools but had become perhaps the best-educated man in Edgefield County, had run for the council in 1972 and 1974, carrying what would have been his district but losing countywide because no white would vote for him. That was just the start of the adversity he faced. His church was burned to the ground. His residence was drawn out of his local voting precinct. The county attorney tried to remove his name from the voting rolls.

Judge Robert Chapman, a conservative Nixon appointee on the district court, first heard the case in 1975. He took five years to rule, unexpectedly announcing on April 17, 1980, that Edgefield's at-large council violated Section 2 of the VRA. "There is bloc voting by the whites on a scale that this Court has never before observed," Chapman wrote. "Whites absolutely refuse to vote for a black."

Derfner had never been so surprised in his life. Chapman had only once ruled for the plaintiffs in a civil rights case. Then, five days later, after the Supreme Court released its decision in *Mobile*, Chapman was forced to reverse his opinion. It was a familiar story for blacks in Strom Thurmond's hometown, a place that epitomized the savagery of the post-Reconstruction South, where whites seized power violently in 1876 and refused to give it up.

"It was the most unrepresentative place you'd ever seen in your life," Derfner said. "Blacks had nothing, and yet they were a huge part of the population." Whites owned stately antebellum mansions, surrounded by lush peach fields, while blacks lived in tar-paper shacks with no sewage systems, paved roads, or playgrounds.

Following Judge Chapman's ruling, McCain's lawyers discovered that Edgefield had not cleared its shift to at-large elections in 1966 with the federal government as required under Section 5. The DOJ did approve a subsequent change of the size of the council in 1971 but had been kept in the dark about Edgefield's adoption of a new electoral system. McDonald and Derfner sued the county under Section 5.

The Civil Rights Division drafted a friend-of-the-court brief backing the black plaintiffs in August 1981. Reynolds signed off on it, then received a call from Thurmond and pulled the brief twenty-four hours before the case was to be heard in South Carolina district court. Reynolds based his decision on "new information" but declined to say what it was. "I do it all the time," Reynolds said of overruling the division's recommendation. "That's a routine kind of experience I have these days."

It was yet another setback for Edgefield's black voters. McDonald said it would have been "enormously helpful for somebody from the Justice Department to affirm their position that the use of at-large voting had never been precleared." A three-judge court in South Carolina subsequently ruled against McCain. What McDonald called "this seemingly interminable lawsuit" dragged on.

As the Senate debated the VRA reauthorization, Edgefield had still not elected a black county representative in over one hundred years. "Without extension," McCain told the Senate, "there is no hope of ever getting a black elected to county government in Edgefield; there is no hope, in fact, of blacks in my county ever achieving true racial equality."

Events in Edgefield County showed the absurdity of the Reynolds-Roberts-Thernstrom-Hatch argument that the House version of Section 2 of the VRA would lead to quotas or proportional representation. "It was a scare tactic," Derfner said. "It was a fear that was not justified. In a lot of cases we were talking about, there were no blacks elected. We were trying to get from none to some."

In the seven southern states originally covered by Section 5, blacks made up 25 percent of the population but held only 5 percent of elected seats. Twelve of South Carolina's forty-six counties had black voting majorities, but the at-large elected state senate had no black members, making it the only all-white legislative body in the South.

Seventeen years after passage of the VRA, blacks and other minorities remained severely underrepresented across the country. It was next to impossible to find the inverse of Edgefield, a county where whites made up 44 percent of the population but had no elected voice.

On March 1, 1982, following Reynolds's testimony, the Reagan administration won a major victory when the Senate Subcommittee on the Constitution passed a ten-year extension of the VRA that preserved the Supreme Court's intent test for Section 2. The Senate Judiciary Committee deadlocked on how to proceed. Hatch and Thurmond appeared to be on the verge of killing the House bill.

Senator Bob Dole of Kansas, the powerful chairman of the Finance Committee, stepped in to broker a compromise. Dole advised fellow Republicans to make "the extra effort to erase the lingering image of our party as the cadre of the elite, the wealthy, the insensitive . . . Our job now is to demonstrate concern to blacks and others who doubt our sincerity." Dole adopted the House-backed effects test for Section 2 but inserted language quoting the Supreme Court's "totality of circumstances" standard from *White v. Regester* and added a disclaimer that a lack of proportional representation was not enough to justify a Section 2 violation.

Joe Rauh dubbed Dole "the Dirksen of the '80s," the critical Republican moderate who, at a pivotal moment in the debate, embraced the cause of

civil rights. "It was no compromise at all," Rauh said. "We got everything
we wanted." Opponents of the law could hardly disagree.

Reynolds attended an all-night meeting where Kennedy and Dole ham-
mered out the final language of the bill. "It was a compromise we were not
pleased with," Reynolds said. Roberts was furious. "There is no reason to
change the permanent nationwide provisions of the Voting Rights Act from
an intent test to a results test," he wrote in response to an editorial praising
the bill.

Color-blind critiques of Dole's compromise quickly emerged from conservative commentators. "In forty years of covering politics, I cannot recall a
more lamentable legislative error," wrote the syndicated columnist James Kilpatrick, a longtime defender of segregation. "For the first time since the days
of Reconstruction, the Dole amendment would institutionalize racist policies at the very core of our public life." Kilpatrick asked rhetorically, "What
is this verb, 'dilute'? We are creating by this language a 'protected class of
citizens'—that is, black citizens—whose block power must not be 'diluted.'"

The Senate Judiciary Committee passed the Dole compromise, 14–4, on
May 4. A dozen new cosponsors signed on within twenty-four hours. Thurmond voted against it, but VRA supporters lobbied him to support the
final bill. Every member of the South Carolina House delegation had signed
on, as had the South Carolina senator Fritz Hollings and South Carolina's
governor, Richard Riley. Derfner knew Thurmond was meeting with black
mayors to query their views on the law. "Whatever Senator Thurmond says
to you," he told Mayor Charlie Ross of Lincolnville, "tell him you like the
Kennedy-Dole compromise."

Dole sold the bill to the upper echelons of the Reagan administration.
"White House is on board," he told Neas on May 3. The North Carolina
senator Jesse Helms, who had replaced Thurmond as the Senate's leading
civil rights critic, vowed to filibuster "until the cows came home." After
Helms railed for five days against "Big Brother in Washington," the Senate
voted, 97–0, to silence him.

The Senate passed the Dole compromise on June 18 by a vote of 85–8,
the largest margin for the VRA in the body's history. Only four of twenty-
two senators from the South—Helms and John East of North Carolina,
Jeremiah Denton of Alabama, and Harry Byrd of Virginia—opposed the
bill. When the Louisiana senator Russell Long walked in to cast his yes vote,

a reporter asked why he opposed an intent test for Section 2. "The road to hell is paved with good intentions," Long responded. Even Thurmond, who didn't want to antagonize his state's growing bloc of black voters, backed the VRA for the first time in his life.

The House passed the Senate bill on a nearly unanimous voice vote five days later. The extension lasted for twenty-five years, three and a half times longer than the 1975 reauthorization. Despite the most conservative president since Herbert Hoover and the most conservative Congress since the 1950s, it was the strongest and most bipartisan Voting Rights Act ever enacted.

Reagan signed the bill in the Rose Garden on June 29. "The right to vote is the crown jewel of American liberties," the president said, "and we will not see its luster diminished." In sharp contrast with LBJ in 1965, who spoke for twenty minutes and handed out fifty pens, Reagan used only four minutes and one pen, although he did attend a posh reception in the East Room afterward with civil rights leaders like Jackson and Coretta Scott King.

Rauh, the liberal lion, had been right in early 1981. The civil rights community had challenged Reagan on voting rights, and it had won. "Our fondest hopes in 1981 were exceeded," he said.

On October 31, 1983, Tom McCain and fifty blacks from Edgefield County traveled to Washington for Supreme Court oral arguments in *McCain v. Lybrand*. They sat at the front of the courtroom, hoping for a long-overdue resolution to their case. Nine years after filing the original lawsuit, the ACLU lawyer Laughlin McDonald argued for the black plaintiffs. The Department of Justice didn't submit a brief until the Supreme Court asked for one, and this time Reynolds did not overrule his Civil Rights Division staff, which maintained that the at-large county council plan had never been properly cleared by the DOJ.

The Supreme Court unanimously agreed four months later, requiring the county to adopt five single-member districts. In the 1984 election, three blacks—Willie Bright, an AT&T technician; Sarah Williams, a schoolteacher and dry cleaner's owner; and Albert Talbert, a barber—were elected to the council for the first time since Reconstruction. The swearing-in ceremony took place at the Edgefield County Courthouse, next to Thurmond's statue. "We were able to get representation only because of the Voting Rights Act," McCain said.

As its first official action, on New Year's Day 1985, the council hired McCain as county administrator. "The change in the method of elections had a tremendous impact on everything, on all walks of life," said the council's chairman, Willie Bright, who served for twenty-two years. "We showed we could run the government and do it effectively and fairly. We paved roads for the first time in the black communities, improved garbage collection, changed road signs, got blacks in every office in the court house, changed the land fill, got a black magistrate, and started a rural fire department. We made a lot of changes and it was all new."

Following the 1982 reauthorization, similar transformations occurred throughout the country, especially in the South. "The amendment really started things up again," said McDonald. "Cases are being filed. Cases are being won. Cases that have languished are being resurrected."

That included Mobile, where a retrial in Judge Pittman's courtroom showed that the city's at-large elections were adopted not as part of a Progressive Era reform, as its defenders claimed, but for far more nefarious racial reasons. Peyton McCrary, a professor of history at the University of South Alabama, found the "smoking gun," a 1909 letter from the former Mobile congressman Frederick Bromberg in the Mobile *Register* explaining the change from district to at-large elections. "We have always, as you know, falsely pretended that our main purpose was to exclude the ignorant vote," Bromberg wrote, "when, in fact, we were trying to exclude not the ignorant vote but the Negro vote." Pittman, for a second time, abolished the city's at-large elections in 1982, this time for good.

In July 1985, for the first time in the port city's history, three African-Americans were elected to the seven-member city council: Irmatean Watson, a pharmacist, and two ministers, Charles Tunstall and Clinton Johnson. The former commissioner Arthur Outlaw, a racial moderate who had opposed the city's decision to appeal the original *Mobile* ruling, became the new mayor. Twenty-five hundred Mobilians attended the swearing-in ceremony.

A year later ninety-three-year-old Wiley Bolden addressed a meeting of the council. A decade after filing the *Mobile* case, seeing the three African-American commissioners "gratifies me more than you can know," Bolden said.

6

CHALLENGING THE CONSENSUS

On a sweltering afternoon in June 1983, Brad Reynolds, Jesse Jackson, and half a dozen lawyers from the Civil Rights Division barreled through the Mississippi Delta in a twenty-six-foot Winnebago that Jackson called the Justice Buggy. The much-maligned civil rights czar had made the trip, on Jackson's invitation, to investigate violations of the VRA before Mississippi's statewide elections that fall.

As was often the case with the loquacious Jackson, they were running behind schedule. Their driver from Memphis, who had a Fuzzbuster radar detector, sped along the desolate two-lane highway between Greenville and Jackson. It was raining ferociously, and the sky above the cotton fields turned a disquieting purple. Jackson and Reynolds were at the front of the bus arguing passionately about affirmative action. It was like an odd buddy sitcom.

Suddenly lightning and thunder hit at the same time. The bus shook and nearly skidded off the road. "See, Brad," Jackson responded, "God don't like that shit you're saying."

Even the tightly coiled Reynolds had to laugh. He was deep behind enemy lines with Jackson in the delta. "Jackson kept saying: 'If we would accompany him to Mississippi, he would show us,'" said the deputy attorney general for civil rights Jim Turner. "And by golly, he did."

Eighteen years after the VRA's passage, Mississippi remained a center of massive resistance. At every stop on the two-day tour, from Greenwood to Belzoni to Canton, black voters approached Reynolds with horror stories about contemporary voting discrimination. White neighborhoods were annexed to dilute black representation; county supervisor districts were gerrymandered to fragment black voters; white plantation bosses and factory owners forced black employees to work overtime on Election Day; voters had to register twice for county and municipal elections; polling places were moved from black to white neighborhoods. A black attorney said a local white man had even posed as a Justice Department official to intimidate black voters. "I never heard of anything like that before," Reynolds responded over eggs and grits in a diner in Belzoni.

It was an eye-opening experience for Reynolds. "I've heard the difficulties you have in access to registrars," he said to amens at the Pleasant Green Holiness Church in Canton. "I've heard about the polling places that were moved . . . and intimidation at the ballot box. I urge you to step forward so I can hear your story." He called the VRA "the most precious of the civil rights statutes on the books" and pledged that "we are going to enforce the Voting Rights Act as vigorously as you expect it to be enforced." (Reynolds's critics dismissed the trip as a ploy by the Reagan administration to court black voters ahead of the 1984 presidential election.)

At the end of every stop, he and Jackson—the aristocratic lawyer in a shirt and tie and the country preacher in a beige leisure suit—joined hands and sang "We Shall Overcome."

A day after returning to Washington, Reynolds dispatched ten federal registrars to five counties in Mississippi—former civil rights battlegrounds like Canton, Greenwood, and Ruleville—for the first time in eight years.

Examiner Neilan Burns, a retired federal employee from Atlanta who had been deputized as an examiner, opened a makeshift office in Ruleville's tiny post office in Sunflower County, the home of Fannie Lou Hamer and the segregationist Mississippi senator James Eastland.

"Do you solemnly swear to faithfully support the Constitution of the United States and the State of Mississippi, so help you God?" he asked Tommie Lee Petty, a black farmhand who worked for a white plantation owner.

"Yes, sir," Petty responded.

It was just like the old days in August 1965, when federal officials signed up black voters in droves. In June 1983, the examiners enrolled over a thousand new voters in one weekend. Jackson's "Southern Crusade" signed up forty thousand blacks from May to July.

In 1967, Petty had registered in the county seat of Indianola, twenty-seven miles away, but had not registered separately for city elections under Mississippi's dual registration law. (The law was challenged in the late 1980s under Section 2.) "We weren't allowed to vote in Mississippi for a long time," he said. "Never been allowed here to do too much." He'd still never voted. "Figured it wouldn't do no good. They whites going to get who they want anyhow." Though Sunflower County was 65 percent black, the county board of supervisors—the most powerful local officials—was all white.

Such was the case across Mississippi. Blacks made up 35 percent of the population but only 7 percent of elected officials. Of the 410 county supervisors in eighty-two counties, just 27 were black. Under Section 5, Mississippi counties were required to submit new redistricting maps for the board of supervisors before the 1983 election. The DOJ objected to an unprecedented thirty-six plans that discriminated against black voters in places like Starkville, where Oktibbeha County officials intentionally fragmented Mississippi State University into three districts to prevent black officeholders from getting elected with student support.

Federal courts postponed elections in fourteen counties while nondiscriminatory districts were drafted. During the first round of balloting that August, more than three hundred federal observers monitored voting in eleven counties. Fourteen observers were sent to tiny Tunica County on the Mississippi River near the Tennessee border, one of the poorest areas in the country, which Jackson called "America's Ethiopia." On August 2, the teacher James Dunn became the first black county supervisor in Tunica history.

Elsewhere in Mississippi, blacks took control of supervisor boards in Humphreys County, where Lewis and Bond once embraced the white mayor of Belzoni, and Holmes County, the home of the state representative Robert Clark. In total, the number of black supervisors nearly doubled in 1983 and 1984, from twenty-seven to fifty.

The flurry of activity showed what was possible when the VRA was vigorously enforced. That's what civil rights activists had been trying to tell Reynolds and Reagan for the past three years. "Just to focus on Mississippi is selective enforcement," Jackson said after the trip. "We need comprehensive enforcement of the Voting Rights Act."

If Mississippi briefly spotlighted the pro-VRA side of Reynolds, Louisiana showcased the civil rights skeptic that the public was more accustomed to seeing.

In late December 1981, Louisiana submitted its redistricting plan for Congress following the 1980 census for DOJ approval. The department had sixty days to decide whether to accept or reject the plan. The submission "sent up a lot of alarm bells" in the Civil Rights Division, Reynolds admitted.

The original plan overwhelmingly passed by the Louisiana legislature created a majority-black congressional district in New Orleans, which was 55 percent black and in 1978 had elected Ernest "Dutch" Morial as its first black mayor. The new district would give voters in New Orleans the opportunity to elect the first black congressman in the state's history. At the time there were only two black members of Congress from the entire South: Harold Ford, Sr., from Memphis and Mickey Leland from Houston.

Louisiana's Republican governor, David Treen, quickly expressed his displeasure with the legislature, stating: "Any bill in that form is unacceptable and without question will be vetoed." Treen had started out in politics as a member of the States' Rights Party of Louisiana, whose main political platform was the defense of segregation. He had run unsuccessfully for Congress three times as a Republican in the 1960s, opposing civil rights laws in voting, education, and housing. He was finally elected in 1972 and served until 1980, voting against nearly every piece of civil rights legislation, including the VRA extension of 1975.

Treen defended his veto threat in Reynoldsesque color-blind terms. "What I did do was to question the appropriateness of a deliberate, conscious drawing of congressional district lines for the deliberate purpose of achieving a majority black district," he told DOJ lawyers. "I observed that such motives were inconsistent with our goal of a homogeneous society. In fact, it is demeaning to blacks to suggest that they must be in an absolute majority in order to effect the election of a member of their race. It is also demeaning to them that they will always vote along racial lines." It was a fact in Louisiana, however, that few whites would vote for a black candidate, and that explained why African-Americans made up 29 percent of the population but held no elected statewide posts.

The legislature had not overridden a veto by the governor since the nineteenth century. The two most powerful entities in Louisiana, local pols joked, were God and the governor, and even that was debatable. In response to Treen's threat, a small group of legislators and state officials secretly met in the subbasement of the state capitol to draft a new congressional map without a majority-black district. No black legislators or officials were part of the process. Representative Peppi Bruneau of New Orleans, the chairman of the subcommittee in charge of redistricting, told Lawrence Chehardy, the tax assessor of Jefferson Parish, "We already have a nigger mayor, and we don't need another nigger bigshot." Governor Treen stayed until late in the night to review the plan.

The new maps fragmented black voters in New Orleans into two congressional districts where they would be a distinct minority—one in liberal, urban Orleans Parish and the other in conservative, suburban Jefferson Parish, two places with little in common. Whites retained decisive control in both. The effort to marginalize black voters by strategically removing black wards but not white ones left the districts horrifically misshapen. The Second Congressional District, represented by the Democrat Lindy Boggs, the widow of the former House majority leader Hale Boggs, became known as the "Donald Duck" gerrymander, with its head and tail on one side of the Mississippi River and its fat body on the other.

Robert Kwan, a staff attorney in the Civil Rights Division, sent Reynolds a twenty-nine-page single-spaced memo explaining why the DOJ should object to the plan. "It is clear in our view that the Governor was acutely aware of the racial consequences of his actions, and those racial considerations formed the basis of his actions," Kwan wrote. "We conclude that the State has not met its burden of proving the lack of a racial purpose and recommend the interposition of a Section 5 objection."

But Treen had one important thing going for him: a close friendship with Reynolds. Reynolds spoke to Treen nine times on the phone about the plan and paid a personal visit to Louisiana, where he stayed in the governor's mansion and took a helicopter tour of New Orleans with Treen, who assured him the state had done nothing improper. Though the DOJ received over one hundred letters from black legislators and community leaders opposing the plan, Reynolds didn't speak with any of them.

In the spring of 1982, top officials in the Civil Rights Division— Jim Turner; Gerry Hebert; the voting section chief, Gerry Jones; and the litigation director, Paul Hancock—met with Reynolds to discuss the case. The staffers all agreed with Kwan's assessment, urging an objection. But it was clear that Reynolds had been influenced by his friendship with Treen, who'd convinced him that the plan was based on political considerations—protecting the Republican congressman Bob Livingston in Jefferson Parish—not racial ones.

"Your problem, Brad, is that you are biased because you have a friendship with Treen, and you're not going to believe that he could be a product of this intentionally discriminatory plan," said Hebert, the supervising attorney on the case.

Turner walked to the chalkboard and said, "I'm going to say this one time." He wrote down the factors DOJ lawyers considered when analyzing a potentially discriminatory redistricting plan: the racial views of the decision makers; irregularities in the legislative process that disadvantaged minorities; deviation from normal map-drawing procedures; the discriminatory effect of the plan; the burden of proof on the submitting authority. "All these factors are present," he told Reynolds. "You should object. I'm going home." Turner threw the chalk at the board and stormed out of the meeting.

Reynolds overruled the advice of his attorneys and declined to object. "If you can't convince people to stop even intentional discrimination, that says a lot," Hebert said.

The NAACP Legal Defense Fund filed suit against the plan under Section 2 in the Eastern District of Louisiana. Barbara Major, a black community activist in New Orleans, became the lead plaintiff in *Major v. Treen*. Lani Guinier, a thirty-three-year-old LDF lawyer from New York who'd previously worked as a special assistant to Drew Days at the DOJ, produced an eight-foot map of the duck district, which she displayed prominently in the courtroom. The LDF retained Jerris Leonard, the former assistant attorney general for civil rights under Nixon, as an expert witness. Leonard called the legislature's plan "one of the most egregious and blatant racial [gerrymanders] that I have seen . . . and [one] of only two cases that I can think of where legislative bodies intentionally, overtly intentionally, went out of its way to disenfranchise black voters."

In October 1983, the three-judge district court unanimously ruled for the plaintiffs, concluding that "the contours of the First and Second Congressional Districts . . . operate to deny or abridge the rights of minority voters, who are accorded less opportunity than other members of the electorate to participate in the political process and to elect representatives of their choice." It was the first time since 1965 that a congressional redistricting plan approved by the Justice Department had been struck down in court. The legislature subsequently drew a majority-black district, which Lindy Boggs continued to represent until her retirement in 1990, when Louisiana elected its first black member of Congress.

A year later Guinier gave a presentation about the case at her office in New York, inviting all the chiefs of the Civil Rights Division. She brought the large map of the duck district that she had used in court. "Thank you for inviting me to lunch," Reynolds said when Guinier finished her presentation. "I didn't know I was to be the main course."

After his landslide reelection in 1984, Reagan named Ed Meese, who had been his "ideological alter ego" as White House counselor, as his new attorney general. In his first press conference at the Justice Department in March 1985, Meese announced that he was promoting Reynolds to associate attorney general, the number three position at the DOJ, which required Senate confirmation.

Room 228 of the Dirksen Office Building was packed when Thurmond's Judiciary Committee began hearings on Reynolds's nomination on June 4, 1985. Never had a nomination for associate attorney general attracted so much attention.

"Mr. Chairman, it is no secret that many of us have serious reservations about this nomination," said Ted Kennedy. "Mr. Reynolds has been the architect of most, if not all, of the administration's retreat on civil rights."

Reynolds's hearings became a referendum on Reagan's civil rights policies. The long list of complaints by civil rights activists against the administration included pushing for tax exemptions for segregated schools, fighting tooth and nail against the VRA reauthorization, firing the longtime Republican head of the Civil Rights Commission and three commissioners who criticized Reagan's "color-blind" policies, prosecuting black civil rights activists in Alabama for voter fraud, siding with North Carolina over black plaintiffs in the first Supreme Court challenge to Section 2, and opposing consent decrees in fifty cities for minority and women hiring in government jobs.

Civil Rights Division lawyers often celebrated when they lost cases in court because Reynolds had forced them to make arguments at odds with the previous positions of the division. "It's like *Through the Looking Glass*," said Muriel Spence, a division lawyer who left in 1983 to join the ACLU. "Everything is exactly the opposite of the way it's supposed to be." The NAACP even asked Congress to abolish the Civil Rights Division. "I have difficulty thinking of a single civil rights matter in which I would welcome participation of the US Justice Department," said the NAACP counsel Thomas Atkins.

"Under Mr. Reynolds, the civil rights division has changed sides," said LBJ's attorney general Nick Katzenbach. "It no longer is an advocate for blacks or minorities. It has never happened before under a Democratic or Republican president. It didn't happen under Nixon or, before that, under Eisenhower. It's a total change of policy."

Reynolds's mentor Erwin Griswold distanced himself from his former protégé. "I must say I find him more ideological and more rigid and more ungiving than I would have anticipated," he told *The Washington Post*.

Under Meese, the Justice Department had become even more reactionary. Reynolds's chief deputy, Chuck Cooper, became head of the Office of Legal Counsel, the top lawyer for all government agencies, and chose as his top aide a former assistant to the solicitor general named Samuel Alito. Stephen Markman, Orrin Hatch's counsel on the Judiciary Committee, took charge of judicial selection as head of the Office of Legal Policy. All three young founders of the Federalist Society were hired by the DOJ. (John Roberts moved to the White House counsel's office.) "This was not the traditional Republican Party," said Neas. "This was a new breed. This was the beginning of the radical right."

The same coalition behind the VRA reauthorization of 1982, Neas's Leadership Conference on Civil Rights, mobilized to oppose Reynolds. It dubbed him "the Scrooge of the Justice Department." His lax enforcement of the VRA became the centerpiece of the case against Reynolds. "What we tried to do was demonstrate that the DOJ with Brad Reynolds in the lead was trying to repudiate what had been a bipartisan consensus on civil rights that went back to the mid 1950s," Neas said. "They were not just repudiating but upending how these civil rights laws had been enforced."

Lani Guinier and Gerry Hebert urged Senator Joe Biden of Delaware, the ranking Democrat on the committee, who was known for his aggressive prosecutorial style, to focus on the *Major v. Treen* case. Biden was the same age as Reynolds and from the same state. "I happen to agree with you on busing," he told Reynolds. "I happen to agree with you on your view of quotas. What I have questions about is the degree to which you think that the entire civil rights agenda has been promoted too much by this country."

Biden brought up *Major v. Treen* early in his questioning and returned to it often.

"Do you recall whether or not this issue was discussed by you with the voting section staff?" Biden asked.

"I certainly discussed the Louisiana redistricting on a number of occasions with people in the voting section," Reynolds said.

"And would it be fair to characterize the disagreement you had with the voting section staff as one of the more serious disagreements you have had in your tenure there with your staff?" Biden followed up.

"Well, Senator, there was serious disagreement on it," Reynolds responded. "I would say that."

"The reason why I am focusing on that case rather than on all the different cases," Biden said, "is because I want to make sure I get a pretty good idea of how you approach these things, what your thought process is, because your critics suggest, as you well know, not that you are not intellectually competent to hold the post, not that you are not by background qualified to hold the post, and not that you are unfair, but simply that you are very insensitive to the concerns of minority persons."

Voting rights lawyers like Guinier of the LDF and Frank Parker of the Lawyers' Committee for Civil Rights Under Law supplied the most damning testimony against Reynolds. "The Assistant Attorney General speaks in lofty tones about the need for colorblindness," Guinier said. "Yet, where a race-conscious effort is taken to assure re-election of white incumbents, he declines to act."

Major v. Treen was one of thirty cases in which Reynolds ignored the recommendation of the Civil Rights Division to object to a discriminatory voting change and one of five cases in which a voting change cleared by the department was later overturned in court.

The Section 2 unit of the voting section had filed only ten new lawsuits from 1982 to 1985, Parker told the committee, and none in Louisiana,

Mississippi, South Carolina, Texas, or Virginia. Voting rights lawyers grumbled that the ACLU voting rights project in Atlanta, which had three lawyers, filed more new cases than the twenty-seven lawyers at the DOJ's voting section. Whereas the Nixon and Ford administrations had blocked over 5 percent of voting submissions under Section 5, that figure fell to 1 percent under Reagan.

Parker later estimated that private lawyers filed ten times as many voting cases as the Justice Department during the Reagan years. Of the 1,792 voting rights cases filed in federal court between 1981 and 1988, the U.S. government initiated only 4 percent of new lawsuits.

"You have been active in the voting rights litigation, you were at the Justice Department, you are very familiar with voting rights cases," the Ohio Democratic senator Howard Metzenbaum told Guinier. "You know Mr. Reynolds' testimony in this area. Do you agree that he has provided strong advocacy in the voting rights area, or are you in disagreement with his position?"

"My brief answer is that I disagree strongly, as strongly as I possibly could, with his statement that he is vigorously enforcing the Voting Rights Act," Guinier responded.

Metzenbaum then asked her: "I wonder if you would rate Mr. Reynolds in your own mind: A, he is against discrimination of all kinds; B, he is reasonable; C, he is objective and impartial in racial cases; D, he is somewhat prejudicial against black rights; and E, he is a bigot. Where would you rate him because I am having trouble?"

"F," she responded.

In an attempt to portray himself as a champion of the VRA, Reynolds repeatedly told Congress one thing when he'd done another. He said that he'd discussed the Louisiana redistricting case with black officials and their lawyers, but Bill Quigley, the principal lawyer representing the black plaintiffs, said that "neither I nor any of the people that objected were ever allowed to meet with Mr. Reynolds."

The committee held two days of contentious hearings in early June 1985. After a two-week break, Thurmond reconvened on June 18 to give Reynolds a chance to clarify his statements. Instead, he dug himself a deeper hole.

During the VRA reauthorization hearings in 1982, Reynolds had told Senator Arlen Specter of Pennsylvania that he believed the DOJ should not intervene in a case challenging at-large elections in Burke County, Georgia, which had a black population of 53 percent but no black county commissioners. In the lower courts, the DOJ had filed a lengthy amicus brief supporting the black plaintiffs. Specter obtained a memo during Reynolds's confirmation hearings showing that Reynolds had urged Solicitor General Rex Lee to intervene *against* the black plaintiffs in Georgia, contradicting his testimony in 1982. The Supreme Court subsequently ruled, 6–3, in *Rogers v. Lodge* in July 1982 that the election system was intentionally discriminatory.

"Wasn't your response to me deceptive?" Specter asked Reynolds.

"I apologize to you if I left an impression otherwise," Reynolds responded.

"Well, Mr. Reynolds, I find that hard to accept," Specter said.

Toward the end of the last day of hearings, Biden asked Reynolds: "Maybe you could answer for me why, if you believe as you do, that you have been so vigorous in the support of and the concern for minorities in this country, they don't seem to like you very much?"

Reynolds responded: "I think that what we are talking about here is a difference of opinion on fundamental principles that are highly emotional. And I have, for whatever reasons, become the personification of those issues."

In a sign of just how important the nomination was for the administration, Reagan devoted his weekly radio address to defending Reynolds, whom he called "a tireless fighter against discrimination" and "a brilliant and dedicated lawyer." Reagan called the GOP senators Specter and Mathias to urge them to back Reynolds.

But ten days after the hearings ended, Specter and Mathias joined eight Democrats in defeating Reynolds's nomination, 10–8. "It is now clear that Mr. Reynolds does not support the approach that Congress, for the past 20 years, has taken to the problem of assuring civil rights," Mathias said.

Thurmond tried and failed three times to advance the nomination to the full Senate, despite the committee's no vote.

"The chairman has railroaded the vote," Metzenbaum said.

"I have not railroaded anything," Thurmond angrily responded.

Reynolds blamed the vote on "the pro-busing/pro-quota lobby," but it was his opposition to voting rights—and his contradictory testimony about his actions in that area—that sank his nomination. The detailed attention to cases like *Major v. Treen* "helped shift the focus of Reynolds' confirmation hearings from the murky political ground of busing and quotas to the moral high ground of voting rights," noted *The Washington Post*.

Reynolds's defeat reaffirmed the bipartisan consensus in Congress for civil rights—and voting rights in particular. "The traditionalists won; the radical revisionists of the Reagan administration are, for the present, routed," wrote the *Los Angeles Times*.

Reynolds dismissed his defeat as partisan politics and vowed to continue as head of the Civil Rights Division. Reagan told him: "Don't you go anywhere. I'm counting on you to stay."

"I got battered around quite a bit," Reynolds said afterward. "The lines were always drawn on the politics of it. The Democrats were ready to bash the administration and play the race card as much as they could, because they thought it was politically advantageous for them to do that. So anything and everything that I did was labeled racist by the other party."

But the civil rights lawyers who worked under Reynolds, Democrats and Republicans, shared the Senate's bipartisan critique. "The basic criticisms of Brad were substantial and correct," Jim Turner said.

The irony was that without his promotion, Reynolds would still be their boss, and under Meese he'd become more powerful than ever. Following his defeat, the *National Review* called Reynolds "one of the heroes of the Reagan revolution."

In the early 1960s two black teenagers, Milton F. Fitch, Jr., and George K. Butterfield, Jr., jumped into the large segregated swimming pool in their hometown of Wilson, North Carolina. After they were caught, the city drained the entire pool before reopening it for whites.

Fitch was tall and dark skinned; Butterfield, short and exceptionally light skinned. He looked Italian, with an olive complexion and black hair, and in most places could've easily passed for white. But not in Wilson, an eastern North Carolina tobacco town of one hundred thousand where the railroad track separated the white mansions on the west side from the shotgun houses on the historically black east side where Fitch and Butterfield lived. Thanks to the tobacco harvest, the west side of Wilson had the highest number of millionaires per capita in North Carolina. The east side had few paved roads and such a poor sewer system that the streets flooded whenever it rained.

The two boys came from prominent activist families. Fitch's father became the city's first black postman since Reconstruction and the North Carolina coordinator for the SCLC. Butterfield's father, a dentist, served as Wilson's first black elected official in the twentieth century. Nonetheless, their sons attended segregated schools.

In 1953, G. K. Butterfield, Sr., joined the Wilson City Council. He was reelected in 1955 and, after supporting the white mayor, was put in charge of the city's budget committee. Butterfield traveled to Raleigh to present the city's budget to the state legislature, as was the custom. After the presentation, the white state representative from Wilson sponsored an act changing the city's elections from ward districts, like Butterfield's on the east side, to at large. Butterfield lost the next election. Another African-American wouldn't be elected to the city council for the next two decades.

After attending college and law school together at North Carolina Central University, a historically black college in Durham, Fitch and Butterfield opened a small law firm in Wilson on the east side of the tracks. They tried repeatedly to integrate the city's political system. Butterfield ran for the city council in 1977 and lost. So did Fitch Sr. in 1979. Fitch Jr. lost by eight votes in 1981.

Winning election to the state legislature wasn't any easier. State representatives hailed from multimember districts, where black voters were submerged in large white areas to prevent black candidates from getting elected. House District 8 consisted of Wilson, Edgefield, and Nash counties, where blacks made up 40 percent of the population but all four state representatives were white. The same was true of major cities like Charlotte, Durham, Raleigh, and Winston-Salem, where few, if any, blacks had been elected to the state legislature as late as 1980.

In the early 1980s, Butterfield talked with Julius Chambers, the leading civil rights lawyer in North Carolina, about challenging the state legislature's multimember districts under Section 2. The Supreme Court had invalidated similar districts in the Texas legislature in *White v. Regester* in 1973.

Chambers had been born a decade before Butterfield, 150 miles west of Wilson in the small rural town of Mount Gilead. His father, Shine, worked as a car mechanic and had saved up to send Julius to a prestigious private school before a white customer refused to pay for two thousand dollars of work on his eighteen-wheel rig. No white lawyer would take Shine's case, and Julius had to attend the dilapidated segregated public school twelve miles away, which lacked even a library. That's when he decided he wanted to become a lawyer.

Chambers finished high school in May 1954, the same month as *Brown v. Board of Education*, became student body president of North Carolina College in Durham, got a master's in history from the University of Michigan, and then served as the first black editor of the law review at the University of North Carolina–Chapel Hill. Despite having graduated at the top of his class, Chambers was not invited to the year-end banquet at the segregated Chapel Hill Country Club.

In early 1965, after opening the state's first integrated law firm, Chambers filed suit to desegregate Charlotte's public schools. While speaking at a mass meeting at a church in the coastal town of New Bern, Chambers heard a loud boom. He went outside to find his car in flames. "What are we going to do?" asked his law partner Geraldine Sumter.

"We're going to go back inside and finish the meeting," Chambers said. "There's nothing we can do about that car."

Later that year, after Chambers filed suit to desegregate the Shrine Bowl, an all-star game between high school football players from North Carolina and South Carolina, dynamite blew out the window in his front bedroom while Chambers and his wife were in bed.

After Chambers won landmark discrimination cases in education and employment in the early 1970s, his Charlotte law office was firebombed, forcing him to relocate the practice to a hotel. His stoic persistence and religious sense of drive made him the state's most effective civil rights lawyer.

Chambers eagerly took on the case challenging the North Carolina legislature in 1981, targeting six multimember districts in large urban areas where few blacks had been elected. "There were parallels between this case and *Major v. Treen*," said Guinier, who worked with Chambers. "The state was trying to bury the power of black voters." Ralph Gingles, a lawyer in Gastonia who had worked for Chambers as a law student one summer, became the lead plaintiff.

At the beginning of 1984, a three-judge district court in North Carolina unanimously ruled in Chambers's favor. In Wilson's House District 8, for example, Butterfield testified that 90 percent of whites refused to vote for a black candidate. The racial polarization in voting was "so extreme," the court said, "that, all other factors aside, no black has any chance of winning election in the district as it is presently constituted."

After Chambers filed the lawsuit, eleven new black representatives were elected to the state legislature in 1982; they included six from the challenged districts. North Carolina said that was proof that multimember districts were not discriminatory. The court disagreed.

"The success that has been achieved by black candidates to date is, standing alone, too minimal in total numbers and too recent in relation to the long history of complete denial of any elective opportunities to compel or even arguably to support an ultimate finding that a black candidate's race is no longer a significant adverse factor in the political processes of the state—either generally or specifically in the areas of the challenged districts," wrote Judge James Dickson Phillips, a Carter appointee.

North Carolina, backed by the Reagan administration, appealed to the Supreme Court in the first major test of the 1982 reauthorization of the VRA. In its brief before the Court, the federal government supported a southern state over minority plaintiffs in a voting case for the first time since 1965.

The administration hoped to win in court the fight it had lost in Congress in 1982 over Section 2. "If left undisturbed," said the solicitor general's brief, which had been written by Brad Reynolds and Chuck Cooper, the lower court's decision "means that wherever there has been discrimination in the past and some measure of racial polarization in voting in the present, district courts will be free to strike down virtually any scheme that does not—or even those that do—deliver electoral successes proportional to minority voting strength."

"Reduced to its essentials, the argument is the familiar one emanating from Reagan officials these days," responded Laughlin McDonald of the ACLU, "that anything more than tokenism in civil rights is a quota or a form of prohibited affirmative action."

The ten major cosponsors of the 1982 reauthorization in Congress—five Democrats and five Republicans, led by Bob Dole—filed a response before the Supreme Court rebuking the government's position. The administration's interpretation of the law "would pose as significant an impediment to the enforcement of Section 2 as the specific intent rule of *City of Mobile v. Bolden* (1980), rejected by Congress in 1982," they wrote. The RNC and the North Carolina Republican Party, believing that multimember districts also deprived Republicans of fair representation, backed the members of Congress.

The oral arguments before the Court in late December 1985 mirrored the debate over Section 5 in the *Allen* case seventeen years earlier. North Carolina and the Reagan administration maintained that because blacks participated in the political process without hindrance in North Carolina, there could be no violation of the VRA. "We contend that by applying the law as the court did and by fashioning the remedy in the manner in which it did, that it expanded the scope far beyond the intent of Congress in the passing of this Act," said North Carolina's attorney general, Lacy Thornburg.

Chambers, who had become the third director-counsel of the LDF in 1984, following in the footsteps of legendary civil rights lawyers Thurgood Marshall and Jack Greenberg, argued for the black plaintiffs. He was used to battling southern states, but this was the first time he faced the federal government as "the enemy" before the Supreme Court.

Chambers contended that the "totality of circumstances" in North Carolina clearly showed that blacks were disadvantaged when it came to electing candidates from multimember districts. "We have substantial racial bloc voting," he said. "We have substantial racial appeal. We have substantial submergence of blacks in each of the districts. We have all the factors that make for dilution of black votes."

The Supreme Court unanimously agreed on June 30, 1986, in *Thornburg v. Gingles.* "The language of Section 2 and its legislative history plainly demonstrate that proof that some minority candidates have been elected does not foreclose a Section 2 claim," wrote Justice William Brennan. Where an electoral system "generally works to dilute the minority vote, it cannot be defended on the ground that it sporadically and serendipitously benefits minority voters."

Brennan devoted half of his forty-seven-page opinion to rebuking the Reagan administration's brief, point by point. (In a highly publicized speech at the University of Missouri that year, Reynolds had called Brennan's "radical egalitarianism . . . perhaps the major threat to individual liberty" in the United States.)

In a sign of the growing voting rights divide on the Court, four justices—Sandra Day O'Connor, William Rehnquist, Lewis Powell, and Warren Burger—joined "the Court's judgment, but not its opinion." Wrote O'Connor: "In my view, the Court's test for measuring minority voting strength and its test for vote dilution, operating in tandem, come closer to an absolute requirement of proportional representation than Congress intended when it codified the results test in Section 2."

She was referring to the three factors that Brennan deemed necessary to win a vote dilution suit under Section 2: first, "the minority group must be able to demonstrate that it is sufficiently large and geographically compact to constitute a majority in a single-member district"; second, "the minority group must be able to show that it is politically cohesive"; third, the minority group must "demonstrate that the white majority votes sufficiently as a bloc to enable it—in the absence of special circumstances—usually to defeat the minority's preferred candidate."

The 1982 reauthorization of the VRA and the new *Gingles* test facilitated a great increase in minority voting power. The number of successful Section 2 cases skyrocketed from 3 in 1981, after the *Mobile* decision, to 175 in 1988, according to the California Institute of Technology historian Morgan Kousser. Section 2 became the sword of the VRA, the offensive weapon used to strike down discriminatory electoral schemes, while Section 5 became the shield, the defensive mechanism preemptively protecting minority voters from discriminatory voting changes.

The *Gingles* case had an enormous immediate impact across the South, including in North Carolina. As a result of newly drawn single-member districts, the number of blacks in the state legislature increased from four in 1981 to nineteen by 1990. Toby Fitch was elected to represent Wilson. He was to become house majority leader, the second most powerful position in the body, serving for nineteen years.

Butterfield filed suit against the Wilson county commission and school board to redraw their district lines, helping to elect three black officeholders to each of the previously all-white institutions. After facing another lawsuit based on *Gingles*, North Carolina also drew new judicial districts, which resulted in the election of eight new black judges in 1988.

One of them was Butterfield. He took up residence as a state superior court judge on the third floor of the Wilson County Courthouse, overlooking the white marble steps where he had protested Jim Crow laws twenty-five years earlier. "I never thought I'd have a key to the courthouse," he said.

In the 1980s, the courts and Congress, with the prodding of determined local activists and lawyers, repeatedly prevented the Reagan administration from enacting its most extreme civil rights policies, especially in the field of voting rights. Despite these setbacks, the administration developed a long-term strategy for implementing its vision, which centered on changing the courts.

Starting in 1981, Bruce Fein, an assistant to the deputy attorney general, organized a White House–Justice Department Judicial Selection Committee, chaired by Meese, to interview and screen prospective candidates for the bench. The effort grew in prominence during Reagan's second term, when Stephen Markman, after serving as Senator Hatch's counsel and the Washington director of the Federalist Society, became head of the Office of Legal Policy. Reagan put in place "the most thorough and comprehensive system for recruiting and screening federal judicial candidates of any administration ever," Markman said.

He worked closely with Reynolds and Cooper to make sure ideologically committed conservative justices were appointed. "I'm convinced that the right decided in 1982–1983, with the Federalist Society, that the judiciary was their strategy," Neas said. "If they were going to remake civil rights laws, they would have to stack the courts."

In 1986, when Chief Justice Burger announced his retirement, Reynolds persuaded Meese and Reagan to nominate Rehnquist as his replacement. As with his initial nomination in 1971, Rehnquist's past and present views on voting rights became a major topic of debate during his second round of confirmation hearings in July and August 1986.

His challenges to minority voters in Phoenix in the 1960s attracted renewed scrutiny. James Brosnahan, the assistant U.S. attorney in Phoenix from 1961 to 1963, traveled to Washington to testify against Rehnquist. In 1971, Rehnquist told Congress, "In none of these years did I personally engage in challenging the qualifications of any voters." Brosnahan testified: "This does not comport with my recollection of the events I witnessed in 1962, when Mr. Rehnquist did serve as a challenger."

On Election Day 1962, the U.S. attorney's office in Phoenix received numerous complaints that voters at predominantly black and Hispanic precincts in South Phoenix were being challenged aggressively, without cause, at the polls. "It was my opinion in 1962 that the challenging effort was designed to reduce the number of black and Hispanic voters by confrontation and intimidation," Brosnahan said.

After receiving a complaint from the FBI, Brosnahan went to investigate at the Mary McLeod Bethune School. "At that polling place I saw William Rehnquist, who was known to me as an attorney practicing in the city of Phoenix," he said. "He was serving on that day as a challenger of voters; that is to say . . . the complaints had to do with his conduct."

Multiple witnesses—the Arizona state senator Manuel Peña, the former Democratic Party chair Charles Pine, the Democratic activist Michael Mirkin—relayed similar accounts to the Senate Judiciary Committee. Sydney Smith, a clinical psychologist, said he saw Rehnquist approach two black men and tell them: "You are not able to read, are you? You have no business being in this line trying to vote. I would ask you to leave."

Kennedy asked Rehnquist directly about the allegations.

Kennedy: "Have you ever personally challenged any individual in any precinct?"

Rehnquist: "I do not think so."

Kennedy: "Well, you would know it, would you not, if you did?"

Rehnquist: "I am not entirely sure. I cannot recall ever challenging any person . . . but if you are asking me about whether over a period from 1953 to 1969 I ever challenged a voter at any precinct in any election, I am just not sure my memory is that good."

Rehnquist's alleged conduct toward minority voters heightened anxiety about his voting rights record on the Court. "Consistent with Rehnquist's harassment of black Phoenix voters, Justice Rehnquist has repeatedly voted against racial minorities in cases concerning the right to vote," testified Julius Chambers. On eighteen occasions Rehnquist had written or joined opinions trying to limit the scope of the VRA.

Kennedy filibustered the nomination. "Imagine what America would be like if Mr. Rehnquist had been the Chief Justice and his cramped and narrow view of the Constitution had prevailed in the critical years since World War II," the Massachusetts senator said. "The schools of America would still be segregated. Millions of citizens would be denied the right to vote."

But the Senate had become familiar with Rehnquist over his fifteen years on the Court, and he was well liked by his colleagues. Bob Dole, who had partnered with Kennedy on the VRA, led the effort to end the filibuster. Rehnquist was confirmed, 65–33, on September 17, 1986. The former Lone Ranger, whom *The New York Times* called "once a lonely dissenter on the Court's extreme right wing," had become its new leader.

Ten minutes after Rehnquist's confirmation, the Senate unanimously confirmed the court of appeals judge Antonin Scalia as Rehnquist's replacement. Scalia was even more conservative than Rehnquist but attracted little scrutiny because of the Rehnquist nomination. "We couldn't fight on two fronts at once," Neas said.

Nominating Scalia immediately after Rehnquist was a brilliant strategic move by the Reagan administration. In the span of ten minutes, the Supreme Court shifted significantly to the right.

Emboldened by the confirmations of Rehnquist and Scalia, the president nominated Robert Bork, the solicitor general from 1973 to 1977 and a court of appeals judge under Reagan, to fill a third vacancy on the Supreme Court after Justice Powell retired in 1987.

Like Rehnquist, Bork took a dim view of the civil rights laws of the 1960s. Like Scalia, he subscribed to an originalist interpretation of the Constitution, believing that the courts should defer to the views of the founders rather than base their decisions on contemporary circumstances, an ideology that Meese popularized in a series of high-profile speeches beginning in 1985. The originalist philosophy advocated a passive approach to the problem of racial discrimination.

As a Yale law professor in the early 1960s Bork opposed the Civil Rights Act of 1964. "The principle of such legislation is that if I find your behavior ugly by my standards, moral or aesthetic, and if you prove stubborn about adopting my view of the situation, I am justified in having the state coerce you into more righteous paths," he explained. "That is itself a principle of unsurpassed ugliness."

As a professor, government advocate, and judge, Bork also defended the poll tax in Texas and the literacy test in Virginia, questioned the constitutionality of the VRA in 1965 and 1970, and criticized the Court's "one person, one vote" doctrine.

The first black Democrats elected to Congress from the South since Reconstruction, Barbara Jordan and Andrew Young, testified against Bork on the first day of his confirmation hearings on September 21, 1987. Thanks to C-Span, it was the first time that many Americans had ever watched a judicial confirmation hearing.

"Had Judge Bork's truncated view of the First Amendment prevailed," Young, who had been elected mayor of Atlanta in 1981, told Congress, "Dr. Martin Luther King, Jr., would not be a venerated national hero. He would instead be serving a jail sentence in Alabama and the non-violent method of social change might never have found root on American soil."

The Leadership Conference on Civil Rights organized a formidable Block Bork coalition, with a two-million-dollar ad campaign, the most sophisticated effort yet to defeat a Supreme Court nominee. People for the American Way ran TV ads featuring Gregory Peck, best known as Atticus Finch in *To Kill a Mockingbird*. "Robert Bork wants to be a Supreme Court Justice, but the record shows that he has a strange idea of what justice is," Peck said. "He defended poll taxes and literacy tests, which kept many Americans from voting."

Unlike Rehnquist, Bork had a confrontational demeanor that won him no new allies in the Senate. The Reagan administration, with Reynolds in charge of Bork's confirmation, had badly overplayed its hand. On October 23, 1987, six Republicans joined fifty-two Democrats to torpedo Bork's nomination, 58–42.

The impact of the VRA led to Bork's defeat. In 1965, sixteen of twenty-two southern senators had opposed the VRA. Twenty-three years later, sixteen of twenty-two southern senators voted against Bork.

That included the crucial swing votes of Senators Terry Sanford of North Carolina, Howell Heflin and Richard Shelby of Alabama, and John Breaux of Louisiana, all of whom were elected in either 1984 or 1986 after losing the white vote but carrying more than 75 percent of the black vote. The country's growing black electorate helped Democrats regain the Senate in 1986 and defeat Bork a year later.

"I think, more than anything, the defeat of that nomination was testimony to the effectiveness of the Voting Rights Act," said William Taylor, vice-chairman of the Leadership Conference on Civil Rights. "There were substantial black constituencies in every one of those eleven states, and the senators representing those states had to take into account those constituencies when they were casting their vote."

After Reagan's initial replacement for Bork, the court of appeals judge Douglas Ginsburg, withdrew his nomination following the revelation that he had smoked marijuana in college, the president chose Judge Anthony Kennedy of the Ninth Circuit Court of Appeals to fill the vacancy. The Senate unanimously confirmed him in February 1988. Kennedy was less conservative than Bork but more conservative than his predecessor, Justice Powell. Reagan's four Supreme Court appointees—O'Connor, Rehnquist, Scalia, and Kennedy—all were more conservative than the justices they replaced and soon formed the core of the Rehnquist Court's "Federalism Five."

The Supreme Court was just one aspect of the administration's judicial strategy. By the end of his time in office, Reagan had appointed half of all federal judges: 78 to the court of appeals and 280 to the district court. To a startling degree, the judges reflected the ideology and makeup of the Reagan administration: of the appointees, 94 percent were white, 95 percent were male, and 95 percent were Republican.

Reagan's judicial appointments became the most enduring legacy of his counterrevolution. Presidents and Congresses come and go, but judges serve for a generation. "The new federal judiciary," Neas wrote in 1989, "may accomplish what Edwin Meese, William Bradford Reynolds, and their allies were unable to achieve."

Reynolds agreed. "I think they had a major impact," he said. "They were very very helpful in reshaping civil rights policies from when Reagan first started."

Weary of leaving anything to chance, the Justice Department developed comprehensive marching orders for new judicial appointments and future administrations. Markman's Office of Legal Policy on February 19, 1988, issued its "Guidelines on Constitutional Litigation," a detailed booklet expressing the Reagan administration's view of the law.

The guidelines were deeply influenced by Meese's originalist jurisprudence and Rehnquist's views on federalism. They specifically targeted Congress's powers under the enforcement clauses of the Reconstruction amendments, which formed the basis of the VRA and the landmark civil rights laws of the 1960s. Supreme Court decisions named as "inconsistent" with the Reagan administration's views included a series of cases upholding the constitutionality of the VRA and its subsequent reauthorizations.

In September 1987, Harvard University Press and the Twentieth Century Fund published Abigail Thernstrom's long-awaited book *Whose Votes Count? Affirmative Action and Minority Voting Rights*, the first substantive, book-length critique of the VRA.

She argued the law was "an emergency measure taken with the expectation that it would be lifted as soon as conditions allowed." Yet "as the emergency subsided, emergency powers paradoxically expanded . . . the more potent the legislation became, the fewer were the objections raised."

Thernstrom attributed the VRA's powerful longevity to "the myth of moral simplicity," which had "largely insulated the voting rights issue from debate." Her targets included Justice Department bureaucrats, opportunistic politicians, voting rights lawyers, the mainstream media, and liberal foundations, all colluding to promote the VRA. Even the Reagan administration, she maintained, had been too meek to take on the civil rights establishment. "In the enforcement of minority voting rights its record has differed little from that of its predecessors," she argued.

Thernstrom portrayed herself as one of the few intellectuals brave enough to challenge voting rights orthodoxy. "Voting rights has become another immensely complex affirmative action issue, distinctive only in not being acknowledged as such," she wrote. To Thernstrom, the election of the first black officeholders in places like Mobile, Alabama; Edgefield County, South Carolina; Wilson, North Carolina; and Selma, Alabama, were not historic achievements but examples of pernicious social engineering.

"It is scarcely an exaggeration to say that affirmative action in the electoral sphere has only adherents," she wrote. "The opposition to busing and to affirmative action goals and timetables is loud and clear; protest against racial gerrymandering to increase minority officeholding is too muted to be heard."

The book received mixed reviews in the mainstream press. "She argues what she thinks, not what she can prove," Adam Clymer wrote in *The New York Times*.

And it was skewered mercilessly by voting rights experts. The book "so distorts the evidence that it cannot be taken seriously as scholarship," wrote Pam Karlan, associate counsel at the LDF, and Peyton McCrary, professor of history at the University of South Alabama, in a detailed critique in the University of Virginia *Journal of Law & Politics*.

"Thernstrom's work, however, is not only careless," Karlan and McCrary wrote. "Rather, it is crafted to serve a conservative political agenda. Judicial acceptance of her interpretation would cripple the Voting Rights Act as a tool for enabling minorities to elect representatives of their choice."

But the book won a hero's embrace in conservative and neoconservative political circles. "She has shown an unusual degree of intellectual courage in challenging the acceptable wisdom on the Voting Rights Act," wrote John Fund in *The Wall Street Journal*. "Her book is a first-rate contribution on an issue of enormous significance, equal electoral opportunity; and her analysis is all the more welcome since the goal of proportional representation has occasioned so little public debate," seconded Harold Stanley in *The New Republic*.

Despite her criticism of the Reagan administration as too friendly to voting rights, which civil rights activists, who'd been battling the administration since day one, viewed as laughable, top officials in Reagan's DOJ embraced Thernstrom's book. "The political appointees were reading it," said Gerry Hebert. "The rest of us read it and thought it was nonsense. A lot of the arguments she raised were arguments we had to knock down with John Roberts and Brad Reynolds and Chuck Cooper."

Whose Votes Count? appeared at the perfect moment for Thernstrom. Like her *Public Interest* essay, which came out at the dawn of the Reagan era, her book was published just as Reagan's disciples took control of the courts. The book became "a virtual bible among conservative jurists," wrote Adam Shatz in *The American Prospect*. The judges and advocates embracing Thernstrom's arguments were to shape the direction of voting rights law for decades to come.

7

THE REALIGNMENT

On October 31, 1985, John Lewis and Julian Bond had lunch at the Marriott Hotel in downtown Atlanta. Congressman Wyche Fowler, a liberal white Democrat who had represented Georgia's Fifth District since Andrew Young became UN ambassador in 1977, had privately announced he was going to run for the Senate. That left an opening for the coveted congressional seat in metro Atlanta.

Bond and Lewis met at noon to discuss the impending vacancy. They both were forty-six, close friends since the first SNCC convention in Raleigh during Easter weekend in April 1960. When Lewis was beaten and hospitalized on Bloody Sunday, Bond coordinated SNCC's press response from Atlanta. He still called Lewis Mr. Chairman from his days as leader of SNCC.

"Mr. Chairman, what are you going to do?" Bond asked Lewis.

"I'm going to run for Congress," Lewis replied. "What are you going to do?"

"I'm going to run for Congress," Bond responded.

It was a very short lunch. "I'll see you on the campaign trail," Lewis said.

The Bond versus Lewis contest symbolized how few opportunities there were for black politicians twenty years after the passage of the VRA. In

1986, there were only four majority-black districts in the entire South and a mere two African-Americans from the region in Congress. "Outside Atlanta, there was no place a black person could be expected to be elected to the Congress," Bond said. "So it was this seat or none."

That's how two icons of the civil rights movement, who had been best friends in the 1960s and 1970s, ended up as fierce opponents on the campaign trail.

After heading the Voter Education Project for seven years, Lewis had first run for the Fifth District in 1977 against Fowler. "I was drawn to it because of my work with VEP and SNCC but also because of the assassination of Dr. King and Bobby Kennedy," he said. "I just felt like I had to pick up where they left off."

After losing badly, he followed Young to Washington, working as the associate director of ACTION, which directed federal volunteer programs. He traveled two hundred thousand miles in three years to forty-two states, writing long memos to the White House urging the Carter administration to boost antipoverty funding for beleaguered communities like poor whites in Appalachia. The Washington bureaucracy was not for him. "In Washington I have found so many people unwilling to take a chance, to take a risk," he said. "I really want to be out there agitating."

He returned to Atlanta and won an at-large seat on the city council in 1981, representing the entire city. "I had strong biracial support in the city," he said. "So I felt like if we had the necessary resources and we got out there with Julian one on one, I would prevail."

Bond had his own reasons for wanting to run. Indeed, Lewis had urged Bond to run for Congress in 1972 before Young got in. As a state senator in 1980 Bond introduced legislation increasing the black population in the Fifth District from 50 percent to 69 percent, which would virtually guarantee his victory.

The Georgia legislature, which was still dominated by whites, blocked Bond's bill. "I'm not going to draw a nigger district if I can help it," said Representative Joe Mack Wilson, a Democrat from Marietta who was chair of the house redistricting committee. Instead, the legislature increased the black population of the Fifth District to 57 percent, but whites remained 54 percent of registered voters. As in 1972, when the legislature tried to remove black voters from the district before Young ran, the Justice Department once again refused to approve the plan under Section 5. A federal court found it was enacted with intentional discrimination. In response, the legislature increased the district's black voting-age population to 65 percent, making it a majority-black district for the first time.

Bond began as a huge favorite. He'd been a household name since the Georgia legislature refused to seat him in 1966. He'd been nominated for vice president at the Democratic convention in 1968 at twenty-eight, hosted *Saturday Night Live* in 1977, and earned $150,000 a year on the lecture circuit. The Temptations performed at a lavish fundraiser for his campaign, endorsements came from Rosa Parks and Ted Kennedy, and checks rolled in from Hugh Hefner, Bill Cosby, Frank Zappa, and Paul Simon. Andrew Young, Atlanta's mayor, officially stayed neutral, but his closest advisers backed Bond.

Bond drove a Peugeot; Lewis, a blue Chevy. Bond opened a campaign office in a spacious tire dealership, featuring a five-foot-tall replica of his face on the cover of *Ebony*. Lewis worked out of a dingy storefront six blocks away, next to the Gospel Light Rescue Mission. Lewis couldn't match Bond's celebrity and sex appeal, so he instead emphasized his blue-collar roots. "It is time to send a tugboat to Washington and not a showboat," he said.

The Morehouse College political scientist professor Tobe Johnson dubbed the race "Julian the patrician against John the plebian." A cartoon in *The Atlanta Journal-Constitution* depicted Bond as Goliath and Lewis as David. "I wonder what power is behind that shepherd boy?" asked a towering Bond, outfitted with sword and armor.

Lewis, crouching in a loincloth, clutched a bone and a rock. "One more chance to save the 5th district voters!" he said.

Bond bested Lewis, 47 to 35 percent, in the first round of voting. Bond won the black vote by two to one. Lewis won the white vote by two to one. Because neither candidate garnered over 50 percent, the race went to a runoff.

As he'd done his entire life, Lewis outworked Bond in the runoff, going through two pairs of shoes on the campaign trail. He'd start the day at the crack of dawn, shaking hands at MARTA train stations, and end late in the night at twenty-four-hour grocery stores. "I went from door to door literally running," he said. "I think it's paying off."

"Beat City Hall! Beat City Hall!" his supporters chanted outside his small storefront headquarters on Election Night. The crowd fell silent as Lewis's staff recorded the vote. Then came a deafening cheer as the results were announced. Lewis had recorded a stunning upset, narrowly defeating Bond by two thousand votes, 52 to 48 percent. He'd won 84 percent of the white vote and 41 percent of the black vote, uniting moderate whites and working-class blacks in his own version of Jesse Jackson's Rainbow Coalition.

At 10:50 p.m., Lewis stepped up to the microphones to announce his victory. "For a boy who grew up poor in Alabama, son of a sharecropper, we have come a distance," he said. "We have witnessed a nonviolent revolution. Today we sent a message."

"John Lewis got his voters to the polls. I think a lot of Julian's people were so busy getting dressed for the victory party that they forgot to vote," quipped the SCLC's chairman, Joe Lowery. The *Washington Post* columnist David Broder dubbed it "a victory for all the infantry 'grunts' in the world over the Air Force glamour boys."

Lewis easily defeated the Republican Portia Scott, editor of the *Atlanta Daily World*, in the general election. He took a thirteen-hour train ride to Washington for his inauguration in the One Hundredth Congress. He was accompanied by forty friends, who carried red, white, and blue balloons, cold champagne, and cartons of jambalaya.

Lewis was only the second African-American to represent Georgia in Congress in the twentieth century, after Young. At the swearing in at the U.S. Capitol, he stood next to the newly elected congressman Joseph Kennedy of Massachusetts, the son of his idol, RFK. Mike Espy, a thirty-two-year-old attorney, joined Lewis as the first black congressman from Mississippi since Reconstruction.

"This is a long way from the red clay hills of Alabama," Lewis marveled. "I've traveled a lot of miles from Troy, Alabama, and from the Edmund Pettus Bridge."

The arrival of Lewis and Espy doubled the number of black southern congressmen, from two to four, which showed how woefully underrepresented African-Americans remained in Congress. They constituted 17 percent of eligible voters in Dixie but held only 3 percent of House seats.

Jesse Jackson ran for president in 1984 and 1988 on a platform of greater minority representation. "We're locked out of the Congress, the Senate and the Governor's mansion," Jackson said in his keynote speech at the Democratic convention in San Francisco in 1984. "If you want a change in this nation, you enforce that Voting Rights Act . . . We can save the cotton, but we've got to fight the boll weevils."

This demand for representation grew louder as the 1990 census and the crucial decennial redistricting cycle approached. According to the historian Morgan Kousser, there were more southern black state legislators in 1870 (nearly three hundred) than in 1990 (roughly two hundred).

After spending eight years battling the Reagan administration, minority voters found an unlikely ally in the incoming Bush administration.

During the 1988 presidential campaign, a group called Americans for Bush ran an infamous television ad featuring Willie Horton, a black convicted murderer who, during a weekend furlough in Massachusetts, twice raped a white woman. The ad attacked Bush's opponent, Michael Dukakis, governor of Massachusetts at the time, for opposing the death penalty and allowing "first-degree murderers to have weekend passes from prison." The racist overtones of the ad were hard to miss.

Though the ad was not officially broadcast by the Bush campaign, it was widely believed to be the brainchild of the Bush campaign manager Lee Atwater, a blues-playing bad boy from South Carolina.

After Bush's election, Atwater became chairman of the RNC. "Do something about redistricting," were his first words to the RNC counsel Ben Ginsberg, a redheaded Jewish Republican from Pennsylvania.

Despite the racial appeals of the 1988 campaign, Atwater wanted Ginsberg to form an improbable partnership with black Democrats in the South to overthrow the white Democrats who had controlled the region since the end of Reconstruction. The creation of new majority-black districts, Atwater believed, would siphon black voters away from adjoining white Democratic districts, making those districts whiter and more conservative, giving Republicans their best chance at breaking the South's one-party stranglehold.

"The fact is that minorities remain grossly underrepresented in Congress, state legislatures and local boards and commissions," Ginsberg told the Congressional Black Caucus Foundation in September 1990. "The culprit is the gerrymander . . . It has been done to Republicans . . . and to racial minority groups."

In 1990, there were sixty-six Democrats from the South in the House of Representatives, compared with forty Republicans. Despite the region's increasing conservatism at the presidential level, white southern Democrats retained a decisive majority in the House in part by strategically dispersing black voters—who voted heavily Democratic—across white Democratic districts, so that each district had just enough black voters to help elect white Democratic candidates. Creating new majority-black districts, Ginsberg believed, would concentrate black voters in a few predominantly urban and rural districts, allowing Republicans to pick up a large number of seats in rural and suburban areas where the party performed strongly but was underrepresented. Under his strategy, minorities won new seats and Republicans did too.

Ginsberg viewed the 1982 amendments to the VRA and the *Thornburg v. Gingles* decision, which prevented the continued dilution of minority votes, as a powerful new tool. "As passed by Congress and interpreted by the courts, the Voting Rights Act now requires the drawing of majority-minority districts wherever possible," he said. "Of course, the notion of Republicans aiding racial minorities cuts against political stereotypes. But it is a natural alliance born of the gerrymander."

Ginsberg worried that he would "get the living hell beat out of me" before the black caucus. Instead, he spoke to polite applause.

On the twenty-fifth anniversary of the VRA, John Lewis, now in Congress, endorsed the "unholy alliance" between black Democrats and the GOP.

"One GOP tactic—working with black Democrats to create majority-black congressional districts during the 1992 reapportionment—is viewed with concern by many Democrats, black and white," Lewis wrote in *The Washington Post*. "A particular worry is that such overtures to black Democrats will threaten Democratic biracial coalitions.

"No one, though, should fear the prospect of minority-led biracial and multi-racial coalitions. The prospect is a natural development of American politics and society, which have come a long way since 'Bloody Sunday.' We should embrace the consequences of the Voting Rights Act."

The RNC set up a tax-exempt foundation called Fairness for the 90s, funded by some of the biggest donors in the conservative moment, to deliver technical expertise and, in Ginsberg's words, "truly space-age" computer software to aid black and Hispanic civil rights organizations in the drawing of new districts. The GOP pundit Peter Brown called it "the ulti-mate political one-night stand."

Democrats controlled the state legislatures, which drew new maps for themselves and Congress, in every southern state. Thus Ginsberg needed either black Democrats to persuade their white colleagues to adopt new majority-minority districts or, failing that, for the courts or the Depart-ment of Justice to step in. The Bush Civil Rights Division was prepared to do just that.

George H. W. Bush had initially nominated William Lucas, a black Re-publican with no civil rights experience, to be his assistant attorney general for civil rights. After the Senate Judiciary Committee rejected Lucas's nom-ination, Bush nominated John Dunne, a moderate Republican state senator from New York who was close friends with Attorney General Dick Thorn-burgh, to run the Civil Rights Division. He was easily confirmed.

Dunne adopted a very different approach to civil rights enforcement from his predecessor, Brad Reynolds. "I came to the department with the view that I should attempt to enforce the law in the spirit of those who made the law," Dunne said.

Dunne traveled to Selma early in his tenure to show his support for the VRA and made a point of meeting regularly with the career lawyers in the Civil Rights Division, who had been alienated under Reagan. Dunne supported the creation of new majority-minority districts. "I thought it was the correct strategy and in keeping with the spirit of the Voting Rights Act," he said.

So did attorneys in the Civil Rights Division. "What happened in 1991 and 1992—and I was one of the people responsible for this—was we went out and gave speeches to the National Conference of State Legislatures, the National Urban League, the NAACP, the Southern Legislative Conference and said, 'If you can draw a majority-black district, even if it's bizarre in shape, you're going to have to justify your failure not to draw that district,'" explained Gerry Hebert, who was deputy chief of the voting section. "We were not concerned about the political ramifications of the districts. If it helped Republicans, so be it. Our job was to help blacks and Latinos get elected."

Few in the department realized just how controversial this position would be.

North Carolina became the epicenter of the 1990s redistricting fight.

Following the *Gingles* decision, the number of black elected officials in the state had increased dramatically, from 245 in 1980 to 453 in 1990. In 1991, Dan Blue, Jr., a lawyer and mathematician from Raleigh, had been elected the speaker of the North Carolina House of Representatives, becoming the first black leader of any southern legislative chamber since Reconstruction. He appointed Toby Fitch from Wilson as one of the cochairs of the house redistricting committee.

As a result, black politicians enjoyed unprecedented influence during the redistricting process in North Carolina. They resolved early on to balance demands for greater black representation—there had been no black members of Congress from North Carolina since 1901—with the need to preserve large Democratic majorities in the state legislature and Congress.

The initial plan passed by the legislature created a new majority-black congressional district in rural eastern North Carolina, which had the highest concentration of black voters and had been the center of black political power in the state after the Civil War. But Blue and Democratic leaders were careful not to concentrate too many black voters in one place. While African-Americans constituted 51 percent of registered voters in the First Congressional District, they still made up more than 20 percent of registered voters in six of the state's eleven other districts, which protected the white Democrats who depended on black support.

Republicans, however, wanted Democrats to draw two or even three new majority-black districts. The GOP representative David Balmer from Charlotte proposed a new seat stretching from Charlotte to Wilmington that would be 45 percent black and 7 percent Lumbee Indian, in which, Balmer argued, blacks and Native Americans could join together to elect their preferred candidate. The plan faced stiff resistance inside the legislature; one of Balmer's interns, who drafted the plan, titled the computer file "Just Dreamin' a Bit Too Much."

Civil rights groups, including the ACLU and the North Carolina NAACP, which usually sided with Democrats on civil rights issues, backed the GOP's proposal for an additional majority-black district. "Basically, the NAACP position from the very onset was that we wanted to see a maximization of the black voting strength in North Carolina," said Mary Peeler, executive director for the North Carolina NAACP. Before the legislature had even passed its congressional plan, four Republican members of Congress from North Carolina wrote a letter to Dunne urging the Justice Department to intervene in the redistricting process against Democrats by supporting the creation of multiple majority-black congressional seats.

Democratic leaders, including Blue and Fitch, traveled to Washington to plead their case before the DOJ. "If blacks go too far they will find themselves confined to 'political reservations' with less political influence than they have today," Fitch argued.

An intense debate about what to do occurred within the DOJ. Veteran lawyers inside the department, led by Jim Turner, urged Dunne to approve the legislature's plan under Section 5. One majority-black district was enough, Turner argued. Dunne's general counsel, David Simon, who had close ties to Ginsberg, urged him to reject it, because Republicans and the civil rights groups had made a persuasive case that an additional majority-minority district could be drawn.

Dunne sided with the GOP and civil rights groups. "The proposed configuration of the district boundary lines," he wrote to the legislature in December 1991, "appear[s] to minimize minority voting strength."

North Carolina Democrats were furious. "What the Republicans are trying to do," Blue said, "is corrupt the Voting Rights Act to the extent they can go beyond what its goal and mission is and use it for their political advantage."

Blue and other Democrats believed that Balmer's proposed district would elect a white Republican instead of a black Democrat because blacks and Native Americans in eastern North Carolina had little in common. In the basement of the North Carolina legislative building, Gerry Cohen, special counsel to the legislature, drafted a new map for the state's Twelfth Congressional District.

In the 1980s, Cohen had drawn the state's redistricting maps with colored pencils and Magic Markers. Now he had a state-of-the-art computer that could print color maps and process complex demographic data. The state had purchased fifty megabytes of storage for five hundred thousand dollars. "It was the next generation of Magic Markers," he said.

Cohen drew a new majority-black district stretching 150 miles from Durham to Charlotte along the I-85 freeway and what had previously been the North Carolina railroad corridor, where blacks had settled after the Civil War to work in the mills. It surgically picked up concentrations of black voters along the way in cities like Greensboro and Winston-Salem.

It had a highly unusual shape, resembling a "string of pearls" or a "serpentine monstrosity," depending on one's perspective. The district was so narrow at points that southbound drivers on I-85 were in one district and northbound drivers in another. "I love the district because I can drive down I-85 with both car doors open and hit every person in the district," joked Representative Mickey Michaux, a Democrat from Durham. Despite its odd shape, the district accomplished two competing objectives for North Carolina Democrats, creating a new majority-black congressional seat while protecting white Democratic incumbents.

Democrats once again submitted the maps for DOJ approval. This time Dunne acquiesced. "The North Carolina people really wanted to stick it to us," he said. "It was ridiculous, but I figured we just had enough of this. If they wanted to play that game, let them do it."

His decision reverberated for years. For critics of the VRA, North Carolina's Twelfth District symbolized all that was wrong with the law and how it was enforced, a cynical form of affirmative action in the electoral sphere. In *The Washington Post*, Abigail Thernstrom called it "a Republican-civil rights conspiracy."

"The policies of the voting section of the Civil Rights Division are now indistinguishable from those of the NAACP," she wrote dismissively.

In 1990, Harvey Gantt, the first black student at Clemson in 1963 and the first black mayor of Charlotte from 1983 to 1987, ran for the U.S. Senate against Jesse Helms. Gantt, a soft-spoken architect, led Helms days before the election until the Helms campaign ran an ad titled "White Hands."

It featured a pair of white hands crumpling a job rejection letter. "You needed that job, and you were the best qualified, but they had to give it to a minority, because of a racial quota," said the ominous narration. "Is that really fair? Harvey Gantt says it is. Gantt supports Ted Kennedy's racial quota law that makes the color of your skin more important than your qualifications. You'll vote on this issue next Tuesday. For racial quotas, Harvey Gantt. Against racial quotas, Jesse Helms."

Helms won the election by six points, his racial appeal proving the difference.

After the creation of the Twelfth Congressional District, Gantt's campaign manager, Mel Watt, called his old boss.

"I'm ready to manage your campaign," Watt said.

"I'm not running," Gantt responded. "Why don't you run?"

So Watt threw his hat in the ring. He had the perfect political pedigree, as a partner in Julius Chambers's law firm and Gantt's longtime campaign manager. But his upbringing made him the most improbable of congressional candidates.

Watt had grown up, literally, in Dixie, a rural neighborhood outside Charlotte near the airport. His house had no electricity, plumbing, or running water. You could see the ground through the wooden floor and the stars through the tin roof. Watt's mother, who dropped out of school in the sixth grade, had three boys by eighteen and was divorced at twenty-two, when Watt was five. She raised the boys on her own, cleaning homes to get by.

Watt, who was born in 1945, attended segregated schools for K–12, passing three white schools on his fifteen-mile bus ride to York Road High School, the closest black school. He was one of only seventeen black students in his incoming freshman class of two thousand at the University of North Carolina. He was assigned three white roommates. Before the end of the day, all of them had moved out. "Get the hell out of that room with that nigger," he overheard the father of one of his roommates saying on the phone.

Watt's life changed the day before he left for college, when he met Chambers, whom he called the godfather of civil rights in North Carolina. Chambers shared an office building with Watt's dentist on East Trade Street in Charlotte. They stayed in touch while Watt attended college.

Chambers offered Watt a job after he finished Yale Law School, but he turned it down. When he called back Chambers and said he'd changed his mind, Chambers said he'd already filled the position. Watt went to New York and worked for the LDF, which Chambers was to run two decades later.

On the day Watt moved back to Charlotte, Chambers's office was firebombed in the middle of the night. Watt took a job with the firm and never again left home.

He specialized in business law and economic development, "helping re-define what civil rights was," he said. Chambers became his mentor. They shared a coolness born of their life struggles. "Mel is not flamboyant," said his law partner Leslie Winner, who argued the *Gingles* case. "But he's as steady as you go." He was laid-back and good-looking, with a distinctive black mustache.

Watt's conciliatory personality made him an ideal candidate for the fractious Twelfth Congressional District, which inspired controversy even before it existed. "There were upsides to it and downsides to it from a politi-cal perspective," he said. "From the law firm's perspective, we were inter-ested in maximizing minority representation. It was consistent with what we were trying to do."

Watt edged out Durham's Mickey Michaux, a longtime civil rights ac-tivist, in the Democratic primary and defeated Barbara Gore Washington, a black Republican, with 70 percent of the vote in the general election.

Majority-black districts in the South like the Twelfth were often oddly shaped and were created in part to help Republicans, but without them, people like Mel Watt would never have made it to Washington.

Days before the 1992 election, John Lewis took a six-day bus tour through the South to campaign for the Clinton-Gore ticket and the unprecedented number of black candidates, like Watt, running for Congress.

"If someone had told me in 1961 that we would have black elected officials across the South, that I would be in Congress, I would have told them they were crazy," he said. "The future of black America is at stake in this election."

Ten years after the 1982 extension of the VRA, the *Los Angeles Times* proclaimed 1992 "the year of the minority."

On January 5, 1993, the new class of the Congressional Black Caucus (CBC) took their oaths in the courtyard of the grand National Building Museum in Washington. There were so many new black members they could barely fit on the podium. It was the largest class of African-Americans ever to assemble in Congress.

Seventeen black members of Congress, thirteen of them from the South, were elected in 1992; all were from newly created majority-black districts. The number of Hispanic members of Congress also jumped from twelve to eighteen. It was the most diverse Congress in U.S. history. "It was transformative," Watt said. "It was a dramatic demonstration of the power of the Voting Rights Act."

DOJ objections to statewide redistricting plans in Alabama, Georgia, Louisiana, Mississippi, North Carolina, Texas, and Virginia led to the creation of new majority-black districts, which made the dramatic increase in minority representation possible. Five southern states elected black members of Congress for the first time in the twentieth century: Earl Hilliard of Alabama; Corrine Brown, Alcee Hastings, and Carrie Meek of Florida; Eva Clayton and Mel Watt of North Carolina; Jim Clyburn of South Carolina; and Bobby Scott of Virginia.

Judge Leon Higginbotham, the chief judge of the U.S. Court of Appeals for the Third Circuit, administered the oath to the black freshmen. He excitedly called the new class "members of the most distinguished delegation to ever appear in Washington, as important and more significant than when Thomas Jefferson went to Philadelphia on July 4, 1776."

The forty members of the CBC rose and pledged to "champion the rights of those who suffer from discrimination."

George H. White of North Carolina had been the last black member of Congress to serve after Reconstruction before he was chased out by a vicious white supremacy campaign in 1901. "This, Mr. Chairman, is perhaps the Negro's temporary farewell to the American Congress; but let me say, Phoenix-like he will rise up some day and come again," White had said in his emotional farewell speech on the House floor.

The absence was much longer than temporary: it took ninety years for a black Democrat from North Carolina to return to Congress.

"We are, in fact, that Phoenix that he spoke of rising from those ashes," the CBC's chair, Kweisi Mfume, said.

The celebration ended abruptly. Two months after Watt's swearing in, five white residents of Durham, led by the Duke University law professor Robinson Everett, filed a lawsuit challenging the Twelfth District as an unconstitutional racial gerrymander. It was the first of many challenges to come.

A few days after the presidential inauguration in 1993, Lani Guinier hosted a dinner party at a friend's house in Northwest Washington, D.C., for her Yale Law School classmates Bill and Hillary Clinton. The Clintons had been guests at her wedding, and during her days as a civil rights lawyer she'd even sued Bill once when he was governor of Arkansas. The guests at the small gathering included Watt, who discussed voting rights with the new president. The dinner symbolized how a white southern president, who grew up in Jim Crow Arkansas, had embraced the new wave of black political power.

Three months later Clinton personally nominated Guinier to be his assistant attorney general for civil rights with an announcement in the courtyard of the Justice Department. "I want it to set an example in the practice of law and in the protection of civil rights that will make all Americans proud," the president said.

Attorney General Janet Reno introduced Guinier, to a loud ovation, as "a remarkable woman who is no stranger to the Justice Department." She had been a special assistant to Drew Days in the Civil Rights Division during the Carter administration before spending the Reagan years at the LDF and the Bush years at the University of Pennsylvania.

The tall and striking Guinier wore a checked black blazer with a red pocket square, her frizzy black hair pulled back in a ponytail. "If confirmed by the Senate, I eagerly anticipate leading a new and highly regarded Civil Rights Division that works to enforce, not repeal, the civil rights laws as passed by Congress," she said to cheers. She grinned and gave a thumbs-up to the crowd.

After twelve years of Reagan and Bush, lawyers in the Civil Rights Division were excited to welcome back one of their own. "No nominee for the post has ever been better prepared than Lani Guinier," *The New Yorker* wrote.

She'd grown up in the working-class neighborhood of St. Albans, Queens, the daughter of a Jewish mother and a Guyanese father, who became the first chair of Afro-American studies at Harvard. She'd wanted to be a civil rights lawyer since she was twelve, when she watched the LDF lawyer Constance Baker Motley escort James Meredith into the University of Mississippi. Guinier attended Barnard and then Yale Law, where she lived on the third floor of the house where Motley had grown up.

As a civil rights lawyer during the 1980s Guinier had been a fierce opponent of the Reagan Justice Department, defending black voters from bogus voter fraud charges in the Alabama Black Belt and attacking discriminatory electoral systems in states like North Carolina and Louisiana. When asked at a press conference following her nomination who was responsible for damaging the reputation of the Civil Rights Division, Guinier responded, "William Bradford Reynolds." She told the story of the *Major v. Treen* case, when Louisiana, with Reynolds's blessing, deliberately avoided drawing the state's first majority-black congressional district. Those days were now over.

"Ms. Guinier," *The New York Times* wrote, "is poised to lead a counter-counter-revolution" in civil rights.

But Guinier and her supporters woefully underestimated just how potent the counterrevolution to the civil rights laws of the 1960s had become.

A few weeks before Clinton's announcement, Abigail Thernstrom told her friend Clint Bolick, over dinner at the Jefferson Hotel in Washington, that the president would nominate the "very radical" Guinier.

"Clint, you're going to love her," Thernstrom said. She did not mean "love" affectionately. Bolick, a thirty-five-year-old Reagan vet, had worked in the Justice Department under Reynolds and in the Equal Employment Opportunity Commission under Clarence Thomas, the godfather to his son. He was now president of the Institute for Justice, one of many new conservative legal groups to emerge from the Reagan years.

Thernstrom had long been a vocal critic of Guinier's civil rights record. When they appeared at a Harvard conference on new ways of allocating political power in the early 1990s, Thernstrom attacked Guinier with such vehemence during her introductory remarks that the audience nearly booed her off the stage.

Bolick had never heard of Guinier until that dinner. But two days after her nomination, he published a scathing op-ed in *The Wall Street Journal* calling Guinier one of "Clinton's Quota Queens."

"Ms. Guinier sets the standard for innovative radicalism," he wrote. "Guinier argues that proportional legislative representation for minority groups, which the Voting Rights Act of 1965 presently is constructed to guarantee, is not enough. Instead, she demands equal legislative outcomes, requiring abandonment not only of the 'one person, one vote' principle, but majority rule itself . . . Ms. Guinier would graft onto the existing system a complex racial spoils system that would further polarize an already divided nation."

Thernstrom amplified Bolick's critique. "[Guinier] isn't your garden-variety civil rights advocate," she wrote in *The New Republic*. "Her proposals make existing affirmative action programs look tame." She called Guinier "the voice of black separatism."

Clinton's civil rights nominee had become Angela Davis in a pantsuit.

The controversy centered on a series of dense law review articles Guinier had written as she entered academia: "Keeping the Faith: Black Voters in the Post-Reagan Era" (*Harvard Civil Rights–Civil Liberties Law Review*, 1989); "The Triumph of Tokenism: The Voting Rights Act and the Theory of Black Electoral Success" (*Michigan Law Review*, 1991); and "No Two Seats: The Elusive Quest for Political Equality" (*Virginia Law Review*, 1991).

Guinier's articles focused on the third generation of voting rights problems facing minority voters. In the first generation of voting rights cases post-1965, the VRA outlawed the literacy tests and poll taxes that prevented blacks from registering to vote. The second generation of cases, in the 1970s and 1980s, dismantled the gerrymandered districts and at-large electoral systems that prevented minority voters, once they registered in large numbers, from electing their preferred candidates.

In the third generation of cases, Guinier focused on how minority elected officials could secure not just representation but a fair share of political power. "My point is simple," she wrote. "Fifty-one percent of the people should not always get 100 percent of the power." She called the American political system "the tyranny of the majority."

Guinier looked south for unorthodox solutions, drawing on her voting rights work for the LDF.

In Alabama, hundreds of jurisdictions had been ordered by the federal courts to adopt single-member districts in the 1980s to boost black representation. But in some counties, black voters were too dispersed to be represented in a single district. One of those places was Chilton County, the "Peach Capital of the World," south of Birmingham, which had long been governed by an all-white county commission and school board. In 1988, the county adopted a system called cumulative voting, by which each voter got seven votes to cast for the seven-member commission. A voter could use all seven votes for one candidate or spread them out among multiple candidates. Similar systems were used in corporate board elections to accommodate minority factions.

In the first election held under cumulative voting, Bobby Agee, a funeral home director, became the first African-American elected to the county commission. Three Republicans were also elected to the previously all-Democratic commission. "The system has been fair, because for the first time you have represented all aspects of the community," Agee said. Two years later, Agee's peers elected him commission chairman. The "one voter, seven votes" system was confusing at first, but it boosted minority representation without the squabbling and polarization that accompanied the drawing of new majority-minority districts in states like North Carolina, Guinier believed. She urged other places to adopt the reform, which had become known as the "Chilton County Experience."

In Mobile, Guinier saw how black and white officeholders could share governing power. Following the landmark *Mobile v. Bolden* case, four whites and three blacks sat on the newly integrated city council. To ensure that black interests were not ignored, the Justice Department required that all legislation pass with five votes, meaning that the white majority had to secure at least one black vote. The "supermajority requirement," said the council's vice president, Clinton Johnson, was "the best thing to have happened to Mobile . . . It has created an environment for greater harmony and cooperation between the races."

Guinier made clear that "the enforcement of this representational right does not require legislative set-asides, color coded ballots, electoral quotas, or 'one black, two votes' remedies." She had long opposed quotas, which had denied her father a scholarship to Harvard in 1929.

Nor would the reforms she proposed overtake conventional enforcement of the VRA. "I am not articulating a grand moral theory of politics," she wrote. "Nor do I argue that these proposals are statutorily or constitutionally required."

Guinier did not anticipate the vehemence of the attack against her. "Within the academic world, my articles had not been controversial," she wrote. "They had been widely circulated and warmly received even by dissenting conservative scholars who had substantive, legitimate disagreements with my ideas but nevertheless respected my efforts."

But Washington was not the ivory tower. Few journalists or senators bothered to read Guinier's intricately argued articles or investigate the sources of her ideas. Instead, they relied on Bolick's and Thernstrom's critiques. Meanwhile, the Clinton administration did little to defend her, failing to assign a full-time staffer to her nomination for nearly a month, as she was attacked every day in the press.

From a suite of offices across the street from the Justice Department, Bolick ran an around-the-clock war room against Guinier, sending her articles and talking points against her nomination to congressional aides, journalists, editorial writers, and key opinion leaders in Washington. In May and June 1993, the phrase "Quota Queen" appeared in 330 different articles.

"The 'Q' word stuck," Guinier wrote.

Democratic senators began to complain to the Clinton administration. Bob Dole, who had personally thanked Guinier for her work on the 1982 VRA reauthorization, claimed on the Senate floor that he'd never met her. "If nothing else, Ms. Guinier has been consistent in her writings," he said. "Consistently hostile to the principle of one person–one vote, consistently hostile to majority rule, and a consistent supporter not only of quotas, but of vote-rigging schemes that make quotas look mild."

Clinton, who had not read the articles before nominating Guinier, read them on a helicopter trip to Maryland in early June and invited Guinier to the White House to make her case. Two dozen Senate Democrats had by then asked the president to withdraw her nomination.

Guinier met with the president for an hour in the Oval Office, where she described her arguments in minute detail. Shortly after she returned to the Justice Department, the president called. "I have decided to withdraw the nomination," he told her. "You made the best case I can imagine, but you didn't change my mind."

Ten minutes later Guinier watched on TV as Clinton announced her withdrawal in a hastily planned press conference. "At the time of the nomination, I had not read her writings," the president said. "In retrospect, I wish I had. Today, as a matter of fairness to her, I read some of them again in good detail. They clearly lend themselves to interpretations that do not represent the views that I expressed on civil rights during my campaign."

One hundred twenty demonstrators marched outside the White House to protest Clinton's decision, carrying signs that read, QUAYLE CAN'T SPELL / CLINTON DOESN'T READ and REAGAN BACKED BORK / BUSH BACKED THOMAS / CLINTON BACKED DOWN.

Unlike Reynolds, Guinier never got a chance to defend herself before the Senate.

In early 1993, Ruth Shaw, a Durham bookkeeper, attended the funeral of a friend's mother. When she reached the casket, the son of the deceased, Robinson Everett, asked her an unusual question given the setting. Would she join a lawsuit he was filing challenging North Carolina's Twelfth Congressional District?

Standing by the casket, Shaw said yes. She became the lead plaintiff in *Shaw v. Barr*, which alleged that Mel Watt's district violated the rights of white voters to "participate in a 'color-blind' electoral process."

A three-judge district court in North Carolina initially dismissed the case. "The plaintiffs here have not alleged—nor could they prove under the circumstances . . . that the redistricting plan was adopted with the purpose and effect of discriminating against white voters such as plaintiffs on account of their race," wrote Judge James Dickson Phillips, who had written the *Gingles* decision. Everett and two other plaintiffs didn't even live in the challenged district.

Everett, a longtime moderate Democrat whose mother had been the first woman to argue a case before the North Carolina Supreme Court and whose father had been Durham's first city attorney, appealed to the U.S. Supreme Court. It heard the case, now titled *Shaw v. Reno*, on April 20, 1993, nine days before Clinton nominated Guinier.

In court, Everett showed a map of the district that he called "political pornography."

"We take the color-blind Constitution to be more than an idle aspiration, particularly under present conditions," he argued.

The federal government defended North Carolina.

"We do not believe that the principle of the color-blind Constitution requires a state to be blind to the fact that its citizens regrettably may vote along racial lines," replied Deputy Solicitor General Edwin Kneedler.

In a contentious 5–4 decision on June 28, 1993, three weeks after Clinton withdrew Guinier's nomination, the Court sided with Everett.

"We believe that reapportionment is one area in which appearances do matter," Justice O'Connor wrote for the Court's conservative majority.

"A reapportionment plan that includes in one district individuals who be-long to the same race, but who are otherwise widely separated by geograph-ical and political boundaries, and who may have little in common with one another but the color of their skin, bears an uncomfortable resemblance to political apartheid."

The opinion read as if Thernstrom had written it. Indeed, O'Connor cited *Whose Votes Count?* on page eight of her opinion.

In the 1977 case *United Jewish Organizations of Williamsburg, Inc. v. Carey,* which inspired Thernstrom to write about voting rights, the Court had ruled, 7–1, that "race-conscious plans can be legitimate if they are in-tended to make up for past discrimination and are adopted to comply with the Voting Rights Act."

O'Connor's opinion essentially overruled *UJO.* "A covered jurisdic-tion's interest in creating majority-minority districts in order to comply with . . . Section 5 of the Voting Rights Act does not give it *carte blanche* to engage in racial gerrymandering," she wrote. Such districts must be "narrowly tailored to further a compelling governmental interest" other than race.

Four irate dissents were filed by Justices White, Blackmun, Stevens, and Souter.

"It is particularly ironic that the case in which today's majority chooses to abandon settled law," wrote Blackmun, "is a challenge by white voters to the plan under which North Carolina has sent black representatives to Congress for the first time since Reconstruction."

Black Democrats in Congress were outraged.

"This is the greatest threat to the Voting Rights Act since it was written in August 6, 1965," said John Lewis. "If it wasn't for the Voting Rights Act, it would still be primarily white men in blue suits in Congress."

Mel Watt, who had the most to lose in the case, took particular um-brage at O'Connor's description of his district as racial apartheid, a phrase the Court had never used before.

The opinion "suggests that a Congressional district which is 53 percent black, as my Congressional district is, and 47 percent white, is racial apart-heid; while a Congressional district which is 80 percent white and 20 percent black is somehow an integrated Congressional district," he said at a news conference on Capitol Hill. "It talks about black people not being able to represent the interests of white constituents, while assuming that white representatives can adequately represent the interests of black people."

The *Shaw* case turned history on its head, with the Court's majority invoking the equal protection clause of the Fourteenth Amendment, adopted in 1868 to protect black citizens, to dismantle districts that benefitted black candidates. "The Supreme Court discovered an entirely new constitutional right for white voters," Guinier told the annual NAACP convention in Indianapolis.

Never before had the Supreme Court objected to a congressional district simply because of its shape. At a congressional hearing, the Massachusetts congressman Barney Frank showed a map of a district resembling a one-armed crab. "It is a rather bizarre district," he said. "It is mine. I didn't ask for it; it is what the legislature gave to me. And I guess I want to know—is this OK because I am white?"

With the exception of the *Mobile v. Bolden* case in 1982, the Supreme Court had always taken an expansive view of the VRA since its enactment. That changed in 1993 with *Shaw v. Reno*. The replacement in 1991 of Thurgood Marshall with Clarence Thomas—two men with diametrically opposed views on racial equality, with nothing in common other than the color of their skin—decisively shifted the Rehnquist Court to the right on civil rights issues.

The Supreme Court—and lower courts as well, now filled with Reagan and Bush appointees—exhibited a new kind of hostility to the VRA. In the years following *Shaw*, eight of seventeen majority-black congressional districts in the South would be redrawn. The legal and political backlash against the VRA, and the law's supporters, continued to grow.

On January 4, 1995, Newt Gingrich ascended from the back of the House of Representatives, where he'd sat for sixteen years as a lonely member of the minority party, to take his new position on the rostrum as Speaker of the House. "It's a whole new world," a Republican congressman shouted from the floor.

Republicans picked up fifty-four seats in the House in the 1994 election, retaking the chamber for the first time in forty years. The Republican Party and the country's political landscape, most notably in the South, had transformed suddenly and dramatically. "The year of the minority" gave way to "the year of the angry white male."

Few states illustrated this shift better than Gingrich's home state of Georgia. In 1990, Gingrich was the only Republican, and Lewis the only minority, in Georgia's nine-member House delegation. The rest were white male Democrats.

In 1992, the Georgia legislature, under pressure from the DOJ, created two new majority-black districts. Black voters were moved out of surrounding white Democratic districts to create the new seats. As a result, two black Democrats, Sanford Bishop and Cynthia McKinney, joined Lewis in Congress, and three white Republicans from adjoining districts joined Gingrich's side. Democrats still controlled the House delegation seven to four.

Two years later Georgia elected eight Republicans and three Democrats to the House, a stunning change from 1990 and 1992. All three Democrats were African-American. In the span of four years, every white Democratic congressman in Georgia had lost or retired.

"Racial gerrymandering," wrote the *Newsweek* columnist George Will, "is one reason that Newt Gingrich is speaker."

The same phenomenon occurred throughout the South, including in North Carolina. In 1992, Democrats controlled the North Carolina delegation eight to four. Two years later, those numbers had flipped. Even the craftiest of gerrymanders failed to protect white Democratic incumbents. Before the 1990 redistricting cycle, 44 percent of white Democratic districts in the South were at least 20 percent black; after the creation of thirteen new black Democratic districts in 1992, only 25 percent of white Democrats had as many black constituents, making them far more vulnerable to a Republican challenge.

In 1990, the North Carolina Democrat Tim Valentine's Second District was 37 percent black. In 1992, the black population of his district shrank to 20 percent after black voters were shifted to the majority-black districts of Mel Watt and Eva Clayton. The six-time incumbent was narrowly reelected that year, but in 1994 he lost by twelve points to the Republican David Funderburk, Reagan's ambassador to Romania, whom Valentine described as "to the right of Jesse Helms."

In 1992, Democrats controlled twenty-eight more House seats than Republicans in the South. After the Republican revolution of 1994, Republicans held a majority of southern House districts for the first time since Reconstruction. They constituted the largest block of House Republicans: the

Speaker of the House, majority leader (Dick Armey), and majority whip (Tom DeLay) all were hard-edged southern conservatives. "With the Southern Republicans you get a more aggressive, assertive conservatism," said the GOP pollster Whit Ayres of Atlanta. "This is a conservatism that has been built on confronting Democrats and liberals, not accommodating them."

Twenty members of the Congressional Black Caucus lost committee or subcommittee chairmanships after 1994. Thirty-six of thirty-eight black House members found themselves in the minority. "Proponents of black voting rights have won the ballot," Guinier wrote shortly after Gingrich's swearing in, "but may be losing the war."

Republicans also won control of seventeen state legislative bodies, including in Florida, South Carolina, and North Carolina, for the first time in the twentieth century.

"What has long been apparent is only now fully understood: herding black voters into their own 'majority-minority' districts is a boon to the GOP," Thernstrom wrote in *The New York Times*.

Many commentators, like Thernstrom, overstated the impact of racial gerrymandering on the Democrats' collapse. Democrats lost twenty-four House seats in states without any majority-minority districts. Clinton's unpopularity, a series of corruption scandals in the House, the failure of health care reform, and the passage of an assault weapons ban all contributed to the GOP's takeover.

"Racial redistricting alone does not explain Republican gains in 1994, but it played an important subsidiary role," concluded the American University political scientist David Lublin. At least fifteen districts changed hands as a result, he estimated.

The South had been voting Republican at the presidential level since Nixon's southern strategy in 1968, but the 1994 congressional results definitively confirmed LBJ's prediction that he'd lost the South for a generation by signing the Civil Rights Act and the VRA.

"Maintenance of Negro voting rights is essential to the GOP," Nixon's Machiavellian strategist Kevin Phillips had written in *The Emerging Republican Majority* in 1969. "Negroes are slowly but surely taking over the apparatus of the Democratic Party in a growing number of Deep Southern Black Belt counties, and this cannot help but push whites into the alternative major party structure—that of the GOP."

Phillips's prediction became a reality in 1994, when Democratic congressional candidates in the South received 91 percent of black votes but only 35 percent of white votes. Southern whites shifted to the GOP in larger numbers than any other demographic group. The twenty-six majority-minority districts in the South elected twenty-four minority members of Congress. The ninety-nine majority-white districts elected ninety-nine white members.

Twenty years after Phillips's book, Ben Ginsberg had followed his blueprint at the RNC, advocating the drawing of new political maps that turned the Democratic Party into a predominantly black party in the South and thereby shifted the region to the GOP. He jokingly called his master plan "Project Ratfuck."

8

THE COUNTERREVOLUTION (II)

On November 7, 2000, Willie Steen, a navy vet who served in the Persian Gulf during Desert Storm, went to cast his ballot for president at the St. Francis Episcopal Church in Tampa, Florida.

He brought his ten-year-old son, Willie, Jr., to the polls for the first time. They waited a half hour to reach a poll worker. When Steen gave the poll worker his name, she searched a list of registered voters in the precinct and told him, "You can't vote. You're a convicted felon."

"You must be mistaken," a shocked Steen replied. "I've never been arrested in my life." He worked at a hospital, the Tampa Orthopedics Center, that wouldn't employ anyone with a felony conviction.

The poll worker gave him a number to call at the board of elections, but no one picked up. The seventy-five people behind him in line grew antsy. Few would look him in the eye.

He left in embarrassment, struggling to explain to his son what had just happened. After fighting for his country abroad, he wasn't able to exercise his most fundamental right at home. "I felt I was shafted," Steen said. "I think there were a lot of things that weren't done properly. My name was dragged through the mud."

He later found out he'd been confused with a convict named Willie O'Steen, who had committed a felony between 1991 and 1993, when Steen was in the Persian Gulf. Little did Steen know that the same thing was happening to voters across the state of Florida, particularly to voters like him, who were African-American.

Before the election, Florida sent its sixty-seven county election supervisors a list of fifty-eight thousand alleged felons to purge from the voting rolls. Florida was one of eight states that prevented ex-felons from voting. Blacks made up only 15 percent of registered voters in the state, but 44 percent of those on the purge list, which turned out to be littered with errors.

Elsewhere in Tampa, Wallace McDonald was one of 3,258 alleged felons who received a letter from the Hillsborough County supervisor of elections, Pam Iorio, telling him he was ineligible to vote. In 1959, when he was twenty-three, McDonald fell asleep on a bench while waiting for a bus and was arrested for vagrancy. He was ordered to work on a municipal garbage truck for his sentence. He was fined thirty dollars when he walked off the job in protest.

But he'd never been accused of a felony until he received the state's notification forty-one years later. "I could not believe it, after voting for all these years since the 50s, without a problem," McDonald said. He hired a lawyer, who confirmed he was not a felon, but Iorio refused to reinstate him to the voter rolls.

In St. Petersburg, Floredia Walker showed up at her usual polling place at Pleasant Grove Church. She too appeared on the felon list and was told she couldn't vote.

Walker worked for the department of corrections, where she was subject to background checks and, like Steen, couldn't hold her job with a criminal record. Fifteen years earlier a thief had stolen her purse and used her driver's license. Walker had immediately contacted the department of corrections and explained what had happened. "I thought it was all taken care of," she said. She was never told she was ineligible to vote. She'd even received a new voter registration card a month before the election.

"I was devastated," she said. "I've voted in every election. I've even worked the polls. There was never a problem in the past."

Steen, McDonald, and Walker had little in common except for two things: they were African-American and were planning to vote for Al Gore.

Hanging chads, butterfly ballots, the antics of the Florida secretary of state, Katherine Harris, and thousands of Jews accidentally voting for Pat

Buchanan in Palm Beach were among the stories that captured the headlines during the chaotic thirty-six-day Florida recount between Gore and George W. Bush. The widespread and wrongful purging of registered voters, which disproportionately targeted African-American voters, was the most consequential—and least discussed—aspect of the Florida election.

"The parties and the candidates did not want to focus on the racial impact of decisions that were made in Florida," said the civil rights lawyer Judith Browne Dianis. "It was one of those moments when race was being swept under the rug."

Edward Hailes, the staff director of the U.S. Commission on Civil Rights, arrived in Florida two days after the election to begin investigating reported civil rights violations. Crucial details about the state's voter purge emerged only after voters had been turned away from the polls.

In 1868, to prevent newly emancipated African-Americans from exercising the franchise, Florida passed a law banning anyone with a criminal conviction from voting unless the governor pardoned him or her. During slavery, blacks were far more likely to be arrested than whites, for crimes such as looking at a white woman. Following the Civil War, every southern state had a felon disenfranchisement law on the books; the ban had spread to three-fourths of the country by 1920. Seventeen states restored voting rights for ex-felons in the 1960s and 1970s, but Florida's law remained in effect.

The modern impetus for the voter purge occurred in 1997 in Miami, when the former mayor Xavier Suarez ("Mayor Loco") faced off against the incumbent Joe Carollo ("Crazy Joe"). Suarez narrowly defeated Carollo, but evidence soon emerged that hundreds of dead voters and felons illegally voted absentee on his behalf. A court overturned the results and reinstated Carollo as mayor.

Weeks later the Florida legislature passed a law requiring an annual purge of the voter rolls by a private entity. A four-million-dollar contract went to the Boca Raton–based Database Technologies (DBT), a company recommended by a conservative advocacy group called the Voting Integrity Project, which since the early 1990s had advocated aggressive voter purges to prevent fraud.

On the orders of state officials, new names were added to the purge list for the 2000 election if there was only a 70 percent match between a name on the voter rolls and a name on the state's felon database. That meant that voters could be tagged as felons even when middle initials, suffixes, nicknames, and even race and sex data didn't perfectly match. Hence the confusion of Steen with O'Steen.

DBT warned the state that it was compiling "false positives." Bucky Mitchell, a senior attorney for the division of elections, told the company, "Obviously, we want to capture more names that possibly aren't matches and let the supervisors make a final determination rather than exclude certain matches altogether." Voters were deemed guilty until proven innocent. The election supervisors became responsible for Florida's intentionally lax record keeping.

Blatant warning signs were ignored by the state. In May 2000, after the first batch of names was released, the elections supervisor in Madison County found herself on the purge list. Ion Sancho, the elections supervisor for Tallahassee's Leon County, was the only election official to go through the list one by one. "We went for a five-for-five match," he said. "Those were criteria such as name, birth date, race, sex, Social Security number. When we applied that to this list of 697 that we got in 2000, I could verify only 33."

Because of these errors, twenty counties disregarded the state's list. But it was still used by a majority of election supervisors, including in heavily populated swing areas like Tampa and St. Petersburg.

The NAACP sued Florida after the election for violating the VRA. As a result of the settlement, DBT ran the names on its 2000 purge list using stricter criteria. The exercise turned up twelve thousand voters who shouldn't have been labeled felons. That was twenty-two times Bush's 537-vote margin of victory. But it was too late for their votes to count.

On Election Night, Bush led Gore by 1,784 votes. Because of the closeness of the election, an automatic recount began two days later in every county. Hundreds of lawyers flocked to Florida. Ben Ginsberg, national counsel for the Bush campaign, called it "Woodstock for constitutional lawyers."

Ted Cruz, a twenty-nine-year-old domestic policy adviser on the Bush campaign and a former law clerk for Justice Rehnquist, constructed Bush's legal team. One of his first calls was to John Roberts, whom Cruz knew from the close-knit network of former Rehnquist clerks, nicknamed the Cabal.

"We started to assemble a team of the best lawyers and in particular the best Supreme Court lawyers in the country, and John's name naturally came near the top of the list," Cruz said. Roberts, now in private practice, caught the next flight to Tallahassee.

Roberts edited legal briefs, including the campaign's fifty-page submission to the Supreme Court, and prepared the former Reagan assistant attorney general Theodore Olson for oral arguments. He also provided counsel to Florida's governor, Jeb Bush. Roberts's name appeared on no briefs, but his influence was unmistakable. "He is one of the finest legal writers of his generation," Cruz said. "His editing pen was invaluable."

The parties had very different objectives. The Bush campaign wanted as few disputed ballots counted as possible. The Gore campaign, which trailed by 327 votes after the automatic recount, wanted as many disputed ballots counted as possible. When the Florida Supreme Court ordered a statewide manual recount on December 8, which favored Gore, the Bush campaign appealed to the U.S. Supreme Court.

John Lewis was among those seated in the packed courtroom on December 11, 2000, for oral arguments. As he watched the news from Florida on television on Election Night, he thought of how he had almost died on the Edmund Pettus Bridge. "It's important to bear witness," he said. "This day is as important for me as March 7, 1965, when I attempted to march from Selma to Montgomery . . . We won that battle and we come back 35 years later and see that people's votes aren't counted."

The next day the Supreme Court halted Florida's recount, thereby declaring Bush the winner of the election. No justice put his name on the unsigned 5–4 opinion.

The Court asserted that the recount violated the equal protection clause of the Fourteenth Amendment because there was no uniform statewide standard for counting disputed ballots in each county. In a draft of her dissent, Justice Ginsburg noted in a footnote that if there was any equal protection violation in Florida, it was because black voters encountered a disproportionate number of problems voting. Justice Scalia, her closest friend on the Court, objected to Ginsburg's "Al Sharpton" footnote, and she took it out.

When one read the *Bush v. Gore* opinion, it was as if the disenfranchisement of black voters had never occurred.

Three weeks after the court's decision, Gore, as president of the Senate, had the misfortune of presiding over the certification of electors for Bush during a joint session of Congress in the House of Representatives.

The Congressional Black Caucus contested the result.

"Mr. President, I object to the certificate from Florida," said Representative Alcee Hastings, a former judge from Broward County.

"The gentleman from Florida, Mr. Hastings, will present his objection," Gore said. "Is the gentleman's objection in writing and signed by a member of the House of Representatives and by a senator?"

"Mr. President," Hastings replied, "and I take great pride in calling you that, I must object because of the overwhelming evidence of official misconduct, deliberate fraud and an attempt to repress . . ."

"Objection!" Republican members yelled.

Gore banged his gavel for order. "No debate is allowed in the joint session," he said.

"To answer your question, Mr. President," Hastings said, "the objection is in writing; signed by a number of members of the House of Representatives, but not by a member of the Senate." No senator would join the CBC's challenge of the Florida electors, thus preventing the objection from being heard.

"Are there other objections?" Gore asked.

One by one, black Democrats, from Florida and across the country, took to the House floor to object.

"Mr. Vice President, I rise to object to the fraudulent 25 Florida electoral votes," said the California representative Maxine Waters.

"Is the objection in writing and signed by a member of the House and a senator?" Gore asked again.

"The objection is in writing and I don't care that it is not signed by a member of the Senate," Waters said to loud Democratic applause. "Mr. Vice President, there are gross violations of the Voting Rights Act from Florida . . ."

Republicans shouted Waters down.

One by one, Gore surreally ruled out of order the black members of Congress, who were protesting *his* wrongful defeat.

"We did all we could," Hastings said.

"The chair thanks the gentleman from Florida," Gore said wryly.

When Gore officially declared Bush the winner, 271 electoral votes to 266, twenty members of the CBC walked out in protest.

"It's going to be very difficult, almost impossible, for many of us to forget what happened," Lewis said.

In January and February 2001, the Civil Rights Commission listened to thirty hours of testimony from more than one hundred witnesses during three field hearings on the election in Florida. Those interviewed included Jeb Bush, Katherine Harris, Florida's attorney general, and numerous county elections supervisors.

"Despite the closeness of the election, it was widespread voter disenfranchisement, not the dead-heat contest, that was the extraordinary feature in the Florida election," the commission's final report concluded. "After carefully and fully examining all the evidence, the Commission found a strong basis for concluding that violations of Section 2 of the Voting Rights Act occurred in Florida."

Black ballots were nearly ten times as likely to have been rejected as white ballots, the commission reported. African-Americans cast more than half of the 180,000 "spoiled" ballots. When it came to the voter purge, the commission found that top officials at the division of elections were responsible for "encouraging an error-laden strategy that resulted in the removal of a disproportionate number of eligible African-American voters from the rolls."

No one could ever determine precisely how many legitimately registered voters were prevented from voting. But the commission staff director, Edward Hailes, did the math the best he could: if 12,000 voters were wrongly purged from the rolls and 44 percent of them were African-American and 90 percent of African-Americans voted for Gore, that meant 4,752 black Gore voters, almost nine times Bush's margin of victory, could have been barred from the polls. It wasn't a stretch to conclude that the purge cost Gore the election. "We did think it was outcome determinative," Hailes said.

Abigail Thernstrom, whom Bush had appointed to the Civil Rights Commission at the beginning of his presidency, filed a strenuous dissenting statement, joined by Commissioner Russell Redenbaugh, a Philadelphia businessman appointed by Bush's father. "The obvious explanation for a high number of spoiled ballots among black voters is their lower literacy rate," they wrote. They acknowledged that "without question, some voters did encounter difficulties at the polls, but the evidence fails to support the claim of systematic disenfranchisement."

The civil rights panel had focused on the wrong set of voting problems in Florida, they asserted. "The Commission should have looked into allegations of voter fraud," the two commissioners wrote, "not only with respect to ineligible felons, but allegations involving fraudulent absentee ballots in nursing homes, unregistered voters, and so forth. Across the country in a variety of jurisdictions, serious questions about voter fraud have been raised."

Despite the dissenting statement, a majority of commissioners called on the Department of Justice to immediately prepare litigation against Florida under the VRA. By then, however, it was too late. The Bush administration followed Thernstrom's heed and prioritized prosecutions of voter fraud over investigations into voter disenfranchisement.

One thousand miles north of Florida, a similar electoral fiasco unfolded in St. Louis.

On Election Day 2000, Mahina Nightsage, a forty-one-year-old community organizer, went to her polling place of twenty years at 10:30 a.m. But this time she found that her name was not on the registration rolls. Her local election judge did not have a phone to call the board of elections, and the line was busy for over an hour when Nightsage tried to call them herself. She finally reached her alderman, who told her to visit the elections board downtown and see what happened.

When she arrived at 300 North Tucker Street at 12:30 p.m, Nightsage saw a scene that resembled an election in a third-world country. Hundreds of voters were lined up around the block and packed inside, standing on tables to get the board of elections' attention. Nightsage waited two and a half hours before the board processed her paperwork and she was able to return to her polling place to vote for Gore.

Not everyone was as lucky. "There were many people who had been waiting for hours, and they just left," Nightsage said. Only three workers from the board of elections were on hand to assist voters. The line of jilted voters in the heavily Democratic city was predominantly African-American.

"The sight of hundreds of African Americans waiting for hours upon hours simply to exercise their constitutional right to vote sent shock waves to [the] pit of my stomach," wrote Denise Lieberman, a lawyer for the Missouri ACLU who was stationed at the board of elections. "As I looked around the room that afternoon, I couldn't help but feel as though I had been transported back in time, back to a time of poll taxes and literacy tests, back to a time (not all that long ago, really), when the color of your skin determined whether you had a right to vote."

The problems started well before the 2000 election, when the St. Louis Board of Election Commissioners sent voter registration cards to all eligible voters. Those whose mail was returned as "Attempted–Not Known," "Not Deliverable as Addressed," or "Forwarding Order Expired" were labeled "inactive" and removed from the rolls. More than fifty thousand voters in St. Louis were placed on inactive status between November 1996 and November 2000. None of them were notified about the change in their status.

Thus thousands of voters like Nightsage arrived at the polls on Election Day only to learn that they were no longer on the rolls and could not vote until a local election judge received authorization from the board of elections by telephone or in writing. Election judges in more than a third of the city's voting precincts had to call the board of elections because of voter registration problems. At least half of the election officials couldn't get through to election headquarters because the line was busy. Hence the flood of angry voters sent downtown.

The Gore campaign filed an emergency suit late that afternoon asking a court to keep the polls open an extra three hours so that everyone could vote. Nightsage was among those who testified before the St. Louis Circuit Court judge Evelyn Baker. Baker ordered the polls open until 10:00 p.m. in St. Louis. The Bush campaign filed an immediate appeal. Forty-five minutes later, the Missouri Court of Appeals rescinded Baker's order and closed the polls. Only a hundred additional voters had been able to cast ballots during the brief additional time. "As of 10:00 PM on election day," a Justice Department lawsuit later stated, "individuals were still standing in line at the downtown headquarters of the Board of Elections."

Baker's order infuriated Missouri Republicans, who gathered at an Election Night party at the St. Louis Marriott West Hotel. The Missouri senator John Ashcroft watched in disbelief as election returns showed him losing to a dead man.

Ashcroft's opponent in the closely watched Senate race, Missouri's governor, Mel Carnahan, had died in a plane crash three weeks before the election. His name remained on the ballot, and his wife, Jean, ran in his stead. "I'm Still with Mel" became her campaign slogan.

Republicans viewed the extended poll hours as a last-ditch attempt to illegitimately oust Ashcroft from office. "I know there are very serious allegations of fraud and corruption as it related to the conduct of the election in the city of St. Louis," Ashcroft said.

Missouri's senior senator, the Republican Kit Bond, was far more blunt. "Democrats in the city of St. Louis are trying to steal this election," he screamed into the microphone at the Marriott, slamming his right fist on the podium in anger.

How else could a sitting senator lose to a dead man?

Ashcroft lost by forty-nine thousand votes, a result that would not have been determined by a hundred extra people voting from 7:00 to 7:45 p.m. Nevertheless, Bond sent the FBI and the U.S. attorney's office a 250-page report alleging "a major criminal enterprise designed to defraud voters." Less than two month's later, Bush nominated Ashcroft as attorney general, and a new right-wing voter fraud movement was born.

A month before the 2002 election, three hundred FBI agents and U.S. attorneys traveled to Washington for the first annual Voting Integrity Symposium, which Ashcroft called an "unprecedented gathering of the nation's justice officials." It was the first meeting of the attorney general's new "Voting Access and Integrity Initiative," a major joint project of the DOJ's Civil Rights Division and Public Integrity Unit.

Though the initiative was supposed to combat voting discrimination and voter fraud, the latter cause clearly took priority. Voting integrity had become the shorthand for targeting fraud. Deputy Attorney General Larry

Thompson described it as "an issue that I know is close to the attorney general's heart."

Ashcroft spoke in the ornate Great Hall of the Justice Department. At a cost of eight thousand dollars, the devout attorney general had installed massive navy drapes covering the bare-chested art deco statues of Lady Justice and her male counterpart, Majesty of Justice.

The dour Ashcroft painted a bleak picture of the country's electoral security. "Votes have been bought, voters intimidated and ballot boxes stuffed," he said. "The polling process has been disrupted or not completed. Voters have been duped into signing absentee ballots believing they were applications for public relief. And the residents of cemeteries have infamously shown up at the polls on election day . . . Political war stories like these are often told with a grin, but these failures of our democracy are no laughing matter. There is nothing funny about winning an election with stolen votes."

Ashcroft called for "a new ethic of enforcement of our voting rights," which kicked off a multiyear probe into alleged voter fraud abuses, beginning with 120 new election fraud investigations. The new emphasis on voter fraud represented a major shift in priorities for the Civil Rights Division and its voting section, which had previously focused on enforcing the Voting Rights Act and protecting minority voters from discrimination. Ashcroft's new initiative "was done with absolutely no consultation at all with the voting section," said Joe Rich, chief of the voting section, who had been with the Civil Rights Division since 1968.

Rich and the voting section quickly became a target of the department's new conservative political appointees.

In late 2001 Ashcroft hired three GOP operatives for the Voting Access and Integrity Initiative. Hans von Spakovsky, the former head of the Fulton County Republican Party in Atlanta, became the brains of the operation.

Von Spakovsky's unusual name, which sounded like a nineteenth-century Austrian villain's, came from his Russian father, who met his German mother at a displaced persons camp in Bavaria after World War II and immigrated to the United States in 1951. They were fierce anti-Communists who settled in Huntsville, Alabama. After graduating from MIT and Vanderbilt Law School, von Spakovksy volunteered as a GOP poll watcher at an inner-city housing project in Atlanta. During his first election, he said he observed election officials asking voters which party they belonged to, which was forbidden in a general election.

Voter fraud became von Spakovsky's obsession. "For too long in this country, we have taken our elections for granted and have assumed that the type of fraud we read about in Third World countries 'could not happen here,'" he wrote in a letter published in *The Wall Street Journal* in 1995. "Well, it very easily could and does."

At the DOJ, von Spakovsky initially worked on the Help America Vote Act (HAVA), Congress's response to the 2000 election. After its passage in 2002, he was promoted to the "front office" of the Civil Rights Division, the home of the powerful political appointees, as special counsel to the assistant attorney general for civil rights. He soon became the de facto head of the voting section. Six former career attorneys in the voting section called him "the point person for undermining the Civil Rights Division's mandate to protect voting rights."

"The first stirrings of a new movement to restrict voting came after the 2000 Florida election fiasco," wrote Wendy Weiser of the Brennan Center for Justice, "which taught the unfortunate lesson that even small manipulations of election procedures could affect outcomes in close races." HAVA was supposed to prevent another Florida. But many of the problems that plagued Florida in 2000 resurfaced in Ohio four years later.

In November 2003, Ebony Malone, a twenty-year-old food service cook, registered to vote in downtown Cleveland. She received her voter registration card three months later. Shortly thereafter, she moved and updated her registration address. But she never received a new registration card. Then, in October 2004, a worker from the community organizing group ACORN told her she was on a list of voters whose eligibility would be challenged at the polls by the Republican Party.

"I am worried that I will be unable to vote on Election Day," she said in a court declaration.

Malone's name appeared on the GOP's challenge list because of a mailing the Ohio Republican Party chairman, Robert Bennett, sent to 232,000 newly registered voters between January and August 2004, urging them to vote Republican. Thirty-five thousand letters were returned as undeliverable, which the GOP saw as evidence of impending voter fraud. "The potential for these fraudulent registrations to produce fraudulent votes at the ballot box is very real," Bennett said.

It just so happened that more than half the challenged voters lived in Ohio's two most populous counties—Cuyahoga (Cleveland) and Franklin (Columbus)—which were overwhelmingly Democratic and heavily minority.

The DNC sued the RNC, claiming that a prior court ruling prohibited the party from engaging in such voter caging. In 1981, during a New Jersey gubernatorial election, the RNC launched a "Ballot Security Task Force" that sent letters to voters in predominantly African-American and Hispanic precincts. When forty-five thousand letters were returned as undeliverable, the RNC tried to remove the voters from the rolls and hired off-duty cops to patrol polling sites in the black and Hispanic neighborhoods of Newark and Trenton. They posted large signs on Election Day reading: THIS AREA IS BEING PATROLLED BY THE NATIONAL BALLOT SECURITY TASK FORCE. IT IS A CRIME TO FALSIFY A BALLOT OR TO VIOLATE ELECTION LAWS. After the election, the DNC won a court settlement ordering the RNC to "refrain from undertaking any ballot security activities."

When the Ohio case went to federal court, the Justice Department, four days before the election, sent a highly unusual letter to the District Court judge Susan Dlott that backed the Ohio GOP's position. Voter challenges, wrote the assistant attorney general for civil rights, Alex Acosta, struck "a balance between ballot access and ballot integrity." This was Ashcroft's strategy in action.

Von Spakovsky spearheaded the effort, according to Civil Rights Division lawyers. "Hans wrote the brief," said Joe Rich. "It was done with absolutely no input from the voting section."

The intervention raised eyebrows because the DOJ had not been a party to the case, nor had the court asked for its opinion, and the Civil Rights Division didn't like to take sides in a partisan election dispute days before an election. Von Spakovsky's letter amounted to "cheerleading for the Republican defendants," said Rich's deputy, Bob Kengle. "It was doubly outrageous, because the allegation in the litigation was that these were overwhelmingly African-American voters that were on the challenge list."

The court ruled against the RNC, finding that voters like Malone "faced irreparable injury in that her constitutional right to vote was threatened." The challenges had to stop.

But elsewhere in Ohio, Secretary of State Ken Blackwell, the Bush campaign's cochair, reprised the role of Katherine Harris, issuing a series of directives limiting the availability of provisional ballots, now mandated by HAVA, and requiring that voter registration forms be accepted only on eighty-pound paper stock. His decisions were immediately challenged in court.

Days before the election, hundreds of Democrats, including John Lewis, marched from the state capitol to Blackwell's office in Columbus, carrying signs reading, NOT THIS TIME!, and chanting, "Count every vote."

"We cannot forget what happened in Florida," a fired-up Lewis told the crowd. "And it will not happen here."

But on Election Day in 2004, history repeated itself.

When Tanya Thivener, a thirty-eight-year-old mortgage broker, arrived at her polling place in a majority-black neighborhood of Columbus, she found a line stretching out the door. She waited in line to cast a ballot for four hours, including one hour in the rain. She watched dozens of voters abandon the polls in disgust.

"A lot of people left in the four hours I waited," she said. "A lot of them were young black men who were saying over and over: 'We knew this would happen.'"

After finally voting for John Kerry, she drove to her mother's house in a white, heavily Republican suburb of Franklin County. How long had she waited to vote? Thivener asked her mom. Fifteen minutes, she replied.

Thivener couldn't believe it.

Even though HAVA allocated $3.9 billion for states to modernize their election systems, county election officials in Ohio allocated far fewer voting machines than necessary to accommodate the high voter turnout in the nation's top battleground state. That was especially true in heavily populated Democratic cities like Columbus, Cleveland, Toledo, and Akron and on college campuses like Kenyon, where students waited in line for up to ten hours.

Overwhelmingly Democratic precincts in Columbus received seventeen fewer voting machines in 2004 than 2000, while heavily Republican precincts got eight more machines. That explained the gaping difference in wait times between Thivener and her mother. The Franklin County Board of Elections, which was narrowly controlled by Republicans, used half as many polling machines as its own analysis recommended.

By midmorning the Ohio Democratic Party had filed an emergency court appeal asking for additional voting machines in Franklin and Knox counties. "The massive lines are deterring voters from waiting to cast their ballots," the lawsuit stated. "The situation is dire."

The party produced affidavits from fifteen election judges and poll watchers describing the long lines.

"At 12:35, there are approximately 90 voters in line," wrote Josh Schoenberger at Precinct 25-F in northeastern Columbus. "The wait in line at this precinct is approximately 3 hours. The line has been this long all day. I have personally observed voters leaving without having voted due to the long lines. The precinct is predominately African American."

"I am serving as a presiding judge, a position I have held for some 15+ years in precinct 40," wrote Richard Frost from his polling place near Ohio State University. "In all my years of service, the lines are by far the longest I have seen, with some waiting as long as four to five hours. I expect the situation to only worsen as the early evening heavy turnout approaches. I have requested additional machines since 6:40 a.m. and no assistance has been offered."

The District Court judge Algernon Marbley finally ordered that voters be given paper ballots in the early evening. By then, however, the damage had been done.

A postelection survey by the pollsters Cornell Belcher and Diane Feldman for the DNC estimated that 3 percent of Ohio voters left their polling places without voting because of the long lines. That number, 174,000, was larger than Bush's 118,000 margin of victory in the Buckeye State.

"The Election Day experience for most African American voters was starkly different from that of most white voters in Ohio," Belcher and Feldman found. African-Americans waited an average of fifty-two minutes to vote, compared with eighteen minutes for white voters. Twice as many black voters reported experiencing problems at the polls. The long lines became known as a "time tax."

Edward Hailes, the former staff director for the Civil Rights Commission, spent the 2004 election in Ohio. "There were the same issues in Ohio that we found in Florida in 2000," he said.

The CBC once again protested the certification of the presidential electors because of the widespread irregularities in Ohio. This time they found a senator, Barbara Boxer of California, willing to sign on to the challenge, for the first time since 1877. It did little good. The Senate voted, 74–1, and the House voted, 267–31, to uphold the election results.

"Get over it," said the GOP representative Ric Keller of Florida.

"How can we get over it when people died for the right to vote?" Lewis responded.

On the fortieth anniversary of the VRA, a sticky Saturday in August 2005, Lewis was once again marching. This time twenty thousand people joined him on the streets of Atlanta; they included veterans of the Selma to Montgomery march like the comedian Dick Gregory and the singer Harry Belafonte. They chanted, "Keep the vote alive!"—the theme of the day—as they marched one mile down Martin Luther King, Jr., Drive, from the Richard B. Russell Federal Building downtown to Morris Brown College, blocks away from where Lewis once ran SNCC.

"Forty years later, we're still marching for the right to vote," Lewis said when the marchers reached Morris Brown's large football stadium. "The Voting Rights Act was good in 1965, and it's good in 2005 . . . We're being too quiet with this administration. We've got to talk back to the Bush Administration. Keep your eyes on the prize!"

Lewis didn't want to hear any platitudes about how much racial progress America had made. The manipulation of the electoral system for partisan advantage had been a defining feature of the 2000 election in Florida and the 2004 election in Ohio. The new wave of GOP-led voter disenfranchisement efforts uniquely targeted black voters, who had become the most loyal group of Democratic voters. After the 2004 election, Republicans intensified their drive to restrict access to the ballot by hyping the threat of voter fraud.

Atlanta was chosen as the site of the march because five months earlier Georgia had passed the first law requiring government-issued photo identification to cast a ballot.

After the 2004 election, Republicans took control of state government in Georgia for the first time since 1871. When the legislature convened in early 2005, the GOP representative Sue Burmeister of Augusta introduced the voter ID bill.

A devout Lutheran from Wisconsin, Burmeister kept a Bible on her desk next to a business card holder with a cross on it and wore a silver pin on her lapel showing tiny feet inside a womb, signifying the sanctity of life. Her inspiration for the law came from reading the *Wall Street Journal* columnist John Fund's book *Stealing Elections*, which claimed that "at least eight of the 19 hijackers who attacked the World Trade Center and the Pentagon were actually able to register to vote in either Virginia or Florida." (There was no proof, however, that they *did* register to vote.) If terrorists could register to vote, Burmeister reasoned, what would stop other criminals from manipulating U.S. elections?

"It's about protecting the security of our elections," she said. "The bill does get at the heart of voter fraud. The reason voter fraud isn't caught at the polls is because there is no picture ID requirement."

Before 2005 Georgians could vote with seventeen different types of identification, including a Social Security card, student ID, and birth certificate. Burmeister's proposal allowed only six forms of government-issued photo ID: a Georgia driver's license, a Georgia ID card, a U.S. passport, a government employee ID card, a military ID, and a tribal ID.

The debate in the Georgia legislature proved highly contentious. Governor Sonny Perdue admitted that three hundred thousand registered Georgians did not have driver's licenses or state ID cards. Census data showed that blacks were five times more likely than whites to not have cars, and thus not own driver's licenses, and were disproportionately more likely to lack the other forms of required ID. Only 56 of 159 counties in Georgia issued driver's licenses or photo IDs, and none were in metro Atlanta. Moreover, the state planned to charge twenty to thirty-five dollars for an ID card, which Lewis called "a modern-day poll tax."

The law's critics pointed out that Georgia Republicans had not provided any evidence of specific cases of voter fraud that the new law would stop. "I cannot recall one documented case of voter fraud during my tenure as Secretary of State or Assistant Secretary of State that specifically related to the impersonation of a registered voter at voting polls," Secretary of State Cathy

Cox, who'd been in office since 1996, wrote to Governor Perdue. The bill did not require a photo ID for absentee ballots, Cox noted, where the potential for fraud was much greater. (Elderly voters and members of the military, two heavily GOP voting blocs, often voted absentee.)

The bill passed on an emotional party line vote in both chambers. Members of the Georgia Legislative Black Caucus walked out of the legislature to protest the final vote. The state representative Randal Mangham of Decatur dropped a pair of shackles on Burmeister's desk. "This is wrong!" shouted Senator Vincent Fort of Atlanta as he exited. "What's happening today is just an updated form of Jim Crow."

Georgia submitted the legislation to the Justice Department for approval under Section 5 on June 13, 2005. Lewis urged the Civil Rights Division to reject it. "We have struggled too long and too hard to see, in Georgia and other parts of our country, people moving to violate the very spirit and letter of the Voting Rights Act of 1965," he said. If the DOJ approved the law, warned Jesse Jackson, it would "spread like a virus" to other states.

Since he was a young activist in Nashville, Lewis had looked to the Civil Rights Division as a "sympathetic referee." Those days were now over.

In May 2002, the *National Review* published "Fort Liberalism: Can Justice's Civil Rights Division Be Bushified?," the blueprint for a radical restructuring of the Civil Rights Division.

"There may be no part of the federal government where liberalism is more deeply entrenched," wrote the national correspondent John J. Miller. Even Brad Reynolds and the Reagan administration had failed to disrupt the bipartisan consensus favoring vigorous enforcement of the country's civil rights laws, particularly the VRA. The second-generation counterrevolutionaries in the Bush administration shouldn't make the same mistake.

"Republicans should work to gain more control over the civil rights division and its renegade lawyers," Miller wrote. "Republican political appointees should seize control of the hiring process." He recommended firing longtime section chiefs and bringing in new lawyers with strong conservative credentials.

New hires in the Bush Civil Rights Division, like von Spakovsky, eagerly embarked on the new assignment. "Searching for a conservative in the Civil Rights Division prior to 2001 was like Diogenes searching for an honest man in ancient Greece," von Spakovsky wrote.

Exactly a year after the *National Review* article, Ashcroft tapped Brad Schlozman, a thirty-three-year-old Kansan with no prior civil rights litigation experience, to undertake an extreme makeover of the Civil Rights Division as deputy assistant attorney general for civil rights. Schlozman had a high-pitched nasal voice and a frat boy persona. He'd previously worked with Reynolds, whom he considered a mentor, at the law firm Howrey & Simon, where he bragged to colleagues that he made up "a four-member Vast Right-Wing Conspiracy."

Schlozman was put in charge of hiring and supervision for the voting, criminal, appellate, special litigation, and employment litigation sections. "I too get to work with mold spores, but here in Civil Rights, we call them Voting Section attorneys," he wrote to a former colleague in July 2003. "My tentative plans are to gerrymander all of those crazy libs right out of the section."

Schlozman embarked on a hiring spree of "RTAs," short for "right-thinking Americans," recruiting a dozen lawyers from the Federalist Society, the National Republican Lawyers Association, and the Bush-Cheney campaign. Sixty-four percent of Schlozman's hires were self-identified Republicans or conservatives. Only nineteen of forty-five lawyers Schlozman hired for the voting, employment, and appellate sections had any civil rights experience, and nine of them had *opposed* civil rights enforcement efforts.

"When we start asking about, 'what is your commitment to civil rights?' . . . How do you prove that?" he said in a voice mail to the special litigation section chief, Shanetta Cutlar. "Usually by membership in some crazy liberal organization or by some participation in some crazy cause . . . So, I mean, I just want to make sure we don't start confining ourselves to, you know, politburo members because they happen to be a member of some, you know, psychopathic left-wing organization designed to overthrow the government." An internal Justice Department review subsequently found that Schlozman "improperly considered political and ideological affiliations in the recruitment and hiring of career attorneys in the Civil Rights Division," violating DOJ guidelines and federal civil service laws.

Veteran civil rights lawyers with decades of experience began leaving in droves; they included the well-respected chief of the voting section, Joe

Rich, and his deputy, Bob Kengle, who took early buyouts. Throughout all their years working for Democratic and Republican administrations, from Nixon to Clinton, they'd never been treated with such disdain by political appointees who bitterly opposed the very laws they were meant to enforce.

"You take an oath to uphold the laws of the United States," Kengle said. "These guys didn't believe in the laws of the United States. They came in to work for an institution for which they had the utmost contempt."

In May 2005, Schlozman was promoted to acting head of the Civil Rights Division. He handed the keys to the voting section to von Spakovsky. The career lawyers who remained likened the voting section to Vichy France during the Nazi occupation.

On June 2005, a week after Georgia submitted its voter ID law for DOJ approval, an article appeared in the *Texas Review of Law & Politics*, a conservative legal journal, entitled "Securing the Integrity of American Elections: The Need for Change." Its author, writing under the pseudonym Publius (the same moniker used by the authors of *The Federalist Papers*, in honor of the Roman consul Publius Valerius Publicola), was identified as "an attorney who specializes in election issues."

"It is unfortunately true that in the great democracy in which we live, voter fraud has had a long and studied role in our elections," the article began. It continued: "putting security measures in place—such as requiring identification when voting—does not disenfranchise voters and there is no evidence to suggest otherwise."

Only a year later did the news emerge that Publius was in fact Hans von Spakovsky.

The explosive revelation was hardly surprising. Von Spakovsky had been writing in favor of voter ID laws before practically anyone else. "Requiring official picture identification such as a driver's license with a current address would immediately cut down on a large amount of fraud," he wrote in *The Wall Street Journal* in 1995. Two years later, he recommended, "Georgia should require all potential voters to present reliable photo identifications at their polling locations to help prevent impostors from voting."

DOJ ethics guidelines clearly stated that von Spakovsky, given his longstanding advocacy for voter ID laws and the strong viewpoints in his then-anonymous article, should have recused himself from consideration of

Georgia's voter ID law. Instead, he became the leading proponent for Georgia Republicans during the Section 5 review. (Career lawyers in the voting section suspected he'd also helped the Georgia legislature write the law.)

The new chief of the voting section, John Tanner, was eager to please Schlozman and von Spakovsky. When Schlozman asked Tanner how he liked his coffee, Tanner replied, "Mary Frances Berry style—black and bitter." Berry had headed the U.S. Commission on Civil Rights from 1993 until 2004.

Tanner assigned one of Schlozman's new hires, Joshua Rogers, to work on the five-member team reviewing the Georgia law. Rogers was a graduate of the University of Mississippi Law School and a member of the Federalist Society and the Christian Legal Society. He knew little about the VRA when he joined the review team. "He had no familiarity with Section 5," said Heather Moss, a civil rights analyst in the voting section who worked on the Georgia review. "He would ask me simple questions like, 'What is preclearance?'"

Von Spakovsky began secretly e-mailing Rogers copies of his articles, and arguments and analysis in favor of the Georgia ID law. He told him to password protect his computer so that no other attorneys on the team could see their correspondence. "They chose to put him on the case because of his political leanings and personal connection with von Spakovsky," Moss said.

Von Spakovsky also dismissed concerns about Georgia's law in meetings with the review team. "You can get a voter ID at any Kroger's in Georgia," he told Moss during an early presentation she gave.

"How could you not know that?" Tanner angrily asked her afterward.

When Moss did more research, she found out that the grocery chain had issued photo IDs at select locations in Georgia during a pilot project in 2000, but that the program was not in place anymore and hadn't been for a while.

"We went in with the attitude that we were going to do the traditional civil rights analysis," Moss said. "They were looking for evidence to preclear it."

Despite von Spakovsky's best efforts, the review did not reflect positively on his home state.

Rogers interviewed Burmeister about why she introduced the law. According to the DOJ's records of the conversation: "Burmeister said that if there are fewer black voters because of the bill, it will only be because there is less opportunity for fraud. She said when black voters in her precinct are not paid to vote, they do not go to the polls."

Her racially inflammatory assertions, indicating that the law may have been enacted with a discriminatory purpose, set off alarm bells among the review team.

Atlanta's mayor, Shirley Franklin, presented a very different perspective on the issue, telling the story of her eighty-four-year-old mother, who had recently moved from Philadelphia to Atlanta and could not obtain a new photo ID for voting. She visited multiple DMV offices before finding one that was open. Her expired Pennsylvania driver's license was rejected as sufficient documentation to obtain a Georgia ID card, and she was told to produce a copy of her birth certificate. But Franklin's mother had been born at home in North Carolina and, like many elderly African-Americans who grew up during Jim Crow, never had a birth certificate. After voting for forty years, she would be disenfranchised by the new law.

Citing the high number of voters without ID, the disparate rates of ID possession among blacks and whites, the number of DMV offices that did not issue IDs, the cost of the ID, and the underlying documents needed to obtain an ID (ranging from $20 for an ID card to $210 for naturalization papers), four of five members of the Georgia review team urged that the law be rejected under Section 5.

"While no single piece of data confirms that blacks will [be] disparately impacted compared to whites, the totality of evidence points to that conclusion," they wrote in a fifty-one-page analysis.

The four-member majority of the review team presented its recommendation to Tanner on August 25, 2005. The next day Georgia officials told the voting section lawyers that the state had overstated the number of people with driver's licenses or ID cards by six hundred thousand. The review team asked Tanner for more time to examine this crucial information, which made the case for rejecting the law even stronger. But Tanner said no and told them he'd already decided to approve the law.

Rogers had submitted a dissenting memo, after consulting with von Spakovsky, that Tanner used as the basis for his swift approval letter. Contrary to DOJ protocol, the detailed analysis recommending a rejection of the law was never even sent to the political appointees in the Civil Rights Division, not that it would have made a difference with Schlozman in charge.

A few years later, during a speech before a Latino group in Los Angeles, Tanner explained his reasons for approving the law. He cited data showing that elderly voters in Georgia were more likely to lack voter IDs. "Anything that disproportionately impacts the elderly has the opposite impact on minorities," he claimed. "Minorities don't become elderly the way white people do. They die first." His statement was both racist and factually wrong: blacks made up 40 percent of the elderly voters in Georgia who lacked the newly required forms of voter ID.

To supporters of the VRA, the Georgia review process epitomized the corruption of the Bush Civil Rights Division. "You could ask anyone who's done Section 5 enforcement for thirty years, there's never been anything like that," Joe Rich said.

Rogers, von Spakovsky's conduit, received a $450 bonus for his work on the case. Tanner reprimanded the four other members of the team. The retribution didn't end there.

The deputy chief of the Section 5 unit tried to give Moss a negative performance evaluation, alleging that her personal political views influenced her work. Her supervisor resigned in protest rather than acquiesce.

Within a year all four members of the Georgia review team who recommended a Section 5 objection had left the voting section. They were part of a broader exodus from the section, which lost over half of its lawyers during the Bush years.

VRA enforcement came to a standstill. From 2001 to 2005 the DOJ objected to only forty-eight voting changes out of eighty-one thousand submitted, ten times fewer than during the first four years of the Reagan administration. Georgia's wasn't the only controversial voting change the department had approved. Two years earlier the political appointees had signed off on an unprecedented midyear congressional redistricting plan in Texas engineered by the House majority leader, Tom DeLay. The plan eliminated the seats of six white Democrats and dismantled two majority-minority districts, leading the voting section review team to unanimously recommend that it be blocked. As in Georgia, the career staff was overruled.

In the first five years of the Bush administration, the Civil Rights Division filed only one case alleging voting discrimination in the Deep South—on behalf of white voters in Noxubee County, Mississippi, for the first time in the history of the VRA, against a black Democrat accused of voter fraud.

Veterans of the voting section could only shake their heads at the irony. "During the second Bush administration," said Paul Hancock, who spent twenty years in the Civil Rights Division, "people were referring to Brad Reynolds as the good old days."

Shortly after the 2006 election, David Iglesias, the U.S. attorney for New Mexico, received a call from Mike Battle, director of the executive office for U.S. attorneys, who told Iglesias he was being replaced. He was not alone. On the orders of the White House, initiated by the deputy chief of staff Karl Rove, seven U.S. attorneys were fired in one week.

Iglesias had the dream Republican résumé: the child of Southern Baptist missionaries, a naval lawyer who had been an inspiration for Tom Cruise's character in *A Few Good Men*, the cochair of Lawyers for Bush in 2000. He was one of only two U.S. attorneys to create a special Election Fraud Task Force following Ashcroft's antifraud initiative in 2002, and taught a "voting integrity symposium" at the DOJ in 2005.

Iglesias's task force received more than one hundred complaints of voter fraud prior to the 2004 election. "Vote fraud issues are intensifing [*sic*], and we are looking for you to lead," Allen Weh, the chairman of the New Mexico Republican Party, wrote to him.

Gore had won New Mexico by 366 votes in 2000, and Republicans were looking for any edge they could get in 2004. "I believe the [voter] ID issue should be used (now) at all levels—federal, state legislative races," Michael Rogers, the former counsel for the state Republican Party, wrote to New Mexico Republican activists, including Iglesias. "This is the single best wedge issue, ever in NM."

New Mexico Republicans wanted Iglesias to file indictments against employees of the left-leaning voter registration group ACORN for submitting false registration forms. But after the election, Iglesias told Weh there wasn't enough evidence to justify the prosecutions. Weh then asked the White House to replace Iglesias.

"As you are aware the incumbent, David Iglesias, has failed miserably in his duty to prosecute voter fraud," Weh wrote to the Rove deputy Scott Jennings, copying Rove on the e-mail. "If we can get a new US Atty that takes voter fraud seriously . . . we'll make some real progress in cleaning up a state notorious for crooked elections."

Before the 2006 election, Bush and Rove complained to Attorney General Alberto Gonzales about Iglesias.

"Is anything ever going to happen to that guy?" Weh asked Rove at a White House Christmas party.

"He's gone," Rove replied.

Iglesias wasn't the only U.S. attorney fired for failing to bring voter fraud cases. In 2004, the Democrat Christine Gregoire defeated the Republican Dino Rossi by 129 votes in the Washington State governor's race. After two recounts declared Gregoire the winner, Washington Republicans pushed John McKay, the U.S. attorney for the Western District of Washington, to investigate alleged election irregularities. The chief of staff to the Republican congressman Doc Hastings called McKay to ask about the status of the investigation. "There was no evidence," McKay said, "and I am not going to drag innocent people in front of a grand jury."

McKay, another Bush appointee, was widely respected in Washington State. A DOJ performance evaluation in 2006 called him an "effective, well-regarded, and capable leader." But when McKay interviewed at the White House for a federal judgeship opening, the White House counsel, Harriet Miers, asked him to explain why he had "mishandled" voter fraud prosecutions. Soon he was out of a job.

Of the twelve U.S. attorneys whom the Bush administration dismissed or considered removing as part of what became known as Attorneygate, five worked in places identified by Rove in 2006 as voter fraud hot spots, including Missouri, New Mexico, and Washington.

"It's like the boogeymen parents use to scare their children," Iglesias said of voter fraud accusations. "It's very frightening, and it doesn't exist. U.S. attorneys have better things to do with their time than chasing voter-fraud phantoms."

Ashcroft's much-hyped Voting Access and Integrity Initiative didn't turn up much new evidence either. The major probe by the Justice Department between 2002 and 2007 resulted in only eighty-six convictions out of three hundred million votes cast during that period.

There were a handful of cases of double voting. Thirty people were convicted of small vote-buying schemes for local sheriff or judgeship races. A smattering of immigrants and felons mistakenly registered to vote or voted.

Rarely did the punishment fit the crime. Usman Ali, a native of Pakistan who owned a jewelry store in Tallahassee, accidentally filled out a voter registration card while renewing his driver's license. Though he never voted, he was deported on misdemeanor charges after living in the United States for more than a decade.

In Milwaukee, Kimberly Prude voted absentee in 2004 while on probation, which she didn't think prevented her from voting. She spent over a year in jail for her offense.

In Alaska, Rogelio Mejorada-Lopez, a Mexican immigrant who managed a gas station, received a voter registration card in the mail after applying for U.S. citizenship. He voted, mistakenly believing he was eligible, and faced deportation after sixteen years in the United States.

These were minor mistakes, not evidence of a massive criminal conspiracy on the magnitude that Ashcroft, Rove, and many others in the Bush administration alleged. "They were sure there was fraud," said Joe Rich, "but they could never find it."

Not a single voter was charged for going to the polls and impersonating an eligible voter. But that didn't stop voter ID proponents, like von Spakovsky, from arguing that voter ID laws were urgently needed.

In March 2006, Bush gave von Spakovsky a recess appointment to the Federal Election Commission. Von Spakovsky was also appointed to the advisory board of the Election Assistance Commission, created by HAVA to analyze the country's election problems.

The commission hired two well-respected experts, the Republican Job Serebrov and the Democrat Tova Wang, to produce a comprehensive study on voter fraud. "There is widespread but not unanimous agreement that there is little polling place fraud, or at least much less than is claimed, including voter impersonation, 'dead' voters, non-citizen voting and felon voters," a draft of the report stated. After von Spakovsky complained to the commission's GOP leadership, the wording in the final report was changed to "There is a great deal of debate on the pervasiveness of fraud."

Von Spakovsky's interventions also suppressed the release of a study on voter ID laws by election experts at Ohio State and Rutgers, which found that identification requirements for voters reduced Hispanic turnout by 10 percent and black and Asian-American turnout by 6 percent in 2004.

No matter how much evidence emerged to the contrary, the voter fraud myth would not die. The University of California–Irvine law professor Rick Hasen dubbed von Spakovsky, Rove, and their ilk "The Fraudulent Fraud Squad."

In early 2005, the CBC met with President Bush in the White House Cabinet Room. In two years the temporary provisions of the VRA, last renewed in 1982, were set to expire.

"Do we have your support in extending and strengthening the 1965 Voting Rights Act when it comes up for renewal in 2007?" Congressman Jesse Jackson, Jr., asked the president.

Bush answered that he didn't know enough about the law to comment on it and would take a position once there was new legislation in Congress. His answer stunned the black members. "I thought the president either needs to fire his staff or pay more attention during Black History Month," said Congressman Emanuel Cleaver of Missouri.

Given the administration's fixation on voter fraud and dismantling of the Civil Rights Division, the prospects for the VRA's renewal didn't look good.

But the administration had also launched a very public effort to court black voters. Following Bush's reelection, the RNC chairman, Ken Mehlman, Bush's campaign manager in 2004, traveled thousands of miles to speak at black churches and civic organizations, trying to rebrand the GOP as "the party of Lincoln and Frederick Douglass." At the NAACP's ninety-sixth annual convention in Milwaukee in July 2005, he publicly apologized for the Republican Party's southern strategy.

"By the '70s and into the '80s and '90s, the Democratic Party solidified its gains in the African-American community, and we Republicans did not effectively reach out," Mehlman told three thousand black delegates at the Midwest Airlines Arena. "Some Republicans gave up on winning the African-American vote, looking the other way or trying to benefit politically from racial polarization. I am here today as the Republican chairman to tell you we were wrong."

Four days before Mehlman's speech, Congressman James Sensenbrenner, the Republican chairman of the House Judiciary Committee, told the NAACP that he was preparing to reauthorize the VRA.

"I am here to tell you publicly what I have told others privately—including the head of the Congressional Black Caucus, Representative Mel Watt—that during this Congress we are going to extend the Voting Rights Act," Sensenbrenner announced to a sustained standing ovation, punctuated by organ chords.

"Just like its enactment and its 1982 extension, this bipartisan effort will succeed," he predicted. "While we have made progress and curtailed injustices thanks to the Voting Rights Act, our work is not yet complete. We cannot let discriminatory practices of the past resurface to threaten future gains. The Voting Rights Act must continue to exist—and exist in its current form."

The White House and GOP leadership in Congress, which controlled the House and Senate, quickly signaled they were on board.

Beginning in early 2005, Sensenbrenner and Watt, a member of the Judiciary Committee since 1992 and the new chair of the CBC, began secretly meeting to plot the strategy for the VRA's reauthorization.

They were the ultimate political odd couple. Sensenbrenner was an heir to the fortune of the Kimberly-Clark Corporation, which manufactured tampons, and represented the wealthiest and most Republican district in Wisconsin, comprising the overwhelmingly white northern and western suburbs of Milwaukee. He had a near-perfect conservative voting record from the American Conservative Union and had been one of the floor managers during Bill Clinton's impeachment. Watt, one of the most liberal members of Congress, grew up in stark poverty and represented the working-class urban areas of the North Carolina piedmont. He'd endured four reconfigurations of his district since the *Shaw v. Reno* decision, becoming the poster child for VRA litigation.

The sixty-two-year-old Sensenbrenner was large and volatile, with a thick Wisconsin accent and a fondness for oversize Cadillacs and mammoth cigars. "He is commonly described as 'prickly,' 'cantankerous' and 'unpleasant,' " *The New York Times* once wrote. "And this is by his friends." When Democrats denounced the Patriot Act, which Sensenbrenner introduced, during a Judiciary Committee hearing in 2005, Sensenbrenner abruptly stormed out with the gavel. The footage ended up on *The Daily Show. Rolling Stone* dubbed him the Dictator.

Despite their very different philosophies and personalities, Watt and Sensenbrenner formed an unlikely bond. "Sensenbrenner and I had taken diametrically opposed positions on the Judiciary Committee," Watt said. "What I came to understand about him, and what he came to understand about me, is that if we believed in something, we would fight for it."

Though Sensenbrenner once described himself as "not the most civil-righteous individual in the House of Representatives," he had led the effort to reauthorize the VRA in 1982 as a young member of Congress, taking on the Reagan administration and Senate Republicans. He believed that the GOP could remain the party of Lincoln by embracing the VRA. "The Voting Rights Act of 1965 has been the most successful piece of civil rights legislation ever passed by the Congress," he testified before the Senate. He displayed one of the pens Reagan had used to sign the VRA extension in his Capitol Hill office.

Watt and Sensenbrenner agreed on three major points: first, the VRA needed to be reauthorized before the 2006 election, after which Sensenbrenner would be replaced as House Judiciary Committee chairman by the Texas representative Lamar Smith, who did not share Sensenbrenner's affinity for the law. Second, the law had to be reauthorized, not rewritten, in order to assure quick passage. Any attempt to have states with more recent voting problems—like Ohio—approve their voting changes with the federal government would doom the entire effort. Third, Watt would police the left and Sensenbrenner would police the right to maintain a bipartisan consensus.

"You go and fight off the people who want to do away with the Voting Rights Act and I'll go and fight off the people who want to dramatically change the Voting Rights Act," Watt told Sensenbrenner.

Less than a year after the NAACP convention, Sensenbrenner, Watt, John Lewis, and the congressional leadership of both parties gathered on the steps of the Capitol to introduce the Fannie Lou Hamer, Rosa Parks, and Coretta Scott King Voting Rights Act Reauthorization and Amendments Act of 2006, renewing the VRA for another twenty-five years.

"Like other landmark civil rights bills, the renewed and restored bill that we introduced today is good for all Americans," Watt said. "It is not a Republican bill, it is not a Democratic bill, it is not a House bill or a Senate bill. And it is not a bill solely for minorities. This is a bipartisan, bicameral bill that unites us as a country by ensuring that all Americans may have their voices heard."

Naming the bill after three female pioneers of the civil rights movement "allows us to ensure that rights they fought for remain for future generations," Watt said.

The reauthorization of the law seemed assured. But opponents of the VRA weren't going to give up without a fight.

In 1990, Ed Blum, a thirty-eight-year-old stockbroker at Paine Webber, moved from the Houston suburbs to the museum district downtown, into the Eighteenth Congressional District, drawn and once represented by Barbara Jordan. It was known as "the black seat." When Blum went to vote that year, he realized there was no Republican challenger running against the Democrat Craig Washington, who had succeeded Jordan and Mickey Leland in Congress. So two years later Blum decided to run himself.

"I believe most of you are asking yourselves, 'Why is this poor son-of-a-bitch doing this to himself—doesn't he know he can't win?'" Blum said on the campaign trail. "Go ahead and nod your heads—be honest." He explained: "The 550,000 people living in this district should have a choice when it comes time to vote for their representative."

Blum's parents were liberal Jewish Democrats, and he had volunteered for the McGovern campaign while attending the University of Texas. But he became a Republican during the Reagan years after reading the neoconservative magazine *Commentary*, which fervently subscribed to the color-blind conservatism championed by the Reagan administration. "My mom and dad were Roosevelt-Truman Democrats," Blum said. "Our household was pro–civil rights. I am probably the first Republican that my mother ever met."

Blum decided to knock on as many doors as possible. He took one side of the street, and his wife, Lark, took the other. "Even with detailed street maps," Blum said, "it was nearly impossible to determine who was in the district. I couldn't always tell who I was running to represent." Black and

Hispanic voters who lived side by side frequently resided in different congressional districts. "This didn't happen just once," he said. "It happened dozens and dozens of times."

After the 1990 census, Texas gained three new congressional seats. To create a new majority-Hispanic seat in Houston, some Hispanic voters were moved from the Eighteenth District and put into the new Twenty-ninth District, which fitted together like a jigsaw puzzle. The once-compact inner-city Eighteenth now stretched from the Intercontinental Airport in the north to the Astrodome in the south, resembling a broken window with four jagged corners.

Blum lost the election by thirty points. Six months later he read about the *Shaw v. Reno* case in *The New York Times*. "I thought that if there was a good case in North Carolina, there very well may be a good case in Texas," he said.

He recruited six other plaintiffs, including a retired high school government teacher named Al Vera, to challenge three majority-minority districts in Houston and Dallas, including the Eighteenth, as unconstitutional racial gerrymanders. He paid a lawyer from Monroe, Louisiana, seven thousand dollars a month from his own pocket to represent them. "Our guiding philosophy is that you cannot segregate America in order to integrate Congress," Blum said. He used the tactics of civil rights lawyers to challenge civil rights orthodoxy, modeling his new organization after the LDF and MALDEF, which he called the Campaign for a Colorblind America Legal Defense and Educational Foundation.

A three-judge district court in Texas, made up of Reagan and Bush appointees, ruled in his favor. The challenged districts "bear the odious imprint of racial apartheid," wrote Judge Edith Jones, borrowing Justice O'Connor's infamous language from the *Shaw* decision. The case, *Bush v. Vera*, went all the way to the Supreme Court, where O'Connor once again wrote a contentious 5–4 decision upholding the lower court's finding that "the districts' shapes are unexplainable on grounds other than race and, as such, are the product of presumptively unconstitutional racial gerrymandering."

Blum attracted high-profile new allies in the conservative legal establishment. Clint Bolick filed an amicus brief on his behalf. Thernstrom praised the decision as "a victory for those who favor a colorblind society." The districts were redrawn to become more compact and racially diverse.

Blum had found his "moral cause." He filed similar lawsuits attacking majority-minority districts in Florida, New York, South Carolina, and Virginia. "I didn't really have much fear that Congress would become all white again in the Deep South," he said.

In 1997, he underwrote a referendum to end Houston's minority contracting program, which set voluntary goals for minority- and women-owned businesses. Houston became the first city to challenge affirmative action following the passage of Proposition 209 in California, a landmark 1996 ballot initiative barring the consideration of race or ethnicity in state government hiring and public university admissions. The polarizing issue brought national attention to Houston. "In my judgment, were such a thing to pass," said Houston's mayor, Bob Lanier, "it would send a chilling shock throughout this diverse community."

Blum's hardball tactics, including releasing photos of the homes of black contractors to the media, sparked an unprecedented backlash among black voters, who turned out in record numbers to defeat the ballot initiative and elect Lee Brown, the former chief of police in Houston and drug czar under Bill Clinton, as the city's first black mayor.

After the election, Paine Webber asked Blum to end his anti–affirmative action efforts. He resigned in protest. Thernstrom defended him in *The New York Times*. "We're supposed to be having a national conversation on race and his views fall within the parameter of that discussion," she told the paper. "You don't want a society in which people feel intimidated or that their jobs are on the line because of their political views."

Blum became a folk hero to critics of racial preferences. LET A THOUSAND BLUMS BLOOM, the *New York Post* proclaimed.

He moved to Washington and became a fellow at the American Enterprise Institute. In 2005, he and Thernstrom cofounded the Project on Fair Representation to lobby against the VRA's reauthorization.

They fired the first shot in a *Wall Street Journal* op-ed on July 15, 2005. "Draconian federal intrusion into local elections was justified when it was the only way to enfranchise Southern blacks—but 40 years on, it's an unconstitutional travesty," they wrote.

Their message was simple: the times had changed, but the VRA had not. They focused their opposition on Section 5, based on their belief that the Department of Justice was forcing states to draw misshapen majority-minority districts to comply with the law. "The justification for creating these bizarrely-shaped, bug splat districts was that Section 5 of the Voting Rights Act required it," Blum said. "If Section 5 was creating this mischief, then Section 5 needed to be updated or struck down."

Blum and Thernstrom became a ubiquitous couple. They appeared on panels sponsored by the Federalist Society and the U.S. Civil Rights Commission and wrote frequently for conservative publications like *The Wall Street Journal* and *National Review*. A study they commissioned on the increase in minority voting power in the South circulated widely on Capitol Hill. Blum testified before the House, and Thernstrom testified twice before the Senate.

"Bull Connor is dead," Blum told the House Subcommittee on the Constitution. "And so is every Jim Crow–era segregationist intent on keeping blacks from the polls."

Two Republican representatives from Georgia, Lynn Westmoreland and Charlie Norwood, became Blum and Thernstrom's chief advocates in Congress. Norwood, a dentist from Augusta, entered the House in 1994 as a close ally of Newt Gingrich's. Westmoreland, a conservative Republican from suburban Atlanta who ran his family's construction business before entering politics, joined the House in 2005 and became best known for sponsoring a bill to place the Ten Commandments in Congress.

During the VRA debate, Westmoreland played the role of Strom Thurmond. "The pre-clearance portions of the Voting Rights Act should apply to all states, or no states," he argued. "Singling out certain states for special scrutiny no longer makes sense."

The opponents of Section 5 found common cause with outspoken critics of illegal immigration, like the Iowa congressman Steve King, who wanted to end the VRA's protections for language-minority voters. Shortly after the new legislation was introduced with much fanfare in Congress, Westmoreland and his allies led a revolt during a meeting of the House Republican Caucus, chanting, "Pull the bill, pull the bill."

The House majority leader, John Boehner, who hoped to schedule a quick vote before Memorial Day, postponed consideration of the bill indefinitely.

Watt and Sensenbrenner saw the resistance coming. "We knew, coming into the first reauthorization in twenty-four years, that the argument would be made that the South had changed and that Section 5 was no longer necessary and/or it was an unconstitutional federal encroachment on what has traditionally been the prerogative of the state," Sensenbrenner said. "That's why we held extensive hearings and compiled twelve thousand pages of testimony."

Beginning in October 2005, the House and Senate held the first of twenty-one hearings on the VRA, the most since 1965.

Both sides conceded that dramatic progress had occurred since 1965. The percentage of black registered voters in the South had more than doubled, from 31 percent to 73 percent. The number of black elected officials had skyrocketed from fewer than 500 nationwide in 1965 to 10,500 by 2005. The number of black members of Congress had increased from 5 to 43.

Opponents of the VRA, like Blum and Thernstrom, saw this as evidence that the temporary provisions of the VRA were no longer necessary. Supporters of the VRA, while acknowledging the extraordinary gains, highlighted ongoing instances of voting discrimination, from Georgia's voter ID law to Texas's mid-decade redistricting plan to lesser-known voting changes blocked by Section 5. In fact, the attorney general had objected to more discriminatory voting changes from 1982 to 2004 than between 1965 and 1982.

To break the legislative logjam, the House leadership allowed the Republican dissidents to offer four amendments during the floor debate. "It was necessary to allow them to offer their amendments," Watt said, "and it was necessary to defeat them, resoundingly."

"This rewrite is outdated, unfair, and unconstitutional," Westmoreland declared on the House floor on July 13, 2006, during the final debate on the VRA. "It is true when the Voting Rights Act was first passed in 1965, Georgia needed federal intervention to correct decades of discrimination. Now, 41 years later, Georgia's record on voter equality can stand up against any other State in the Union."

To reinforce his point, Westmoreland boldly quoted John Lewis. "Under oath in federal court five years ago, Congressman Lewis testified: 'There has been a transformation. It's a different state, it's a different political climate, it's a different political environment. It's altogether a different world we live in. We've come a great distance. It's not just in Georgia, but in the American South, I think people are preparing to lay down the burden of race.'"

"Will my colleague from Georgia yield?" Lewis asked across the chamber.

"I will not yield any time," Westmoreland responded defiantly. "The House is voting today to keep my state in the penalty box for 25 years based on the actions of the people who are now dead."

When Westmoreland finished, Lewis rose to defend himself. "It is true that years ago I said that we are in the process of laying down the burden of race," he said, pointing at Westmoreland. "But it is not down yet and we are not asleep yet. The Voting Rights Act was good and necessary in 1965, and it is still good and necessary today. So don't misquote me. Don't take my words out of context."

An hour later, Lewis returned to the House floor to make his closing argument.

"We cannot separate the debate today from our history and the past we have traveled," he said, holding a large black-and-white photo of himself crossing the Edmund Pettus Bridge with Hosea Williams on March 7, 1965. "When we marched from Selma to Montgomery in 1965, it was dangerous. It was a matter of life and death."

Sensenbrenner and Watt did the hard work behind the scenes, but Lewis became the public face of the VRA's reauthorization. No one could match the moral force of his testimony.

He showed another blown-up image of himself lying on the bridge, preparing to take a blow to the head from an Alabama state trooper. "We must pass this act without any amendment," he said passionately, holding the photo in his right hand. "It is the right thing to do, not just for us, but for generations yet unborn." He pounded his left fist on the lectern for emphasis. "When historians pick up their pens and write about this period, let it be said that those of us in the Congress in 2006, we did the right thing, and our forefathers and our foremothers would be very proud of us."

Sensenbrenner spoke after Lewis. "We need the Voting Rights Act," he said, "because in the last 25 years the covered jurisdictions have not come clean."

Sensenbrenner rattled off the number of DOJ objections to discriminatory voting changes since 1982: 91 in Georgia, 105 in Texas, 112 in Mississippi, 96 in Louisiana, 73 in South Carolina, 46 in Alabama, 45 in North Carolina. "Now, I think these figures ought to make it very clear that we need this bill," he said.

In a theatrical flourish, he took bound copies of the twelve thousand pages of House committee hearings out of a cardboard box and tossed them on the table in front of him; landing with a loud thump, the pages slid off onto the House floor. "It is one of the most extensive considerations of any piece of legislation that the United States Congress has dealt with in the 27½ years that I have been honored to serve as a member of this body," he said.

Representative Norwood offered the first of four amendments, basing the Section 5 coverage formula on data from the last three presidential elections rather than from the 1964, 1968, and 1972 elections. That sounded appealing in theory, but in practice the only state fully covered under Norwood's proposal would have been Hawaii. "The amendment not only guts the bill, but turns the Voting Rights Act into a farce," Sensenbrenner responded. The amendment was defeated, 318 to 96.

Representative Louis Gohmert of Texas offered an amendment to reauthorize the VRA for ten years instead of twenty-five. It went down, 288 to 134.

Representative Steve King introduced an amendment to end the VRA's language-minority protections. It failed, 238 to 185.

Westmoreland offered the last amendment, to require that the DOJ's voting section review all nine hundred jurisdictions subject to Section 5 within three years to see if they deserved to be released from federal oversight. He noted that his proposal had the support of liberal law professors like Rick Hasen of UC Irvine.

"This amendment expands federal authority by people who have been complaining about federal authority since the Voting Rights Act was passed 41 years ago," Sensenbrenner replied. "Let's not turn the VRA on its head." It was defeated, 302 to 118.

After seven hours of debate, the House passed the final bill by an overwhelming vote of 390 to 33, a nearly identical margin to 1982.

A week later, the Senate passed the House bill by a resounding vote of 98–0. Ted Kennedy invited Lewis to be his guest on the Senate floor for the final passage. They celebrated in the ornate President's Room, where LBJ had signed the VRA forty-one years earlier. "This is a historic day," Lewis said.

As in 1970, 1975, and 1982, opponents of the VRA, on and off the Hill, had failed to shatter the bipartisan consensus for the law in Congress.

"The title of the Act alone—containing the names of Fannie Lou Hamer, Rosa Parks, and Coretta Scott King—was politically intimidating, clearly the inspiration of a marketing genius," Thernstrom wrote afterward.

"For Republicans, uncritical support for the Voting Rights Act has become a way to prove the GOP's race credibility," lamented the *National Review*'s John Miller, who had written the blueprint for the Bush administration's takeover of the Civil Rights Division. Miller's article ignored the good-faith efforts of Republicans like Sensenbrenner, but there was some truth to what he was saying.

The Bush administration endorsed the law's renewal because it believed that opposing the VRA would damage the Republican Party, especially given the GOP's dismal standing with black voters following Hurricane Katrina and with the midterm elections upcoming. The Bush Justice Department had actively subverted the law and prevented lawyers from working on its renewal, but Brad Schlozman testified in favor of the VRA extension on the orders of the White House. The law's long-standing popularity meant that opponents had to tread carefully. That was why Republicans on the Senate Judiciary Committee bizarrely published a report criticizing the legislation only after they all were on record voting for it.

A week after Congress passed the bill, Bush signed it on the South Lawn, surrounded by members of the Hamer, Parks, and King families. The first black mayor of Selma, James Perkins, traveled to Washington for the occasion. Sensenbrenner stood directly behind the president.

Despite the prior actions of his administration, the president proclaimed himself a staunch supporter of voting rights. "Today, we renew a bill that helped bring a community on the margins into the life of American democracy," he said. "My administration will vigorously enforce the provisions of this law, and we will defend it in court."

The last part of Bush's statement was more prescient than he knew. Eight days after the signing ceremony, Blum filed a case from Texas challenging the constitutionality of Section 5.

"We needed 218 votes in the House," Westmoreland said, "but we'll only need five votes on the Supreme Court."

9

OLD POISON, NEW BOTTLES

Barack Obama held the final rally of his campaign, on the night before the 2008 election, in Manassas, Virginia, the site of the first major battle of the Civil War. At 10:30 p.m., he strode onstage at the Prince William County Fairgrounds, and saw a sea of ninety thousand supporters—black and white, young and old. At the top of the hill, the words "Vote for Change" shone in bright white letters.

"What a scene," Obama said. "What a crowd. Thank you, Virginia."

It was an improbable setting for an improbable campaign. In 1965, only 438 blacks, fewer than 20 percent of eligible African-American voters, were registered to vote in Prince William County. Virginia hadn't voted for a Democratic presidential candidate since LBJ in 1964. The last time so many people had gathered in Manassas, other than to attend the county fair, had been in August 1862, when Robert E. Lee's Confederate forces routed the Union in the Second Battle of Bull Run.

Obama had spent the day campaigning in Jacksonville, Florida, and Charlotte, North Carolina, before arriving in Virginia, targeting three southern states where he more than likely would not have been able to vote in 1965 and where his parents could not have married.

"Tomorrow, at this defining moment in history, you can give this country the change that we need," Obama said. "It starts here in Virginia. It starts here in Manassas. This is where change begins."

John Lewis couldn't sleep that night. He was up at 4:00 a.m. and at the polls by 7:15. He shook hands with every one of the two hundred voters in line early at Westlake High School in southwestern Atlanta. "Historic day," he kept repeating.

As a young civil rights activist Lewis never imagined he would live to see the day when a black man could be elected president. "An African-American president wasn't even part of my dream back then," he said. "I just wanted black people to vote so we could elect more progressive whites. If someone had told me I was going to be in this position in my lifetime, I would have said, 'What have you been drinking? Or smoking?'"

Lewis and Obama bonded early. Lewis invited the Illinois senator to give the keynote speech at his sixty-fifth birthday party in Atlanta in 2005 and predicted he would one day be president. Lewis had initially endorsed Hillary Clinton on the basis of his longtime friendship with the Clintons, but changed his allegiance after Obama decisively won Georgia's Democratic primary. "I think the candidacy of Senator Obama represents the beginning of a new movement in American political history," he said. "And I want to be on the side of the people, on the side of the spirit of history."

Lewis spent Election Night with Andrew Young and the King family at MLK's Ebenezer Baptist Church in Atlanta. Two thousand people packed the historic church, watching the returns on two giant video screens. Lewis grew emotional when he took the pulpit, reflecting on all he had been through to reach this moment. "It is an unbelievable night," he said. "It is a night of thanksgiving."

At 11:00 p.m., when the networks called the election for Obama, the church erupted in delirious celebration. Lewis jumped in the air and yelled, "Thank God, hallelujah, hallelujah!" Ebenezer's pastor, the Reverend Raphael Warnock, asked the audience to clasp hands and recite "Lift Ev'ry Voice and Sing."

"Sisters and brothers, it looks like we have moved from Bloody Sunday to Triumphant Tuesday," Warnock said.

Watching the celebration in Chicago's Grant Park, Lewis said, "The struggle, the suffering, the pain, and everything we tried to do to create a more perfect union, it was worth it."

The 2008 electorate was the most diverse in American history. Of the five million new voters in 2008, two million were black, two million were Hispanic, and six hundred thousand were Asian. Obama lost white voters to John McCain by twelve points but won 75 percent of the combined black, Hispanic, and Asian vote, which increased by four points over 2004. Ronald Brownstein of the *National Journal* dubbed Obama's base of minorities, young voters, women, and college-educated whites the "coalition of the ascendant."

These electoral changes were particularly dramatic in the South. Not only did Obama carry the three southern states where he had campaigned the day before the election, but the biggest increases in voter turnout occurred in Georgia, North Carolina, Louisiana, Mississippi, and Virginia.

Unexpected changes were happening across Dixie. Six months after Obama's election, James Young became the first black mayor of Philadelphia, Mississippi. The fifty-three-year-old Pentecostal minister defeated a three-term white incumbent by forty-six votes, in a town that was 56 percent white.

Young was nine when Chaney, Goodman, and Schwerner were murdered in Philadelphia. He remembered his father sitting in the living room with a gun at night. Young had been the first black student to integrate his sixth-grade class a few years later. He became an EMT, working the grounds at the Neshoba County Fair when Ronald Reagan spoke, and a county supervisor before deciding to run for mayor in August 2008, inspired by the Obama campaign.

"Obama's election sent a message to our people that it was possible," he said. "If we can elect a black man as president we can elect a black man as mayor of Philadelphia."

The forty-fourth anniversary of Bloody Sunday, in the wake of Obama's election, was a joyous occasion in Selma. "Because of what you did, we got the Voting Rights Act in 1965," Lewis told an overflow crowd at Brown Chapel. "Because of what you did, Barack Obama is the President of the United States."

Two years earlier Obama had spoken at the same church and marched across the Edmund Pettus Bridge with Lewis. "Don't tell me I don't have a claim on Selma, Alabama," Obama said. "Don't tell me I'm not coming home when I come to Selma, Alabama. I'm here because somebody marched. I'm here because y'all sacrificed for me. I stand on the shoulders of giants."

The featured speaker at the celebration in 2009 was Eric Holder, the first black attorney general. Holder sat next to Lewis, whom he called "one of my personal heroes." Peggy Wallace Kennedy, the daughter of George Wallace, introduced the attorney general.

It was an unlikely meeting, given the histories of the Holder and Wallace families. Holder's late sister-in-law, Vivian Malone of Mobile, had been one of the first two African-American students to enroll at the University of Alabama. In June 1963, Wallace personally blocked her entry to the university. President Kennedy dispatched Nick Katzenbach to tell Wallace to step aside. After a heated, nationally televised standoff, Kennedy federalized the Alabama National Guard to escort Malone into the school.

She became the first African-American graduate of the university. She later worked in the DOJ's Civil Rights Division and became director of the Voter Education Project after Lewis. "I so wish Vivian had lived to see this moment," Holder said. He hung a portrait of Katzenbach in his office and one of Bobby Kennedy in his conference room.

Peggy Wallace Kennedy told her own story of those turbulent years. "Watching from behind the gates of the Alabama Governor's Mansion, I knew in my heart that their cause was just, but unlike them, I did not let my voice be heard," she said. "For many years, I wandered in the world of indifference, until I heard the voice of Barack Obama. He inspired me to believe in myself and to join with millions of others who laid claim once again to faith and pride in America." She introduced Holder with tears in her eyes.

"The world that existed on Bloody Sunday is all but unrecognizable to us now," Holder said. "We are all the beneficiaries of Selma. I am a beneficiary of Selma."

The attorney general had grown up far from Selma, the son of immigrants from Barbados who settled in the diverse neighborhood of East Elmhurst, Queens, where his neighbors included Louis Armstrong, Dizzy Gillespie, Willie Mays, and Malcolm X. After graduating from Columbia

University Law School, Holder found his first job at the LDF. He then rose through the ranks of the DOJ, becoming deputy attorney general during the Clinton administration. He called the Civil Rights Division "the crown jewel" of the Justice Department and planned to make restoring its credibility one of his top priorities. "Under my leadership, in all that it does, the Civil Rights Division will reflect the spirit of the movement that inspired its creation," he said in Selma.

Following his speech, Holder, Wallace, and Lewis locked arms and sang "We Shall Overcome." "In one snapshot, there it was: civil rights in America from 1955 to 2009," reported NPR's Nina Totenberg.

That day Holder touted the historic progress that had been made but warned against complacency in the long fight for civil rights. "We stand closer to the dream of Dr. King than ever before, but we've got to keep marching," he said. "Some take a view that when it comes to civil rights, we have already reached the Promised Land. But we know better. And some take a view that justice and equality have been achieved for all Americans, but I know better."

In particular, longtime critics of the VRA argued that Obama's ascendance signified that constitutional protections for previously disenfranchised minority groups were no longer necessary. "It says that the road we started down in 1965 with the Voting Rights Act has come to an end," Abigail Thernstrom told *The New York Times* in August 2008. "We don't need to talk about disfranchisement in the same way anymore." She called Obama's election "victory in the voting rights battle."

Two months after Obama's election, the Supreme Court agreed to hear a challenge to Section 5 of the VRA brought by Ed Blum. "We must commit ourselves to continuing to defend the Voting Rights Act, which is under attack," Holder said.

Chief Justice Rehnquist died on September 3, 2005, at the age of eighty. John Roberts was one of eight pallbearers at his funeral. Two days after Rehnquist's death, Bush nominated Roberts to succeed his former boss as chief justice.

The White House released fifteen thousand pages of records documenting Roberts's tenure in the Reagan administration, which revealed his extensive efforts to limit the scope of the VRA in the early 1980s.

Lewis testified before the Senate Judiciary Committee against Roberts's nomination. "Judge Roberts's memos reveal him to be hostile toward civil rights, affirmative action and the Voting Rights Act," Lewis said. He cited a memo in which Roberts wrote that violations of the VRA "should not be made too easy to prove."

"Had Judge Roberts's narrow reading of the Voting Rights Act prevailed, fewer people of color would be serving in Congress and at both the state and local level today," Lewis continued. "We cannot afford to elevate an individual to such a powerful lifetime position whose record demonstrates such a strong desire to reverse the hard-won civil rights gains that so many of us sacrificed so much to achieve."

Roberts, Lewis concluded, "was on the wrong side of history."

Members of the Judiciary Committee pressed Roberts to explain his current views on the VRA.

"I'm deeply troubled by a narrow and cramped and, perhaps, even a meanspirited view of the law that appears in some of your writings," Senator Kennedy told him. "It appears that you did not fully appreciate the problem of discrimination in our society. It also seems that you were trying to undo the progress that so many people had fought for and died for in this country."

Kennedy asked him, "You do agree[,] don't you, Judge Roberts, that the right to vote is a fundamental constitutional right?"

"It is preservative, I think, of all the other rights," Roberts responded. "Without access to the ballot box, people are not in a position to protect any other rights that are important to them."

"I'm just trying to find out on the Voting Rights Act whether you have any problem at all, and trouble at all, in terms of the constitutionality of the existing Voting Rights Act that was extended by the Congress?" Kennedy asked.

"The existing Voting Rights Act, the constitutionality has been upheld, and I don't have any issue with that," Roberts answered.

"Will you on the Court fairly apply the Voting Rights Act?" the Iowa senator Charles Grassley followed up.

"Any issues that come before me under the Voting Rights Act, I will confront those with an open mind and decide them after full and fair consideration of the arguments, in light of the precedents of the Court, and in light of a recognition of the critical role that the right to vote plays as preservative of all other rights," Roberts responded.

The nominee told the Senate: "I come before the committee with no agenda. I have no platform." He used a baseball analogy to describe his judicial philosophy. "Judges are like umpires," he said. "Umpires don't make the rules, they apply them. The role of an umpire and a judge is critical. They make sure everybody plays by the rules, but it is a limited role. Nobody ever went to a ball game to see the umpire."

The Senate confirmed Roberts, 78 to 22. "They had faith that he would continue to do the right thing," Lewis said.

But it soon became clear that the chief justice's views on voting rights hadn't moderated since the Reagan years.

In 2002, Don Zimmerman, a libertarian Ron Paul supporter, won election to the local utility board in an upscale suburb of Austin. When Zimmerman wanted to move the utility's polling place from a neighbor's garage to a nearby school, he had to receive approval from the federal government under Section 5, which covered all voting changes in Texas. Zimmerman complained to Greg Coleman, a former clerk for Clarence Thomas. Coleman contacted Blum, who was looking for a jurisdiction to challenge the 2006 reauthorization of the VRA.

Coleman represented the utility, and Blum's Project on Fair Representation paid the legal bills. After the VRA's reauthorization, Blum stopped working with Thernstrom and focused exclusively on challenging the law through the courts, getting funding from a consortium of influential conservative funders called Donors Trust. The utility's brief called Section 5 "an unconstitutional overextension of Congress's enforcement power to remedy past violations of the Fifteenth Amendment." Blum lost in the lower courts and appealed to the Supreme Court, which heard oral arguments in *Northwest Austin Municipal Utility District No. 1 v. Holder* (*NAMUDNO*) one hundred days after Obama's inauguration.

Chief Justice Roberts said almost nothing during the first thirty minutes of the trial, when Coleman spoke for the plaintiffs. But he interrupted the Obama administration's deputy solicitor general, Neal Katyal, a former national security adviser to Holder, within a minute.

Roberts: "Here, as I understand it, one-twentieth of 1 percent of the submissions [from states to the DOJ] are not pre-cleared. That, to me, suggests that they are sweeping far more broadly than they need to, to address the intentional discrimination under the Fifteenth Amendment."

Katyal: "I disagree with that, Mr. Chief Justice. I think what that represents is that Section 5 is actually working very well; that it provides a deterrent."

Roberts: "Well, that's like the old elephant whistle. I have this whistle to keep away the elephants. Well, there are no elephants, so it must work."

Katyal: "I agree that if we were just standing up with no record whatsoever, that's one thing, but Congress heard testimony, they found example after example of [voting discrimination]."

Five minutes later Roberts again interrupted Katyal as he spoke about modern-day voting discrimination in Texas.

Roberts: "Well, let me focus on that historical aspect. Obviously no one doubts the history here and that the history was different [between states]. But at what point does that history stop justifying action with respect to some jurisdictions but not with respect to others that show greater disparities?"

Katyal: "Congress has said that the Court should be particularly worried about trying to predict the future and say that discrimination is now over."

Roberts: "Well, so your answer is that Congress can impose this disparate treatment forever because of the history in the South?"

Katyal: "Absolutely not."

Roberts: "When do they have to stop?"

Katyal: "Well, Congress here said twenty-five years was the appropriate reauthorization period."

Roberts: "Well, they said five years originally and then another twenty years. I mean, at some point it begins to look like the idea is that this is going to go on forever."

Roberts sounded far more like an aggressive player than an umpire simply calling balls and strikes. In a case on school integration in Seattle and Louisville a few years earlier, he'd succinctly described his color-blind views on race, writing in the last sentence of his opinion, "The way to stop discrimination on the basis of race is to stop discriminating on the basis of race."

John Lewis, on his first visit to the Court since *Bush v. Gore*, listened anxiously to the oral arguments. "It reminded me of some of the same debate of 1965," he said after. "This Act is one of the most progressive pieces of legislation the country ever passed, and it changed America forever. We don't need to go back." His testimony against Roberts now sounded prescient.

On the basis of Roberts's questioning, many legal experts expected the Court to overrule Congress's overwhelming judgment and strike down Section 5, which would have been unthinkable before Roberts and Samuel Alito, his peer in the Reagan administration, joined the Court. Jeffrey Rosen of *The New Republic* reported that the four liberal justices "threatened to write a strong dissent that would have accused the majority of misconstruing landmark precedents about congressional power." Roberts or Justice Anthony Kennedy, the swing vote, got cold feet, and the Court eventually punted, exempting the utility from Section 5 oversight (known as a bailout) without resolving the larger constitutional questions.

But in a hopeful sign for the plaintiffs, the conservative majority expressed strong skepticism about the continued relevance of Section 5. "The historic accomplishments of the Voting Rights Act are undeniable, but the Act now raises serious constitutional concerns," Roberts wrote for the 8–1 majority. "The Act imposes current burdens and must be justified by current needs. The Act also differentiates between the States in ways that may no longer be justified."

Blum called the decision "an excellent first chop on the log." During the 2006 congressional debate, few Republicans publicly challenged the VRA, and no other jurisdiction covered by Section 5 joined the *NAMUDNO* lawsuit. The Court's opinion "emboldened many in the Republican Party to feel more comfortable criticizing Section 5," Blum said. Roberts's words guaranteed that there would be another challenge to the VRA very soon.

NAMUDNO wasn't the first major voting rights case to come before the Roberts Court. Six days after Obama's surprise victory in the Iowa caucus, the Court heard a challenge to Indiana's voter ID law, which had passed at the same time as Georgia's in 2005, brought by the state representative Bill Crawford, Democrat of Indianapolis, the longest-serving black state lawmaker in the country.

Indiana's voter ID law was the first of its kind to reach the Supreme

Court. (Georgia's law was initially blocked by a federal court as a "poll tax," then approved after the legislature passed a revised bill providing for a free voter ID.) Crawford's brief called the law "a severe burden on the fundamental right to vote," particularly for poor, elderly, disabled, and minority voters who lacked the government-issued IDs required to cast a ballot.

A 2006 study by the Brennan Center for Justice found that up to 11 percent of U.S. citizens—twenty-one million eligible voters—did not have government-issued photo IDs; they included 25 percent of African-Americans, 18 percent of seniors sixty-five and over, and 15 percent of those making less than thirty-five thousand dollars a year. "Let's not beat around the bush," wrote Judge Terence Evans of the Seventh Circuit Court of Appeals. "The Indiana voter photo ID law is a not-too-thinly veiled attempt to discourage election-day turnout by certain folks believed to skew Democratic."

Indiana called its law "an eminently reasonable effort to combat in-person voter fraud." The Supreme Court sided with the state. Writing for a 6–3 majority, Justice John Paul Stevens said Indiana had a legitimate "interest in deterring and detecting voter fraud" and "protecting public confidence in elections." He did concede that "the record contains no evidence that the fraud [the law] addresses—in-person voter impersonation at polling places—has actually occurred in Indiana."

The only example of voter impersonation cited by Stevens stretched back to New York City in 1868, when operatives for Boss Tweed allegedly paid people to vote multiple times by altering their facial hair. The absence of any recent evidence of voter impersonation led Justices Souter, Breyer, and Ginsburg to dissent. "The State responds to the want of evidence with the assertion that in-person voter impersonation fraud is hard to detect," Souter wrote. "But this is like saying 'the man who wasn't there' is hard to spot."

Just as *NAMUDNO* encouraged new challenges to the VRA, so the *Crawford* decision signaled that states could implement new voting restrictions merely by invoking the threat of voter fraud, even if such fraud had not actually occurred. Taken together, the two cases set a chilling precedent for voting rights in the Obama era.

The state representative Debbie Riddle, a horse breeder and a grandmother of ten from suburban Houston, arrived at the empty Texas capitol two days before the beginning of the 2011 legislative session. She camped out on the cold floor so that she could be the first lawmaker in line to file a new voter ID bill.

Riddle had a penchant for attracting controversy. She once said that public education "comes from Moscow, from Russia. It comes straight out of the pit of hell." In an interview with CNN, she claimed that pregnant Middle Eastern women were coming to the United States to deliver babies "with the nefarious purpose of turning them into little terrorists who will then come back to the U.S. and do us harm." *Texas Monthly* gave her its Joseph McCarthy "Have You No Sense of Decency?" Award.

Riddle's bill was one of ten voter ID measures introduced in the Texas legislature in the 2011 session. Texas's governor, Rick Perry, declared the voter ID bill an emergency item, which meant it could pass in the first sixty days of the new legislative session. He predicted the legislation would be approved "so fast it'll make your head spin."

When asked for an example of voter fraud to support her new bill, Riddle said she'd once seen a Latina woman at her polling place who couldn't speak English and needed assistance. "She was not only limited in English, she really didn't know any English," Riddle said. Even though the VRA provided help for language-minority voters in Texas, Riddle was "perplexed how anyone could come in and attempt to vote and have just a complete disconnect of the entire process." In addition to voter ID, Riddle introduced legislation modeled after Arizona's toughest-in-the-nation anti-immigration law, which the Department of Justice denounced as racial profiling. The changing demographics of Texas and the push for voter ID went hand in hand.

Texas Republicans had begun pushing for voter ID in 2005, after the census declared Texas the country's fourth majority-minority state, with blacks, Hispanics, Asians, and other minorities narrowly overtaking whites. Democrats in the Texas senate needed a third of the body to block the bill but were missing a crucial vote. Senator Mario Gallegos, the first Hispanic state legislator from Houston, was recovering at home from a liver transplant that his body was rejecting. When Texas Republicans scheduled a hasty vote on the bill, Gallegos rushed back to Austin against the advice of his doctors. "If not for voter ID, I wouldn't be here; that's how serious the issue is for me," Gallegos said.

When Gallegos returned, another Democratic senator, Carlos Uresti of San Antonio, was in bed with a nasty flu. Uresti received a call that he was needed immediately on the senate floor to vote against the voter ID bill. He sprinted up the steps of the capitol, arriving moments before his name was called. He voted no, then promptly vomited in the senate lounge.

After the legislature failed to pass the voter ID bill in 2005, the Texas attorney general, Greg Abbott, announced a major investigation into voter fraud the following year, much as the Bush administration had done in Washington. "In Texas, an epidemic of voter fraud is harming the electoral process and it's time we rooted it out," he declared.

His targets were people like Willie Ray, a sixty-nine-year-old black city councilwoman in Texarkana, and her granddaughter Jamillah, who were charged with voter fraud for mailing absentee ballots on behalf of home-bound elderly voters. They had violated an obscure Texas law mandating that the addresses of those mailing the ballots be included on the envelope, which Ray forgot to do. "A lot of blood has been shed for the rights of people to vote," Ray said after pleading guilty to a misdemeanor. "I just hope those rights are not taken away or people are frightened so bad they won't vote."

Abbott's critics pointed out that of the twenty-two cases of election fraud prosecuted by his office over a six-year period, none would have been stopped by a voter ID law. His investigation also had disturbing partisan and racial overtones. All of Abbott's prosecutions involved Democrats, primarily Latinos and African-Americans. A PowerPoint presentation developed by his office to educate local officials about voter fraud showed a slide of black voters standing in line to vote. Another slide showed a sickle-cell anemia postage stamp featuring a black woman holding a baby. None of the seventy-one slides included any white voters, suggesting that voter fraud was something that only Democrats of color did.

Voter fraud fears went national in 2008. Republicans ratcheted up attacks on ACORN that had begun during the Bush administration, seizing on evidence that ACORN employees had registered fictitious voters like Mickey Mouse. (ACORN canvassers in states like Nevada, who made eight dollars an hour, earned a bonus for submitting more than twenty-one new voter registration names a day, so they sometimes submitted fake names to make extra money.) There was no evidence that Mickey Mouse had actually voted—under HAVA, new registrants had to provide some type of proof of identity, be it a driver's license, utility bill, or bank statement—but that didn't stop John McCain from alleging in his final debate with Obama that ACORN "is now on the verge of maybe perpetrating one of the greatest frauds in voter history."

After the 2008 election, one poll found that 52 percent of Republicans believed that ACORN had stolen the election for Obama. The Republican fixation with voter fraud became a "new Southern strategy," the Rutgers University political science professor Lori Minnite wrote in her book *The Myth of Voter Fraud.* "The reddest base of the Republican Party has been energized by the tarring of Democrats as cheaters and the association of Democrats with a radicalized crime-prone underclass."

The relentless focus on ACORN and voter fraud, combined with major GOP gains in the 2010 election, significantly boosted the prospects for passing new voting restrictions, including voter ID in Texas. Republicans picked up twenty-one seats in the Texas house, giving them a huge majority. And Lieutenant Governor David Dewhurst quickly eliminated the requirement that the bill needed two-thirds support in the senate, preventing Democrats from filibustering it again.

As Texas became increasingly diverse, the GOP caucus grew whiter and more conservative. Of the 120 Republican members of the Texas legislature, there were only 5 Hispanics, 1 Asian, and no African-Americans. Democrats, by contrast, had 11 whites, 17 blacks, 32 Hispanics, and 2 Asians in their caucus. This stark racial contrast helped explain the parties' radically different views on voter ID.

The voter ID bill introduced in 2011—the fourth time the legislature had tried to pass the measure—was significantly tougher than the legislation debated in prior sessions or the laws adopted by Georgia and Indiana. Whereas Riddle's bill required one form of government-issued ID or two types of nonphoto ID to cast a ballot, legislation brought to the floor by Senator Troy Fraser, a childhood friend of Governor Perry's, allowed only five forms of government-issued ID to vote: a driver's license, a personal ID card issued by the Department of Public Safety, a U.S. military ID card, a U.S. passport, and a U.S. citizenship certificate. Unlike Indiana's and Georgia's laws, Texas's bill did not allow student IDs or expired driver's licenses. The Texas legislature did, however, adopt an amendment adding a concealed handgun permit to the list of accepted voter IDs.

As in Georgia, Fraser's bill did not require voter IDs for absentee ballots, which Republicans used more frequently than Democrats and which was the form of voting by which voter fraud was far and away most likely to occur. Abbott's investigation turned up no instances of voter impersonation, but more than half of his prosecutions involved absentee ballot fraud.

During the house debate, Representative Rafael Anchia, a Hispanic Democrat from Dallas, aggressively quizzed the bill's sponsor, Representative Patricia Harless, about the purpose of the bill. Anchia was a rising star in Texas politics whom the press dubbed "El Gobernador" and "the Hispanic Obama." He represented a district that was nearly three-fourths Hispanic, where a quarter of his constituents lived below the poverty line. Harless, a conservative evangelical Christian and member of the Texas Tea Party Caucus, ran a used car dealership with her husband in suburban Houston.

Anchia: "Describe how voter impersonation works."

Harless: "Someone shows up to the poll with a voter's registration card that may not be theirs and casts a vote with that card."

Anchia: "How often does that happen in the state of Texas[,] do you think?"

Harless: "I'm not advised."

Anchia: "Why does [the bill] ignore mail-in ballots?"

Harless: "This bill is only addressing one type of voter fraud, in-person voter fraud."

Anchia: "But that's really interesting to me because we've got a bill that addresses a narrow type of fraud that you even acknowledged you have no cases of."

Harless: "I did not say I have no cases of."

Anchia: "Give me a case."

Harless: "I said that they were not part of our testimony."

Anchia: "So there's no cases on the House floor of impersonation. You are yet very, very concerned about the integrity of elections, correct?"

Harless: "Uh-huh."

Anchia: "Yet this bill doesn't deal with the type of voter fraud that we've seen most prevalently in the State of Texas[,] which is mail-in ballots, correct?"

Harless: "There are other pieces of legislation that—"

Anchia: "Have you filed a bill on mail-in ballots?"

Harless: "No, sir."

Under sustained questioning from Anchia, Harless admitted: "This is about restoring confidence in the election process . . . And to get off on the fraud argument or how often it happens or if it even happens, we will never agree on that . . . We can stay here all day long discussing the fraud but that is not what this bill is about. This bill is about protecting, deterring, and detecting possible fraud in the elections."

"The goal post has moved," Anchia responded in a passionate speech against the bill, "because, as the author's pointed out, this is no longer about voter impersonation. This is about the integrity of elections.

"Really? Do we really believe that? Because if this was about the integrity of elections, then we would clearly be focused on the place where seventy percent of all the Attorney General's investigations and prosecutions have been, which is in mail-in ballots. Yet this bill specifically ignores mail-in ballots.

"And my fear is, members, that the way this bill is crafted, it's going to have a disproportionate impact on the poor. It's going to have [a disproportionate impact] on African-Americans and Hispanics. And I hope that this is not what it's about, because we know it's not about voter impersonation. We still don't have one case here on the House floor. And we know it's not about the integrity of elections, because if it was about the integrity of elections, it would be about mail-in ballots. So we know it's not about those things. And I fear, members, that it's about something else, and it's about fewer people voting."

Five months after the Texas legislature convened in Austin, Perry signed Texas's voter ID law, the strictest in the country, at the state capitol. Thirty Republican legislators packed the small reception room. "This is what democracy is really all about," Perry said.

A rare Republican dissent came from Royal Masset, the former executive director of the Texas Republican Party. Masset supported voter ID laws until he began taking care of his invalid ninety-one-year-old mother, a registered voter in Austin who did not have a driver's license, a passport, a handgun permit, or any of the documentation required to vote or needed to obtain the correct ID. He accused Texas Republicans of "using sheer racism to pump their own political points" by attempting to suppress Democratic voters.

"Anyone who says all legal voters under this bill can vote doesn't know what he is talking about," Masset wrote on his blog. "And anyone who says that a lack of IDs won't discriminate against otherwise legal minority voters is lying."

Texas was far from alone in pushing to restrict access to the ballot. In 2011 and 2012, 180 new voting restrictions were introduced in forty-one states, with twenty-seven new laws taking effect in nineteen states, nearly all of them controlled by Republicans. The right to vote had become deeply politicized. The country hadn't seen anything like it since the end of Reconstruction, when every southern state placed severe limits on the franchise.

The election of the first black president and the resurrection of new barriers to the ballot box were not a coincidence. "The proposal of restrictive voter-access legislation has been substantially more likely to occur where African-Americans are concentrated and both minorities and low-income individuals have begun turning out at the polls more frequently," reported a study from the University of Massachusetts–Boston.

"As minorities grow in the political process, it's in the interest of one of the parties to tamp down voter turnout," said Mel Watt. "It's the same system that other people went through when there were poll taxes and literacy tests. This is just another iteration of that."

Before 2010, only Indiana, Georgia, and Missouri had passed strict voter ID laws. Nine states controlled by Republicans adopted them following the 2010 election: Alabama, Kansas, Mississippi, Pennsylvania, South Carolina, Tennessee, Texas, Virginia, and Wisconsin.

The accelerated push for voter ID laws didn't emerge from nowhere. In 1980, Paul Weyrich, the tart-tongued first director of the Heritage Foundation, convened a gathering of fifteen thousand evangelical Christians for Ronald Reagan. Acolytes described Weyrich as "the Lenin of social conservatism." He said in his speech: "I don't want everybody to vote. Elections are not won by a majority of people, they never have been from the beginning of our country and they are not now. As a matter of fact, our leverage in the elections quite candidly goes up as the voting populace goes down."

Weyrich was also a key founder of a group called the American Legislative Exchange Council (ALEC), which paired conservative state legislators with large business interests to draft model legislation for states. For many years ALEC was the most influential organization that no one had ever heard of.

In the summer of 2009, ALEC drafted model voter ID legislation based on Indiana's voter ID law. A cover story in ALEC's magazine praised voter ID laws as "a strong step toward the prevention of fraud at the polls." (The group also launched an initiative called "Cracking Acorn," featuring a graphic of a hammer smashing an acorn, which urged states to defund the group.)

ALEC's Public Safety and Elections Task Force adopted the voter ID measure during a meeting in Atlanta in July 2009. The drafting and discussion were led by three conservative state legislators, including the Arizona state senator Russell Pearce, the author of Arizona's controversial anti-illegal immigration law, which the Supreme Court later struck down. A mix of fifty state legislators, corporations, and conservative advocacy groups, including the NRA, overwhelmingly approved the measure.

Of the sixty-two voter ID bills introduced in thirty-seven states in 2011 and 2012, more than half were sponsored by members of ALEC, including in Texas. The bills were virtually identical. "We're seeing the same legislation being proposed state by state by state," said Heather Smith of Rock the Vote.

The new restrictions went well beyond voter ID. They were designed to impede voters at every step of the electoral process, targeting the very methods that the Obama campaign had used so successfully in 2008 to expand the electorate, like intensive voter registration drives and early voting.

During the 2008 election, the number of registered voters in the United States increased by 5 percent, from 177 million to 187 million. In the twenty-nine states that recorded party affiliation, roughly two-thirds of new voters registered as Democrats. Obama won nearly 70 percent of the country's 15 million first-time voters.

GOP-controlled states responded by making voter registration more difficult. Alabama, Kansas, and Tennessee required proof of citizenship to register. Maine repealed Election Day voter registration. Florida and Texas added stringent requirements for third-party registration groups.

Florida required that anyone who registered new voters had to hand in the forms to the state board of elections within forty-eight hours and comply with a barrage of onerous bureaucratic requirements. Those who submitted

late forms would face a thousand-dollar fine, as well as possible felony pros-
ecution. The measure was drafted by Bucky Mitchell, the elections official
who had overseen Florida's disastrous voter purge in 2000.

The law turned civic-minded volunteers, like Dawn Quarles, a public
school teacher from Pace, Florida, into inadvertent criminals. She was the
first person fined by the state for failing to turn in seventy-six registration
forms from her students within forty-eight hours, even though she hadn't
even heard about the new law. "We have the worst voter turnout of any Western democracy and this is the reason why," Quarles said.

The normally mild-mannered League of Women Voters denounced the
law as "good old-fashioned voter suppression" and shut down voter registration drives in the state for the first time in seventy years because its
volunteers were unable to comply with the state's stringent requirements.
Black and Hispanic citizens in Florida were twice as likely as whites to
register through such drives.

Florida's registration law took effect one day after it passed, under an
emergency statute—as in Texas—designed for "an immediate danger to the
public health, safety or welfare." Sponsors of the bill invoked ACORN to
justify the law, even though there had been only thirty-one suspected cases
of voter fraud in Florida during the previous three years, resulting in three
arrests statewide. There were more shark attacks in Florida than cases of
voter fraud. "No one could give me an example of all this fraud they speak
about," said Mike Fasano, a Republican state senator who bucked his party
and voted against the registration law.

In addition to making it harder to register to vote, five states—Florida,
Georgia, Ohio, Tennessee, and West Virginia—cut short their early voting
periods.

After the recount debacle in Florida in 2000 and the long lines in Ohio
in 2004, allowing voters to cast their ballots before Election Day had
emerged as a popular bipartisan reform. "I think it's great," Florida's
governor, Jeb Bush, said in 2004. "It's another reform we added that has
helped provide access to the polls and provide a convenience. And we're
going to have a high voter turnout here, and I think that's wonderful." Early
voting was particularly important for lower-income and minority voters,
who had a harder time taking off work on Election Day and were more

likely to vote at underresourced polling places with fewer poll workers and voting machines, which led to longer lines and more frequent problems.

But Republican support for early voting receded after the Obama campaign utilized the reform as a key part of its strategy in 2008. Nearly 30 percent of the electorate voted early, and those voters favored Obama over McCain by ten points. The strategy proved especially effective in Florida, where blacks outnumbered whites by two to one among early voters, and in Ohio, where Obama received fewer votes than McCain on Election Day but ended up winning the state because of his advantage among early voters in cities like Cleveland and Columbus.

After 2008, early voting was shrunk from fourteen to eight days in Florida and from thirty-five to eleven days in Ohio. Both states also banned voting on the Sunday before the election, when black churches held Souls to the Polls rallies. "In the races I was involved in in 2008, when we started seeing the increase of turnout and the turnout operations that the Democrats were doing in early voting, it certainly sent a chill down our spines," said Wayne Bertsch, a Republican campaign consultant in Florida.

Ex-felons who had paid their debt to society also lost their right to vote in Florida and Iowa. Charlie Crist, Florida's Republican governor from 2007 to 2011, had repealed the state's felon disenfranchisement law and restored the voting rights of 154,000 former prisoners who had been convicted of nonviolent crimes. But in March 2011, after only thirty minutes of public debate, Florida's governor, Rick Scott, overturned his predecessor's decision, instantly disenfranchising 97,491 ex-felons and prohibiting another 1.1 million prisoners—nearly 20 percent of African-American voters in Florida—from being allowed to vote after serving their sentences. "In record time, Florida's Cabinet brought us back to Jim Crow–era laws," *The Miami Herald* editorialized.

In total, the new restrictions made it more difficult for more than five million Americans to vote, a larger number than the margin of victory in the 2000 and 2004 presidential elections. States with new voting restrictions accounted for 218 of the 270 electoral votes needed to win the presidency. This new attack on voting rights had an unprecedented breadth and depth— it wasn't just concentrated in the South, as during Jim Crow—nor did it target only one segment of the population. Young voters, African-Americans,

Hispanics, the elderly, and the poor all were impacted by this massive re-structuring of the country's voting rules.

Since the VRA outlawed literacy tests and poll taxes, states had focused on diluting the power of the growing minority vote rather than denying access to the ballot. In the decades after 1965, the fight over voting rights had centered on the value of the vote, not on the right to vote itself. But after Obama's election, the climax of decades of struggle to win greater represen-tation, vote denial efforts returned with a vengeance. The high point of the Second Reconstruction spawned a Second Redemption backlash.

The new measures were more sophisticated and less obvious than the poll taxes and literacy tests of yesteryear, but they had the same intended effect: to control who could participate in the democratic process and to once again make voting a privilege, not a fundamental right. As the demo-graphics of the country became younger, more diverse, and more progres-sive, the Republicans who took power after 2010 wanted the electorate to be older, whiter, and more conservative, as it had been in 2010, compared with 2008. "Of the 11 states with the highest African-American turnout in 2008, 7 have new restrictions in place," reported the Brennan Center for Justice. "Of the 12 states with the largest Hispanic population growth between 2000 and 2010, 9 passed laws making it harder to vote."

"There has never been in my lifetime, since we got rid of the poll tax and all the Jim Crow burdens on voting, the determined effort to limit the fran-chise that we see today," Bill Clinton told a group of student activists in July 2011. "Why is all of this going on? This is not rocket science. They are try-ing to make the 2012 electorate look more like the 2010 electorate than the 2008 electorate."

A few unusually candid Republican leaders eventually admitted that fraud wasn't the real issue; race and political power were. The Pennsylvania house majority leader told GOP activists that the state's voter ID law would "allow Governor Romney to win the state of Pennsylvania." The GOP chair-man in Columbus, Ohio, defended cutbacks in early voting hours by telling *The Columbus Dispatch*: "I guess I really actually feel we shouldn't contort the voting process to accommodate the urban—read African-American—voter-turnout machine." The author of South Carolina's voter ID law dis-tributed packets of peanuts to his constituents with cards that read: "Stop Obama's nutty agenda and support voter ID."

In February 2011, Obama awarded the Presidential Medal of Freedom to John Lewis. "Generations from now, when parents teach their children what is meant by courage, the story of John Lewis will come to mind," the president said. Two months later Lewis was honored during the fiftieth anniversary of the Freedom Rides. Despite these accolades, Lewis did not feel like celebrating that July when he delivered an impassioned speech on the floor of the House of Representatives about the right to vote.

"Voting rights are under attack in America," Lewis said, his voice echoing through the nearly empty chamber. "There's a deliberate and systematic attempt to prevent millions of elderly voters, young voters, students, minority and low-income voters from exercising their constitutional right to engage in the democratic process."

Much to his dismay, Lewis said, "no one seemed to be listening." He pleaded with his friends in the Obama administration to urgently take up the fight.

In December 2011, Holder traveled to the LBJ Library in Austin, Texas, to deliver a major speech on voting rights. Before his talk, the attorney general looked up at a video screen in the library's auditorium and saw a picture of his sister-in-law standing next to Rosa Parks and Martin Luther King as LBJ handed out the pens he'd used to sign the VRA. He'd never known Vivian had been present on that historic day.

"I am concerned about some of the legislation that has been passed that recently goes against that arc of history and is tending to restrict, in ways subtle and not so subtle, the ability of the American people to cast their ballots," Holder said. He quoted Lewis's speech from the House floor and warned, "We are failing to live up to one of our nation's most noble, and essential, ideals."

The LBJ Library was a fitting setting for Holder's speech, not just for its history but because Texas had recently embodied how conservative officials were trying to limit the power of an increasingly diverse electorate.

The state's redistricting plan for Congress and the statehouse initially drew the ire of the Justice Department. Texas gained 4.3 million new residents from 2000 to 2010, and 90 percent of that growth came from minority residents. Because of the population increase, the state gained four congressional seats following the 2010 census. Yet under the redistricting maps drawn by Texas Republicans in 2011, the number of majority-minority districts actually declined, from eleven to ten. Three of the four new seats went instead to white Republicans. The League of Women Voters called the plan "the most extreme example of racial gerrymandering among all the redistricting proposals passed by lawmakers so far this year."

Even though Texas had to clear its election changes with the federal government, the counsel to the state's congressional Republicans referred to key sections of the VRA as "hocus-pocus." The Justice Department objected to the new maps in fall 2011.

Six months later the DOJ objected to Texas's voter ID law. Texas's own data showed that between 600,000 and 795,000 registered voters lacked government-issued IDs and Hispanic voters were anywhere from 46 percent to 120 percent more likely than white voters to not have one. (The state submitted no information on how many blacks and Asians lacked IDs.) "Even using the data most favorable to the state, Hispanics disproportionately lack either a driver's license or a personal identification card issued by [the state], and that disparity is statistically significant," wrote Tom Perez, the assistant attorney general for civil rights.

There were other, less noticeable burdens attached to the new law. To obtain the free voter ID provided by the state, prospective voters had to provide supporting documentation confirming their identities, the cheapest option being a birth certificate for twenty-two dollars. Getting to a Department of Motor Vehicles office in Texas could be a trying affair. There were no DMV offices in 81 of the 254 counties in Texas, and some voters would have to travel up to 250 miles to get to one. Not surprisingly, counties with significant Hispanic populations were less likely to have a DMV office, while Hispanic residents in such counties were twice as likely as whites to not have the right ID, nor to have a car. Public transportation was virtually nonexistent outside major cities in Texas, making getting a voter ID all the more difficult.

Victoria and Nicole Rodriguez, eighteen-year-old twins from San Antonio and freshmen at St. Mary's University, were two of the hundreds of thousands of registered voters without acceptable voter IDs. The Rodriguez sisters never had driver's licenses because it was too expensive for their mother to add them to her car insurance. Their father worked during business hours, and their mother took care of their grandmother, meaning they'd have to get the bus to the closest DMV office, which took an hour round-trip.

Victoria testified for the Justice Department when a federal court in Washington heard the Texas voter ID case in June 2012. "I was able to use my student ID on the airplane when they flew us out to DC," she said. "And I was able to get into the hotel, just with my student ID. And I was able to get into the district court, just with my student ID. But I wasn't able to use it to vote."

In June 2012, the GOP-controlled House of Representatives voted to hold Holder in contempt of Congress for allegedly failing to provide documents in the Operation Fast and Furious gunrunning scandal—a first for a sitting cabinet member. The Congressional Black Caucus walked out of the House chamber in protest.

The word "embattled" stuck to Holder like gum on a shoe. *The New York Times* had described Holder as "mild, self-deprecating, even eager to please" in a profile after Obama's election, but that was not how he was regarded in Washington. He'd been a controversial attorney general from the start, a target for the right since he'd said, during Black History Month in 2009, that America had been a "nation of cowards" when it came to discussing race.

He was also under siege from the left for failing to reverse the Bush administration's erosion of civil liberties or to prosecute Wall Street banks for fraud. To the right, he might as well have been a member of the Black Panther Party. Indeed, foes like Hans von Spakovsky accused him of killing an investigation into the New Black Panther Party that had begun in the waning days of the Bush administration.

During a congressional hearing on the case, the Texas representative John Culberson, a Houston Republican, told him: "There's clearly evidence, overwhelming evidence, that your Department of Justice refuses to protect the rights of anybody other than African Americans to vote."

"I would disagree very vehemently with the notion that there's overwhelming evidence that that is in fact true," Holder responded.

Holder returned to Texas the day after the state's voter ID trial had begun to defend his department's efforts to protect voting rights, speaking at the NAACP convention in Houston. He singled out Texas for particular scrutiny, noting that a handgun permit was an acceptable voter ID in the state but a student ID was not. "Especially in recent months, Texas, *Texas*, has—in many ways—been at the center of our national debate about voting rights issues," Holder said.

He explained why the DOJ had objected to the law. "Many of those without IDs would have to travel great distances to get them—and some would struggle to pay for the documents they might need to obtain them." He then added a much-discussed line that was not in the prepared text of the speech: "We call those poll taxes." Audience members applauded loudly. "Let me be clear," Holder continued, "let me be very clear: we will not allow political pretexts to disenfranchise American citizens of their most precious right."

Holder's poll tax comment set off a barrage of debate, but it was technically accurate. A poll tax in Alabama in the 1960s cost roughly ten dollars, adjusted for inflation, while the birth certificate needed to obtain an allegedly free voter ID in Texas cost twice as much.

In the late summer of 2012, the federal district court in Washington sided with the DOJ in the Texas redistricting and voter ID cases. On August 28, the court found that Texas's redistricting maps were "enacted with discriminatory purpose." Two days later the court rejected Texas's voter ID law for three reasons: "(1) a substantial subgroup of Texas voters, many of whom are African American or Hispanic, lack photo ID; (2) the burdens associated with obtaining ID will weigh most heavily on the poor; and (3) racial minorities in Texas are disproportionately likely to live in poverty."

Notably, the court found that the law did, in fact, amount to a modern-day poll tax. "A law that forces poorer citizens to choose between their wages and their franchise unquestionably denies or abridges their right to vote," the court wrote. Federal courts also blocked South Carolina's voter ID law for 2012 and overturned Florida's restrictions on early voting in the five counties in the state subject to Section 5.

These victories for Holder's DOJ signaled a major shift in the voting wars. Suddenly, Republicans pushing new voting restrictions found themselves on the defensive.

In states not subject to Section 5, civil rights groups like the NAACP and ACLU successfully filed suit to halt restrictive voting laws in crucial swing states like Ohio, Pennsylvania, and Wisconsin. On the eve of the election, state or local courts had blocked ten major voting restrictions, including voter ID laws (Missouri, Pennsylvania, Texas, and Wisconsin), limits on voter registration drives (Florida), cutbacks to early voting (Ohio), partisan voter purges (Iowa), hurdles to student voting (New Hampshire), and the disqualification of provisional ballots (Ohio).

Two Sundays before the election, Lewis traveled to Florida to speak at an Empowerment Sunday rally at Bo Diddley Plaza in Gainesville, urging black voters to cast their ballots after attending church. He told the story of Bloody Sunday and linked it to the present day. "There are forces in America that are trying to make it harder, more difficult for people to cast a vote," he said. "We must not let that happen."

A week later Lewis was in Ohio on the Sunday before the election. The Ohio GOP had tried to prevent early voting three days before the election, but the Obama campaign had successfully sued to reinstate those days. As he approached the Hamilton County Board of Elections, in Cincinnati, Lewis saw the line of voters stretching for nearly a mile around multiple blocks, with thousands waiting for hours in the damp cold. "This is very, very moving," Lewis said as he walked the line. "This is living testimony that people who tried to make it hard and difficult and who put up stumbling blocks and road blocks—it's just not working."

In Texas, with the voter ID law blocked, Victoria and Nicole Rodriguez were able to vote for the first time in their lives.

Despite the perseverance of many, the barriers and confusion resulting from the push to restrict voting rights turned the 2012 race into a case study of how not to run an election.

Floridians had six fewer days to vote, which led to much longer lines at the polls. Desiline Victor, a ninety-seven-year-old Haitian immigrant, had had no problems voting for the first time in her life in 2008. But when she went to her polling place in North Miami in 2012 on the first day of early voting, she waited for three hours before being told to return later in the day. When she returned that evening, poll workers moved her to the front of the line and she was able to cast a ballot. "I was happy when I finally cast my ballot," she said. "But I was also upset. In this great nation why should anybody have to stand in line for hours, and make two trips, to vote?"

Richard Jordan wasn't so lucky. He worked as a painter and went to his polling place in East Orlando at 4:30 p.m. on Election Day after finishing a ten-hour shift. After he had waited for three hours, the line had barely moved. His back hurt, and he needed water. Though he'd voted for more than a decade, Jordan reluctantly left without voting. The polls didn't close at his precinct until 11:00 p.m. Jordan was one of an estimated two hundred thousand Floridians who didn't vote in 2012 because of long lines.

"I want to thank every American who participated in this election," Obama said during his victory speech in Chicago, "whether you voted for the very first time or waited in line for a very long time." He then added, "By the way, we have to fix that."

The last voter in Florida cast his ballot at 2:03 a.m. in Miami, seven hours after the polls closed and four hours after Obama's victory speech. Across the country, blacks and Hispanics waited twice as long as whites to vote.

Still, voting rights activists greeted the election results with great relief. The new restrictions hadn't swung the election and, if anything, seemed to have backfired on the GOP. Compared with 2008, 1.7 million more blacks, 1.4 million more Hispanics, and 550,000 more Asians went to the polls, versus 2 million fewer whites. The turnout rate among black voters exceeded that of whites for the first time on record, according to the Census Bureau. While the turnout rate fell among nearly every demographic group, the largest increase came from blacks sixty-five and over. Those, like Lewis, who had lived through the days when merely trying to register could get you killed were the ones most determined to defend their rights in 2012.

A year after his visit to the LBJ Library, Holder traveled to Boston following the election to give another major speech about voting rights at the JFK Library. The fight was far from over, he warned. "The unfortunate reality is that, even today, too many citizens have reason to fear that their right to vote, their access to the ballot—and their ability to have their votes counted—is under threat," he said. Just three days after Obama's reelection, the Supreme Court agreed to hear a new challenge to Section 5, which Holder called the "keystone of our voting rights."

It all started with a two-vote election in Alabama.

Before local elections in 2008, the town of Calera, in central Alabama, redrew its city boundaries. Locals used to call the once-sleepy area, fifty-five miles north of Selma, Pineville. It had one main road, U.S. 31, and a quaint two-block downtown, surrounded by woods. Its main attraction was the Heart of Dixie Railroad Museum. But over the past decade, Calera had become the fastest-growing city in the state, increasing from three thousand to twelve thousand people, and adding new businesses like Walmart and Cracker Barrel off the busy I-65 highway running from Birmingham to Montgomery.

The black voting-age population in Calera had also grown, from 13 percent in 2004 to 16 percent in 2008, but the new maps eliminated the city council's lone majority-black district, represented by Ernest Montgomery since 2004. Montgomery was only the second black officeholder in the town's history.

Calera decreased the black voting-age population in Montgomery's district from 71 to 30 percent by adding three overwhelmingly white subdivisions while failing to include a large surrounding black neighborhood. A day before the election the DOJ objected to the change. Calera could have preserved the majority-black district, the city's demographer told officials in Washington, but the city council chose not to. Calera held the election in defiance of Justice Department orders, and Montgomery lost by two votes. "I had no knowledge of any of this until after the election," he said.

Montgomery was a soft-spoken precision machinist who built water valves for companies and municipalities. He held the same job since graduating from technical school and had been married to his high school sweetheart for thirty-four years. He spent all his time at work, with the city council, or helping out at his church.

Montgomery was born in 1957, when 85 percent of whites, but only 17 percent of blacks, were registered to vote in Calera's Shelby County. He grew up going to segregated schools until junior high, when he was bused to a predominantly white school. "I can remember a lot of violence, a lot of talking," he said. "White parents said they would be dead before they'd allow their children to go to school with black children." The Klan had an active presence in Shelby County, shooting up the church of a preacher who was involved with the civil rights movement and castrating a black man accused of impregnating a white lady.

Still, Montgomery didn't think race was as big an issue in Calera as it was in other parts of the state. That changed in 2008, when he knocked on doors in the lily-white subdivisions of his new district, which he knew well from his time on the city planning commission, and was told by residents that they were supporting his opponent, an office manager for a food supply company who'd lived in the town for only three years. When he asked why, they couldn't give him a good reason. Montgomery could come to only one conclusion: "They voted against me because of the color of my skin."

The DOJ negated the 2008 election results, and after a year of negotiations, Calera moved from single-member districts to an at-large election plan for the city council. Montgomery was easily elected under the new system, winning the largest number of votes of any candidate, while his opponent from 2008 received the second fewest. After the two elections, "I realized how important Section 5 is," Montgomery said.

That would have been the end of it—if Ed Blum hadn't read the objection on the DOJ's website and called Shelby County's lawyer, Frank "Butch" Ellis, urging him to challenge Section 5.

Ellis had been the county's lawyer since 1964. He had a long history in the area. His father, Handy, had been chairman of the Alabama delegation at the 1948 Democratic convention that walked out in protest after Harry Truman endorsed a civil rights platform.

Shelby County, a wealthy, white-flight exurb of Birmingham, was one of those southern counties that moved from solidly Democratic to deeply Republican after the 1960s. Romney won 76 percent of the vote there in 2012. The Alabama Republican Party held its Election Night party at a gun range in Shelby County, where attendees fired away while awaiting election returns. Its nine-member county commission consisted of eight white men and one white woman. It wasn't the type of place that much liked the VRA, especially under the control of a black president and black attorney general. Blum and Ellis filed the suit in early 2010. The brief claimed that "Section 5's federalism cost is too great" and the statute had "accomplished [its] mission."

Civil rights groups found it highly ironic that a county in Alabama, of all places, would make such a claim. "The Voting Rights Act is Alabama's gift to our country," Debo Adegbile, counsel for the NAACP Legal Defense Fund, said at a mass meeting in Shelby County. The disputed election in Calera was "a textbook example of why you need Section 5," said Sam Bagenstos, the deputy assistant attorney general for civil rights under Holder. The

DOJ had objected to four other discriminatory annexations in Shelby County since 1975 under the Ford, Carter, Reagan, and Clinton administrations. Kevin Myles, southeast regional director for the NAACP, compared the challenge with "a fox filing a lawsuit saying the chicken coop is too secure."

Yet Blum called Shelby County "the ideal plaintiff because they are unable to bail out of Section 5." Unlike in the *NAMUDNO* case, the Supreme Court would be forced to consider the constitutionality of Section 5 head-on. Blum's suit became a cause célèbre in the conservative moment, attracting support from Republican attorneys general in Alabama, Alaska, Arizona, Georgia, South Carolina, South Dakota, and Texas.

The rhetoric used by outspoken critics of the VRA was reminiscent of the Civil War. When asked about Section 5 at a Republican presidential debate in South Carolina, Rick Perry declared, "Texas is under assault by the federal government. I'm saying also that South Carolina is at war with this federal government and with this administration."

Shelby County lost in the district court and appeals court, but by the time the lawsuit reached the Supreme Court, the bipartisan consensus that supported the VRA for nearly fifty years, including in 2006, had collapsed. There had been more lawsuits challenging the constitutionality of Section 5 in 2011 and 2012 than during the previous four decades combined.

Shelby County v. Holder pitted the traditionalists in the GOP, who had long backed the VRA, against the ascendant counterrevolutionaries.

The counterrevolution's most influential players in the Reagan and Bush II administrations—Brad Reynolds, Chuck Cooper, Hans von Spakovsky, and Brad Schlozman—filed an amicus brief supporting *Shelby County*. It faulted the DOJ for refusing to approve voter ID laws in Texas and South Carolina in 2012. "Rather than heed this Court's repeated calls for restraint, Congress' and DOJ's recent actions have only worsened the grave constitutional flaws of Section 5."

The brief drew a heated response from Dick Thornburgh, the attorney general from 1988 to 1991, and the heads of the Civil Rights Division under Clinton, Bush I, Carter, and Ford. "Far from raising constitutional concerns, the recent enforcement of Section 5 demonstrates its continued necessity and vitality," they wrote.

The Supreme Court heard oral arguments on the morning of February 27, 2013, a day after the 144th anniversary of Congress's passing the Fifteenth Amendment.

Ernest Montgomery sat in the packed courtroom, alongside civil rights icons like John Lewis. Blum was there too, hoping for an entirely different outcome.

History had come full circle. Shelby County's lawyer, Bert Rein, had once clerked for Justice John Harlan, one of two justices to dissent in the *Allen v. State Board of Elections* case, which established Section 5 as a centerpiece of the VRA in 1969.

Rein began by referring to the *NAMUDNO* case. "Those Justices recognized that the record before the Congress in 2005 made it unmistakable that the South had changed," he said. "They questioned whether current remedial needs justified the extraordinary federalism and cost burdens of preclearance."

Justice Sotomayor interjected. "Assuming I accept your premise, and there's some question about that, that some portions of the South have changed, your county pretty much hasn't," she said. "Why would we vote in favor of a county whose record is the epitome of what caused the passage of this law to start with?"

"Well, I don't agree with your premises," Rein responded, "but let me just say, number one, when I said the South has changed, that is the statement that is made by the eight justices in the *Northwest Austin* case."

As with the prior challenge to the VRA, Roberts said nothing during Rein's presentation. But he interrupted Solicitor General Donald Verrilli, who argued the case for the United States, within a minute.

Roberts: "Do you know which State has the worst ratio of white voter turnout to African-American voter turnout?"

Verrilli: "I do not."

Roberts: "Massachusetts. Do you know where African-American turnout actually exceeds white turnout? Mississippi."

Verrilli: "Yes, Mr. Chief Justice. But Congress recognized that expressly in the findings when it reauthorized the act in 2006. It said that the first generation problems had been largely dealt with, but there persisted significant . . ."

Roberts: "Which State has the greatest disparity in registration between white and African-American?"

Verrilli: "I do not know that."

Roberts: "Massachusetts. Third is Mississippi, where again the African-American registration rate is higher than the white registration rate."

Verrilli: "Congress wasn't writing on a blank slate in 2006, Mr. Chief Justice. It faced a choice. And the choice was whether the conditions were such that it could confidently conclude that this deterrence and this constraint was no longer needed . . . Congress made a cautious choice in 2006 to keep the constraint and to keep the deterrence in place."

The chief justice had his facts wrong. In 2008, Mississippi ranked eighth in black voter turnout, and Massachusetts twenty-sixth. Despite this disparity, the comparison was highly misleading. Massachusetts, 8 percent black, had elected the first black senator since Reconstruction in 1966 and currently had a black governor, while Mississippi, 37 percent black, had never elected a black official to statewide office. Obama won 56 percent of the white vote in Massachusetts in 2012 but only 10 percent in Mississippi. Massachusetts was hardly a racist backwater, and Mississippi was far from a postracial utopia.

Nonetheless confident in his argument, Roberts returned to interrogating Verrilli a few minutes later.

Roberts: "General, is it the government's submission that the citizens in the South are more racist than citizens in the North?"

Verrilli: "It is not, and I do not know the answer to that, your honor, but I do think it was reasonable for Congress . . ."

Roberts: "Well, once you said it is not, and you don't know the answer to it."

Verrilli: "As an objective matter, I don't know the answer to that question. But what I do know is that Congress had before it evidence that there was a continuing need based on Section 5 objections, based on the purpose-based character of those objections, based on the disparate Section 2 rate, based on the persistence of polarized voting, and based on a gigantic wealth of jurisdiction-specific and anecdotal evidence, that there was a continuing need."

Roberts: "A need to do what?"

Verrilli: "To maintain the deterrent and constraining effect of the Section 5 preclearance process in the covered jurisdictions."

Roberts: "And not impose it on everyone else?"

To Roberts and his conservative colleagues, those states with the longest histories of voting discrimination were now the ones being discriminated against.

"If Alabama wants to have monuments to the heroes of the civil rights movement, if it wants to acknowledge the wrongs of its past, is it better off doing that if it's an independent sovereign or if it's under the trusteeship of the United States government?" Justice Kennedy, the ostensible swing vote, asked Verrilli.

"Of course this is aimed at states," Justice Breyer responded. "What do you think the Civil War was about?"

To rebut the conservative justices, Verrilli repeatedly invoked Congress's overwhelming reauthorization of the VRA in 2006. But to critics of the VRA, the legislation's popularity paradoxically served as evidence of its unconstitutionality.

"I think it is attributable, very likely attributable, to a phenomenon that is called perpetuation of racial entitlement," Justice Scalia said fifty-one minutes in. "It's been written about. Whenever a society adopts racial entitlements, it is very difficult to get out of them through the normal political processes. I don't think there is anything to be gained by any senator to vote against continuation of this act. And I am fairly confident it will be reenacted in perpetuity unless a court can say it does not comport with the Constitution . . . You have to show, when you are treating different states differently, that there's a good reason for it. This is not the kind of a question you can leave to Congress."

After the courtroom murmured with shock, Justice Sotomayor asked Rein, "Do you think that the right to vote is a racial entitlement in Section 5?"

"No," he responded.

"Why should we make the judgment, and not Congress, about the types and forms of discrimination and the need to remedy them?" Sotomayor followed up.

"I think the problem to which the Voting Rights Act was addressed is solved," Rein said.

"You said the problem has been solved," Justice Kagan interjected. "But who gets to make that judgment really? Is it you, is it the Court, or is it Congress?"

"I think the question is Congress can examine it, Congress makes a record; it is up to the Court to determine whether the problem indeed has been solved," Rein responded.

"Well, that's a big new power that you are giving us, that we have the power now to decide whether racial discrimination has been solved," Kagan said. "I did not think that that fell within our bailiwick."

The argument was most notable for what was not said. Remarkably, there was no discussion of the new voting restrictions in 2012 that, as Lewis put it, "dramatized the need for Section 5."

The justices did not hear, for example, that six of the nine fully covered states under Section 5 had passed new voting restrictions since 2010, including voter ID laws (Alabama, Mississippi, South Carolina, Texas, and Virginia), limits on early voting (Georgia), and restrictions on voter registration (Alabama and Texas), compared with only one-third of noncovered jurisdictions during the same period. Nor did they hear that the Justice Department and federal courts had blocked four major discriminatory voting changes from becoming law in 2012 under Section 5.

What had changed in recent years wasn't so much the South as the fact that states like Kansas and Ohio and Pennsylvania and Wisconsin had adopted southern-born barriers to the ballot box. But when the potent remedy of the VRA was needed the most, a majority on the Court seemed to believe that the illness of voting discrimination had been cured.

A law that eight justices had praised as "a valid effectuation of the Fifteenth Amendment" in 1966 had been transformed into a "racial entitlement" that only the Supreme Court was brave enough to end. Scalia's comment captured the headlines, but he was only stating, in more graphic form, the prevailing views of the Roberts Court.

When the Court recessed at eleven-thirty, Lewis hurried across the street to catch the unveiling of the new statue of Rosa Parks at the U.S. Capitol.

Congressman Jim Clyburn of South Carolina was the only speaker at the ceremony to note the irony of Congress's honoring Parks at the same time that the Supreme Court was hearing a challenge to the legislation bearing her name.

"One hour ago, I sat across the street witnessing the opening arguments of a voting rights case before the United States Supreme Court—a case that many feel could turn the clock back on much of the progress that has been made, and for which we pause today to honor Rosa Parks," he said.

Lewis got to the Capitol at the tail end of the ceremony, but his mind was elsewhere. He said he almost cried when Justice Scalia compared the VRA with a "racial entitlement."

"So what happened to the Fourteenth and Fifteenth Amendments?" he asked, shaking his head. "What happened to the whole struggle to make it possible in the twentieth century, and now the twenty-first, for every person to be able to cast a free and open vote?"

He was also deeply disturbed by the conservative justices' preoccupation with the sovereign dignity of states like Alabama.

"You heard it all those years in the South: 'Why you picking on the South? Why you selected the South? Why you select Alabama?'" Lewis exclaimed. "Alabama selected herself. It's history—Alabama and Georgia, and the eleven states of the old Confederacy, they did it.

"Places like Georgia, Alabama, Mississippi, they forget recent history. We're not talking about something that took place a hundred years ago, but a few short years ago. And some of it is still going on right today. And if you get rid of Section 5 of the Voting Rights Act, many of these places will slip back to the habits of the past."

On May 20, 1961, Lewis and two dozen Freedom Riders traveling through the South were assaulted by a frenzied mob at the Greyhound bus station in Montgomery, Alabama. Lewis was struck over the head with a Coca-Cola crate and left lying unconscious in a pool of blood. The Freedom Riders sought refuge at the First Baptist Church, pastored by Ralph Abernathy, disguising themselves as members of the choir to avoid police scrutiny. Three thousand white supremacists surrounded the church the next night and hurled Molotov cocktails through the stained glass windows. "That night was unbelievable," Lewis remembered. "I thought some of us would die." After tortured deliberation, President Kennedy sent in federal marshals to escort the Freedom Riders to safety.

On March 2, 2013, when Lewis returned to the First Baptist Church on a civil rights pilgrimage to Alabama with two hundred guests, including thirty members of Congress, Chief Kevin Murphy, head of the Montgomery Police Department, unexpectedly apologized to him. "We enforced unjust laws," Murphy said. It was the first apology Lewis had ever received from a law enforcement official in the Deep South, after forty arrests and countless near-death experiences. They embraced, as the congregation cheered and wept, and Murphy gave Lewis his badge.

"Chief Murphy, my brother, I accept your apology," Lewis responded. "I don't think I'm worthy of this." Then he joked: "Actually, do you think I could get another?" Lewis kept the badge in his pocket for days. "I want to say to all of you here, it shows the power of love, the power of peace, the power of nonviolence," he said.

The Montgomery Advertiser featured Murphy's apology on its front page. Next to it, however, was a story about how if the Supreme Court overturned Section 5, Republicans might dismantle the majority-black legislative districts protected under the law, which illustrated the South's continuing racial divide. Obama, the article noted, won 95 percent of the black vote in Alabama in 2012, but only 15 percent of the white vote. "Whites won't vote for blacks in Alabama," said the state senator Hank Sanders of Selma. "That's the state of race relations."

The next morning Lewis rode from Selma to Montgomery, following in reverse the route he'd marched forty-eight years earlier. Selma was now a stronghold of black political power, with a black mayor, a black congresswoman, and six black city council members. But economically, it was like so many other poor towns across the country, with too few jobs and too much crime. Lewis's bus passed scores of dilapidated houses on its way to Brown Chapel, a sobering reminder of the gains yet to be won.

He embraced Holder when he walked into the historic redbrick church. Lewis asked to be a "regular pew member," and listened intently as the Reverend James Forbes of Riverside Church in New York animatedly told the story of Cain and Abel, linking the blood of the brothers to Bloody Sunday. "Y'all need to know that God watches voting," Forbes said. "It doesn't matter what kind of voter suppression method."

After the service, Holder spoke at the foot of the Edmund Pettus Bridge, behind a giant American flag draped over an old brick building. "Although our nation has indeed changed, although the South is far different now, and although progress has indeed been made, we're not yet at the point where the most vital part of the Voting Rights Act, Section 5, can be deemed unnecessary," he said.

The large crowd began chanting, in what had to be a first, "Section 5! Section 5!"

Three months later, on June 25, 2013, John Roberts calmly read the highlights of his majority opinion in *Shelby County v. Holder* from the bench.

The chief justice noted the dramatic increase in black registration and "examples of progress more poignant than the numbers," such as black mayors in Selma and Philadelphia, Mississippi.

"Any racial discrimination in voting is too much, but our country has changed in the past 50 years," Roberts said. "When taking such extraordinary steps as subjecting state legislation to preclearance in Washington and applying that regime only to some disfavored states, Congress must ensure that the legislation it passes speaks to current conditions. The coverage formula, unchanged for 40 years, plainly does not do so and therefore we have no choice but to find that it violates the Constitution."

In a shrewd political maneuver, Roberts and the four concurring conservative justices had invalidated not Section 5 of the VRA but instead Section 4, the formula devised in 1965 that eliminated literacy tests in the states with the worst histories of voting discrimination and instructed them to approve their voting changes with the federal government to prevent future discrimination. These states had now been freed from federal oversight. Roberts's opinion turned Section 5 into a zombie, a body with no life in it.

The same Court that had upheld the constitutionality of Section 5 on four previous occasions had finally accomplished what longtime opponents of the VRA in the legislative and executive branches, including a young Roberts in the 1980s, had failed to do. Eight years earlier, Roberts told the Senate that the constitutionality of the VRA had been settled. In fact, curbing the VRA and similar laws aimed at remedying historic discrimination had become his signature project as chief justice. The Court's five conservative justices all had been appointed by Reagan or served in his administration. The *Shelby County* decision showcased how the counterrevolution against civil rights had captured the highest echelons of power in the United States.

After Roberts finished, eighty-one-year-old Ruth Bader Ginsburg, the oldest member of the Court, read a ten-minute summary of her fiery dissent.

"The Court points to the success of Section 5 in eliminating the tests and devices extant in 1965 and in increasing citizen's registration and ballot access," she said in her high-pitched New York City accent. "Does that provide cause to believe Section 5's potent remedy is no longer needed?"

Her thirty-seven-page written dissent with Justices Breyer, Kagan, and Sotomayor was much more scathing. "In the Court's view, the very success of Section 5 of the Voting Rights Act demands its dormancy," read the first line. It continued: "Throwing out preclearance when it has worked and is continuing to work to stop discriminatory changes is like throwing away your umbrella in a rainstorm because you are not getting wet."

The scope and longevity of the VRA were a decision best made by Congress, not the courts, Ginsburg said. "It was the judgment of Congress that 40 years has not been a sufficient amount of time to eliminate the vestiges of discrimination. That judgment of the body empowered to enforce the Civil War Amendments by appropriate legislation should garner this Court's unstinting approbation."

She viewed the *Shelby* decision as a radical act of judicial activism by five justices appointed to the Court on the basis of their stated belief in judicial restraint.

"Congress approached the 2006 reauthorization of the VRA with great care and seriousness," her written dissent read. "The same cannot be said of the Court's opinion today . . . Hubris is a fit word for today's demolition of the VRA."

She closed her remarks from the bench by invoking the pivotal events that led to the passage of the VRA. "The arc of the moral universe is long," Ginsburg said, quoting King's famous line at the end of the march from Selma to Montgomery, "but it bends toward justice *if* there is a steadfast commitment to see the task through to completion.

"That commitment has been disserved by today's decision."

Armand Derfner, who argued the *Allen* case in 1969, was among the spectators sitting in the hushed courtroom. "Everybody was just kind of numb," he said.

The VRA's formula was far from perfect—it covered only five counties in Florida and forty counties in North Carolina and did not apply to recent violators like Ohio—but Derfner knew from four decades as a voting rights lawyer that a flawed Section 5 was far better than none.

By chance, he'd sat next to Blum on the plane from Charleston to Washington for the oral arguments in the case. He asked Blum the same question a conservative white southerner on the Richmond City Council had asked him decades earlier: "How can a nice man like you do such awful things?"

Blum celebrated on the steps of the Supreme Court following the ruling. "This decision restores an important constitutional order to our system of government, which requires that all fifty states are entitled to equal dignity and sovereignty," he said.

Elected officials across the South, who were prevented from implementing discriminatory voting changes under Section 5, swiftly praised the decision. "Eric Holder can no longer deny #VoterID in #Texas after today's #SCOTUS decision," the Texas attorney general, Greg Abbott, tweeted minutes after.

"The Supreme Court did itself proud," Abigail Thernstrom wrote in *The Wall Street Journal*. "The court's ruling Tuesday will benefit black America."

The first black attorney general and first black president strenuously contested Thernstrom's prediction.

"This decision represents a serious setback for voting rights," Holder said at the Department of Justice, "and has the potential to negatively affect millions of Americans across the country."

Obama was in Senegal, touring Goree Island, where Africans had been sent as slaves to board ships to the Americas, when he commented on the decision. "I might not be here as President had it not been for those who courageously helped to pass the Voting Rights Act," he said.

Alvin Holmes of Montgomery, the longest-serving black legislator in the Alabama House of Representatives, remarked: "I know Dr. Martin Luther King Jr. is turning over in his grave."

In Calera, Ernest Montgomery couldn't believe the decision. "Disappointed isn't even the word for it," he said.

Lewis stayed away from the Supreme Court that day. He couldn't bear to be in the courtroom when the justices struck down his signature achievement. "It would've been too much," he said.

He watched the news in his congressional office, a shrine to the civil rights movement. The walls were lined with black-and-white photos of Lewis speaking at the March on Washington, marching in Selma, conferring with LBJ, and touring the South with Julian Bond. He received the news from two TVs mounted above busts of LBJ and RFK.

"I'm shocked, dismayed, disappointed," he said that morning. "I take it very personally." He felt like crying but put on a brave face for the cameras.

Since the 1950s the Supreme Court had been an ally to civil rights activists like Lewis. Now it was his greatest foe.

"These men never stood in unmovable lines," Lewis said. "They were never denied the right to participate in the democratic process. They were never beaten, jailed, run off their farms or fired from their jobs. No one they knew died simply trying to register to vote. They are not the victims of gerrymandering or contemporary unjust schemes to maneuver them out of their constitutional rights."

A year earlier Lewis learned from the PBS show *Finding Your Roots* that his great-great-grandfather Tobias had registered and voted in Alabama after becoming an emancipated slave following the Civil War—something that Lewis and his family could not do until nearly one hundred years later. He wept when he heard the news. It underscored how fragile the right to vote had been throughout American history.

"History did not end in 1965," Roberts wrote in the *Shelby* decision. But to Lewis, the chief justice's opinion ignored the long history of voting discrimination that led to the VRA and the persistent attempts to restrict voting rights after 1965 that made the law, particularly Section 5, so essential. Between 1965 and 2013, more than three thousand discriminatory voting changes had been blocked by the courts and the Justice Department under Section 5. Roberts emphasized only the progress that had been made since 1965, disregarding the history in the decades after that told a much more complicated and somber story.

Lewis's amicus brief before the Court highlighted "the unfounded belief that our history of voting rights has been one of consistent progress." In fact, "the narrative of voting rights, as evidenced by the story of Congressman Lewis' own ancestors, is one of a cycle of retrenchment and reconstruction."

Roberts's opinion was a striking product of the states' rights federalism doctrine championed by his mentor, Justice Rehnquist, who had wanted to return America to the principles of the pre–Civil War Constitution. Roberts based the *Shelby* decision on what he called "a 'fundamental principle of equal sovereignty' among the states," which he first cited in the *NAMUDNO* case. It was a doctrine rooted in the darkest chapter of American history.

In the infamous 1857 case *Dred Scott v. Sandford*, the Supreme Court ruled that African-Americans, whether free or enslaved, could not be full citizens of the United States because to do so would violate the equal sovereignty of the slave states. "Shelby County is the first decision since Dred Scott to invoke the doctrine of equal sovereignty where the right to vote was involved," the civil rights lawyers Jim Blacksher and Lani Guinier wrote in the *Harvard Law & Policy Review* following the decision.

The Reconstruction Amendments were passed after the Civil War to give full citizenship to black Americans and to make clear that the federal government's interest in prohibiting racial discrimination trumped the sovereignty of the former slave states. The Supreme Court, however, refused to aggressively administer the amendments and to protect the voting rights of newly enfranchised black Americans like Tobias Lewis.

Jackson Giles, the president and founder of the Colored Men's Suffrage Association of Alabama, had registered and voted in Montgomery for thirty years before he was disenfranchised by the poll tax and literacy test requirements of the 1901 Alabama Constitution. Giles had taken the case to the Supreme Court on behalf of five thousand black residents of Montgomery, alleging that Alabama's new voter registration laws violated the Fourteenth and Fifteenth Amendments.

In a 6–3 decision in 1903, Justice Oliver Wendell Holmes stated that the Supreme Court did not have the authority to invalidate the disenfranchising provisions of Alabama's constitution. Holmes told Giles that "relief from a great political wrong, if done, as alleged, by the people of a state and the state itself, must be given by them or by the legislative and political department of the government of the United States."

Lewis and civil rights activists sought that relief six decades later by appealing to the Congress and the president to pass the VRA. "Perhaps no statute in American history has been the subject of more sustained consideration by Congress than the VRA," wrote Congressmen Sensenbrenner and Watt in their amicus brief. Now the Supreme Court was overruling that extensive judgment of Congress, whose power Holmes had conferred on the legislative body instead of the courts, once again failing to protect voting rights by invoking states' rights, as it had done after the Civil War.

"This Court's expansive reading of state sovereignty," Lewis's brief stated, led to "the end of Reconstruction."

The Supreme Court's failure to enforce the Fifteenth Amendment doomed the First Reconstruction. Would the gutting of the VRA curtail the second one?

10

AFTER SHELBY

A week after the *Shelby County* decision, three hundred people in Raleigh packed into the white-columned Christian Faith Baptist Church on an overcast Monday afternoon. "Supporters on the right, civil disobedience on the left," they were told. The racially and socioeconomically diverse crowd had the feel of an Obama campaign revival. Eighty people took the left side of the pews, wearing green armbands to signal their intention to get arrested at the legislative building downtown, nearly all of them for the first time.

It was the ninth week of the Moral Monday protests, as they came to be known, which started when Republicans in North Carolina, who controlled the legislature and the governorship in 2013 for the first time since the McKinley era, introduced the toughest voting restrictions in the country. The proposed voting changes included requiring strict voter ID, cutting early voting by a week, eliminating same-day registration during the early voting period, ending the two-thousand-dollar child dependency tax deduction for parents whose college students vote where they attend school, and rescinding the automatic restoration of voting rights for ex-felons. Pro-democracy groups dubbed the legislation the Screw the Voter Act of 2013 and the Longer Lines to Vote Bill.

"When I say what'd you want, you say voting rights," the Reverend

Curtis Gatewood, vice president of the North Carolina NAACP, instructed the crowd.

"What do you want?"

"Voting rights!"

"What do you want?"

"Voting rights!"

The activists held clear, simple signs: PROTECT EVERY AMERICAN'S RIGHT TO VOTE; STOP VOTER ID AND FIGHT VOTER SUPPRESSION; DO NOT PENALIZE PARENTS AND COLLEGE STUDENTS FOR VOTING.

Gatewood passed the microphone to the Reverend William Barber II, president of the North Carolina NAACP and the leader of the Moral Monday protests. He was a charismatic preacher in the MLK mold, a big man with a soaring voice who was built like an offensive lineman. He wore pinstriped pants and a matching vest over his clerical collar, leaning his large frame on a ratty cane, which he'd used since suffering from a rare form of debilitating arthritis.

"What do we do when they try to take away voting rights?" he asked.

"We fight, we fight, we fight," the crowd shouted, standing and punching their fists in the air.

Barber was born in Indiana two days after the March on Washington. "Civil rights is in my DNA," he said.

When he was four, his parents, native North Carolinians, uprooted the family from Indianapolis to the tiny rural town of Roper, North Carolina, two hours east of Raleigh, so that Barber could integrate the schools. Barber went to a segregated kindergarten and first grade until North Carolina integrated the schools in 1971, seventeen years after *Brown v. Board of Education*. His father taught science at a previously all-white high school; his mother became the school's first black office manager. "My parents could've stayed out of the South," he said. "They could've stayed in the Midwest and done quite well. But they made a decision to come back."

Barber became president of the North Carolina NAACP in 2005 and transformed the organization from a social club to an activist movement, as it had been in the 1960s, with one hundred branches and twenty-four thousand members. His brain trust included veterans of the civil rights movement like Bob Zellner, the first white field secretary of SNCC.

Zellner had grown up in East Brewton, Alabama, near the Florida border. His grandfather and father were in the Klan, but Zellner rebelled and joined John Lewis on the Freedom Rides. He first met Barber on SNCC's fiftieth anniversary in Raleigh.

Barber and Zellner were among the first wave of arrestees in early April. The house passed a strict voter ID bill that month, but it languished in the senate, along with the other proposed voting restrictions. Then, on the day of the *Shelby* decision, Tom Apodaca, the chairman of the senate rules committee, announced, "Now we can go with the full bill." North Carolina, where forty counties had previously been subject to Section 5, no longer had to endure the "legal headaches" of having its voting changes approved by the federal government, Apodaca said.

"That's not only historically insensitive, that's racially insensitive," Barber said in church, to cries of "amen." He rattled off the names of Evers, Chaney, Goodman, Schwerner, Liuzzo, King—the martyrs in the fight for voting rights. "We come here to say that if you think you gonna take away our voting rights, you gonna have a headache," he announced to loud cheers.

When he arrived at the legislative plaza downtown, Barber was met by two thousand supporters, who formed a long row as the protesters walked into the North Carolina legislature.

"Why do we come here?" he asked.

"Justice!" the crowd yelled.

Inside the lobby of the legislature, activists packed into two floors as Barber led a rousing rendition of "Ain't Gonna Let Nobody Turn Me Around." Protesters could see the state senate chamber through the glass, its members seemingly oblivious of what was happening right outside. (The next day, in a perfect encapsulation of state politics, the senate abruptly attached new abortion restrictions to a bill banning Sharia law.)

"You have five minutes to disperse or you will be arrested," announced the chief of police through a bullhorn.

Eighty-one people were arrested in the peaceful protest, bringing the total number of arrests to 616 since April.

A large crowd gathered across the street to cheer the arrestees as they were herded on buses to the county detention center. Cars honked in solidarity. Barber sang his favorite gospel song, "I've Got a Feeling Everything's Gonna Be All Right."

"Why are people going to jail?" a young boy asked his father. "Because they're standing up," his dad answered.

Two hours later the arrestees began to return to the church. Mary Lucas, a retired physical therapist from Pittsboro, entered to cheers, clutching a manila envelope with her arrest papers and wearing an "I Went to Jail with Rev. Barber" pin.

It was her first protest and first arrest. "I skipped the civil rights movement and I wished I hadn't," she said. She described her arrest as "really liberating. As a retired person, what do I have to lose?"

Barber viewed the protests as a model for resistance across the country. "We believe North Carolina is the crucible," he said. "If you're going to change the country, you've got to change the South. If you're going to change the South, you've got to focus on these state capitols." That's where the new voting restrictions originated after 2010.

A new wave of civil rights activism became especially important after the *Shelby* decision. "The silver lining of that ruling is we now know we must build movements, like we did in the 1960s, from Montgomery up, from Raleigh up, from congressional districts up," Barber said. "States now become national battles."

The Moral Monday movement started in the same place where the 1960s civil rights movement began—in Greensboro, on the campus of North Carolina A&T University.

At 4:30 p.m. on February 1, 1960, four freshmen at A&T—Joseph McNeil, Franklin McCain, Ezell Blair, Jr., and David Richmond—sat down at the lunch counter at Woolworth's and refused to leave until they were served. Twenty students came the next day; three hundred, two days later. The sit-ins spread to Winston-Salem, Durham, Raleigh, and Charlotte. Two months later SNCC was founded at Shaw University, in Raleigh.

Fifty-three years later, after studying the VRA and the civil rights movement in his state and local government class, Tyler Swanson, a nineteen-year-old political science major at A&T, proposed a similar demonstration.

He wanted to march to the local DMV office and chain himself to the door to protest the voter ID bill.

His government professor, Derick Smith, a veteran activist, thought that would be too radical and urged Swanson and his classmate Nnamdia Gooding to march from the A&T Four statue on campus to the government plaza instead. Barber traveled to Greensboro on April 12 and marched downtown with fifty students and NAACP members, who chanted, "We / don't need / no voter ID."

Swanson, who had grown up fifteen minutes away in the small town of McLeansville, put on his Sunday best for the occasion, wearing a khaki baseball cap, gold sunglasses, a navy blazer, and a plaid tie. "I've got news for this general assembly today: we don't approve of this voter ID law," he said through a bullhorn.

"That's right," Barber affirmed.

"We will not stop until everybody has the right to exercise their vote without being disenfranchised," Swanson continued. "Don't take off your marching shoes because we're going to need them again."

The modest protest soon led to something much bigger. Smith called Swanson, Gooding, Quisha Walker of Bennett College, and the A&T NAACP's president, Kyle Keith, the "Greensboro 4 of 2013."

"There's a lot of history here," Swanson said. "We were continuing that legacy."

North Carolina Republicans used the same rhetoric to argue for voter ID as in Texas.

"We call this restoring confidence in government," said the North Carolina speaker of the house, Thom Tillis, an ALEC legislator of the year in 2011. "There is some evidence of voter fraud, but that's not the primary reason for doing this. There are a lot of people who are just concerned with the potential risk of fraud."

But unlike in Texas, which ranked forty-eighth in voter turnout in 2012, North Carolina had the most progressive election laws in the South.

It didn't always used to be that way. In 1996, North Carolina ranked forty-third in voter turnout. To expand voter participation, the state adopted electoral reforms like early voting in 2000, the counting of out-of-precinct ballots in 2005, and same-day registration during the early voting period in 2007. As a result, North Carolina had skyrocketed from thirty-seventh in voter turnout in 2000 to eleventh by 2012.

These reforms had a particularly beneficial impact on African-American voters. In March 1965, when LBJ introduced the VRA, 46.8 percent of black North Carolinians were registered to vote, compared with 96.8 percent of whites. Decades after the passage of the VRA, the gap had narrowed but remained significant. But between 2000 and 2012, black turnout increased by 65 percent, and in 2008 and 2012 African-Americans registered and voted at a higher rate than whites for the first time in state history.

"North Carolina has the best election laws in the country," Barber testified before the house elections committee. "We've had elections for 237 years without voter ID. And only after the massive turnout of African-Americans, Latinos, progressive whites, students and the elderly fundamentally changed the electorate in the South did false witness and distortion about fraud begin."

Ten days after the Greensboro protest, the North Carolina House of Representatives stripped student IDs from private colleges from the list of acceptable voter IDs, affecting eighty-nine thousand students at thirty-six institutions. Students from across the state, with tape over their mouths, packed the house gallery in protest. "We Will Be Heard!" said the black tape over Swanson's lips.

"Dr. King said that our lives end the day we become silent about things that matter," said Shemia Curry of Bennett College in Greensboro. "So I think this is a perfect opportunity to stand up for something we believe in."

"What type of legacy are you really leaving?" Representative Rodney Moore, Democrat of Charlotte, asked his Republican colleagues during the house debate. "See those children up there?" He turned and pointed at the gallery. "Those children have been there for the last three hours with tape around their mouths because they understand what this bill has the potential to do, which is take their voice away."

After the house passed the voter ID bill, 81–36, Barber led the students in singing, "Ain't gonna let no vote turn me around."

The next day a picture of the students ran on the front page of the Raleigh *News & Observer*, under the headline VOTER ID TAKES CLOSER STEP TO LAW.

———

The changes enacted by the North Carolina legislature extended far beyond voting. Since January, the new Republican majority had adopted the most rigidly conservative agenda in the country, eliminating the earned-income tax credit for 900,000; declining Medicaid coverage for 500,000; ending federal unemployment benefits for 170,000; cutting pre-K for 30,000 kids; shifting ninety million dollars from public education to voucher schools; and slashing taxes for the top 5 percent while raising taxes on the bottom 80 percent.

For decades, North Carolina had a reputation as a moderate oasis amid a sea of deep red. It had largely avoided the turbulence of the civil rights years and had become known for good schools and sensible governance. Now it was giving Mississippi a run for its money. "The legislature is filled with lawmakers who view [Jesse] Helms as a role model," wrote the *News & Observer* columnist Rob Christensen.

Barber decided enough was enough. "At that point we had to go to moral civil disobedience to dramatize how extreme, how immoral, and how shameful this was," he said. On April 29, Barber, Zellner, and fifty protesters marched into the legislative building singing freedom songs, blocked the tall gold doors to the senate, and refused to leave. "Voter ID is the first of the voter suppression bills they're planning," he said. "What the voter ID represents is a line in the sand. People of conscience must draw a line somewhere." He called it a "peaceful pray-in."

Seventeen preachers, academics, activists, and students were arrested for failure to disperse. The crowd outside chanted the name of each arrestee as he or she was loaded onto a white school bus and sent to jail. Most were held for eight hours and released at 2:15 a.m.

"It's a whole new beginning for the movement," said a bleary-eyed Zellner.

The NAACP leaders Barber and Gatewood weren't released until 4:15 a.m. "I was never more proud to be with my brothers and sisters from all different backgrounds than I was today," Barber said. "It's 4:15 in the morning. I am tired in my body, but not a bit tired in my soul."

The arrestees published an open letter titled "Why We Are Here." "We will become 'the trumpet of conscience' and 'the beloved community' that Rev. Dr. Martin Luther King Jr. called upon us to be," they wrote.

There were 30 arrests a week later, 49 a week after that, including Swanson and Smith, 57 a week later, and 115 arrests in the fifth week of protests.

"It really caught on like in the old days," Zellner said. "We've been waiting for a renewal of the civil rights movement, and this is it." The protests were building something the South hadn't seen since the 1960s: a multiracial, multi-issue movement centered on social justice.

On June 24, ninety-two-year-old Rosanell Eaton showed up at the protests and told Barber she wanted to be arrested.

"Rosanell, you don't have to do this, you know," Barber told her.

"I know what I have to do," she replied, pushing aside her walker and marching into the legislative building in a black hat and matching pantsuit.

Inside the building, she told her story to the packed crowd.

She was born in Franklin County, in the piney woods outside Raleigh, the youngest of eight. Her father was the only black man to own his farm in the area but died on Christmas Eve after a mule accident. The landlord ripped off her mother, and the family lost the land. "That made me want to be independent," she said.

When she turned twenty-one, she told her mother she wanted to register to vote, which was nearly unthinkable for African-Americans in North Carolina at the time. "I was interested in registering people, so I would be able to lead others or help others," she said. She and her mother rode a mule-pulled wagon seven miles to the county seat of Louisburg, where three white male registrars were sitting in the courthouse.

"What can I do for you, little lady?" a registrar asked her.

"I came down to see if I could register to vote," she replied.

The registrar told her to stand up straight, look straight ahead, keep her arms by her side, and recite the Preamble to the Constitution. After she did that word for word, they gave her a written literacy test, which she also passed. "Ma'am, you ought to be proud of this little lady," the registrar told her mother. Eaton was one of the first black registered voters in Franklin County, which later became one of forty North Carolina counties covered under Section 5.

She cast her first ballot, for FDR, in 1944. When the civil rights movement took off, she registered voters for the SCLC and the NAACP and joined the march from Selma to Montgomery. "I knew John Lewis," she said. "He was young. I was always the oldest." She traveled to Washington and watched from the gallery when LBJ signed the VRA.

Her activism didn't go unnoticed. A cross was burned on her lawn. Shots were fired at her house.

She worked as a third-grade teacher and a librarian, bringing voter registration forms with her everywhere she went. She personally registered over four thousand voters before losing count. On the thirtieth anniversary of the VRA, she was honored alongside Rosa Parks and Jesse Jackson in Selma, receiving the Invisible Giant Award from the National Voting Rights Museum.

"I'm ninety-two years old," she said in the legislature. "I've been in the movement for seventy-five years. I marched with Martin Luther King . . . Now I am just disgusted." Barber repeated her speech, and the crowd cheered loudly. "I can't stand and let these bills be passed and not have a voice."

She was arrested with 120 others, for the first time in her life. "I never had a ticket or nothing," she said. "It was very exciting . . . It was worth going to jail to speak out against the voter ID bill."

The next day the Supreme Court handed down the *Shelby* decision.

Three weeks after *Shelby*, the North Carolina Senate significantly toughened the house's voter ID bill, eliminating student IDs from public universities, out-of-state driver's licenses, and county, municipal, and public employee IDs from the list of acceptable voter IDs. The bill was stricter than the Texas voter ID law blocked by the courts in 2012 under Section 5.

Four days later the North Carolina senator Josh Stein, a Democrat from Raleigh, checked his legislative e-mail at 9:00 p.m. and saw that the senate's voter ID bill, already the most restrictive in the country, had been drastically expanded. He posted a summary of the new bill on his Facebook page:

> I just received a proposed committee substitute on the voter ID bill that turns a 14 page bill into a 57 page elections bill monstrosity . . . It will keeps [sic] tens of thousands of registered voters from participating in their democracy because of two instances of in person voter fraud out of more than 20 million votes cast over past 6 elections in NC.
>
> If anyone had any doubt about the bill's intent to suppress voters, all he/she has to do is read it. The bill now does the following:

- shortens early voting by 1 week,
- eliminates same day registration and provisional voting if at wrong precinct,
- prevents counties from offering voting on last Saturday before the election beyond 1 pm,
- prevents counties from extending poll hours by one hour on election day in extraordinary circumstances (like lengthy lines),
- eliminates state supported voter registration drives and preregistration for 16/17 year olds,
- repeals voter owned judicial elections and straight party voting,
- increases number of people who can challenge voters inside the precinct, and
- purges voter rolls more often.

We will debate the bill in Rules Committee tomorrow at 2 pm. This is a sad day for our democracy.

Stein was stunned. The legislature was due to leave town at the end of the week, and senate leaders had just proposed eliminating or curtailing nearly every single reform in the state that encouraged people to vote. The bill even eliminated Citizens Awareness Month, which the state board of elections used to promote voter registration.

Millions of North Carolinians would be affected by the new restrictions. More than 2.5 million voted early in 2012, nearly 100,000 used same-day registration, 50,000 registered in high schools through preregistration in their civics classes, and 300,000 registered voters didn't have government-issued IDs.

At a packed senate rules committee meeting the next afternoon, Stein, who taught election law at Campbell University Law School, pressed the bill's Republican sponsor, Bob Rucho, to explain the many controversial provisions of the new bill.

He began with early voting. "The first week of early voting, about 900,000 people voted," Stein said. "Something like 85 percent of the state thinks early voting is a good thing and shouldn't be shrunk. Seventy-five percent have voted early at one point or another. Why are we eliminating a week of early voting?"

Senator Rucho was a sixty-five-year-old dentist from Matthews, North Carolina, born in Worcester, Massachusetts, who spoke in a Boston-by-way-of-Wilmington accent. He'd made national headlines during the 2012 election, when he tweeted after the Supreme Court upheld Obama's health care law, "Justice Robert's pen & Obamacare has done more damage to the USA then the swords of the Nazis, Soviets & terrorists combined."

Rucho said he had supported early voting when the concept was first introduced. "It was designed to open up the opportunity for [voter] access. It's been altered over the years, maybe tainted in one direction." Rucho didn't elaborate on how it had been tainted but said in another interview, "It got abused. It was never designed to give one group an advantage over another." He was likely referring to the fact that Democrats used early voting more often than Republicans in North Carolina, and blacks at a greater rate than whites. Seventy percent of African-Americans voted early in 2012, compared with half of white voters.

"That's 900,000 people that need to vote another time," Stein responded, referring to the first week of early voting. "The likely result will be longer lines on Election Day."

He moved on to the statistics on voter fraud he'd received from the board of elections, which showed just two cases of voter impersonation from 2000 to 2012, when twenty-one million votes were cast, totaling 0.0000095 percent of total votes. "What evidence of in-person voter fraud is compelling you to impose the ID requirement?" he asked.

"Senator Stein, you can't live in this society without identification," Rucho responded. "Everyone has a form of ID."

"The notion that everyone has a photo ID is just wrong," Stein said to applause. Senator Apodaca, who presided over the meeting, told the gallery to be quiet.

Stein asked why the state had eliminated preregistration for sixteen- and seventeen-year-olds.

"My son turned 18, went through the school process and was pre-registered and the like and it was very confusing as to when he was supposed to do that," Rucho explained. "What this does is offer some clarity and some certainty as to when that child or that young person is eligible to vote and registered to vote. That's what it's designed to do."

"Did your son not know he was 17 on Election Day?" Stein said, to laughs. The debate continued on the floor of the senate.

"Why are you making it harder for seniors, young people and minorities to vote?" Stein asked. "Might it be because these folks disproportionately vote Democratic?"

He noted that as in Texas, North Carolina exempted absentee ballots from the voter ID requirement, even though the state board of elections found twenty-four times as many cases of absentee ballot fraud, compared with cases of voter impersonation. He suggested that was because Republicans constituted 31 percent of registered voters in 2012 but cast half of all absentee ballots.

After the senate passed the bill on a party-line vote that evening, Swanson and a dozen young activists staged a sit-in in Tillis's office, urging him to stop the bill.

"Today we witnessed the most morally backwards voter suppression law in the United States so far," Joshua Vincent, a graduate student at North Carolina Central University, told Tillis's staff. "We're not here to get arrested, but to instruct House Speaker Thom Tillis and elected officials, as is our constitutional right, to kill House Bill 589."

The young activists sat and waited for Tillis, chanting, "I believe that we will win," the anthem of the Dream Defenders in Florida, who had occupied the Florida capitol after George Zimmerman had been acquitted in the death of Trayvon Martin in July 2013. Tillis never showed. After half an hour Vincent and five others were led out in handcuffs, bringing the total number of Moral Monday arrests to 951.

The next day the bill was sent from the senate to the house by a special messenger for immediate consideration.

The first to rise in opposition was eighty-three-year-old Mickey Michaux, who had been elected in 1972 as Durham's first black representative and appointed in 1977 as the South's first black U.S. attorney since Reconstruction. He was now the longest-serving member of the North Carolina General Assembly.

"I want you to understand why this means so much to so many people," he said on the house floor with tears in his eyes. "In 1965, when the Voting Rights Act was passed, that gave us a great deal of hope. We began to come into the halls of the legislature, city councils, the mayor's races, all of these things happened. Had it not been for the Voting Rights Act, you would not see some of us sitting here today."

He looked at his Republican colleagues and told them, "Now you're putting back what many of us fought our lives for and gave our lives for . . . Forget all of the gains of the 20th century. That's what you're doing with this bill you are trying to pass tonight. I would ask you to take these 57 pages of abomination and confine it to the streets of hell for the rest of eternity."

Every member of the Democratic minority, including five Democrats who'd voted for the house's less restrictive voter ID bill in April, spoke against the bill. Only one Republican member, the house elections committee's chairman, David Lewis, a tobacco farmer from Dunn, North Carolina, defended it. When the voter ID proposal was first introduced in March, Tillis had promised a "deliberative, responsible and interactive approach." That pledge was thrown out the window after the *Shelby* decision.

"It was the most emotional two hours I've ever spent in public office," said Representative Rick Glazier, a Democrat from Fayetteville. "This was, for many of our members, a feeling that their life's work was being rolled back in one two-hour session."

After the bill passed at 10:39 p.m., Democratic house members locked arms, bowed their heads, and observed a moment of silence.

Swanson watched from the nearly empty gallery. He'd used the very reforms the legislature was targeting, registering when he got his driver's license at sixteen and voting early for President Obama during his first election in 2012. "It was a very gloomy day in the General Assembly," he said.

Not since the end of Reconstruction had a state adopted so many voting reforms and then repealed them just a few years later. "I have been trying to think of another state law passed since the 1965 Voting Rights Act to rival this law but I cannot," wrote the law professor Rick Hasen of UC Irvine.

North Carolina became the immediate case study for what a post–Section 5 world would look like, a striking refutation of Roberts's belief that voting discrimination was largely a thing of the past and that Section 5 was no longer needed.

By chance, Attorney General Holder announced that same day that the Justice Department was suing to block Texas's redistricting maps, which had been found intentionally discriminatory under Section 5. "This is the Department's first action to protect voting rights following the *Shelby County* decision," he said, "but it will not be our last."

Two days later North Carolina's governor, Pat McCrory, announced he would sign the bill. "Just because you haven't been robbed doesn't mean you shouldn't lock your doors at night or when you're away from home," he said.

An AP reporter asked him how three parts of the bill—cutting early voting, eliminating same-day registration, and ending high school registration—would help prevent voter fraud.

"There is plenty of opportunity for voter registration—online, offline, through many methods," McCrory responded. He seemed unaware that North Carolina did not allow voters to register online.

The reporter asked again why the legislature had eliminated preregistration for high school students. "I don't know enough, I'm sorry, I haven't seen that part of the bill," McCrory replied.

After the press conference, Rosanell Eaton and hundreds of Moral Monday members marched to the governor's office with blown-up copies of the bill for McCrory to read.

The North Carolina NAACP filed suit against the law the day McCrory signed it. Eaton was one of the lead plaintiffs.

A few weeks later Eaton traveled to Washington for the fiftieth anniversary of the March on Washington. A large North Carolina contingent made the trip, carrying signs that said, NC NEEDS THE VRA.

John Lewis was a featured speaker that Saturday at the Lincoln Memorial. Fifty years earlier he'd been the youngest speaker at the March on Washington, delivering an emotional plea about the need for the federal government to intervene on behalf of black southerners. His prepared text had been so controversial—"I want to know, which side is the federal government on?"—that the older leaders of the movement, including King, asked him to tone it down.

Now he was the only surviving speaker from that day. "I gave a little blood on that bridge in Selma, Alabama, for the right to vote," Lewis said. "I am not going to stand by and let the Supreme Court take the right to vote away from us!"

Eaton saw Lewis after his speech and urged him to convince Holder to sue North Carolina. The Justice Department had filed suit against Texas's voter ID law two days earlier under Section 2 of the VRA. He'd do what he could, Lewis told her.

At the end of September, on the day of the government shutdown, Holder announced the department would intervene to block North Carolina's voting changes. "I stand here to announce this lawsuit more in sorrow than in anger," the attorney general said. "It pains me to see the voting rights of my fellow citizens negatively impacted by actions predicated on a rationale that is tenuous at best—and on concerns that we all know are not, in fact, real."

As 2014 arrived, tens of thousand of activists in North Carolina—from all backgrounds, races, and causes—marched from Shaw University to the state capitol to kick off a new year of Moral Monday protests. "Just like Dr. King sent out the call and said come to Selma in 1965, we're saying come to Raleigh in 2014," Barber said.

One hundred buses arrived from across the country on the chilly February morning. One particularly illustrative sign read: WELCOME TO NORTH CAROLINA / TURN YOUR WATCH BACK 50 YEARS. An estimated eighty thousand people gathered on Jones Street for the mass gathering, the largest civil rights rally in the South since the Selma to Montgomery march in 1965.

As bad as the past few years had been, 2014 got off to a promising start for voting rights.

In early January, a day after King's eighty-fifth birthday, Congressmen Sensenbrenner and Lewis introduced the Voting Rights Amendment Act of 2014 to restore Section 5. It was a modest bill, covering states with five voting rights violations in the past fifteen years, which applied to only Georgia, Louisiana, Mississippi, and Texas, but it represented a promising start for a post-*Shelby* legislative fix. Nancy Pelosi suggested the law be named "The John Lewis Voting Rights Act."

A week later Obama's Presidential Commission on Election Administration, chaired by the Obama campaign lawyer Bob Bauer and the Romney campaign lawyer Ben Ginsberg, released a comprehensive report advocating new voting reforms to ensure that no voter wait longer than thirty minutes to vote.

Despite the long lines in states like Florida and the backlash in 2012 against efforts to make it harder to vote, the effort received no bipartisan support in Congress. "I don't think it's the federal government's role to make sure there are no long lines," said Representative Candice Miller, Republican of Michigan, chairwoman of the House Administration Committee, which had jurisdiction over election reform.

The VRA fix didn't fare any better. Lewis and Sensenbrenner testified on the bill's behalf before the Senate Judiciary Committee. "The Voting Rights Act is needed now more than ever before," Lewis said.

But neither could convince GOP supporters of the 2006 reauthorization to back the new bill. "They're finding now how difficult it is to find a formula that people will support," said Mel Watt, who left Congress in early 2014 to become director of the Federal Housing Finance Agency. "Politically it's very difficult."

There were nineteen Republican senators still serving who had voted for the VRA in 2006, but none stepped forward to sponsor the new bill. They included the Mississippi senator Thad Cochran, who narrowly defeated a Tea Party challenger by urging blacks to vote for him in the Republican primary. Like his Republican colleagues, Cochran praised the *Shelby County* decision, saying, "I think our state can move forward and continue to ensure that our democratic processes are open and fair for all without being subject to excessive scrutiny by the Justice Department."

Sensenbrenner's clout had also waned in the House. The new chairman of the House Judiciary Committee, Bob Goodlatte of Virginia, had voted for the 2006 reauthorization but also for every amendment to weaken it. The Arizona representative Trent Franks, chairman of the Subcommittee on the Constitution, had been one of the thirty-three House Republicans to vote against the 2006 law. Neither was eager to see the legislation resurrected.

Hans von Spakovsky testified against the bill in the House. "There is no evidence of widespread, systematic discrimination in the covered states or that they are any different from other states, and there's no reason for Congress to take any action," he said. Thernstrom testified against it in the Senate, on the one-year anniversary of the Supreme Court's decision. "The decision in *Shelby County* was absolutely right," she said. "The statute had become a period piece."

For many years, critics of the VRA were a minority of congressional Republicans. Now, for the first time, the likes of von Spakovsky and Thernstrom had a majority of Republicans on their side. The southernization of the Republican Party that had begun when LBJ signed the VRA and accelerated following the 1994 election reached a pinnacle after 2010.

With Congress unwilling to fix the VRA, the fight to protect voting rights shifted from the legislative body to the courts.

In early July, seventy-two-year-old Carolyn Coleman pushed her wheelchair up the steps of the federal courthouse in Winston-Salem to testify against North Carolina's voting law. The Justice Department and advocacy groups like the North Carolina NAACP and ACLU were asking the District Court judge Thomas Schroeder for a preliminary injunction blocking key parts of the law—specifically the cuts to early voting, the elimination of same-day registration, and the prohibition on counting a ballot cast in the wrong precinct—before the midterm elections in 2014. The first hearing was held a year after the law passed.

Coleman had grown up in Savannah, Georgia, and joined the youth division of the Alabama NAACP in 1964. She had concentrated on voter registration and had participated in the last day of the march from Selma to Montgomery.

After the passage of the VRA, Coleman had spent a year registering voters in Mississippi, where her friend Wharlest Jackson, an NAACP leader in Natchez, was killed by a car bomb after receiving a promotion at the local tire plant. A year later Coleman was in Memphis organizing striking sanitation workers when King was assassinated.

She served as president of the North Carolina NAACP and southern voter education director for the NAACP before winning election to the county commission in Greensboro's Guilford County in 2002. She had lobbied hard for reforms like early voting and same-day registration to expand North Carolina's electorate. When the legislature passed House Bill 589, "I was devastated," Coleman testified. "I felt like I was living life over again. Everything that I worked for for the last fifty years was being lost."

Rosanell Eaton testified after Coleman. She was the first one in the courtroom, looking resplendent in her trademark pantsuit and matching hat. "Voting should be free and accessible to everyone and give everybody a chance," she said.

"Mrs. Eaton, why have you dedicated so much of your time and effort over the years to helping people vote and to voting-related activities?" Bridget O'Connor of Kirkland & Ellis, who represented the North Carolina NAACP, asked her.

"Well, I think it is because my foreparents or forefathers didn't have the opportunity of registering and voting," Eaton answered. "So when I was young, I read the history, and then I decided it was just my intention to try and help people to reach the point that they could do something."

Lawyers for the plaintiffs argued that the voting restrictions had been passed to silence black voters like Coleman and Eaton. "The sequence of events leading up to the bill show that HB589 was intended to target the very reforms that had expanded opportunities for African-Americans for over a decade," the Justice Department lawyer Catherine Meza argued in court. African-Americans in North Carolina, Meza pointed out, were twice as likely to vote early, use same-day registration, and vote out of precinct compared with whites. (They were also disproportionately less likely to have government-issued IDs, but the voter ID provision didn't go into effect until 2016 and wasn't discussed much in court.)

Under Section 5, North Carolina would have had a very difficult time proving that the law did not leave African-American voters worse off than before. But showing a violation of the VRA under Section 2 was a much tougher job for the Justice Department and civil rights lawyers. Section 2 had primarily been applied to vote-dilution cases like *Mobile v. Bolden* and *Thornburg v. Gingles*, in which blacks were prevented from being elected to office, not to voting changes that restricted access to the ballot, like voter ID or ending same-day registration.

"The standard here is the totality-of-the-circumstances test—that, as a practical matter, African American voters will have less opportunity to participate in the political process as compared to white voters in their ability to register, to cast a ballot, and to have that ballot counted," Bert Russ of the Justice Department argued.

But as a practical matter, there were few relevant precedents for the DOJ to point to. And the federal government, not the state, now had the burden of proof. This was uncharted territory; like the *Allen* and *Gingles* cases, the North Carolina case could set an important legal precedent.

Lawyers for North Carolina portrayed the voting law as a mere policy dispute, not a case of voting discrimination. "The fact that they prefer them, the fact that they think same-day registration, out-of-precinct provisional balloting, these things are good policy, does not mean that they are legally entitled to them," argued Alexander Peters from the state attorney general's office.

The new law "puts North Carolina in the mainstream of other states with regard to election laws," argued Butch Bowers, a South Carolina–based lawyer representing Governor McCrory. Because other states, like South Carolina, did not have expanded early voting or same-day registration, Bowers suggested there was nothing wrong with curtailing or eliminating those reforms in North Carolina.

The defense presented little evidence of voter fraud to justify the law. At one point, the plaintiffs showed a videotaped deposition of the North Carolina state board of elections director, Kim Strach, who was married to one of the state's lawyers in the case.

"I am not aware of specific instances of voter impersonation," Strach said on tape.

The video showed the plaintiffs' lawyers handing Strach a chart showing just one case of voter impersonation in the 2004 and 2008 elections, when 7.8 million people voted. "I think the number speaks for itself," she said.

Strach sat in the courtroom, mortified as she watched herself on tape. The defense lawyers were furious afterward. "Why did we let them show that edited video? Did we know they were going to show it?" one lawyer asked.

"No!" the other responded.

But Chris Coates, the former head of the voting section during the Bush administration, who argued in defense of North Carolina, said the state was under no obligation to present specific evidence of voter fraud because of the Supreme Court's *Crawford* voter ID decision.

"*Crawford* also says that before a state enacts a voter ID or any other type of voting procedure, that if the interests that they are trying to achieve is combating fraud, that there does not have to be evidence that fraud has been committed in the state," Coates said.

Two days after the forty-ninth anniversary of the VRA, Judge Schroeder, a George W. Bush appointee, denied the preliminary injunction in a lengthy 125-page opinion.

"A preliminary injunction is an extraordinary remedy to be granted in this circuit only upon a 'clear showing' of entitlement," he wrote. "Even assuming Plaintiffs are likely to succeed on the merits, they have not demonstrated they are likely to suffer irreparable harm—a necessary prerequisite for preliminary relief—before trial in the absence of an injunction." The trial to consider the full merits of the voting law, including the voter ID provision, wouldn't occur until the summer of 2015.

Schroeder concluded that even if African-American voters disproportionately used the state's voting reforms, they would still be able to openly participate in the electoral process and would not face "an inequality of opportunity to vote."

The past success of Section 5 paradoxically made the case harder to win under Section 2.

As Schroeder noted, "Vote-denial claims under Section 2 have thus far been relatively rare, perhaps due in part to the fact that since 1965, many jurisdictions—including many North Carolina counties—were under federal control and barred from enacting any new voting procedure without first obtaining 'pre-clearance' under Section 5."

What would have been a slam-dunk case for the Justice Department and civil rights groups before *Shelby* had now become a long slog.

The law was already preventing people from voting. Craig Thomas of Granville County, North Carolina, registered to vote before he deployed to Afghanistan with the U.S. Army. After serving abroad for eighteen months, he went to vote early in the state's primary on April 30. He had returned from Afghanistan to the same house, in the same precinct, but was told at the polls that there was "no record of registration" for him.

In the past, Thomas could have reregistered during the early voting period and cast a regular ballot using same-day registration. But he now had to cast a provisional ballot, which was not counted.

Thomas was one of 454 North Carolina voters who would have had their ballots counted in 2012 but did not have them counted in the 2014 primary because of North Carolina's elimination of same-day registration and prohibition on counting a provisional ballot cast in the wrong precinct.

These new restrictions disproportionately burdened black and Democratic voters. "While black voters make up 22% of all registered voters, they were 39% of those who lost their votes because of the two rule changes," according to a review by Democracy North Carolina after Schroeder's opinion. "Democrats are 42% of the state's registered voters, but 57% of those disenfranchised by the new rules."

This new evidence came before the Fourth Circuit Court of Appeals in Charlotte. On October 1, 2014, just weeks before the election, two of three judges overruled parts of Schroeder's opinion, reinstating same-day registration and out-of-precinct voting for the midterms.

Judge James Wynn, an African-American Obama appointee, pointedly asked the state's lawyers: "Why doesn't North Carolina want people to vote?"

It was a small yet important victory for voters in North Carolina. Nearly one hundred thousand North Carolinians, including twice as many blacks as whites, used same-day registration in 2012. States with same-day registration and early voting, like North Carolina, had the highest voter turnout in the country.

Nine days later—less than a month before the midterms—the Supreme Court overrode the Fourth Circuit and restored the new voting restrictions. The appeals court had erred by reinstating the voting reforms so close to the election. There was a cruel irony behind the Court's last-minute intervention: if it had not been for the *Shelby* decision, Justice Ginsburg noted in her dissent, "these measures likely would not have survived federal preclearance."

Elizabeth Gholar was born in rural southwestern Louisiana in 1938, in the small town of Jennings, the county seat of Jefferson Davis Parish. After growing up in the Jim Crow South, she felt voting was always important. "Because I've earned it," she said. "Because it simply wasn't allowed and it should be now, forever."

In 2013, after retiring as a school cook, she moved to Texas to live with her daughter in Austin. She had a driver's license and birth certificate from Louisiana but ran into problems when she tried to get a driver's license in Texas, which she needed to vote. She was told that the name on her birth certificate, which had been incorrectly filled out by the midwife who had delivered her at home and listed her mother's maiden name, had to match her current name.

Gholar returned to a department of public safety office to apply for a voting-only ID but was once again told she needed a matching birth certificate. She then hired a lawyer in Louisiana to get her an amended birth certificate. She didn't know when or if that would happen and couldn't vote in her new home state in the meantime. She called the cost and time of getting a new birth certificate "another form" of a poll tax.

At that point, she got mad and called the NAACP. That's how Gholar became a key witness in the trial to block Texas's voter ID law for a second time, which took place in early September 2014 in the sleepy coastal city of Corpus Christi.

Lawyers for the NAACP Legal Defense Fund played a video of Gholar's deposition in the packed federal courtroom. "Voting is a right that everybody else had and it's a celebration," she said. "And it's been taken away again."

Judge Nelva Gonzales Ramos of the Southern District of Texas became visibly emotional during Gholar's testimony. Gholar was one of seventeen witnesses who testified about the difficulties of getting a voter ID in the state.

Another was Floyd Carrier. During the state's municipal elections in November 2013, Carrier, an eighty-three-year-old who had been an army paratrooper in the Korean War, brought his expired driver's license, VA card, and voter registration card to the polls in China, Texas, where he'd lived and voted for sixty years.

The poll workers immediately recognized Carrier but would not let him vote because, they said, he didn't have a valid voter ID. "I felt terrible," Carrier told the court, "because all I did for the country and they turn me down, so I just felt like I wasn't a citizen anymore."

His son, the deputy chief of the fire department in Beaumont, had visited three counties in a futile attempt to find his father's birth certificate. He'd waited four months after submitting an application for a new birth certificate, only to find his father's name misspelled when it finally arrived.

Margarito Lara, a seventy-seven-year-old from Sebastian, Texas, shared a similarly agonizing story. Lara began voting when Texas still had a poll tax. Like Carrier, he was born at home, and there was no record of his birth. He'd been trying to get a birth certificate for over a decade, traveling to four different counties with his daughter, and could no longer vote with his expired driver's license or voter registration card.

The stories of longtime voters like Gholar, Carrier, and Lara did not reflect positively on Texas. Nearly 800,000 registered voters lacked acceptable voter IDs in the state, Elizabeth Westfall of the Justice Department said in her opening statement, and "Hispanics and African-Americans make up a disproportionate share." Texas had issued just 279 new voter IDs by the beginning of the trial.

Nine plaintiffs in the case—twice as many potentially disenfranchised voters as there were cases of voter impersonation presented by Texas officials—lacked valid voter IDs. The state conceded at trial that it had successfully prosecuted only four instances of in-person voter fraud over the past twelve years.

Representative Todd Smith, the Republican chairman of the house elections committee from 2009 to 2010, testified that legislators knew that minority voters would be most affected by the new law. "If the question is are the people that do not have photo IDs more likely to be minority than those that are not, I think it's a matter of common sense that they would be," he said. "I don't need a study to tell me that."

But given the politics of voter ID in Texas, even Republican skeptics were forced to vote for the bill, known as SB 14. "I think every Republican member of the legislature would have been lynched if the bill had not passed," Smith admitted.

Three weeks after the trial ended, Judge Ramos, an Obama appointee, struck down the law under Section 2 of the VRA in a searing 147-page decision.

"The Court holds that SB 14 creates an unconstitutional burden on the right to vote, has an impermissible discriminatory effect against Hispanics and African-Americans, and was imposed with an unconstitutional discriminatory purpose," Ramos wrote. "The Court further holds that SB 14 constitutes an unconstitutional poll tax."

Ramos's decision was the most extensive rebuke of voter ID laws issued by a federal court to date, debunking the myths that everyone had a voter ID, that it was easy to get one, that there was an epidemic of voter fraud necessitating the new laws, and that such laws were always constitutional.

She concluded that 608,470 registered voters in Texas—4.5 percent of the electorate—lacked voter IDs, with African-Americans three times as likely as whites not to have one and Hispanics twice as likely. "To call SB 14's disproportionate impact on minorities statistically significant would be an understatement," she wrote.

The judge asserted the law was passed not to combat voter impersonation in Texas, which the record showed was virtually nonexistent, but to make it harder for blacks and Hispanics to vote. "This Court concludes that the evidence in the record demonstrates that proponents of SB 14 within the 82nd Texas Legislature were motivated, at the very least in part, *because of* and not merely *in spite of* the voter ID law's detrimental effects on the African-American and Hispanic electorate," Ramos wrote.

Most important, Ramos's finding of intentional discrimination meant that Texas could be "bailed in" under a little-known provision of the VRA, Section 3, becoming the first state since the *Shelby* decision to once again have to submit its voting changes to the federal government under Section 5.

In contrast with North Carolina, the decision represented a major victory for the Department of Justice and Eric Holder, who had recently announced he was stepping down as attorney general. Two years earlier he'd been widely ridiculed for calling Texas's voter ID law a poll tax. Now a federal court had used those same words.

"Even after the Voting Rights Act was seriously eroded last year, we vowed to continue enforcing the remaining portions of that statute as aggressively as possible," Holder said. "This ruling is an important vindication of those efforts."

The discussion around voter ID laws had shifted significantly since the *Crawford* decision. Judge Richard Posner, who wrote the 2007 opinion upholding Indiana's voter ID law in the Seventh Circuit, said six years later that such laws were "now widely regarded as a means of voter suppression rather than of fraud prevention." Justice John Paul Stevens, the author of the *Crawford* decision, admitted that he now agreed with Justice Souter's dissent in the case. "The impact of the statute is much more serious" on poor, minority, disabled, and elderly voters than he'd initially recognized, Stevens conceded.

A day before the Texas and Wisconsin decisions, the nonpartisan Government Accountability Office released a lengthy study showing that strict voter ID laws in Kansas and Tennessee decreased voter turnout by two to three points from 2008 to 2012, compared with similar states without voter ID laws, leading to 122,000 fewer votes. Turnout dropped most sharply among the newly registered, the young, and African-American voters.

"It can no longer be disputed as mere assertion that voter ID laws are obstacles to citizens who wish to exercise their fundamental right to vote; as this report shows, it is clearly a fact," Holder wrote. "This information should help us move past the ideological arguments that too often dominate the debate on these voting laws, and understand them for what they really are."

But the victory didn't last long. The U.S. Court of Appeals for the Fifth Circuit, one of the most conservative courts in the country, overruled Ramos five days later, reinstating Texas's voter ID law for the 2014 election. The lower court's judgment "substantially disturbs the election process of the State of Texas just nine days before early voting begins," wrote Judge Edith Brown Clement.

The Supreme Court reaffirmed the appeals court ruling on October 18, less than three weeks before the election. It was the first time since 1982 that the Court had approved a voting law deemed intentionally discriminatory by a trial court. Justice Ginsburg stayed up all night writing her dissent and released the opinion at 5:05 a.m. on Saturday. She disagreed with the appeals court's finding that striking the voter ID law before the election would confuse voters and election officials. "The greatest threat to public confidence in elections in this case is the prospect of enforcing a purposefully discriminatory law, one that likely imposes an unconstitutional poll tax and risks denying the right to vote to hundreds of thousands of eligible voters," Ginsburg wrote.

Ten days earlier the Supreme Court had upheld a voting law in North Carolina that Ginsburg believed would have very likely been blocked under Section 5. Now it was upholding a law that in fact had been blocked under Section 5. Indeed, the Texas voter ID law had been struck down by two different trial courts, under two different sections of the VRA, yet remained in effect. "It is a major step backward to let stand a law that a federal court, after a lengthy trial, has determined was designed to discriminate," Holder said.

Four major voting rights cases came before the Supreme Court in the month before the election—from North Carolina, Ohio, Texas, and

Wisconsin—and in three of four instances the Court refused to block laws restricting voting rights.

The post-*Shelby* voting rights landscape most closely resembled the period before 1965, which the VRA was meant to end, when the blight of voting discrimination could only be challenged on a torturous case-by-case basis. The loss of Section 5, combined with an often hostile judiciary, created perpetual uncertainty when it came to protecting voting rights. Roberts's long-held view that violations of the VRA "should not be made too easy to prove" was finally being put into practice.

Voters in fourteen states faced new restrictions at the polls for the first time in 2014, in the first election in nearly fifty years without the full protections of the VRA.

In Texas, Elizabeth Gholar couldn't vote for the first time in sixty years because of the state's voter ID law. She was not alone.

Betty Thorn, an eighty-four-year-old grandmother who lived in an assisted living facility in Austin, had voted in every major election in her lifetime. Days before the election, Thorn's granddaughter Amy Gautreaux took her to a department of public safety office to get a new ID because her driver's license had expired. But Thorn didn't have the correct proof-of-address documents to get a new driver's license, nor did she have the birth certificate required to get a voting-only ID.

"When the voter ID law was announced, I didn't understand the big deal," Gautreaux said. "I figured most people have ID. Now that it's happened to me, I'm devastated. This is what happened to an elderly person who has family to help her. I can only imagine how many don't have any help."

Despite a high-profile governor's race between the Republican Greg Abbott and the Democrat Wendy Davis, voter turnout dropped by 270,000 votes, compared with 2010. Only 28 percent of eligible voters went to the polls, the second-lowest turnout rate in the country.

Nationally, voter turnout plummeted to the lowest level since 1942. In Texas and across the country, the electorate was older, whiter, and more conservative than in 2008 and 2012; that is what Republicans wanted. Nearly twice as many Americans chose not to vote as voted in 2014. Although turnout was down, voting problems were up. Voting rights groups fielded eighteen thousand calls at the 1-866-Our-Vote hotline, a 40 percent increase over 2010.

Some of the biggest problems occurred in North Carolina.

Bryan McGowan spent twenty-two years in the U.S. Marine Corps, including four tours in Afghanistan and Iraq. When he was stationed at Camp Lejeune in North Carolina from 2005 until 2010, McGowan used same-day registration to register and vote during the early voting period in the state.

He relocated to Georgia in 2010 because of his military service and returned to North Carolina in 2014. On October 23, the first day of early voting in the state, McGowan arrived at his new polling place in western North Carolina to update his registration and vote, as he had done in the 2008 presidential election. But this time he was turned away. Because North Carolina had eliminated same-day registration and the state's registration deadline had passed, McGowan was unable to update his registration and vote. "All I want to do is cast my vote," he said.

McGowan's story was not atypical in 2014. As a result of the state's new voting restrictions, voters like McGowan were not able to register during the early voting period. Many voters arrived at the wrong polling location, where they could no longer cast a regular ballot out of precinct. There were longer lines during early voting because the state cut early voting by a week. And there were longer lines on Election Day because of the shorter early voting period, particularly in heavily Democratic urban areas like Durham, Raleigh, and Charlotte, where wait times stretched to up to three hours at some polling places.

Leslie Culbertson of Charlotte arrived at her polling place at Eastover Elementary School expecting to quickly cast her ballot. "The last time I voted here the line was nothing," she said. But this time the wait was an hour, and Culbertson had to leave the polls without voting to pick up her children from school.

Despite the best efforts of the Moral Monday coalition to mobilize voters, the new restrictions affected the outcome of the election. In a fiercely contested U.S. Senate race, the Republican Thom Tillis, who as speaker of the North Carolina House of Representatives had overseen the state's voting law, defeated the Democrat Kay Hagan by forty-eight thousand votes. Nearly five times as many voters in 2010 used the voting reforms eliminated by the North Carolina GOP: two hundred thousand had voted during the eliminated first week of early voting, twenty-one thousand had used same-day registration, and six thousand had cast out-of-precinct ballots. Democracy North Carolina estimated that thirty thousand to fifty thousand voters were kept from the polls because of the new law. The number of voters potentially affected by new barriers to the ballot box exceeded the margin of victory in close races for Senate and governor in North Carolina, Kansas, Virginia, and Florida, according to the Brennan Center for Justice.

It was a grim election for voting rights advocates. Republican officials who led the effort to make it harder to vote, such as Tillis in North Carolina and Abbott in Texas, won election to higher office. The GOP tightened its grip on state governments, controlling more states than at any time since the 1920s, meaning that voters would face more restrictions at the polls in the coming years. The hurdles to participating in the political process kept getting higher.

Four months before the election, eight hundred people attended a Moral March to the Polls rally in Winston-Salem on the first day of the district court hearing in July 2014. Tyler Swanson and Derick Smith stood behind Reverend Barber onstage, holding signs that said, ORGANIZE, REGISTER, VOTE and REPEAL ATTACKS ON VOTING RIGHTS.

"Let us not forget that this bill was passed after *Shelby*—turn to your neighbor and say, 'After *Shelby*'—had destroyed Section 5 preclearance by annihilating Section 4," Barber told the crowd. "America, you better look at North Carolina, because this bill shows the nation what these extreme right-wingers, especially in the South, are willing to do to suppress the vote without having to go through preclearance."

To combat the Supreme Court decision, the North Carolina NAACP had placed fifty young organizers in fifty counties to focus on registering new voters. They called it Moral Freedom Summer 2014, a tribute to the fiftieth anniversary of Freedom Summer, when Lewis and thousands of young activists went to Mississippi and Goodman, Chaney, and Schwerner lost their lives.

"How many of you are going to leave here and remember the blood of the martyrs?" Barber asked. Hundreds of hands went up.

Swanson spent the summer of 2014 organizing in Catawba and Iredell counties in western North Carolina, heavily Republican areas where Obama had won only 34 percent of the vote in 2012.

"A lot of African-Americans had given up on voting," he said. Many of his peers had lost faith in the justice system after the shootings of black teenagers like Trayvon Martin and Michael Brown.

But sitting in the courtroom in Winston-Salem for the first time in his life, Swanson was inspired by the testimony of voting rights activists like Rosanell Eaton. "Hearing what they had to go through, that inspired me to fight even harder."

He registered 115 new voters in a month. It wasn't flashy work, but Swanson felt as if he were making a difference. The North Carolina NAACP registered 5,000 new voters that summer.

The activists of the past had inspired the activists of the future. Swanson said his goal was to move to Georgia and one day represent the congressional seat of his hero, John Lewis.

NOTES

All quotations and dialogue are from the author's interviews and reporting unless otherwise cited in the notes.

PROLOGUE

3 *"This city, on the banks"*: Remarks by John Lewis, Selma, Alabama, March 7, 2015, www.youtube.com/watch?v=7HcKyoVO25g.

4 *"one of my heroes"*: Remarks by Barack Obama, Selma, Alabama, March 7, 2015, www.whitehouse.gov/the-press-office/2015/03/07/remarks-president-50th-anniversary-selma-montgomery-marches.

4 *"Woke up this morning"*: Quoted in "President Obama and the First Family Visit Selma," YouTube, March 8, 2015, www.youtube.com/watch?v=SnaLQNwfejg&app=desktop.

4 *"Jimmie Jackson just wanted"*: Quoted in Roy Reed, "Alabama Victim Called a Martyr," *New York Times*, March 3, 1965.

5 *"We're marching"*: Quoted in *PoliticsNation with Al Sharpton*, MSNBC, Feb. 28, 2013.

5 *"I lost all consciousness"*: John Lewis, interview by Abby Ginsburg, Oct. 20, 2008, The Paley Center for Media, New York, N.Y.

5 *"It is wrong"*: Remarks by Lyndon Johnson, Special Remarks to the Congress: The American Promise, Washington, D.C., March 15, 1965, millercenter.org/president/speeches/speech-3386.

6 *"conscience of the Congress"*: Quoted in Ari Berman, "John Lewis's Long Fight for Voting Rights," *Nation*, June 24–July 1, 2013.

6 *"When Lyndon Johnson signed"*: Ibid.

7 *"one of the crowning achievements"*: Remarks by Barack Obama, Selma.

7 *"heart and soul"*: Quoted in Berman, "John Lewis's Long Fight for Voting Rights."

7 *"shift the advantage of"*: *Allen v. State Bd. of Elections*, 393 U.S. 544 (1969).

7 *"the high price many"*: Brief for the Honorable Congressman John Lewis as Amicus Curiae in Support of Respondents and Intervenor-Respondents, *Shelby County v. Holder*, 570 U. S. ___ (2013).

7 *"The Act gives a"*: *Allen v. State Bd. of Elections.*

8 *"a tool for guaranteeing minority"*: Abigail M. Thernstrom, "The Odd Evolution of the Voting Rights Act," *Public Interest* 55 (1979), 53.

8 *"an instrument for affirmative action"*: Abigail M. Thernstrom, *Whose Votes Count?* (Cambridge, Mass.: Harvard University Press, 1987), 27.

8 *"curfew imposed in the wake"*: Ibid., 46.

8 *"The Marshall Plan was"*: Oral Argument, *Shelby County v. Holder,* 570 U. S. ___ (2013), Feb. 27, 2013.

8 *"Even the name of it"*: Ibid.

9 *"In 1965 the States"*: *Shelby County v. Holder,* 570 U. S. ___ (2013).

9 *"I'm in disbelief"*: John Lewis, interview by Jeff Zeleny, *ABC News,* June 25, 2013, http://abcnews.go.com/blogs/politics/2013/06/courts-decision-puts-dagger-in-heart-of-voting-rights-act/#.UcnG9z712G0.twitter.

10 *"Selma was the last act"*: John Lewis with Michael D'Orso, *Walking with the Wind* (New York: Simon & Schuster, 1998), 361.

11 *"coalition of the ascendant"*: Ronald Brownstein, "Obama's Gamble," *National Journal,* June 28, 2012.

11 *"the greatest attacks on"*: Remarks by Benjamin Jealous, Columbia, S.C., Jan. 16, 2012, www.naacp.org/pages/martin-luther-king-day-speech-2012.

12 *"Our history makes plain"*: Written Testimony of Alexander Keyssar, submitted to the Senate Committee on the Judiciary, June 12, 2006.

1. THE SECOND EMANCIPATION

13 *"Well, what the hell's"*: Quoted in Nick Kotz, *Judgment Days* (New York: Houghton Mifflin, 2005), xv.

14 *"the meat in the"*: Quoted in Remarks by Barack Obama, Lyndon B. Johnson Presidential Library, Austin, Tex., Apr. 10, 2014, www.whitehouse.gov/the-press-office/2014/04/10/remarks-president-lbj-presidential-library-civil-rights-summit.

14 *"I want you to"*: Quoted in Kotz, *Judgment Days,* 245.

14 *"a simple, effective method"*: Ibid.

15 *"to overcome voter apathy:"* Nicholas deB. Katzenbach, "Legislation to Overcome Voter Apathy and Discrimination," Dec. 28, 1964, WHCF HU, Legislative Background: Voting Rights Act, Box 1, LBJ Library.

15 *"eliminate every remaining obstacle"*: Remarks by Lyndon Johnson, Annual Message to the Congress in the State of the Union, Washington, D.C., Jan. 4, 1965, www.presidency.ucsb.edu/ws/?pid=26907.

15 *"Certainly I have absolutely"*: Quoted in Garth E. Pauley, *LBJ's American Promise* (College Station, Tex.: Texas A&M University Press, 2006), 77.

15 *"To southern minds"*: Horace Busby to Bill Moyers and Lee White, "The Voting Rights Message," Feb. 27, 1965, Office Files of Horace Busby, Box 3, LBJ Library.

16 *"Martin, you are right"*: Quoted in Kotz, *Judgment Days,* 244.

16 *"was straight out of"*: Eric F. Goldman, *The Tragedy of Lyndon Johnson* (New York: Knopf, 1969), 309.

16 *"any Negro found upon"*: Quoted in John Herbers, "Black Belt of Alabama Is a Stronghold of 19th-Century Racism," *New York Times,* Feb. 14, 1965.

17 *"When you pay $1.50"*: Ibid.

17 *"Black Belt thinking"*: Ibid.

17 *"Clark's rejoinder to"*: Warren Hinckle and David Welsh, "Five Battles of Selma," *Ramparts,* June 1965.

18 *"backward"*: Quoted in J. L. Chestnut, Jr., and Julia Cass, *Black in Selma* (New York: Farrar, Straus and Giroux, 1990), 179.

18 *"Today marks the beginning"*: Quoted in Charles Fager, *Selma 1965* (New York: Scribner, 1974), 9.

18 *"Give us the ballot"*: Remarks by Martin Luther King, Jr., Address at the Prayer Pilgrimage for Freedom, Washington, D.C., May 17, 1957, mlk-kpp01.stanford.edu/index .php/encyclopedia/documentsentry/doc_give_us_the_ballot_address_at_the_prayer _pilgrimage_for_freedom/.

18 *"criminal provocation"*: Quoted in John Herbers, "67 Negroes Jailed in Alabama Drive," *New York Times*, Jan. 19, 1965.

18 *"All of us should be"*: Quoted in John D. Morris, "Johnson Pledges Alabama Action," *New York Times*, Feb. 4, 1965.

19 *"contributing to the delinquency"*: John Herbers, "Negroes Beaten in Alabama Riot," *New York Times*, Feb. 18, 1965.

19 *"For the state troopers"*: Fager, *Selma*, 74.

19 *"first martyr of"*: Taylor Branch, *At Canaan's Edge* (New York: Simon & Schuster, 2006), 8.

19 RACISM KILLED OUR BROTHER: Fager, *Selma*, 84.

19 *"freedom funeral"*: Roy Reed, "Hero's Burial Set for Slain Negro," *New York Times*, Feb. 27, 1965.

19 *"We are going to"*: Quoted in Roy Reed, "266 Apply to Vote as Selma Speeds Negro Registration," *New York Times*, March 1, 1965.

19 *"It required the atrocities"*: Quoted in Steven F. Lawson, *Black Ballots* (New York: Columbia University Press, 1976), 349.

20 *"civil right No. 1"*: Martin Luther King, Jr., "Civil Right No. 1," *New York Times Magazine*, March 14, 1965.

20 *"We strongly believe that"*: John Lewis and Silas Norman, Letter to King from Executive Committee of SNCC, March 7, 1965, SNCC Files, King Library, Atlanta.

20 *"I've been to Selma"*: Lewis, Ginsburg interview.

20 *"bringing the Gandhian way"*: Lewis, *Wind*, 175.

20 *"This is Selma, Alabama"*: Martin Luther King, Jr., "A Letter from a Selma, Alabama, Jail," *New York Times*, Feb. 1, 1965.

21 *"Segregation now, segregation tomorrow"*: Remarks by George Wallace, Montgomery, Ala., Jan. 14, 1963, http://digital.archives.alabama.gov/cdm/singleitem/collection/voices /id/2952/rec/5.

21 *"I'm not going to"*: Quoted in Gary May, *Bending Toward Justice* (New York: Basic Books, 2013), 82.

21 *"Walk for Freedom"*: Leon Daniel, "Tear Gas, Clubs Halt 600 in Selma March," *Washington Post*, March 7, 1965.

21 *"There was no singing"*: Lewis, *Wind*, 338.

21 *"a sea of blue-helmeted"*: Ibid.

22 *"Tear gas!"*: Roy Reed, "Alabama Police Use Gas and Clubs to Rout Negroes," *New York Times*, March 7, 1965.

22 *"Police are beating people"*: Quoted in "Sunday in Selma," *Harvard Crimson*, March 11, 1965, www.thecrimson.com/article/1965/3/11/sunday-in-selma-pilast-sunday -selma/.

22 *"John, speak to the"*: Lewis, Ginsburg interview.

22 *"I don't know how"*: Lewis, *Wind*, 343.

22 *"the bitter, acrid smell"*: Ibid., 344.

23 *"Thousands of us all"*: Mickey Schwerner telegram to John Lewis, March 8, 1965, SNCC Files, King Library.

23 *"What the public felt"*: Harry McPherson, Memorandum to the President, March 12, 1965, Legislative Background: Voting Rights Act, Box 2, LBJ Library.

23 *"Lyndon Come Lately"*: Goldman, *Tragedy*, 330.

23 *"top billing"*: Lyndon Johnson telephone conversation with Nicholas Katzenbach,

March 8, 1965, Miller Center, http://millercenter.org/scripps/archive/presidential recordings/johnson/1965/03_1965.

23 *"A man dies when"*: Remarks by Martin Luther King, Jr., in Selma, Ala., March 8, 1965, www.youtube.com/watch?v=0On19DRA2fU.

23 *"The march is legitimate"*: SNCC chronology—Selma, SNCC Files, King Library.

24 *"Ivy League Gentlemen"*: Victor Navasky, *Kennedy Justice* (New York: Scribner, 1971), 188.

24 *"a calm enforcer"*: John Neary, "Poker-faced Lawman on the Spot," *Life*, May 6, 1966.

24 *"I would rather die"*: Fager, *Selma*, 103.

24 *"charge of the Bible"*: Hinkle and Welsh, "Five Battles of Selma."

25 *"They were allowed to"*: Quoted in "The Central Points," *Time*, March 19, 1965.

25 *"King has turned around"*: Ibid.

25 *"How many Jim Reebs"*: Quoted in Richard B. Stolley, "Inside the White House: Pressures," *Life*, March 26, 1965.

25 *"Just you wait"*: Ibid.

26 *"Two reasons"*: Ibid.

26 *"You can't stop a"*: Goldman, *Tragedy*, 314.

26 *"If I hadn't left"*: Fager, *Selma*, 118.

26 *"The events of last"*: Quoted in "The Transcript of President Johnson's News Conference," *New York Times*, March 14, 1965.

27 *"The Attorney General can"*: Quoted in Stolley, "Inside the White House: Pressures."

27 *"Mistuh Speak-ah!"*: Johnson, "The American Promise," March 15, 1965, LBJ Library, www.youtube.com/watch?v=5NvPhiuGZ6I.

27 *"At times history"*: Ibid.

27 *"I could feel the"*: Lyndon Baines Johnson, *The Vantage Point* (New York: Holt, Rinehart and Winston, 1971), 165.

27 *"For with a country"*: Johnson, "American Promise."

28 *"I almost fell out"*: Nicholas deB. Katzenbach, *Some of It Was Fun* (New York: W. W. Norton, 2008), 167.

28 *"were poor and they"*: Johnson, "American Promise."

29 *"the most moving, eloquent"*: Quoted in Kotz, *Judgment Days*, 316.

29 *"Mr. President, you made"*: Letter to Lyndon Johnson from Albert Herling, March 17, 1965, Busby Files, Box 3, LBJ Library.

29 *"too long, too tedious"*: Quoted in Pauley, *LBJ's American Promise*, 136.

29 *"near-hysteria generated"*: Ibid., 140.

29 *"the song of the"*: Quoted in "Remarkable Remarks," *Des Moines Register*, Sept. 10, 1965.

29 *"was a considerable force"*: Transcript, Lawrence F. O'Brien Oral History Interview XI, July 24, 1986, by Michael L. Gillette, LBJ Library, www.lbjlib.utexas.edu/johnson/archives .hom/oralhistory.hom/OBrienL/OBRIEN11.PDF.

29 *"We will make it"*: Quoted in Ari Berman, "Jim Crow II," *Nation*, Nov. 11, 2013.

30 *"involved nothing more"*: Williams v. Wallace, 240 F. Supp. 100 (1965).

30 *"so-called march from"*: George C. Wallace letter to Lyndon Johnson, March 18, 1965, Statements of Lyndon Johnson, Box 156, LBJ Library.

30 *"hovering between festivity"*: Roy Reed, "Hundreds Pour into Selma," *New York Times*, March 21, 1965.

30 *"When we get to"*: Ibid.

30 *"He had to die"*: Quoted in Kotz, *Judgment Days*, 320.

30 *"Just got to tramp"*: Quoted in Simeon Booker, "50,000 March on Montgomery," *Ebony*, May 1965.

30 *"We are not afraid"*: Quoted in Roy Reed, "Rights Marchers Push into Region Called Hostile," *New York Times*, March 22, 1965.

31 *"Communist training school"*: Ibid.

31 *"evidence of much fornication"*: Quoted in Gene Roberts and Hank Klibanoff, *The Race Beat* (New York: Knopf, 2006), 390.

31 *"The sex orgies"*: Quoted in William E. Leuchtenburg, *The White House Looks South* (Baton Rouge, La.: Louisiana State University Press, 2005), 224.

31 *"All these segregationists"*: Quoted in Roberts and Klibanoff, *Race Beat*, 388.

31 *"The march was like"*: Lewis, Ginsburg interview.

31 *"That's quite a crowd"*: Quoted in "Civil Rights: Protest on Route 80," *Time*, Apr. 12, 1965.

31 *"We have walked on"*: Ibid.

32 *"There was never a"*: Quoted in *Eyes on the Prize: Bridge to Freedom*, PBS, transcript, Nov. 5, 1985, http://digital.wustl.edu/cgi/t/text/text-idx?c=eop;cc=eop;q1=voting%20rights%20act;rgn=main;view=text;idno=lew0015.0557.063;hi=0.

32 *"The climate of public"*: U.S. Congress. House. Committee on the Judiciary, *Voting Rights—Hearings Before Subcommittee No. 5*, 89th Cong., 1st sess., 1965.

33 *"The lesson is plain"*: Ibid.

33 *"OK, that's your literacy"*: Quoted in Armand Derfner, interview by Marsha J. Tyson Darling, Voting Rights Act Documentation Project, Howard University, May 14, 1995, Washington, D.C.

34 *"What is necessary"*: *Voting Rights—Hearings Before Subcommittee No. 5*, 1965.

34 *"If the president's law"*: Ibid.

34 *"Have you ever seen"*: U.S. Congress. Senate. Committee on the Judiciary, *Voting Rights—Hearings on S. 1564*, 89th Cong., 1st sess., 1965.

34 *"I said it was"*: Ibid.

34 *"about as stupid a"*: Ibid.

35 *"all states which have"*: Quoted in Lawson, *Black Ballots*, 319.

35 *"Congress has attempted on"*: *Voting Rights—Hearings on S. 1564*, 1965.

35 *"I am opposed to"*: Quoted in May, *Bending Toward Justice*, 119.

36 *"good, stiff bourbon"*: Lyndon Johnson telephone conversation with Mike Mansfield and Everett Dirksen, Aug. 4, 1965, Miller Center, millercenter.org/scripps/archive/presidentialrecordings/johnson/1965/08_1965.

36 *"every penny my father"*: Lewis, *Wind*, xv.

36 *"The Montgomery bus boycott"*: Ibid., 48.

37 *"boy preacher"*: Ibid., 50.

37 *"I was like a"*: Quoted in *Freedom Riders*, WGBH American Experience, PBS, 2010.

37 *"Now John, you've got"*: Lewis, *Wind*, 361.

38 *"Today is a triumph"*: Remarks by Lyndon Johnson, Signing of the Voting Rights Act, Washington, D.C., Aug. 6, 1965, http://millercenter.org/president/speeches/speech-4034.

38 *"a great, great speech"*: Quoted in "President Lyndon B. Johnson Signs the Voting Rights Act," CBS News, Aug. 6, 1965.

38 *"a magnificent presentation"*: Ibid.

38 *"C'mon around here"*: Ibid.

38 *"a high point in"*: Lewis, *Wind*, 361.

38 *"I think we just"*: Quoted in Kotz, *Judgment Days*, 154.

2. THE SECOND RECONSTRUCTION

39 *"get those boys by"*: Lewis, *Wind*, 361.

39 *"The Voting Rights bill"*: John Doar to Mr. Pollak, Mrs. Jones, Miss Shelton, Miss Bargielski, "Voting Rights Act of 1965," Aug. 5, 1965, private papers of Stephen Pollak, Washington, D.C.

40 *"The decision to appoint"*: Nicholas deB. Katzenbach, draft memorandum to Victor B. Atkins, Aug. 7, 1965, Pollak papers.

41 *"I hereby certify"*: Nicholas deB. Katzenbach, "Certification of the Attorney General Pursuant to Section 6 of the Voting Rights Act of 1965," Aug. 9, 1965, Pollak papers.

41 *"I never dreamed"*: Quoted in John Herbers, "U.S. Voting Aides Depart for South," *New York Times*, Aug. 6, 1965.

41 *"Why are we here?"*: "Voting Rights Manual for Examiners," Aug. 1965, Pollak papers.

41 *"This morning, in some"*: Quoted in Jeffrey Frederick, *Stand Up for Alabama* (Tuscaloosa, Ala.: University of Alabama Press, 2007), 130.

42 *"When things were going"*: Quoted in Janet Wells, "Why Mrs. Mauldin Registered First," *VEP News*, March 1969, Voter Education Project Organizational Records, Printed and Published Materials, Box 45, Robert Woodruff Library, Atlanta.

42 *NOTICE: IT IS A*: U.S. Civil Service Commission, CSC Form 819, Aug. 1965, Pollak papers.

42 *"It didn't take but"*: Quoted in Wells, "Why Mrs. Mauldin Registered First."

43 *"The whole thing's so ridiculous"*: Quoted in Fred Powledge, "Negroes in Selma Flock to Register," *New York Times*, Aug. 10, 1965.

43 *"He is going to"*: Tom Wicker, "The Negro—News for Mr. Charlie," *New York Times*, Aug. 12, 1965.

43 *"The turnout far exceeded"*: Quoted in David Garrow, *Protest at Selma* (New Haven, Conn.: Yale University Press, 1978), 181.

43 *"I want to get"*: Lyndon Johnson telephone conversation with Nicholas Katzenbach, Aug. 17, 1965, Miller Center, millercenter.org/scripps/archive/presidentialrecordings/johnson/1965/08_1965.

43 *"It was clear"*: "Breakthrough on Voting Rights," *New York Times*, Aug. 15, 1965.

43 *"Our whole philosophy"*: Katzenbach, *Some of It Was Fun*, 174.

43 *"60,000 Register in 3"*: "60,000 Register in 3 Dixie States," *Chicago Defender*, Aug. 26, 1965.

44 *"Chris, you missed just"*: Quoted in Fred L. Zimmerman, "Changing Clinton," *Wall Street Journal*, Aug. 27, 1965.

44 *"Would you like to"*: Ibid.

44 *"We've been occupied"*: Ibid.

45 *"I imagine this will"*: Ibid.

45 *"This is the kickoff"*: Quoted in "Mississippi Suit Attacks Vote Act," Associated Press, Sept. 8, 1965.

45 *"to fight the constitutional"*: Frank J. Mizell, Jr., to George C. Wallace, Oct. 25, 1965, Governors' Papers (Wallace), Alabama Department of Archives and History, Montgomery, Ala.

45 *"remarked that bad laws"*: Ibid.

45 *"arbitrarily, unconstitutionally and unlawfully"*: Quoted in "McLeod's Motion Names Katzenbach Defendant," Associated Press, Sept. 30, 1965.

46 *"wide and profound implications"*: Oral Argument, *South Carolina v. Katzenbach*, 383 U.S. 301 (1966), January 17–18, 1966. Argument includes quotes from Warren, Robinson, McIlwaine, Leverett, Gremillion, and Katzenbach.

47–48 *"After enduring nearly"*: *South Carolina v. Katzenbach*, 383 U.S. 301 (1966).

48 *"The requirement that States"*: Ibid. (Black dissenting).

48 *"What the court has"*: "Milepost of Equal Rights," *Washington Post*, March 9, 1966.

48 *"The right to vote"*: *Harper v. Virginia Board of Elections*, 383 U.S. 663 (1966).

49 *"The division's most important"*: John Doar, "Draft memorandum to Attorneys Assigned to Work on Alabama Elections," March 1966, Pollak papers.

49 *"I was in Paris"*: Quoted in Roy Reed, "Joy, and Fear, in the Black Belt," *New York Times*, May 3, 1966.

50 *"I'm a segregationist"*: Quoted in "Selma Police Director: John Wilson Baker," *New York Times*, March 10, 1965.

50 *"Nobody, Negro or White"*: Quoted in "Big Political Day in Dallas County," *Southern Courier*, Apr. 30–May 1, 1966.

50 *"For law and order"*: Fager, *Selma*, 169.

50 *"We'd rather see Jim"*: Quoted in Gene Roberts, "Alabama Negroes Urged Not to Vote," *New York Times*, Apr. 19, 1966.

50 *"unified Negro vote"*: Quoted in Gene Roberts, "Dr. King Bids Alabama Negroes Conquer Fears and Vote as Bloc," *New York Times*, Apr. 29, 1966.

50 *"Baker wasn't our liberator"*: Chestnut and Cass, *Black in Selma*, 238.

50 *"just a little excited"*: Quoted in Jack Nelson, "Smiling, Unafraid, in Sunday Finest, They Came to Vote," *Los Angeles Times*, May 4, 1966.

51 *"I'm going to vote"*: Quoted in Roy Reed, "Alabama Negro Candidates Lead in 2 Legislative, 3 Sheriff's Votes," *New York Times*, May 4, 1966.

51 *"There are more people"*: Quoted in Nelson, "Smiling, Unafraid, in Sunday Finest, They Came to Vote."

51 *"Man, this is the"*: Quoted in Ray Rogers, "Alabama Negroes Vow to Exercise Rights at Primary," *Los Angeles Times*, May 1, 1966.

51 *"The boxes were so"*: Quoted in Roy Reed, "U.S. Asks Court to Declare Winner in Selma," *New York Times*, May 5, 1966.

51 *"ballot box coup"*: "Selma's Changing Climate," *Washington Post*, May 7, 1966.

52 *"Alabama's Segregation Leader"*: "Elect Alabama's Segregation Leader," *Tuscaloosa News*, Apr. 30, 1962.

52 *"nigger ballots"*: Quoted in Jack Nelson, "Judge's Ruling Poses Threat to Clark's Job," *Los Angeles Times*, May 18, 1966.

52 *"It is not a case"*: Quoted in "Alabama Group Hit in U.S. Vote Fraud Suit," *Los Angeles Times*, May 19, 1966.

52 *"The right to vote"*: Quoted in Gene Roberts, "U.S. Role Upheld in Selma Voting," *New York Times*, May 17, 1966.

52 *"The Court listened to"*: United States v. Executive Com. of Dem. P. of Dallas Co., ALA. 254 F. Supp. 537 (1966).

53 *"I didn't know if"*: Quoted in Julian Bond, *Black Candidates* (Atlanta: Southern Regional Council, 1968), 4.

53 *"This voting bill is"*: Quoted in Harold Stanley, *Voter Mobilization and the Politics of Race* (New York: Praeger, 1987), 50.

53 *"register and vote for"*: Quoted in United States v. State of Alabama, 252 F. Supp. 95 (M.D. Ala. 1966).

54 *"Dr. King's endorsement hung"*: Jack Nelson, "Bloc Voting Lesson Seen in Alabama," *Los Angeles Times*, May 5, 1966.

54 *"It was at Selma"*: Quoted in Dan Carter, *The Politics of Rage* (New York: Simon & Schuster, 1995), 287.

54 *"Jim Crow was still"*: John Dittmer, *Local People* (Champaign, Ill.: University of Illinois Press, 1995), 390.

54 *"register and vote"*: Quoted in Steven F. Lawson, *In Pursuit of Power* (New York: Columbia University Press, 1987), 49.

54 *"I only want James"*: Quoted in Branch, *At Canaan's Edge*, 476.

55 *"If you don't vote"*: Quoted in Gordan A. Martin, Jr., *Count Them One by One* (Oxford, Miss.: University Press of Mississippi, 2010), xi.

55 *"Only thus will ballots"*: Quoted in "Mississippi and the NAACP," *The Crisis*, June–July 1966.

55 *"It is time for all"*: Remarks by Clifton J. Whitley, Jan 9, 1966, University of Southern Mississippi Libraries, http://digilib.usm.edu/cdm/ref/collection/manu/id/1226.

56 *"if voter registration percentages"*: Henry Harris, "A Guest Editorial: Consolidation of Counties," *Daily Times Leader*, reprinted in *Jackson Clarion-Ledger*, Apr. 15, 1966.

56 *"All they are trying"*: Quoted in Frank R. Parker, *Black Votes Count* (Chapel Hill, N.C.: University of North Carolina Press, 1990), 59.

56 *"In 1966"*: Ibid., 3.

57 *"The only common element"*: Oral argument, Allen v. State Bd. of Elections, 393 U.S. 544 (1969), October 15–16, 1968.

57 *"great upsurge in voter registration"*: *Political Participation*, U.S. Commission on Civil Rights, Washington, D.C., May 1968.

58 *"the nation's most dramatic"*: Reese Cleghorn, "Meet Lester Maddox of Georgia," *New York Times Magazine*, Nov. 6, 1966.

58 *"It would have been"*: Quoted in Lawson, *In Pursuit of Power*, 6.

60 *"Yes, you can meet"*: Robert Clark, interview by Harriet Tanzman, Civil Rights Documentation Project, University of Southern Mississippi, Feb. 11, 2000, Hattiesburg, Miss., www.usm.edu/crdp/html/transcripts/manuscript-clark_robert_g.shtml.

60 *"election irregularities"*: "Mississippi House May Expel Negro," *New York Times*, Dec. 9, 1967.

60 *"The 1966 election laws"*: Dittmer, *Local People*, 416.

61 *"The question in these"*: Oral Argument, *Allen v. State Bd. of Elections*. Includes statements of Derfner, Lichtman, Allain, and Pollak.

63 *"The Voting Rights Act"*: *Allen v. State Bd. of Elections*.

63 *"This is reminiscent"*: Ibid. (Black dissenting).

63 *"Four years ago"*: Quoted in Lawson, *In Pursuit of Power*, 39.

63 *"What, sir, do you"*: Ibid., 4.

3. THE SOUTHERN STRATEGY

65 *"the most violent civil"*: Rick Perlstein, *Nixonland* (New York: Scribner, 2008), 15.

65 *" 'Get Whitey!' "*: "Out of a Cauldron of Hate—Arson and Death," *Life*, Aug. 27, 1965.

65 *"All through the South"*: Fager, *Selma*, 204.

66 *"Some old SNCC veterans"*: Quoted in Paul Good, "Odyssey of a Man—and a Movement," *New York Times Magazine*, June 25, 1967.

66 *"Black power"*: Quoted in Roy Reed, "Meredith March Through Mississippi a Year Ago Had Mixed Impact on Rights Struggle," *New York Times*, June 5, 1967.

66 *"That night in Canton"*: Quoted in Good, "Odyssey of a Man—and a Movement."

66 *"No good can come"*: Quoted in Jack Nelson, "Ousted Chairman Tells of New Setup in SNCC," *Los Angeles Times*, July 29, 1966.

66 *"It was lonesome"*: Quoted in Good, "Odyssey of a Man—and a Movement."

67 *"The hostility from white"*: Quoted in Laughlin McDonald, *A Voting Rights Odyssey* (Cambridge, U.K.: Cambridge University Press, 2003), 137.

67 *"Our nation is moving"*: Quoted in Perlstein, *Nixonland*, 239.

67 *"The more laws that"*: Ibid., 109.

67 *"I'm sorry, John"*: Quoted in Lewis, *Wind*, 406.

68 *"the loneliest, longest flight"*: Ibid., 416.

68 *"In 1968, it seemed"*: Andrew Young, *An Easy Burden* (New York: HarperCollins, 1996), 493.

68 *"I'm running for the"*: Quoted in Dan Carter, *From George Wallace to Newt Gingrich* (Baton Rouge, La.: University of Louisiana Press, 1996), 31.

69 *"Thurmond was the only"*: Harry Dent, *The Prodigal South Returns to Power* (New York: John Wiley & Sons, 1978), 77.

69 *"Strom is no racist"*: Ibid.

69 *"We're not going to"*: Quoted in Jack Bass and Walter De Vries, *The Transformation of Southern Politics* (New York: Basic Books, 1976), 27.

69 *"publicly defined the Republican"*: Mary D. Edsall and Thomas Byrne Edsall, *Chain Reaction* (New York: W. W. Norton, 1991), 7.

69 *"The party of our fathers"*: Quoted in Jack Bass and Marilyn W. Thompson, *Strom* (New York: Public Affairs, 2005), 192.

69 *"enormous significance"*: "Thurmond," *National Review*, Sept. 29, 1964.

70 *"I wanna tell you"*: Quoted in Bass and Thompson, *Strom*, 117.

70 *"Southern Manifesto"*: *Congressional Record*, 84th Cong., 2nd sess., vol. 102, part 4. Washington, D.C.: Government Printing Office, 1956.

70 *"Do not be deceived"*: Quoted in Nadine Cohodas, *Strom Thurmond and the Politics of Southern Change* (New York: Simon & Schuster, 1993), 292.

70 *"the most patently unconstitutional"*: Quoted in Joseph Crespino, *Strom Thurmond's America* (New York: Hill and Wang, 2012), 291.

70 *"nothing more nor less"*: Quoted in Horance G. Davis, "The Strangest of Coalitions," *Gainesville Sun*, Oct. 12, 1983.

70 *"Goldwater and Thurmond were"*: Dent, *Prodigal South*, 64.

71 *"seized and beaten by"*: Crespino, *Strom Thurmond's America*, 183.

71 *"The party of Lincoln"*: Jack Nelson, "Goldwater Republicans Tighten Grip in South," *Los Angeles Times*, Sept. 27, 1965.

71 *"We don't see anything"*: Quoted in Robert E. Baker, "Race, Big Government Are Main Issues in SC," *Washington Post*, May 1, 1966.

71 *"Our program for civil"*: Quoted in Theodore H. White, *The Making of the President 1960* (New York: Pocket Books, 1961), 466.

71 *"must not compromise its"*: Quoted in "Be Firm on Rights, Nixon Urges Party," *New York Times*, March 14, 1965.

72 *"riots, violence in the"*: Quoted in Carter, *Politics of Rage*, 327.

72 *"This is the future"*: Quoted in George Packer, "The Fall of Conservatism," *New Yorker*, May 26, 2008.

72 *"The newest of the new"*: Andrew Kopkind, "Back to Goldwater?," *New Republic*, Sept. 17, 1966.

72 *"come a-callin'"*: Quoted in Crespino, *Strom Thurmond's America*, 210.

72 DIXIELAND IS NIXONLAND: "'Dixieland Is Nixonland,' Reads a Big Sign Behind Republican Presidential Candidate, Richard Nixon," May 31, 1968, Allposters.com, www .allposters.com/-sp/Dixieland-Is-Nixonland-Reads-a-Big-Sign-Behind-Republican -Presidential-Candidate-Richard-Nixon-Posters_i9361275_.htm.

72 *"I was doing serious"*: Richard M. Nixon, *RN* (New York: Grosset & Dunlap, 1978), 304.

72 *"They tell me you"*: Quoted in Lewis Chester, Godfrey Hodgson, and Bruce Page, *An American Melodrama* (New York: Viking, 1969), 447.

72 *"strict constructionists"*: Quoted in Dent, *Prodigal South*, 82.

72 *"a whipping boy"*: Quoted in Perlstein, *Nixonland*, 300.

72 *"Nixon affirmed what people"*: Dent, *Prodigal South*, 81.

73 *"offers America the best"*: Ibid., 83.

73 *"Richard Nixon's position"*: Ibid., 87.

73 *"the chief of the Nixon"*: Ibid., 89.

73 *"Harry would sell Strom"*: Quoted in James Boyd, "Harry Dent, the President's Political Coordinator, Says: 'I Gave Thurmond 100% Loyalty and Now I Give Mr. Nixon 100%,'" *New York Times Magazine*, Feb. 2, 1970.

73 *"satisfy some professional civil rights group"*: Quoted in Carter, *Politics of Rage*, 392.

73 *"non-discriminatory"*: John Herbers, "Nixon Holds Most of Support in South by Promising Conservative Stand on Rights," *New York Times*, Aug. 8, 1968.

73 *"He's prostituted himself"*: Quoted in Will Lisner, "Jackie Robinson Splits with GOP over Nixon Choice," *New York Times*, Aug. 12, 1968.

73 *"looting, burning, killing"*: Quoted in Norman Mailer, *Miami and the Siege of Chicago* (New York: World Publishing Company, 1968), 150.

74 *"truly Strom Thurmond's convention"*: Rowland Evans and Robert Novak, "Strom Thurmond's Veto," *Syracuse Post-Standard*, Aug. 13, 1968.

74 *"the Nixiecrats"*: Quoted in "White House Denies Control of Convention," Associated Press, Aug. 16, 1968.

74 *"ran as a racist"*: Quoted in Carter, *Politics of Rage*, 326.

74 *"always couched his views"*: Quoted in Dean J. Kotlowski, *Nixon's Civil Rights* (Cambridge, Mass.: Harvard University Press, 2002), 268.

74 *"I don't talk about"*: Chester, Hodgson, and Page, *An American Melodrama*, 662.

74 *"I think the ideas"*: Quoted in Reg Murphy and Hal Gulliver, *The Southern Strategy* (New York: Scribner, 1971), 1.

74 *Thurmond Speaks for Nixon*: Dent, *Prodigal South*, 106.

74–75 *"Senator Thurmond denied the"*: Quoted in Perlstein, *Nixonland*, 342.

75 *"Help Strom Elect Nixon"*: Quoted in Homer Bigart, "Nixon, After Tour in South, Goes to Hartford Rally and Assails Inflation," *New York Times*, Oct. 5, 1968.

75 *"The first civil right"*: "1968 Nixon vs. Humphrey vs. Wallace," Museum of the Moving Image, New York, N.Y., www.livingroomcandidate.org/commercials/1968/the-first-civil -right.

75 *"I pledge to you"*: Quoted in Carter, *From George Wallace to Newt Gingrich*, 34.

75 *"The fact is that"*: Vernon E. Jordan, Jr., "New Game in Dixie," *Nation*, Oct. 21, 1968.

75 *"The Great White Switch"*: Earl Black and Merle Black, *The Rise of Southern Republicans* (Cambridge, Mass.: Harvard University Press, 2002), 205.

75 *"Strom, you did a"*: Quoted in Dent, *Prodigal South*, 116.

76 *"a small quid for"*: Quoted in Boyd, "Harry Dent, the President's Political Coordinator, Says: 'I Gave Thurmond 100% Loyalty and Now I Give Mr. Nixon 100%.'"

76 *"Uncle Strom's Cabin"*: Quoted in Dent, *Prodigal South*, 6.

76 *"When I voted for"*: U.S. Congress. House. Committee on the Judiciary, *Hearings Before Subcommittee No. 5 on H.R. 4249, H.R. 5538, and Similar Proposals*, 91st Cong., 1st sess., 1969.

76 *"The history of the"*: Ibid.

76–77 *"John, this is extremely"*: Quoted in Kotlowski, *Nixon's Civil Rights*, 78.

77 *"the nation as a whole"*: Ibid., 79.

77 *"The Voting Rights Act"*: Quoted in Leon Panetta and Peter Gall, *Bring Us Together* (New York: Lippincott, 1971), 106.

77 *"As to the whole"*: Quoted in Rick Perlstein, "Exclusive: Lee Atwater's Infamous 1981 Interview on the Southern Strategy," TheNation.com, Nov. 13, 2012, www.thenation .com/article/170841/exclusive-lee-atwaters-infamous-1981-interview-southern -strategy#.

77 *the Heavyweight*: "The Administration: Nixon's Heavyweight," *Time*, July 25, 1969.

77 *"dour, taciturn, formidably efficient"*: Ibid.

77 *"Mr. Southern Strategy"*: Panetta and Gall, *Bring Us Together*, 97.

77 *"I think this is"*: Quoted in Milton Viorst, "The Mitchell Philosophy," *New York Times Magazine*, Aug. 10, 1969.

77 *"I cannot support"*: *Hearings Before Subcommittee No. 5 on H.R. 4249, H.R. 5538, and Similar Proposals*, 1969.

78 *"is like saying"*: Ibid.

78 *"The administration creates a"*: Ibid.

78 *"Your proposed alternative"*: Theodore M. Hesburgh, letter to Hon. John M. Mitchell, U.S. Commission on Civil Rights, Washington, D.C., June 28, 1969.

78 *"by far the most"*: Quoted in Leon Friedman and William F. Levantrosser, *Watergate and Afterward: The Legacy of Richard M. Nixon* (New York: Praeger, 1992), 71.

78 *"into smoke and ashes"*: *Hearings Before Subcommittee No. 5 on H.R. 4249, H.R. 5538, and Similar Proposals*, 1969.

79 *"My Greene County chairman"*: Quoted in Sheryll Cashin, *The Agitator's Daughter* (New York: Public Affairs, 2008), 196.

80 *"the theft of the"*: Oral Argument, *Hadnott v. Amos*, 394 U.S. 358 (1969), Oct. 18, 1968.

80 *"We are going to"*: Quoted in Cashin, *Agitator's Daughter*, 202.

80 *"Soul power"*: Quoted in Martin Waldron, "Alabama Negroes Get Confirmation," *New York Times*, Aug. 2, 1969.

80 *"a victory for justice"*: Quoted in "Greene County Election a 'Victory for Justice,'" United Press International, Aug. 12, 1969.

80 *"The pool is integrated"*: Ibid.

80 *"The provisions of the"*: John T. Nixon, letter to Hon. Birch Bayh, Dec. 16, 1969. U.S. Congress. Senate. Committee on the Judiciary, *Hearings Before the Subcommittee on Civil Rights on S. 818, S. 2456, S. 2507 and Title IV of S. 2029*, 91st Cong., 1st and 2nd sess., 1969–1970.

81 *"At the present time"*: Quoted in Jack Nelson, "Civil Rights Aide Quits, Blasts at Justice Dept.," *Los Angeles Times*, Oct. 17, 1969.

81 *"Jim Crow Must Go"*: "NAACP History: Medgar Evers," NAACP.org, www.naacp.org /pages/naacp-history-medgar-evers.

81 *"We've come a long"*: Quoted in "Evers Takes Mayor's Oath in Mississippi," *Chicago Tribune*, July 8, 1969.

81 *"Don't vote for a"*: Quoted in Bayard Rustin, "The Myths of the Black Revolt," *Ebony*, Aug. 1969.

81 *"the greatest deterrent"*: Quoted in Tom Greene, "Voting Rights Act: Dramatic Results in South," United Press International, Aug. 6, 1970.

81 *"Oh my, this is"*: Quoted in Richard Harwood, "Evers: 'A New Day' for Fayette," *Washington Post*, July 8, 1969.

82 *"We got no jobs"*: Quoted in Anthony Hiss, "Notes and Comment," *New Yorker*, June 14, 1969.

82 *"we're through"*: Quoted in Bruce Eggler, "A Long Way to Go in Mississippi," *New Republic*, June 28, 1969.

82 *"I have stated before"*: U.S. Congress. Senate. Committee on the Judiciary, *Hearings Before the Subcommittee on Civil Rights on S. 818, S. 2456, S. 2507 and Title IV of S. 2029*, 91st Cong., 1st and 2nd sess., 1969–1970. Includes statements of Thurmond, Mitchell, and Rauh.

83 *"civil wrong bill"*: Quoted in May, *Bending Toward Justice*, 205.

84 *"It looks like the Klan"*: Quoted in William Greider, "House Vote Is Bitterly Criticized," *Washington Post*, Dec. 12, 1969.

84 *"repealing the 1960's"*: Russell Baker, "Observer: Elephants in Dixie," *New York Times*, Dec. 15, 1969.

84 *"I believe the time"*: *Hearings Before the Subcommittee on Civil Rights on S. 818, S. 2456, S. 2507 and Title IV of S. 2029*, 1969–1970.

85 *"unconstitutional"*: Quoted in "Nixon Statement on Signing Voting Bill," *New York Times*, June 22, 1970.

85 *"A veto of the anti-South"*: William E. Timmons, memorandum for the President, June 18, 1970, Box 20, HU, WHCF, Nixon Presidential Materials, National Archives, College Park, Md.

85 *"To veto the Voting"*: Ray Price to Len Garment, "Voting Rights Act—to sign or veto," June 18, 1970, Box 60, Haldeman Files, NPM.

85 *"I cannot emphasize how"*: Len Garment, "Memorandum on Voting Rights," June 18, 1970, Box 60, Haldeman Files, NPM.

85 *"Am concerned re volatile"*: Quoted in Kotlowski, *Nixon's Civil Rights*, 91.

85 *"In the five years"*: "Nixon Statement on Signing Voting Bill," *New York Times*, June 23, 1970.

86 *"regional"*: Quoted in Kotlowski, *Nixon's Civil Rights*, 92.

86 *"man in Greene County"*: Quoted in Robert Dewitt, "Rights Leader Slipped Back into Life He Loved," *Tuscaloosa News*, Jan. 27, 1991.

86 *"the black capital of"*: Quoted in Philip D. Carter, "Blacks in Power in Alabama County," *Washington Post*, Jan. 25, 1971.

86 *"This court don't do"*: Quoted in James T. Wooten, "Alabama Judge Is Found Guilty in Keeping Negroes Off the Slate," *New York Times*, Jan. 7, 1971.

86 *"Three hundred thousand nigger"*: Quoted in Carter, *From George Wallace*, 48.

87 *"bloc vote"*: Murphy and Gulliver, *Southern Strategy*, 99.

87 *"spotted alliance"*: Ibid., 101–102.

87 *"This Could Be Alabama"*: Carter, *Politics of Rage*, 393.

87 *"Suppose your wife is"*: Carter, *From George Wallace*, 48.

87 *"The principal factor"*: Ted Pearson, "Wallace Rides Backlash to Narrow Comeback," *Birmingham News*, June 3, 1970.

87 *"It was nigger, nigger"*: Quoted in Carter, *Politics of Rage*, 395.

87 *"as the pillar of"*: Kevin Phillips, *The Emerging Republican Majority* (New Rochelle, N.Y.: Arlington House, 1969), 187.

88 *"The blacks aren't where"*: Quoted in Panetta and Gall, *Bring Us Together*, 187.

88 *"will do for conservative"*: Quoted in Robert Mason, *Richard Nixon and the Quest for a New Majority* (Chapel Hill, N.C.: University of North Carolina Press, 2004), 50.

88 *"follow Phillips['s] plan"*: Quoted in Carter, *Politics of Rage*, 379.

88 *"Use Phillips as an analyst"*: Ibid., 380.

88 *"Since I have been"*: U.S. Congress. House. Committee on the Judiciary, Subcommittee on Civil and Constitutional Rights, *Hearings on Extension of the Voting Rights Act*, 94th Cong., 1st sess., 1975.

89 *"black Moses"*: Quoted in Lawson, *In Pursuit of Power*, 179.

89 *"These Are Your Candidates"*: "These Are Your Candidates," *New York Times*, Apr. 30, 1971.

89 *"In our present state"*: Parker, *Black Votes Count*, 62.

89 *"Charles Evers bill"*: Ibid.

89 *"I believe the history"*: Jim Turner letter to Jerris Leonard, "Mississippi Open Primary Law," Sept. 17, 1970, Department of Justice, private papers of Jim Turner.

90 *"humiliation in bringing the"*: *Evers v. State Board of Election Commissioners*, 327 F. Supp. 640 (S.D. Miss. 1971).

90 *"I have told the"*: Quoted in Kenneth Reich, "Mitchell Calls Voting Act Heavy Burden," *Los Angeles Times*, May 19, 1971.

90 *"All the work that"*: Quoted in Kenneth Reich, "Justice Dept. OKs New Voter Signup in 4 Mississippi Areas," *Los Angeles Times*, March 24, 1971.

91 *"The re-registration process"*: John Lewis, Telegram to Attorney General John Mitchell, Apr. 19, 1971, VEP records, Office Files, Box 95.

91 *"unable to reach the"*: Quoted in Martin Waldron, "Mississippi Blacks to Test Vote Rule," *New York Times*, March 23, 1971.

91 *"It is a palpable"*: "The Vote in Mississippi," *Los Angeles Times*, March 29, 1971.

91 *"de facto repeal"*: Quoted in Lawson, *In Pursuit of Power*, 163.

91 *"difficult to comprehend"*: Quoted in John P. MacKenzie, "Voting Right Switch Asked of Mitchell," *Washington Post*, March 29, 1971.

91 *"The Attorney General is"*: U.S. Congress. House. Committee on the Judiciary, Civil Rights Oversight Subcommittee, *The Enforcement and Administration of the Voting Rights Act of 1965*, 92nd Cong., 1st sess., 1971.

92 *"Our trip was"*: Quoted in "1971 Annual Report, Voter Education Project, Inc.," VEP records, Office Files, Box 162.

93 *"Let the Voice of"*: Ibid.

93 *"I had no idea"*: Quoted in Thomas A. Johnson, "130 Lawyers Arrive to Observe Mississippi Voting," *New York Times*, Nov. 1, 1971.

93 *"Welcome to Belzoni"*: Quoted in Kenneth Reich, "Changing South," *Los Angeles Times*, July 3, 1971.

94 *"He didn't come down"*: Ibid.

94 *"go see Charles Evers"*: Quoted in Lester Salamon, "Mississippi Post-Mortem: The 1971 Elections," *New South*, Winter 1972.

94 *"The strategy of mounting"*: Ibid.

95 *"All my land"*: Ibid.
95 *"two extremes"*: *The Enforcement and Administration of the Voting Rights Act of 1965*, 1971.
95 *"In 1971, the weight"*: Quoted in "What Happened in the South 1971," VEP records, Printed and Published Materials, Box 25.
95 *"hack up Atlanta worse"*: Quoted in McDonald, *Voting Rights Odyssey*, 149.
95 *"a white, moderate, Democratic"*: Ibid.
95 *"There was no question"*: Andrew Young, interview by Jack Bass and Walter De Vries, Jan. 31, 1974. Southern Oral History Program Collection, University of North Carolina, Chapel Hill, http://docsouth.unc.edu/sohp/A-0080/A-0080.html.
95 *"a clear case of"*: Quoted in "Young Calls Reseating Plan Racial," *Atlanta Daily World*, Oct. 15, 1971.
96 *"King was the spear"*: Quoted in Wayne King, "Andrew Jackson Young Jr.," *New York Times*, Dec. 16, 1976.
96 *"New South Coalition"*: Quoted in Hamilton Bims, "A Southern Activist Goes to the House," *Ebony*, Feb. 1973.
96 *"Think Young"*: Ibid.
96 *"Rodney will have an"*: Quoted in "Cook Gets Nixon's Blessings," *Atlanta Daily World*, Nov. 2, 1976.
97 *"What's the Difference"*: Quoted in Stuart Eizenstat and William H. Barutio, "Andrew Young: The Path to History," Apr. 1973, VEP records, Printed and Published Materials, Box 28.
97 *"Cook opposes the concept"*: Ibid.
98 *" for the first time"*: Ibid.
98 *"I lost Old South"*: Quoted in John Hemphill, "South's First Black Since 1870 Is Elected to House by Georgia," *New York Times*, Nov. 9, 1972.
98 *"Andy's victory"*: Quoted in Eizenstat and Barutio, "Andrew Young: The Path to History."
98 *"Even white people had"*: Chestnut and Cass, *Black in Selma*, 262.
98 *"People have got more"*: Quoted in Janet Wells, "Why Mrs. Mauldin Registered First."
99 *"I think within the"*: Remarks by Martin Luther King, Jr., Washington, D.C., Aug. 5, 1965, SCLC Files, King Library, Atlanta.
99 *"By the mid-1970s"*: Bass and De Vries, *Transformation of Southern Politics*, 42.
99 *"the peaceful revolution"*: Quoted in "Voter Education Project 1972 Annual Report," VEP records, Office Files, Box 162.

4. HANDS THAT PICK COTTON

100 *"There was no separation"*: Lewis, *Wind*, 180.
100 *"the central front"*: Ibid., 179.
100 *"an undertaking so wise"*: Remarks by Nicholas deB. Katzenbach, Atlanta, Feb. 28, 1966, www.justice.gov/sites/default/files/ag/legacy/2011/08/23/02-28-1966.pdf.
101 *"a new era of moderation"*: Remarks by John Lewis, Atlanta, Nov. 14, 1976, VEP records, Printed and Published Materials, Box 25.
102 *"Mr. Bond and Mr. Lewis"*: Quoted in James T. Wooten, "Rights Aides Find Southern Blacks Failing to Use Voting Power," *New York Times*, Aug. 8, 1971.
102 *"We come to Louisiana"*: Statement by John Lewis, Baton Rouge, Louisiana Press Conference, Aug. 3, 1971, VEP records, Office Files, Box 48.
102 *"When an oppressed people"*: Quoted in Wooten, "Rights Aides Find Southern Blacks Failing to Use Voting Power."
102 *"the day of tea"*: Quoted in Bob Anderson, "Bond Urges Blacks to Register to Vote," *Advocate* (Baton Rouge), Aug. 4, 1971.
102 *"wear an Afro"*: Ibid.

103 *"a real go-getter"*: William H. Samuel, Jr., to John Lewis–Julian Bond Tour Party, July 31, 1971, VEP records, Office Files, Box 95.

103 *"paper work"*: Weldon Rougeau, Field Report #38-11, VEP records, Office Files, Box 161.

103 *"Unquestionably, the Tensas Parish"*: Ibid.

103 *"there is no use"*: Quoted in *The Voting Rights Act: Ten Years After*, U.S. Commission on Civil Rights, Washington, D.C., 1975.

103 *"Our problem is that"*: Quoted in Wooten, "Rights Aides Find Southern Blacks Failing to Use Voting Power."

103 *"continued, unglamorous, day-to-day"*: Remarks by John Lewis, Leadership Conference on Civil Rights, Washington, D.C., Jan. 27, 1975, VEP records, Office Files, Box 95.

104 *"It is a must"*: Quoted in Portia S. Brookings, "Senators, Rights Leaders Back Extension of Voting Act," *Atlanta Daily World*, Jan. 16, 1975.

104 *"For each state"*: *The Voting Rights Act: Ten Years After*.

105 *"We've come a long"*: Quoted in Lawson, *In Pursuit of Power*, 224.

105 *"We used to sing"*: Quoted in "Back to Selma After 10 Years of Progress," *Brooklyn Recorder*, Apr. 5, 1975.

105 *"forgotten minority"*: Dennis Holder, "The Forgotten Minority," *D Magazine*, Sept. 1986.

105 *"I want to tell"*: U.S. Congress. Senate. Committee on the Judiciary, Subcommittee on Constitutional Rights, *Extension of the Voting Rights Act of 1965*, 94th Cong., 1st sess., 1975.

106 *"Our political lives"*: House, *Hearings on Extension of the Voting Rights Act*, 1975.

106 *"If you are going"*: Senate, *Extension of the Voting Rights Act of 1965*, 1975.

107 *"Now when I try"*: Quoted in Richard A. Shaffer, "Ballot-Box Bias?," *Wall Street Journal*, July 11, 1975.

107 *"For Chicanos it was"*: House, *Hearings on Extension of the Voting Rights Act*, 1975.

107 *"There has been"*: Ibid.

107–108 *"You have made"*: Ibid.

108 *"Thank you, Mr. Rodriguez"*: Ibid.

108 *"Nearly all the forms"*: Hon. Barbara Jordan, "Voting Rights Extension Act," Feb. 19, 1975, House, 94th Cong., 1st sess., *Congressional Record*, 3685.

109 *"Jordan has been a First and an Only"*: Molly Ivins, "'She's as Cozy as a Pile Driver,'" *Washington Post*, Oct. 10, 1972.

109 *"My political career was"*: House, *Hearings on Extension of the Voting Rights Act*, 1975.

109 *"She proved that black"*: Quoted in Albin Krebs, "A Sometimes Political Hails New Politics," *New York Times*, Oct. 23, 1971.

109 *"a black LBJ"*: William Broyles, "The Making of Barbara Jordan," *Texas Monthly*, Oct. 1976.

109 *"My faith in the"*: U.S. Congress. House. Committee on the Judiciary, *Debate on Articles of Impeachment*, 93rd Cong., 2nd sess., 1974.

109 *"If the Voting Rights"*: House, *Hearings on Extension of the Voting Rights Act*, 1975.

109 *"Extension of the Voting"*: Ibid.

110 *"It would be a"*: Senate, *Extension of the Voting Rights Act of 1965*, 1975.

110 *"Let me put it"*: Quoted in William Raspberry, "'We Still Need the Voting Rights Act,'" *Washington Post*, March 10, 1975.

110 *"limited"*: Lawrence Meyer, "Shift Debated in Voting Rights," *Washington Post*, Dec. 26, 1974.

111 *"pain, suffering, humiliation"*: Quoted in Gary Martin and Jeremy Roebuck, "Man Recalls His Struggle with Voter Discrimination in Texas," *San Antonio Express-News*, May 5, 2013.

112 *"multilingualism"*: Quoted in Ernest Holsendolph, "House Votes, 341 to 70, to Extend and Broaden Voting Rights Act," *New York Times*, June 5, 1975.

112 *"heavy consensus"*: Quoted in "Senate Taking Up Voting Rights Act," Associated Press, July 21, 1975.

112 *"The right to vote"*: Quoted in Cynthia Gorney, "Ford Hails Gain in Voting Rights," *Washington Post*, Aug. 7, 1975.

112 *"That was my first"*: Quoted in Mary Beth Rogers, *American Hero* (New York: Bantam, 1998), 247.

113 *"The 1974 class of"*: Bass and De Vries, *Transformation of Southern Politics*, 377.

113 *"It has helped to"*: Quoted in Peter Stuart, "Civil-Rights Act Renewal," *Christian Science Monitor*, June 10, 1975.

113 *"We in Alabama believe"*: Ibid.

113 *"The South has rejoined"*: Quoted in Roy Reed, "House Veterans Readjust to Liberal Trend in South," *New York Times*, Feb. 25, 1975.

113 *"It used to be"*: Bass and De Vries, *Transformation of Southern Politics*, 47.

114 *"I've got $5"*: Quoted in Patrick Anderson, "Peanut Farmer for President," *New York Times Magazine*, Dec. 14, 1975.

114 *"the most liberal person"*: Ibid.

114 *"In Sumter County you could"*: Quoted in "Why Carter Wins the Black Vote," *Time*, Apr. 5, 1976.

114 *"I say to you"*: Quoted in Anderson, "Peanut Farmer for President."

115 *"In 1970 there was"*: Jimmy Carter, interview by Jack Bass and Walter De Vries, 1974, Southern Oral History Program Collection, docsouth.unc.edu/sohp/A-0066/menu.html.

115 *"White politicians no longer"*: Remarks by Andrew Young, Conference on Southern Minority Politics, Washington, D.C., Oct. 8, 1974.

115 DIXIE WHISTLES A DIFFERENT: "Dixie Whistles a Different Tune," *Time*, May 31, 1971.

115 *"Wallace pulled the whole"*: Quoted in Ken Bode, "Why Carter's Big with Blacks," *New Republic*, Apr. 4, 1976.

116 NEW BLACK SUPPORT HELPED: Francis B. Kent, "New Black Support Helped Wallace Win," *Los Angeles Times*, May 9, 1974.

116 *"[Carter's] effort to defeat George"*: Quoted in Paul Delaney, "Carter's Vote Success with Blacks Assayed," *New York Times*, Apr. 14, 1976.

116 *"the best thing that"*: Quoted in Anderson, "Peanut Farmer for President."

116 *"It's a matter of"*: Quoted in James T. Wooten, "Carter Now Aims to Win Florida," *New York Times*, March 1, 1976.

116 *"It was one hundred"*: Remarks by Barbara Jordan, Democratic National Convention, New York, July 12, 1976, www.americanrhetoric.com/speeches/barbarajordan1976dnc.html.

117 *"I'm ready to lay down"*: Quoted in B. Drummond Ayres, Jr., "Democratic Unity Reflects Changes in South," *New York Times*, July 16, 1976.

117 *"a New South really"*: Quoted in B. Drummond Ayres, Jr., "Brings Votes of Liberals and Blacks to Georgian," *New York Times*, July 14, 1976.

117 *"I knew Jimmy when"*: Ibid.

117 *"Is this the New"*: Quoted in Ayres, "Democratic Unity Reflects Changes in South."

117 *"I have had many"*: Ibid.

118 *"Voter Registration Month"*: VEP Press Release, July 2, 1976, VEP records, Printed and Published Materials, Box 25.

118 *"The goal for which MLK"*: Quoted in VEP 1976 Annual Report, VEP records, Printed and Published Materials, Box 27.

118 *"It was our best"*: Ibid.

118 *"Hands That Pick Cotton"*: Lewis, *Wind*, 434.

118 *"All in the Family"*: VEP 1976 Annual Report.

118 *"the great equalizer"*: Ibid.

118 *"You know why I'm"*: Ibid.

118 *"Operation Big Vote"*: Ibid.

118 *"biggest voter registration"*: Paul Delaney, "Blacks Are Pleased by Election Effort," *New York Times*, Oct. 30, 1976.

118 *"We are going all"*: Quoted in Paul Delaney, "Carter Accelerating His 'All Out' Effort to Broaden His Support Among Blacks," *New York Times*, Aug. 14, 1976.

119 *"would be 10 percent"*: Quoted in Lawson, *In Pursuit of Power*, 255.

119 *"I could not stand"*: Quoted in Howell Raines, *My Soul Is Rested* (New York: Penguin, 1977), 23.

119 *"I would urge my"*: VEP Press Release, Oct. 1976, VEP records, Printed and Published Materials, Box 25.

119 *"I heard that it"*: Quoted in Lawson, *In Pursuit of Power*, 255.

119 *"What made a key"*: Dent, *Prodigal South*, 14.

119 *"The black vote in"*: VEP 1976 Annual Report.

120 *"Those tears weren't about"*: Lewis, *Wind*, 439.

120 *"I wish—Lord, how I wish"*: Quoted in "The Election: Jimmy's Debt to Blacks," *Time*, Nov. 22, 1976.

5. THE COUNTERREVOLUTION

121 *"Before you leave Oxford"*: Quoted in Lewis, *Wind*, 254.

122 *"Mississippi's giant house party"*: Trent Watts, "Mississippi's Giant House Party," *Southern Cultures*, vol. 8, no. 2, Summer 2002.

122 *"If it is necessary"*: Quoted in "James K. Vardaman," *Wikipedia*, en.wikipedia.org/wiki /James_K._Vardaman#cite_note-amex-1.

123 *"We want Reagan!"*: Quoted in Douglas E. Kneeland, "Reagan Campaigns at Mississippi Fair," *New York Times*, Aug. 3, 1980.

123 *"George Wallace–inclined voters"*: Quoted in Joseph A. Crespino, "Did David Brooks Tell the Full Story About Reagan's Neshoba County Fair Visit?," Nov. 15, 2007, History News Network, historynewsnetwork.org/article/44535#sthash.1VcZGtwh.dpuf.

123 *"I believe in states' rights"*: "Transcript of Ronald Reagan's 1980 Neshoba County Fair speech," *Neshoba Democrat*, Nov. 15, 2007.

123 *"We want that federal"*: Quoted in Joseph Crespino, *In Search of Another Country* (Princeton, N.J.: Princeton University Press, 2007), 286.

123 *"You've seen in this"*: Quoted in Anthony Lewis, "A Nice Guy Contest?," *New York Times*, Sept. 21, 1980.

124 *"You can't guarantee someone's freedom"*: Quoted in Ronnie Dugger, *On Reagan* (New York: McGraw-Hill, 1983), 197.

124 *"the Constitution very specifically"*: Ibid., 198.

124 *"vindictive, selective application"*: Ibid.

124 *"humiliating to the South"*: Ibid.

124 *"The thought of Philadelphia"*: Andrew Young, "Chilling Words in Neshoba County," *Washington Post*, Aug. 11, 1980.

124 *"Which one is the"*: Quoted in "Ronald Reagan's Neshoba County Speech," C-Span, Apr. 10, 2010, www.c-span.org/video/?293124-1/ronald-reagans-neshoba-county-speech.

125 *"We've loved you"*: Quoted in Dugger, *On Reagan*, 198.

125 *"the so-called social"*: Quoted in Edsall and Edsall, *Chain Reaction*, 141.

125 *"get the government off"*: Remarks by Ronald Reagan, Nov. 3, 1980, www.presidency .ucsb.edu/ws/?pid=85199.

125 *"What the Administration is"*: Quoted in "Firing a Fighter," *Time*, Nov. 30, 1981.

125 *"Our Constitution is color-blind"*: *Plessy v. Ferguson*, 163 U.S. 537 (1896).

126 *"Justice is pictured blind"*: Quoted in Randall Kennedy, "Colorblind Constitutionalism," *Fordham Law Review*, vol. 82, issue 1, 2013.

126 *"Bible"*: Quoted in Ian Haney Lopez, "A Nation of Minorities," *Stanford Law Review*, vol. 59, issue 4, Feb. 2007.

126 *"my four little children"*: Remarks by Martin Luther King, Jr., Washington, D.C., Aug. 28, 1963, www.americanrhetoric.com/speeches/mlkihaveadream.htm.

126 *"Whenever this issue of"*: Martin Luther King, Jr., *Why We Can't Wait* (New York: Harper & Row, 1964), 159.

126 *"You do not take"*: Remarks by Lyndon Johnson, Washington, D.C., June 4, 1965, www .lbjlib.utexas.edu/johnson/archives.hom/speeches.hom/650604.asp.

127 *"equality as a fact"*: Ibid.

127 *"the anti-Stalinist left"*: Quoted in *Arguing the World*, directed by Joseph Dorman (New York: First Run Features, 1998).

127 *"a man of the"*: Ibid.

127 *"Negroes and Jews"*: Nathan Glazer, "Negroes and Jews," *Commentary*, Dec. 1, 1964.

127 *"Democrats for Nixon"*: Quoted in *Arguing the World*.

128 *"In 1964 we declared"*: Nathan Glazer, *Affirmative Discrimination* (New York: Basic Books, 1975), 31.

128 *"in order to get beyond"*: *Regents of the University of California v. Bakke*, 438 U.S. 265 (1978) (Brennan concurring).

128 *"The Disease as Cure"*: Antonin Scalia, "The Disease as Cure," *Washington University Law Review*, vol. 1979, issue 1, 1979.

128 *"stop taking care of"*: Quoted in Adam Shatz, "The Thernstroms in Black and White," *American Prospect*, March 12, 2001.

129 *"never made a dime"*: Ibid.

129 *"become the world's greatest"*: Ibid.

129 *"You cannot do redistricting"*: Oral Argument, *United Jewish Organizations v. Carey*, 430 U.S. 144 (1977), Oct. 6, 1976.

129 *"Compliance with the Act"*: *United Jewish Organizations v. Carey*.

130 *"clearly lost its way"*: Thernstrom, *Whose Votes Count?*, 76.

130 *"the single most important"*: Quoted in Shatz, "The Thernstroms in Black and White."

130 *"Immediate and massive registration"*: Thernstrom, "The Odd Evolution of the Voting Rights Act."

130 *"The Act gives a"*: *Allen v. State Bd. of Elections*.

130 *"definitively altered"*: Thernstrom, "The Odd Evolution of the Voting Rights Act."

130 *"He is envisioning"*: Ibid.

131 *"The Reagan era was"*: Quoted in Shatz, "The Thernstroms in Black and White."

131 *"a duty to [his] race"*: Quoted in Scotty E. Kirkland, "Pink Sheets and Black Ballots," University of South Alabama, 2009, http://books.google.com/books/about/Pink _Sheets_and_Black_Ballots.html?id=OJcOSQAACAAJ.

132 *"At-large election systems"*: U.S. Commission on Civil Rights, *Voting Rights Act: Unfulfilled Goals*, Washington, D.C., Sept. 1981.

132 *"the totality of circumstances"*: *White v. Regester*, 412 U.S. 755 (1973).

133 *"Practically all active candidates"*: *Bolden v. City of Mobile*, 423 F. Supp. 384 (S.D. Ala. 1976).

133 *"Pittmanville"*: Quoted in Brendan Kirby, "Pariah to 'Hero'—How Judge Virgil Pittman Transformed Mobile and His Own Image," Al.com, Jan. 22, 2010, blog.al.com/live /2012/01/pariah_to_hero_--_how_judge_vi.html.

134 *"The election system in"*: Appellee Brief, *City of Mobile v. Bolden*, 1979.

134 *"affirmative action"*: Appellant Brief, ibid.

134 *"Racially discriminatory motivation"*: *Mobile v. Bolden*, 446 U.S. 55 (1980).

134 *"A plurality of the"*: Ibid., (Marshall dissenting).

135 *"principled, simple, and tight"*: Thernstrom, *Whose Votes Count?* 75.

135 *"An act of war"*: Quoted in Kirkland, "Pink Sheets and Black Ballots."

135 *"the biggest step backwards"*: Quoted in Linda Greenhouse, "High Court Voids Victory of Blacks over At-Large Voting in Mobile," *New York Times*, Apr. 23, 1980.

135 *"If most people had"*: Armand Derfner, "The Implications of the City of Mobile Case for Extension of the Voting Rights Act," in *The Right to Vote: A Rockefeller Foundation Conference* (New York: Rockefeller Foundation, 1981).

137 *"litmus test"*: Barton Gellman, "Voting Rights," *New Republic*, June 27, 1981.
138 *"My view is"*: U.S. Congress. House. Committee on the Judiciary, Subcommittee on Civil and Constitutional Rights, *Extension of the Voting Rights Act*, 97th Cong., 2nd sess., 1981. Includes statements from Hyde, Bozeman, and Edwards.
139 *"You're being dishonest if"*: Quoted in "Sound Advice on American Rights," *New York Times*, July 31, 1981.
139 *"first major breakthrough"*: Ralph G. Neas, "Draft Outline for Legislative Campaign on VRA Extension," private papers of Ralph Neas.
140 *"If you move quickly"*: Quoted in Thomas M. Boyd and Stephen J. Markman, "The 1982 Amendments to the Voting Rights Act: A Legislative History," *Washington and Lee Law Review*, vol. 40, issue 40, 1983.
140 *"It was just like"*: Quoted in "60s Flashback," *Time*, Oct. 19, 1981.
140 *"I am sensitive to"*: Quoted in Lee Lescaze, "Reagan Seeks Assessment of Voting Rights Act," *Washington Post*, June 16, 1981.
141 *"Reagan to Extend Voting Act"*: George Skelton, "Reagan to Extend Voting Act," *Los Angeles Times*, Nov. 6, 1981.
141 *"When I look back"*: Quoted in Kathy Sawyer, "A Repentant Harry Dent Will Follow the Lord," *Washington Post*, Aug. 22, 1981.
141 *"If Reagan endorses the"*: Quoted in Raymond Wolters, *Right Turn* (New Brunswick, N.J.: Transaction Publishers, 1996), 54.
141 *"I want to see"*: Ibid.
141 *"You campaigned against quotas"*: Ibid.
142 *"modified"*: Quoted in George Skelton, "An Angry Smith Won Voting Act Concession," *Los Angeles Times*, Nov. 8, 1981.
142 *"I believe that the"*: Quoted in Robert Pear, "Reagan Backs Voting Rights Act but Wants to Ease Requirements," *New York Times*, Nov. 7, 1981.
142 *"Civil Rights is one"*: Michael E. Hammond, "Justice," in *Mandate for Leadership*, ed. Charles L. Heatherly (Washington, D.C.: Heritage Foundation, 1981), 447.
142 *"I don't think he"*: Quoted in Ronald Brownstein and Nina Easton, *Reagan's Ruling Class* (New York: Pantheon, 1982), 399.
143 *"Color-blindness will be"*: William Bradford Reynolds, letter to Arthur S. Flemming, Sept. 29, 1981, Files of the Attorney General, William French Smith, 1981–1985, National Archives at College Park.
143 *"government-imposed discrimination"*: Quoted in Wolters, *Right Turn*, 6.
143 *"a kind of racial spoils"*: Remarks by William Bradford Reynolds, American Bar Association, San Francisco, Aug. 9, 1982.
144 *"There will never be"*: Quoted in Lawson, *In Pursuit of Power*, 256.
145 *"No 'pattern of discrimination'"*: Hammond, *Mandate for Leadership*.
145 *"Since there seems to"*: William Bradford Reynolds, memorandum to William French Smith, Aug. 16, 1981, Files of the Attorney General, William French Smith, 1981–1985, National Archives at College Park.
145 *"We don't oppose the"*: Dan Wasserman, *Dallas Times-Herald*, Feb. 10, 1982.
146 *"a conservative looking for"*: Quoted in Janny Scott, "Roberts's Harvard Roots: A Movement Was Stirring," *New York Times*, Aug. 21, 2005.
146 *"I realize that it"*: Quoted in Fred P. Graham, "Rehnquist Says '52 Memo Outlined Jackson's Views," *New York Times*, Dec. 9, 1971.
146 *"It is about time"*: Quoted in John A. Jenkins, "The Partisan," *New York Times Magazine*, March 3, 1985.
146 *"It has been well-said"*: Quoted in Rick Perlstein, *Before the Storm* (New York: Hill and Wang, 2001), 461.
147 *"ballot security"*: Quoted in Fred P. Graham, "Rehnquist Role in Arizona Elections Is Confirmed," *New York Times*, Nov. 12, 1971.
147 *"Operation Eagle Eye"*: Perlstein, *Before the Storm*, 511.

147 *"Over the years"*: Quoted in Donald Edward Boles, *Mr. Justice Rehnquist, Judicial Activist* (Ames, In.: Iowa State University Press, 1987), 89.

148 *"The Act does not"*: *City of Rome v. United States*, 446 U.S. 156 (1980).

148 *"[I] disagree with the Court's decision"*: Ibid. (Rehnquist dissenting).

148 *"Rehnquist has a constitutional"*: Owen Fiss and Charles Krauthammer, "The Rehnquist Court," *New Republic*, March 10, 1982.

148 *"the boss"*: Quoted in Michael Grunwald and Amy Goldstein, "Few Have Beat of Roberts's Political Heart," *Washington Post*, July 24, 2005.

148 *"John Roberts is proving"*: Quoted in Brad Snyder, "The Judicial Genealogy (and Mythology) of John Roberts," *Ohio State Law Journal*, vol. 71, no. 1149, 2010.

148 *"The initial meeting left"*: Quoted in Jeffrey Toobin, "The Stealth Hard-Liner," *New Yorker*, May 25, 2009.

149 *"This is an exciting"*: Quoted in Robin Toner and Jonathan D. Glater, "Roberts Helped to Shape 80's Civil Rights Debate," *New York Times*, Aug. 3, 2005.

150 *"a bit of a"*: Interview with Theodore Olson, "Profile of Supreme Court Nominee John Roberts," C-Span, Aug. 30, 2005, www.c-span.org/video/?188589-1/profile-supreme -court-nominee-john-roberts.

150 *"Why Section 2 of"*: John Roberts to the Attorney General, "Voting Rights Act: Section 2," Dec. 22, 1981, Correspondence Files of Ken Starr, 1981–83, RG 60 Department of Justice, Box 22, National Archives at College Park.

150 *"Brad Reynolds has expressed"*: Ibid.

150 *"An effects test would"*: John Roberts to Ken Starr, "Q & A's on Intent/Effects," Jan. 5, 1982, Correspondence Files of Ken Starr, National Archives at College Park.

150 *"This meeting presents an"*: John Roberts to the Attorney General, "Talking Points for White House Meeting on Voting Rights Act," Jan. 26, 1982, John G. Roberts, Jr., Misc., RG 60 Department of Justice, Box 30, National Archives at College Park.

151 *"Do not be fooled"*: Ibid.

151 *"I think that if"*: U.S. Congress. Senate. Committee on the Judiciary, Subcommittee on the Constitution, *Bills to Amend the Voting Rights Act of 1965*, 97th Cong., 2nd sess., 1982.

151 *"The frequent writings in"*: John Roberts to Brad Reynolds, "Voting Rights Act," Feb. 8, 1982, Files of William Bradford Reynolds, 1981–1988, RG 60 Department of Justice, Box 14, National Archives at College Park.

151 *"The Reagan Administration is"*: "Voting Rights Are Not Quotas," *New York Times*, March 19, 1982.

151 *"An 'effects' test under"*: Senate, *Bills to Amend the Voting Rights Act of 1965*, 1982.

152 *"Those who have been"*: Ibid.

153 *"Ain't Gonna Let Strom"*: Quoted in Bass and Thompson, *Strom*, 293.

153 *"To blacks in Edgefield"*: Quoted in United Press International, Jun. 28, 1981.

153 *"There is bloc voting"*: *McCain v. Lybrand*, C.A. No. 74–281 (D.S.C., Apr. 17, 1980).

154 *"new information"*: Quoted in Robert Pear, "U.S. Reverses Move to Aid Rights Suit," *New York Times*, Sept. 13, 1981.

154 *"enormously helpful for somebody"*: Ibid.

154 *"this seemingly interminable lawsuit"*: Quoted in Orville Vernon Burton, Terence R. Finnegan, Peyton McCrary, and James W. Loewen, "South Carolina" in *Quiet Revolution in the South*, eds. Chandler Davidson and Bernard Grofman (Princeton, N.J.: Princeton University Press, 1994), 209.

154 *"Without extension"*: Senate, *Bills to Amend the Voting Rights Act of 1965*, 1982.

155 *"the extra effort to"*: Quoted in Lawson, *In Pursuit of Power*, 290.

155 *"the Dirksen of the"*: Quoted in Mary McGrory, "Voting Rights Make Strange Bedfellows," *Washington Post*, May 9, 1982.

156 *"It was no compromise"*: Ibid.

156 *"There is no reason"*: Quoted in "Report on the Nomination of Judge John G. Roberts Jr. to the Supreme Court," NAACP Legal Defense and Educational Fund, Inc., Aug. 31,

2005, www.afge3614.org/docs/Roberts-Report_on_the_Nomination_of_Judge_John _G._Roberts_Jr._to_the_Supreme_Court_of_the_United_States.pdf.

156 *"In forty years of"*: James L. Kilpatrick, "The Voting Rights Bill," *Spartanburg Herald-Journal*, May 23, 1982.

156 *"White House is on"*: Quoted in Neas, "Draft Outline for Legislative Campaign on VRA Extension."

156 *"until the cows came home"*: Quoted in Steven V. Roberts, "Senators Debate Voting Rights Act," *New York Times*, June 10, 1982.

157 *"The right to vote"*: Quoted in Howell Raines, "Voting Rights Act Signed by Reagan," *New York Times*, June 30, 1982.

157 *"Our fondest hopes in"*: Quoted in Barton Gellman, "The New Old Movement," *New Republic*, Sept. 6, 1982.

157 *"We were able to"*: Quoted in Laughlin McDonald, "Voting Rights Litigation in Edgefield County, South Carolina," unpublished, paper provided by author.

158 *"The change in the"*: Ibid.

158 *"The amendment really started"*: Quoted in Barry Bearak, "Bias Easier to Prove," *Los Angeles Times*, June 29, 1983.

158 *"smoking gun"*: Kirkland, "Pink Sheets and Black Ballots."

158 *"We have always"*: Ibid.

158 *"gratifies me more than"*: Ibid.

6. CHALLENGING THE CONSENSUS

160 *"I never heard of"*: Quoted in Art Harris, "Some Schooling in the Mississippi Delta," *Washington Post*, June 16, 1983.

160 *"I've heard the difficulties"*: Ibid.

160 *"the most precious of"*: Quoted in Frank Thorsberg, "Federal Civil Rights Enforcer Tours Mississippi," United Press International, June 16, 1983.

160 *"Do you solemnly swear"*: Quoted in Art Harris, "Federal Registrars Bring the Vote to Mississippi Cotton Fields," *Washington Post*, June 18, 1983.

161 *"Southern Crusade"*: Tom Morgenthau, "A Black Candidate in 1984?," *Newsweek*, June 6, 1983.

161 *"We weren't allowed to"*: Quoted in Harris, "Federal Registrars Bring the Vote to Mississippi Cotton Fields."

161 *"America's Ethiopia"*: Quoted in Michael Hirsley, "PUSH Will Adopt Poor Town in South," *Chicago Tribune*, July 18, 1985.

161 *"Just to focus on"*: Quoted in E. R. Shipp, "In Mississippi, Who Voted Meant as Much as Who Won," *New York Times*, Aug. 7, 1983.

162 *"Any bill in that"*: Quoted in Robert Kwan, "Section 5 Submission Analysis: Reapportionment of Congressional Districts in the State of Louisiana," Department of Justice. Included in U.S. Congress. Senate. Committee on the Judiciary, *The Confirmation of William Bradford Reynolds to Be Associate Attorney General of the United States*, 99th Cong., 1st sess., 1985.

162 *"What I did do"*: Ibid.

163 *"We already have a"*: Ibid.

163 *"Donald Duck"*: Statement of Frank R. Parker, *The Confirmation of William Bradford Reynolds to Be Associate Attorney General of the United States*.

163 *"It is clear in"*: Kwan, "Section 5 Submission Analysis: Reapportionment of Congressional Districts in the State of Louisiana."

164 *"one of the most"*: Quoted in testimony of Lani Guinier, June 5, 1985, *The Confirmation of William Bradford Reynolds to Be Associate Attorney General of the United States*.

164 *"the contours of the"*: *Major v. Treen*, 574 F. Supp. 325 (E.D. La. 1983).

165 *"Thank you for inviting"*: Quoted in Lani Guinier, *Lift Every Voice* (New York: Simon & Schuster, 1998), 86.

165 *"ideological alter ego"*: Cornell W. Clayton, *The Politics of Justice* (Armonk, N.Y.: M. E. Sharpe, 1992), 151.

165 *"Mr. Chairman, it is"*: *The Confirmation of William Bradford Reynolds to Be Associate Attorney General of the United States*.

166 *"It's like* Through the Looking Glass*"*: Quoted in Michael S. Serrill, "Law: Uncivil Times at Justless," *Time*, May 13, 1985.

166 *"I have difficulty thinking"*: Quoted in Mary Thornton, "NAACP Officer Asks Abolition of Justice's Civil Rights Division," *Washington Post*, May 7, 1983.

166 *"Under Mr. Reynolds"*: Quoted in Juan Williams, "In His Mind but Not His Heart," *Washington Post*, Jan. 10, 1988.

166 *"I must say I"*: Ibid.

166 *"the Scrooge of the"*: *The Confirmation of William Bradford Reynolds to Be Associate Attorney General of the United States*.

167 *"I happen to agree"*: Ibid. Includes statements from Biden, Reynolds, Guinier, Metzenbaum, Quigley, and Specter.

169 *"a tireless fighter against"*: Quoted in Robert Pear, "Reagan Defends Justice Dept. Nominee as Opposition Rises," *New York Times*, June 16, 1985.

169 *"It is now clear"*: Quoted in Robert Pear, "Senate Committee Rejects Reynolds for Justice Post," *New York Times*, June 28, 1985.

169 *"The chairman has railroaded"*: Ibid.

169 *"the pro-busing"*: Quoted in Howard Kurtz, "Reynolds' Foes Claim Moral High Ground," *Washington Post*, June 24, 1985.

169 *"helped shift the focus"*: Ibid.

170 *"The traditionalists won"*: "Red Light for Reynolds," *Los Angeles Times*, June 28, 1985.

170 *"Don't you go anywhere"*: Quoted in Wolters, *Right Turn*, 11.

170 *"one of the heroes"*: "Reynolds's Inquisition," *National Review*, July 12, 1985.

172 *"What are we going"*: Quoted in Dannye Romine Powell and David Perlmutt, "Pioneering Civil Rights Attorney and Former NCCU Chancellor Julius Chambers Dies," *News & Observer*, Aug. 4, 2013.

173 *"so extreme"*: *Gingles v. Edmisten*, 590 F. Supp. 345 (E.D. N.C. 1984).

173 *"The success that has"*: Ibid.

173 *"If left undisturbed"*: Brief for the United States as Amicus Curiae Supporting Appellants, *Lacy H. Thornburg, et al., Appellants v. Ralph Gingles, et al.*, No. 83-1968.

173 *"Reduced to its essentials"*: Laughlin McDonald, "The Attack on Voting Rights," *Southern Changes*, vol. 7, no. 5, 1985.

174 *"would pose as significant"*: Brief of Senators Dennis DeConcini, Robert J. Dole, Charles E. Grassley, Edward M. Kennedy, Charles McC. Mathias, Jr., and Howard M. Metzenbaum and Representatives Don Edwards, Hamilton Fish, Jr., Peter W. Rodino, Jr., and F. James Sensenbrenner as Amici Curiae in Support of Appellees, *Thornburg v. Gingles*.

174 *"We contend that by applying"*: Oral Argument, *Thornburg v. Gingles*, 478 U.S. 30 (1986), Dec. 4, 1985.

174 *"the enemy"*: Quoted in Lincoln Caplan, *The Tenth Justice* (New York: Knopf, 1987), 241.

174 *"totality of circumstances"*: Oral Argument, *Thornburg v. Gingles*.

174 *"The language of Section 2"*: *Thornburg v. Gingles*.

174 *"radical egalitarianism"*: Caplan, *Tenth Justice*, 243.

175 *"In my view"*: *Thornburg v. Gingles* (O'Connor concurring).

175 *"the minority group must"*: *Thornburg v. Gingles*.

176 *"I never thought I'd"*: Quoted in William Freivogel, "Voting Rights: Reagan Administration Fought Rear-Guard Action on Enforcement," *St. Louis Post-Dispatch*, March 26, 1989.

176 *"the most thorough and"*: Quoted in David M. O'Brien, "If the Bench Becomes a Brawl," *Los Angeles Times*, Aug. 23, 1987.

176 *"In none of these"*: U.S. Congress. Senate. Committee on the Judiciary, *Nominations of William H. Rehnquist, of Arizona, and Lewis F. Powell, Jr., of Virginia, to Be Associate Justices of the Supreme Court of the United States*, 92nd Cong., 1st sess., 1971.

176 *"This does not comfort"*: U.S. Congress. Senate. Committee on the Judiciary, *Nomination of Justice William Hubbs Rehnquist to Be Chief Justice of the United States*, 99th Cong., 2nd sess., 1986. Includes statements from Brosnahan, Smith, Kennedy, Rehnquist, and Chambers.

177 *"Imagine what America would"*: Quoted in George Lardner, Jr., and Al Kamen, "Kennedy Calls Rehnquist 'Too Extreme,'" *Washington Post*, July 30, 1986.

178 *"once a lonely dissenter"*: "Toward a Rehnquist Court," *New York Times*, June 18, 1986.

178 *"The principle of such"*: Quoted in Adam Serwer, "Principles of Unsurpassed Ugliness," *American Prospect*, Aug 3. 2011.

179 *"one person, one vote"*: U.S. Congress. Senate. Committee on the Judiciary, *The Nomination of Robert H. Bork to Be Associate Justice of the Supreme Court of the United States*, 100th Cong., 1st sess., 1987.

179 *"Had Judge Bork's truncated"*: Ibid.

179 *"Robert Bork wants to"*: Quoted in "Who Torpedoed Judge Bork?," *New York Times*, Oct. 13, 1987.

179 *"I think, more than"*: William Taylor, interview by Marsha J. Tyson Darling, VRA Documentation Project, Jan. 30, 1995.

180 *"Federalism Five"*: Dawn Johnson, "Ronald Reagan and the Rehnquist Court on Congressional Power," *Indiana Law Journal*, vol. 78, issue 1, 2003.

180 *"The new federal judiciary"*: Ralph G. Neas, "The Civil Rights Legacy of the Reagan Years," *USA Today Magazine*, March 1990.

180 *"Guidelines on Constitutional Litigation"*: Quoted in Johnson, "Ronald Reagan and the Rehnquist Court on Congressional Power."

181 *"an emergency measure taken"*: Thernstrom, *Whose Votes Count?*, 46.

181 *"the myth of moral simplicity"*: Ibid., 6.

181 *"In the enforcement of"*: Ibid., 9.

181 *"Voting rights has become"*: Ibid., 6.

181 *"It is scarcely an"*: Ibid., 233.

181 *"She argues what she"*: Adam Clymer, "Black Ballots," *New York Times Book Review*, Oct. 18, 1987.

181–82 *"so distorts the evidence"*: Pamela S. Karlan and Peyton McCrary, "Book Review: Without Fear and Without Research," *Journal of Law & Politics*, vol. 4, Spring 1988.

182 *"She has shown an"*: John H. Fund, "Voting Law Hurts Blacks, Helps GOP," *Wall Street Journal*, Dec. 21, 1987.

182 *"Her book is a"*: Harold W. Stanley, "Fair Shake, Fair Share," *New Republic*, Nov. 30, 1987.

182 *"a virtual bible among"*: Shatz, "The Thernstroms in Black and White."

7. THE REALIGNMENT

184 *"In Washington I have found"*: Quoted in Jacqueline Trescott, "The Valedictory of a Reluctant Bureaucrat," *Washington Post*, Feb. 3, 1980.

184 *"I'm not going to draw"*: Quoted in McDonald, *Voting Rights Odyssey*, 171.

185 *"It is time to send"*: John Lewis, interview by Rebecca Chase, ABC News, Aug. 11, 1986.

185 *"Julian the patrician against"*: Quoted in Fred Grimm, "They Fought Together for Rights; Now They're Fighting for Same Job," *Miami Herald*, March 23, 1986.

185 *"I went from door"*: Quoted in John Lancaster, "Bald, Bulldog-Built Politician Became 'Little Engine That Could,'" *Atlanta Journal-Constitution*, Dec. 4, 1986.

185 *"Beat City Hall!"*: Quoted in Frederick Allen, "Lewis Rewrites Book on Atlanta Voting Patterns," *Atlanta Journal-Constitution*, Sept. 3, 1986.

186 *"For a boy who"*: Quoted in John Lancaster, "Surprise End to Battle Between Comrades in 5th," *Atlanta Journal-Constitution*, Sept. 3, 1986.

186 *"John Lewis got his"*: Quoted in Michael Hirsley, "Even Blacks Underestimated John Lewis' Bid for Congress," *Chicago Tribune*, Sept. 9, 1986.

186 *"a victory for all"*: David S. Broder, "Victory for the Grunts," *Washington Post*, Sept. 7, 1986.

186 *"This is a long"*: Quoted in Scott Shepard, "Fowler, Lewis Take Oath in D.C.," *Atlanta Journal-Constitution*, Jan. 7, 1987.

187 *"We're locked out"*: Remarks by Jesse Jackson, Democratic National Convention, San Francisco, July 18, 1984, www.pbs.org/wgbh/pages/frontline/jesse/speeches/jesse84 speech.html.

187 *"first-degree murderers to"*: "1988 Bush vs. Dukakis," Museum of the Moving Image, www.livingroomcandidate.org/commercials/1988/willie-horton.

187 *"Do something about redistricting"*: Quoted in Michael Kelly, "Segregation Anxiety," *New Yorker*, Nov. 20, 1995.

187 *"The fact is that"*: Quoted in Richard L. Berke, "G.O.P. Tries a Gambit with Voting Rights," *New York Times*, Apr. 14, 1991.

188 *"As passed by Congress"*: Remarks by Benjamin Ginsberg, Congressional Black Caucus Foundation, Washington, D.C., Sept. 28, 1990.

188 *"get the living hell"*: Quoted in Berke, "G.O.P. Tries a Gambit with Voting Rights."

188 *"unholy alliance"*: Quoted in Paul Taylor, "GOP Will Aid Rights Groups in Redistricting," *Washington Post*, Apr. 1, 1990.

188 *"One GOP tactic"*: John Lewis, "Selma and the Triumph of Racial Coalitions," *Washington Post*, Aug. 5, 1990.

188 *Fairness for the 90s*: Thomas B. Edsall, "GOP Goal: Gain Ground by Fostering 'Majority Minority' Districts," *Washington Post*, July 7, 1990.

188 *"truly space-age"*: Quoted in Taylor, "GOP Will Aid Rights Groups in Redistricting."

189 *"the ultimate political"*: Quoted in Jim Sleeper, "The Triumph of Liberalism," *New York Times*, Feb. 4, 1966.

190 *"Basically, the NAACP position"*: Quoted in Van Denton, "A New Political Map," *News & Observer*, Aug. 18, 1991.

191 *"If blacks go too"*: Quoted in Van Denton, "Party Loyalty, Black Gains Clash in Redistricting," *News & Observer*, Jan. 7, 1992.

191 *"The proposed configuration of"*: "Text of Justice Department Letter on North Carolina Redistricting," *Business Wire*, Dec. 18, 1991.

191 *"What the Republicans are"*: Quoted in Denton, "Party Loyalty, Black Gains Clash in Redistricting."

192 *"string of pearls"*: Paul Gronke and J. Matthew Wilson, "Competing Redistricting Plans as Evidence of Political Motives: The North Carolina Case," *American Politics Quarterly*, vol. 27, Apr. 1999.

192 *"serpentine monstrosity"*: Carol M. Swain, "Black Districts: A Bad Idea," *Baltimore Sun*, June 4, 1993.

192 *"I love the district"*: Quoted in Ronald Smothers, "2 Strangely Shaped Hybrid Creatures Highlight North Carolina's Primary," *New York Times*, May 3, 1992.

192 *"a Republican–civil rights conspiracy"*: Abigail M. Thernstrom, "A Republican–Civil Rights Conspiracy," *Washington Post*, Sept. 23, 1991.

192 *"The policies of the"*: Ibid.

192 *"White Hands"*: "Jesse Helms 'Hands' Ad," YouTube, Oct. 16, 2006, www.youtube.com /watch?v=KIyewCdXMzk.

193 *"Get the hell out"*: Mel Watt, interview by Brian Lamb, C-Span, Feb. 11, 2005, www .c-span.org/video/?185481-1/qa-mel-watt.

194 *"If someone had told"*: Quoted in Dennis Patterson, "Black Democratic Congressmen Start Bus Tour in North Carolina," Associated Press, Oct. 12, 1992.

194 *"the year of the minority"*: William J. Eaton, "For Blacks and Latinos, Elections May Make '92 Year of the Minority," *Los Angeles Times*, July 28, 1992.

195 *"members of the most distinguished"*: Quoted in "Congressional Black Caucus Swearing-In," C-Span, Jan. 5, 1993, www.c-span.org/video/?36808-1/congressional -black-caucus-swearingin.

195 *"champion the rights of"*: Ibid.

195 *"This, Mr. Chairman"*: Remarks by Hon. George H. White, Washington, D.C., Jan. 29, 1901, docsouth.unc.edu/nc/whitegh/whitegh.html.

195 *"We are, in fact"*: Quoted in "Congressional Black Caucus Swearing-In," C-Span.

196 *"I want it to"*: Quoted in "Justice Department Address," C-Span, Apr. 29, 1993.

196 *"a remarkable woman who"*: Ibid.

196 *"If confirmed by the"*: Ibid.

196 *"No nominee for the"*: Hendrik Hertzberg, "Idea Woman," *New Yorker*, June 14, 1993.

197 *"William Bradford Reynolds"*: Quoted in Neil A. Lewis, "Lani Guinier's Agenda Provokes Old Enemies," *New York Times*, May 9, 1993.

197 *"Ms. Guinier is poised"*: Ibid.

197 *"very radical"*: Quoted in Michael Isikoff, "Power Behind the Thrown Nominee: Activist with Score to Settle," *Washington Post*, June 6, 1993.

197 *"Clint, you're going to"*: Ibid.

197 *"Clinton's Quota Queens"*: Clint Bolick, "Clinton's Quota Queens," *Wall Street Journal*, Apr. 30, 1993.

197 *"[Guinier] isn't your garden-variety"*: Abigail Thernstrom, "Guinier Miss," *New Republic*, June 14, 1993.

198 *"the voice of black"*: Quoted in "Voting Rights Act Key to Unlocking Guinier's Writings," *St. Petersburg Times*, June 5, 1993.

198 *"My point is simple"*: Lani Guinier, "Who's Afraid of Lani Guinier?," *New York Times Magazine*, Feb. 27, 1994.

198 *"the tyranny of the"*: Lani Guinier, *The Tyranny of the Majority* (New York: Free Press, 1994).

199 *"The system has been"*: Quoted in Jim Yardley, "1 Voter, 7 Votes? County Boosts Minority Clout," *Atlanta Journal-Constitution*, Oct. 23, 1992.

199 *"Chilton County Experience"*: Alvin Benn, "One Person, Seven Votes?," *Montgomery Advertiser*, Nov. 4, 2012.

199 *"supermajority requirement"*: *St. Petersburg Times*, "Voting Rights Act Key to Unlocking Guinier's Writings."

199 *"the enforcement of this"*: Lani Guinier, "Keeping the Faith: Black Voters in the Post-Reagan Era," *Harvard Civil Rights–Civil Liberties Law Review*, vol. 24, 1989.

199 *"I am not articulating"*: Lani Guinier, "The Triumph of Tokenism: The Voting Rights Act and the Theory of Black Electoral Success," *Michigan Law Review*, vol. 89, 1991.

199 *"Within the academic world"*: Guinier, "Who's Afraid of Lani Guinier?"

200 *"The 'Q' word stuck"*: Ibid.

200 *"If nothing else"*: Quoted in Dewey M. Clayton, *African Americans and the Politics of Congressional Redistricting* (New York: Garland Publishing, 2000), 26.

200 *"I have decided to"*: Quoted in Guinier, "Who's Afraid of Lani Guinier?"

200 *"At the time of"*: Quoted in "Transcript of President Clinton's Announcement," *New York Times*, June 4, 1993.

200 QUAYLE CAN'T SPELL: Quoted in Lynne Duke, "Marchers Protest Clinton's Withdrawal of Guinier's Nomination," *Washington Post*, June 8, 1993.

201 *"participate in a"*: Quoted in A. Leon Higginbotham, Jr., Gregory A. Clark, and Marcella David, "Shaw v. Reno: A Mirage of Good Intentions with Devastating Racial Consequences," *Fordham Law Review*, vol. 62, issue 6, 1994.

201 *"The plaintiffs here have"*: Ibid.

201 *"political pornography"*: Oral Argument, *Shaw v. Reno*, 509 U.S. 630 (1993), Apr. 20, 1993.

201 *"We do not believe"*: Ibid.

201 *"We believe that reapportionment"*: *Shaw v. Reno*, 509 U.S. 630 (1993).

202 *"race-conscious plans can"*: *United Jewish Organizations v. Carey*.

202 *"A covered jurisdiction's interest"*: *Shaw v. Reno*.

202 *"It is particularly ironic"*: Ibid. (Blackmun dissenting).

202 *"This is the greatest"*: Quoted in Laughlin McDonald, "The Counterrevolution in Minority Voting Rights," *Mississippi Law Journal*, vol. 65, 1995.

202 *"suggests that a Congressional"*: Quoted in Clayton, *African Americans and the Politics of Congressional Redistricting*, 107.

203 *"The Supreme Court discovered"*: Quoted in Thomas B. Edsall, "Guinier Raps Court Ruling on Remap," *Washington Post*, June 14, 1993.

203 *"It is a rather"*: U.S. Congress. House. Committee on the Judiciary, Subcommittee on Civil and Constitutional Rights, *Voting Rights*, 103rd Cong., 1st and 2nd sess., 1994.

203 *"It's a whole new"*: Quoted in "Gingrich Swearing-In," C-Span, Jan. 4, 1995, www .c-span.org/video/?62500-1/gingrich-swearing.

203 *"angry white male"*: Richard Morin and Barbara Vobejda, "94 May Be the Year of the Man," *Washington Post*, Nov. 10, 1994.

204 *"Racial gerrymandering"*: George F. Will, "The Voting Rights Act at 30," *Newsweek*, July 10, 1995.

204 *"to the right of"*: Quoted in Steven A. Holmes, "Did Racial Redistricting Undermine Democrats?," *New York Times*, Nov. 13, 1994.

205 *"With the Southern Republicans"*: Quoted in Ronald Brownstein, "South Rises Again as Region Takes over GOP Leadership," *Los Angeles Times*, Dec. 4, 1994.

205 *"Proponents of black voting"*: Lani Guinier, "Don't Scapegoat the Gerrymander," *New York Times*, Jan. 8, 1995.

205 *"What has long been"*: Abigail Thernstrom, "Redistricting, in Black and White," *New York Times*, Dec. 7, 1994.

205 *"Racial redistricting alone does"*: David Lublin, "Racial Redistricting Gives Minorities a Voice," *New York Times*, Dec. 8, 1994.

205 *"Maintenance of Negro voting"*: Phillips, *Emerging Republican Majority*, 287.

206 *"Project Ratfuck"*: Quoted in Kelly, "Segregation Anxiety."

8. THE COUNTERREVOLUTION (II)

208 *"I could not believe"*: Quoted in Julian Borger, "How Florida Played the Race Card," *Guardian Observer*, Dec. 4, 2000.

208 *"I thought it was"*: Quoted in Scott Hiaasen, Gary Kane, and Elliot Jaspin, "Felon Purge Sacrificed Innocent Voters," *Palm Beach Post*, May 27, 2001.

208 *"I was devastated"*: Ibid.

210 *"false positives"*: Ibid.

210 *"Obviously, we want to"*: Quoted in David Margolick, Evangelina Peretz, and Michael Shnayerson, "The Path to Florida," *Vanity Fair*, Oct. 2004.

210 *"We went for a"*: Ibid.

210 *"Woodstock for constitutional lawyers"*: Quoted in Gary Fineout and Mary Ellen Klas, "Roberts Gave GOP Advice in 2000 Recount," *Miami Herald*, July 21, 2005.

210 *the Cabal*: Ibid.

211 *"We started to assemble"*: Quoted in Sheryl Gay Stolberg and David K. Kirkpatrick, "Panel Sends Judge 10-Page Questionnaire," *New York Times*, July 28, 2005.

211 *"He is one of"*: Ibid.

211 *"It's important to bear"*: Quoted in Elaine Sciolino, "On the Street, More Arguments Were Heard," *New York Times*, Dec. 12, 2000.

211 *"Al Sharpton"*: Quoted in Jeffrey Toobin, *Too Close to Call* (New York: Random House, 2001), 266.

212 *"Mr. President, I object"*: Quoted in "Congressional Black Caucus Objects to Florida's 25 Electors," CNN.com, Jan. 6, 2001, transcripts.cnn.com/TRANSCRIPTS/0101/06/se.05.html.

213 *"It's going to be"*: Quoted in Lizette Alvarez, "House Leader Differs with Bush on Across-the-Board Tax Cuts," *New York Times*, Dec. 15, 2000.

213 *"Despite the closeness of"*: "Voting Irregularities in Florida During the 2000 Presidential Election," U.S. Commission on Civil Rights, Washington, D.C., June 2001.

214 *"The obvious explanation"*: Abigail Thernstrom and Russell G. Redenbaugh, "The Florida Election Report: Dissenting Statement," Aug. 17, 2001, www.thernstrom.com/pdf/FLelec8-17-01.pdf.

214 *"There were many people"*: Quoted in Dirk Johnson, "Judge Delays Closing of Polls in St. Louis amid Unexpectedly Heavy Turnout," *New York Times*, Nov. 8, 2000.

215 *"The sight of hundreds"*: Denise Lieberman, "Voting Rights as a Race Issue," www.deniselieberman.com/articles/votingrights.htm.

215 *"Attempted–Not Known"*: *USA v. Bd of Elec Com*, 4:02-cv-01235-CEJ (E.D. M.O. 2002).

215 *"As of 10:00 PM"*: Ibid.

216 *"I'm Still with Mel"*: Neil A. Lewis, "In Missouri, Campaign Flourishes After the Death of the Candidate," *New York Times*, Oct. 31, 2000.

216 *"I know there are"*: Quoted in David Scott, "Ashcroft, Talent Decide Against Pursuing St. Louis Voter Fraud Claims," Associated Press, Nov. 8, 2000.

216 *"Democrats in the city"*: Quoted in Johnson, "Judge Delays Closing of Polls in St. Louis amid Unexpectedly Heavy Turnout."

216 *"a major criminal enterprise"*: Quoted in Carolyn Tuft, "Bond Wants Federal Investigation of Problems at City Polls," *St. Louis Post-Dispatch*, Nov. 10, 2000.

216 *"unprecedented gathering of the"*: Remarks by Attorney General John Ashcroft, Washington, D.C., Oct. 8, 2002, www.justice.gov/archive/ag/speeches/2002/100802ballotintegrity.htm.

217 *"an issue that I"*: Quoted in "Voting Integrity Symposium," C-Span, Oct. 8, 2002, www.c-span.org/video/?173086-1/voting-integrity-symposium.

217 *"Votes have been bought"*: Ibid.

218 *"For too long in"*: Hans von Spakovsky, "Letters to the Editor: Some Voting Laws Make Fraud Easier," *Wall Street Journal*, Jan. 4, 1995.

218 *"the point person for"*: Joseph D. Rich, Robert A. Kengle, David J. Becker, Bruce Adelson, and Toby Moore, "Career DOJ Professionals Urge Rejection of von Spakovsky's FEC Nomination," VoteTrustUSA.org, June 14, 2007, www.votetrustusa.org/index.php?option=com_content&task=view&id=2489&Itemid=1221.

218 *"The first stirrings of"*: Wendy R. Weiser, "Voter Suppression: How Bad? (Pretty Bad)," *American Prospect*, Fall 2014.

218 *"I am worried that"*: "Declaration of Ebony Malone," 2:81-cv-03876-DRD-SDW (D NJ 2004).

219 *"The potential for these"*: Quoted in Mark Niquette, "GOP Challenges Voters," *Columbus Dispatch*, Oct. 23, 2004.

219 *"Ballot Security Task Force"*: Quoted in *Democratic National Committee et al. v. Republican National Committee et al.*, "Memorandum in Support of Motions on Behalf of Individual Minority Voters to Intervene and Reopen Case," No. 81-3876, Oct. 30, 2004.

219 *"refrain from undertaking any"*: Ibid.

219 *"a balance between ballot"*: Quoted in Greg Gordon, "Ex-Justice Official Accused of Aiding Effort to Scratch Minority Voters," McClatchy Newspapers, June 24, 2007.

219 *"cheerleading for the Republican"*: Ibid.

219–20 *"faced irreparable injury"*: Democratic National Committee et al. v. Republican National Committee et al., No. 04-4186, Nov. 1, 2004.

220 *NOT THIS TIME!*: Quoted in Paul Farhi and Jo Becker, "Some Fear Ohio Will Be Florida of 2004," *Washington Post*, Oct. 26, 2004.

220 *"We cannot forget what"*: Ibid.

220 *"A lot of people left"*: Quoted in Michael Powell and Peter Slevin, "Several Factors Contributed to 'Lost' Voters in Ohio," *Washington Post*, Dec. 15, 2004.

221 *"The massive lines are"*: The Ohio Democratic Party v. J. Kenneth Blackwell, No. C2 04 1055, Nov. 2, 2004, moritzlaw.osu.edu/electionlaw/docs/ohio/041102LongLine complaint.pdf.

221 *"The Election Day experience"*: Quoted in "Democracy at Risk: The 2004 Election in Ohio," Democratic National Committee, June 22, 2005.

221 *time tax*: "The Time Tax," Advancement Project and OurTime.org, Nov. 18, 2013, b.3cdn.net/advancement/ba719924e82b44bb92_14m6bgjh0.pdf.

222 *"Get over it"*: Quoted in Alan Fram, "Congress Formally OKs Bush Election," Associated Press, Jan. 6, 2005.

222 *"Keep the vote alive!"*: Quoted in Lateef Mungin, "Marchers Support Voting Act," *Atlanta Journal-Constitution*, Aug. 7, 2005.

222 *"Forty years later, we're"*: Quoted in David Stokes, "Thousands Walk to Save Voting Rights," *Atlanta Inquirer*, Voting Rights Issue, 2005, www.atlinq.com/news/voting _rights_2005/march.htm.

223 *"at least eight of"*: John H. Fund, *Stealing Elections* (New York: Encounter Books, 2004), 157.

223 *"It's about protecting the"*: Quoted in Carlos Campos, "Activists Rail Against ID Bill," *Atlanta Journal-Constitution*, March 18, 2005.

223 *"a modern-day poll"*: John Lewis, "Hogwash Can't Hide Prejudice at Polls," *Atlanta Journal-Constitution*, Nov. 21, 2005.

223 *"I cannot recall one"*: Quoted in "ACLU Condemns U.S. Justice Department Decision to Approve Georgia Photo ID Law," ACLU.org, Aug. 26, 2005, www.aclu.org/voting -rights/aclu-condemns-us-justice-department-decision-approve-georgia-photo-id -law.

224 *"This is wrong!"*: Quoted in Doug Gross, "Voting Bill Leads to Democratic Walkout at Capitol," Associated Press, March 11, 2005.

224 *"We have struggled too"*: Quoted in "U.S. Senators Christopher Dodd (D-CT) and Barack Obama (D-IL) and U.S. Representatives John Lewis (D-GA) and John Conyers (D-MI) Hold a News Conference on the Help America Vote Act," Political Transcript Wire, Sept. 20, 2005.

224 *"spread like a virus"*: Quoted in Errin Haines, "Marchers Convene to Preserve Voting Rights Act," Associated Press, Aug. 6, 2005.

224 *"sympathetic referee"*: U.S. Congress. Senate. Committee on the Judiciary, *The 50th Anniversary of the Civil Rights Act of 1957 and Its Continuing Importance*, 110th Cong., 1st sess., 2007.

224 *"Searching for a conservative"*: Hans A. von Spakovsky, "Revenge of the Liberal Bureaucrats," WeeklyStandard.com, Jan. 22, 2009, www.weeklystandard.com/Content /Public/Articles/000./000./016/046wmebv.asp.

225 *"a four-member Vast"*: Quoted in "An Investigation of Allegations of Politicized Hiring and Other Improper Personnel Actions in the Civil Rights Division," U.S. Department of Justice, Office of the Inspector General and Office of Professional Responsibility, Jan. 13, 2009.

225 *"I too get to"*: Ibid.

225 *"RTAs"*: Ibid.

225 *"When we start asking"*: Ibid.

225 *"improperly considered political"*: Ibid.

226 *"Requiring official picture identification"*: von Spakovsky, "Some Voting Laws Make Fraud Easier."

226 *"Georgia should require all"*: Hans A. von Spakovsky, "Voter Fraud: Protecting the Integrity of Our Democratic System," Georgia Public Policy Foundation, March 24, 1997.

227 *"Mary Frances Berry style"*: Quoted in "An Investigation of Allegations of Politicized Hiring and Other Improper Personnel Actions in the Civil Rights Division," Department of Justice.

227 *"Burmeister said that if"*: Robert Berman, Amy Zubrensky, Heather Moss, Joshua Rogers, and Toby Moore, "Section 5 Recommendation Memorandum," Department of Justice, Aug. 25, 2005, www.washingtonpost.com/wp-srv/politics/documents/dojgadocs1_11.pdf.

228 *"While no single piece"*: Ibid.

229 *"Anything that disproportionately impacts"*: Quoted in Paul Kane, "Obama Calls for DOJ Official's Firing," WashingtonPost.com, Oct. 19, 2007, voices.washingtonpost.com/44/2007/10/19/obama_calls_for_doj_officials.html.

230 *"voting integrity symposium"*: Amy Goldstein, "Justice Dept. Recognized Prosecutor's Work on Election Fraud Before His Firing," *Washington Post*, March 19, 2007.

230 *"Vote fraud issues are"*: Quoted in "An Investigation into the Removal of Nine U.S. Attorneys in 2006," U.S. Department of Justice, Office of the Inspector General and Office of Professional Responsibility, Sept. 2008, www.justice.gov/opr/us-att-firings-rpt092308.pdf.

230 *"I believe the"*: Ibid.

231 *"As you are aware"*: Ibid.

231 *"Is anything ever going"*: Quoted in Margaret Talev and Marisa Taylor, "Rove Was Asked to Fire U.S. Attorney," McClatchy Newspapers, March 10, 2007.

231 *"He's gone"*: Ibid.

231 *"There was no evidence"*: Quoted in "Phony Fraud Charges," *New York Times*, March 16, 2007.

231 *"effective, well-regarded"*: Quoted in "An Investigation into the Removal of Nine U.S. Attorneys in 2006," Department of Justice.

231 *"mishandled"*: Quoted in "Phony Fraud Charges," *New York Times*.

231 *"It's like the boogeymen"*: Quoted in Art Levine, "The Republican War on Voting," *American Prospect*, March 19, 2008.

232 *"There is widespread but"*: Quoted in Richard Wolf, "Report Refutes Fraud at Poll Sites," *USA Today*, Oct. 11, 2006.

233 *"There is a great"*: Quoted in Ian Urbina, "Panel Said to Alter Finding on Voter Fraud," *New York Times*, Apr. 11, 2007.

233 *"The Fraudulent Fraud Squad"*: Richard L. Hasen, "The Fraudulent Fraud Squad," *Slate*, May 18, 2007, www.slate.com/articles/news_and_politics/jurisprudence/2007/05/the_fraudulent_fraud_squad.html.

233 *"Do we have your"*: Quoted in Clarence Page, "President Bush on Voting Rights: Is He Savvy or Just Clueless?," *Chicago Tribune*, Jan. 30, 2005.

233 *"I thought the president"*: Ibid.

233 *"the party of Lincoln"*: Quoted in Adam Nagourney, "Lost Horizons," *New York Times Magazine*, Sept. 24, 2006.

233 *"By the '70s and"*: Quoted in Mike Allen, "RNC Chief to Say It Was 'Wrong' to Exploit Racial Conflict for Votes," *Washington Post*, July 14, 2005.

234 *"I am here to"*: Quoted in James Thomas Tucker, "The Politics of Persuasion," *Journal of Legislation*, vol. 33, no. 2, 2007.

234 *"He is commonly described"*: Mark Leibovich, "'Pit Bull' of the House Latches on to Immigration," *New York Times*, July 11, 2006.

235 *the Dictator*: Tim Dickinson, "The Ten Worst Members of the Worst Congress Ever," *Rolling Stone*, Nov. 2, 2006.

235 *"not the most civil-righteous"*: Quoted in Tucker, "Politics of Persuasion."
235 *"The Voting Rights Act"*: Senate, *Bills to Amend the Voting Rights Act of 1965*, 1982.
236 *"Like other landmark civil"*: Quoted in Tucker, "Politics of Persuasion."
236 *"the black seat"*: Lori Rodriguez, "Minority Districts in Danger," *Houston Chronicle*, July 16, 1995.
236 *"I believe most of"*: Quoted in Alan Bernstein, "Clinton's Connections Could Propel Him to Primary Win Here," *Houston Chronicle*, Feb. 16, 1992.
236 *"My mom and dad"*: Quoted in Fabrizio di Piazza, "SCOTUSblog on Camera: Edward Blum (Part Two)," SCOTUSblog, Aug. 6, 2014, www.scotusblog.com/media/scotusblog-on-camera-edward-blum-part-two/.
236 *"Even with detailed street"*: Quoted in Gregory Curtis, "Shape Up," *Texas Monthly*, Oct. 1994.
237 *"This didn't happen just"*: Quoted in Fabrizio di Piazza, "SCOTUSblog on Camera: Edward Blum (Part One)," SCOTUSblog, Aug. 5, 2014, www.scotusblog.com/media/scotusblog-on-camera-edward-blum-part-one/.
237 *"I thought that if"*: Ibid.
237 *"Our guiding philosophy is"*: Quoted in Lori Rodriguez, "Redistricting Is New Game Now," *Houston Chronicle*, Jan. 28, 1995.
237 *"bear the odious imprint"*: Quoted in Sam Howe Verhovek, "Redraw Lines of 3 Districts, Texas Is Told," *New York Times*, Aug. 18, 1994.
237 *"the districts' shapes are"*: Bush v. Vera, 517 U.S. 952 (1996).
237 *"a victory for those"*: Quoted in Judy Wiessler, "Justices Quash Racial Districts," *Houston Chronicle*, June 14, 1996.
238 *"moral cause"*: Quoted in Rodriguez, "Redistricting Is New Game Now."
238 *"I didn't really have"*: Quoted in di Piazza, "SCOTUSblog on Camera: Edward Blum (Part Two)."
238 *"In my judgment"*: Quoted in Julie Mason, "Lanier Announces Effort to Defend Contract Policy," *Houston Chronicle*, Aug. 20, 1995.
238 *"We're supposed to be"*: Quoted in Steven A. Holmes, "Broker Asserts Political Views Drew Pressure," *New York Times*, July 10, 1998.
238 LET A THOUSAND BLUMS: "Let a Thousand Blums Bloom," *New York Post*, July 12, 1998.
238 *"Draconian federal intrusion into"*: Abigail Thernstrom and Edward Blum, "Do the Right Thing," *Wall Street Journal*, July 15, 2005.
239 *"The justification for creating"*: Quoted in di Piazza, "SCOTUSblog on Camera: Edward Blum (Part Two)."
239 *"Bull Connor is dead"*: U.S. Congress. House. Committee on the Judiciary, Subcommittee on the Constitution, *Voting Rights Act: Section 5 of the Act—History, Scope, and Purpose*, 109th Cong., 1st sess., 2005.
239 *"The pre-clearance portions of"*: Quoted in Julian Bond, "Voting Rights Act Remains Pertinent," *Atlanta Journal-Constitution*, June 26, 2006.
239 *"Pull the bill"*: Quoted in Tucker, "Politics of Persuasion."
240 *"This rewrite is outdated"*: Quoted in "House Session," C-Span, July 13, 2006, www.c-span.org/video/?193337-1/house-session. Includes statements of Westmoreland, Lewis, and Sensenbrenner.
243 *"This is a historic"*: Quoted in Seth Stern, "Senate Clears Voting Rights Extension," *Congressional Quarterly Weekly*, July 21, 2006.
243 *"The title of the"*: Abigail Thernstrom, "Reviewing (and Reconsidering) the Voting Rights Act," *Engage*, vol. 7, issue 2, 2006.
243 *"For Republicans, uncritical support"*: John J. Miller, "Every Man's Burden," *National Review*, June 22, 2006.
243 *"Today, we renew a"*: Quoted in "As Bush Signs Voting Rights Act Extension, Activists Urge Enforcement," Associated Press, July 28, 2006.

244 *"We needed 218 votes"*: Quoted in Bob Kemper, "Voting Act OK'd in Tense House," *Atlanta Journal-Constitution*, July 14, 2006.

9. OLD POISON, NEW BOTTLES

245 *"What a scene"*: Remarks by Barack Obama, Manassas, Va., Nov. 3, 2008, www.c-span .org/video/?282202-1/obama-speech-manassas-virginia.

246 *"Historic day"*: Quoted in Steve Hummer, Phil Kloer, Jamie Gumbrecht, and Jim Auchmutey, "Citizens Turn Out in Record Numbers to Vote in Epic Election," *Atlanta Journal-Constitution*, Nov. 5, 2008.

246 *"An African-American president"*: Ibid.

246 *"I think the candidacy"*: Quoted in "Big Backer Goes from Clinton to Obama," CNN .com, Feb. 27, 2008, www.cnn.com/2008/POLITICS/02/27/lewis.switch/.

246 *"It is an unbelievable"*: Quoted in Sharon Cohen, "Obama Victory Sets Off Jubilation," Associated Press, Nov. 5, 2008.

246 *"Thank God, hallelujah, hallelujah!"*: Quoted in "'Hallelujah!' Obama's Triumph Brings Joy, Tears Among US Blacks," Agence France Presse, Nov. 5, 2008.

246 *"Sisters and brothers"*: Quoted in "Jubilation Follows Obama Victory," *Grand Rapids Press*, Nov. 5, 2008.

246–47 *"The struggle, the suffering"*: Quoted in Katharine Q. Seelye, "Live Blogging Election Night," Nov. 5, 2008, NYTimes.com, thecaucus.blogs.nytimes.com/2008/11/05 /live-blogging-election-night/comment-page-6/?_r=0.

247 *"Obama's election sent a"*: Quoted in Chris McGreal, "Mississippi Town Breaks with Its Past to Elect First Black Mayor," *Guardian*, May 22, 2009.

247 *"Because of what you"*: Quoted in Carla K. Peay, "Congressman John Lewis Remembers 'Bloody Sunday,'" *Washington Informer*, March 17, 2009.

248 *"Don't tell me I"*: Quoted in "Obama, Clinton Speeches in Selma, Alabama," *CNN Late Edition with Wolf Blitzer*, CNN, Aug. 4, 2007, edition.cnn.com/TRANSCRIPTS/0703 /04/le.02.html.

248 *"one of my personal heroes"*: Remarks by Eric Holder, Washington, D.C., Jan. 30, 2012, www.justice.gov/opa/speech/attorney-general-eric-holder-speaks-justice-department -2012-dr-martin-luther-king-jr.

248 *"I so wish Vivian"*: Quoted in Sebastian Kitchen, "Holder: We're 'Closer to the Dream,'" *Montgomery Advertiser*, March 9, 2009.

248 *"Watching from behind the"*: Quoted in Nina Totenberg, "Civil Rights History Comes Full Circle in Alabama," *Morning Edition*, NPR, March 19, 2009.

248 *"The world that existed"*: Quoted in "Wallace's Daughter Introduces Attorney General at Selma Celebration," *Tennessee Tribune*, March 19–25, 2009.

249 *"the crown jewel"*: Quoted in Scott Sandlin, "Holder Pushes Diversity at Justice," *Albuquerque Journal*, Sept. 4, 2009.

249 *"Under my leadership"*: Quoted in Jonathan Martin, "Holder Vows to Restore DOJ Civil Rights," Politico, March 8, 2009, www.politico.com/news/stories/0309/19756 .html.

249 *"In one snapshot"*: Totenberg, "Civil Rights History Comes Full Circle in Alabama."

249 *"We stand closer to"*: Quoted in Kitchen, "Holder: We're 'Closer to the Dream.'"

249 *"It says that the"*: Quoted in Rachel L. Swarns, "Blacks Debate Civil Rights Risk in Obama's Rise," *New York Times*, Aug. 25, 2008.

249 *"victory in the voting"*: Abigail Thernstrom, "Victory in the Voting Rights Battle," *Los Angeles Times*, Aug. 31, 2008.

249 *"We must commit ourselves"*: Quoted in Philip Rawls, "Black AG, Wallace's Daughter Celebrate in Selma," Associated Press, March 8, 2009.

250 *"Judge Roberts's memos reveal"*: U.S. Congress. Senate. Committee on the Judiciary, *Confirmation Hearing on the Nomination of John G. Roberts, Jr., to be Chief Justice of*

the United States, 109th Cong., 1st sess., 2005. Includes statements of Lewis, Kennedy, Roberts, and Grassley.

251 *"an unconstitutional overextension of"*: Quoted in Ari Berman, "Why Are Conservatives Trying to Destroy the Voting Rights Act?," *Nation*, Feb. 25, 2013.

251 *"Here, as I understand"*: Oral Argument, *Northwest Austin Municipal Utility District No. 1 v. Holder*, 557 U.S. 193 (2009), Apr. 29, 2009. Includes statements of Katyal and Roberts.

252 *"The way to stop"*: *Parents Involved in Community Schools v. Seattle School District No. 1*, 551 U.S. 701 (2007).

253 *"It reminded me of"*: Quoted in Bob Keefe, "High Court Eyes Voting Rights Act," *Atlanta Journal-Constitution*, Apr. 30, 2009.

253 *"threatened to write a"*: Jeffrey Rosen, "Roberts versus Roberts," *New Republic*, March 2, 2010.

253 *"The historic accomplishments of"*: *Northwest Austin Municipal Utility District No. 1 v. Holder*.

253 *"an excellent first chop"*: Quoted in Damien Cave, "Ruling Prompts a Mixed Response," *New York Times*, June 23, 2009.

254 *"poll tax"*: Quoted in Bill Rankin, "Judge Halts Voter ID Law," *Atlanta Journal-Constitution*, Oct. 19, 2005.

254 *"a severe burden on"*: Brief for Petitioners, *Crawford v. Marion County Election Board*, 553 U.S. 181 (2008).

254 *"Let's not beat around"*: Quoted in Adam Liptak, "Fear but Few Facts in Debate on Voter I.D.'s," *New York Times*, Sept. 24, 2007.

254 *"an eminently reasonable effort"*: Brief of State Respondents, *Crawford v. Marion County Election Board*.

254 *"interest in deterring and"*: *Crawford v. Marion County Election Board*.

254 *"The State responds to"*: Ibid. (Souter dissenting).

255 *"comes from Moscow"*: Quoted in "Worst Legislators; Class of 2009," *Texas Monthly*, July 2009.

255 *"with the nefarious purpose"*: Quoted in "Terror Babies?," *Anderson Cooper 360*, CNN, Aug. 10, 2010.

255 *Joseph McCarthy "Have You"*: "The Worst: Debbie Riddle," *Texas Monthly*, June 2003.

255 *"so fast it'll make"*: Quoted in Dave Montgomery, "Republicans Confident of Passing Texas Voter ID Bill," *Fort Worth Star-Telegram*, Dec. 19, 2010.

255 *"She was not only"*: Quoted in Zachary Roth, "Wave of Voter Suppression Measures Targets Latinos," MSNBC.com, March 27, 2013, www.msnbc.com/politicsnation/wave -voter-suppression-measures-targets-la.

255 *"If not for voter"*: Quoted in Mark Lisheron, "Ill Senator Settles In for Voter ID Fight," *Austin American-Statesman*, May 22, 2007.

256 *"In Texas, an epidemic"*: Greg Abbott, "Helping Stamp Out Voter Fraud in Texas," *Hill Country News*, March 10, 2006.

256 *"A lot of blood"*: Quoted in Polly Ross Hughes, "Some Say Voting Law Being Used to Scare Minorities," *Houston Chronicle*, Sept. 19, 2006.

257 *"is now on the"*: Quoted in Justin Rood, "McCain Acorn Fears Overblown," ABCNews .com, Oct. 16, 2008, abcnews.go.com/Blotter/story?id=6049529.

257 *"new Southern strategy"*: Lorraine C. Minnite, *The Myth of Voter Fraud* (Ithaca, N.Y.: Cornell University Press, 2010), 90.

258 *"El Gobernador"*: Paul Burka, "El Gobernador," *Texas Monthly*, Feb. 2008.

258 *"the Hispanic Obama"*: Eric Celeste, "Is Rafael Anchia the Hispanic Obama?," *D Magazine*, May 2009.

258 *"Describe how voter impersonation"*: Quoted in "House Transcript, March 21, 2011," *Texas Tribune*, www.texastribune.org/session/82R/transcripts/2011/3/21/house/. Includes exchange between Anchia and Harless.

259 *"This is what democracy"*: Quoted in "Gov. Perry: SB 14 Takes a Major Step in Securing the Integrity of the Electoral Process," YouTube, May 27, 2011, www.youtube.com /watch?v=tEifLHSJEZM.

259 *"using sheer racism to"*: Quoted in Juan Castillo, "ID Plan Puts Spotlight on Voter Fraud," *Austin American-Statesman*, May 23, 2007.

260 *"Anyone who says all"*: Royal Masset, "The Voter ID Bill Will Kill My Mother's Right to Vote," Quorum Report, Apr. 23, 2007, blog.chron.com/texaspolitics/2007/04/a -republican-his-mother-and-voter-id/.

260 *"The proposal of restrictive"*: Keith G. Bentele and Erin E. O'Brien, "Jim Crow 2.0? Why States Consider and Adopt Restrictive Voter Access Policies," *Perspectives on Politics*, vol. 11, issue 4, Dec. 2013.

260 *"the Lenin of social"*: Quoted in Lewis H. Lapham, "Tentacles of Rage," *Harper's*, Sept. 1, 2004.

260 *"I don't want everybody"*: Quoted in Ari Berman, "The GOP War on Voting," *Rolling Stone*, Sept. 15, 2011.

261 *"a strong step toward"*: Stephen Elzinga, "The Challenge of Photo ID," *Inside ALEC*, June 2009.

261 *"We're seeing the same"*: Quoted in Berman, "The GOP War on Voting."

262 *"We have the worst"*: Quoted in Bill Kaczor, "Teacher: No Way to Comply with New Fla. Voting Law," Associated Press, Nov. 1, 2011.

262 *"good old-fashioned voter suppression"*: Quoted in Berman, "The GOP War on Voting."

262 *"an immediate danger to"*: Ibid.

262 *"No one could give"*: Ibid.

262 *"I think it's great"*: Ibid.

263 *Souls to the Polls*: "'Souls to the Polls' Aims to Turn Out Early Voters in Ohio," Ed O'Keefe, *Washington Post*, Nov. 4, 2012.

263 *"In the races I"*: Quoted in Dara Kam and John Lantigua, "Early Voting Curbs Called Power Play," *Palm Beach Post*, Nov. 25, 2012.

263 *"In record time"*: "Welcome Back, Jim Crow," *Miami Herald*, March 9, 2011.

264 *"Of the 11 states"*: Wendy R. Weiser and Erik Opsal, "The State of Voting in 2014," Brennan Center for Justice, June 17, 2014, www.brennancenter.org/analysis/state -voting-2014.

264 *"There has never been"*: Quoted in Darren Samuelsohn, "Bill Clinton Likens GOP Effort to Jim Crow Laws," Politico, July 6, 2011, www.politico.com/news/stories/0711 /58419.html#ixzz3KONrYrWi.

264 *"allow Governor Romney to"*: Quoted in Kelly Cernetich, "Turzai: Voter ID Law Means Romney Can Win PA," Politics PA, June 25, 2012, www.politicspa.com/turzai-voter-id -law-means-romney-can-win-pa/37153/.

264 *"I guess I really"*: Quoted in Ray Rivera, "Racial Comment by Republican Official in Ohio Rekindles Battle over Early Voting," *New York Times*, Aug. 22, 2012.

264 *"Stop Obama's nutty agenda"*: Quoted in Rebecca Cohen, "S.C. lawmaker admits positive response to racist email on voter ID bill," McClatchy Newspapers, Aug. 28, 2012.

265 *"Generations from now"*: "Remarks by the President Honoring the Recipients of the 2010 Medal of Freedom," Washington, D.C., Feb. 15, 2011, www.whitehouse.gov/the-press -office/2011/02/15/remarks-president-honoring-recipients-2010-medal-freedom.

265 *"Voting rights are under"*: Quoted in "Rep. John Lewis Condemns Voter Suppression in the U.S.," States News Service, July 19, 2011.

265 *"I am concerned about"*: Remarks by Eric Holder, LBJ Library, Austin, Tex., Dec. 13, 2011, www.lbjlibrary.org/events/an-evening-with-eric-holder.

266 *"the most extreme example"*: Quoted in Ari Berman, "How the GOP Is Resegregating the South," *Nation*, Feb. 20, 2012.

266 *"hocus-pocus"*: Ibid.

266 *"Even using the data"*: Quoted in Ari Berman, "DOJ Blocks Discriminatory Texas Voter ID Law," TheNation.com, March 12, 2012.

267 *"I was able to"*: Quoted in "The Voting Rights Act at Work in Texas," Leadership Conference Education Fund, YouTube, Feb. 4, 2013, www.youtube.com/watch?v=qmZq4 -pfGR4#t=63.

267 *"mild, self-deprecating"*: Jodi Kantor and Charlie Savage, "Getting the Message," *New York Times*, Feb. 15, 2010.

267 *"nation of cowards"*: Ibid.

267 *"There's clearly evidence"*: Quoted in Josh Gerstein, "Eric Holder: Black Panther Case Focus Demeans 'My People,'" Politico, March 1, 2011, www.politico.com/blogs /joshgerstein/0311/Eric_Holder_Black_Panther_case_focus_demeans_my_people .html.

268 *"Especially in recent months"*: Remarks by Eric Holder, NAACP Convention, Houston, July 10, 2012, www.justice.gov/opa/speech/attorney-general-eric-holder-speaks-naacp -annual-convention.

268 *"enacted with discriminatory purpose"*: Quoted in Ari Berman, "Federal Court Blocks Discriminatory Texas Redistricting Plan," TheNation.com, Aug. 28, 2012.

268 *"(1) a substantial subgroup"*: Quoted in Ari Berman, "Federal Court: Texas Voter ID Law Violates Voting Rights Act," TheNation.com, Aug. 30, 2012.

269 *"There are forces in"*: Quoted in "Congressman John Lewis at Empowerment Sunday," YouTube, Oct. 29, 2012, www.youtube.com/watch?v=hv8YeRGysrQ.

269 *"This is very, very"*: Quoted in Barry M. Horstman, "Early Voters Brave Cold and Rain and Hours in Line," *Cincinnati Enquirer*, Nov. 5, 2012.

269 *"I was happy when"*: Quoted in Ryan J. Reilly, "Desiline Victor, Obama's 102-Year-Old Voter, 'Shocked' by Scalia's 'Racial Entitlement' Remark," Huffington Post, March 18, 2013, www.huffingtonpost.com/2013/03/18/desiline-victor-obamas-10_n_2901246 .html.

270 *"I want to thank"*: Remarks by the President on Election Night, Chicago, Nov. 7, 2012, www.whitehouse.gov/the-press-office/2012/11/07/remarks-president-election-night.

270 *"The unfortunate reality"*: Remarks by Eric Holder, John F. Kennedy Library, Boston, Dec. 12, 2012, talkingpointsmemo.com/news/eric-holder-speech-at-john-f-kennedy -presidential-library.

272 *"Section 5's federalism cost"*: Quoted in Berman, "Why Are Conservatives Trying to Destroy the Voting Rights Act?"

272 *"The Voting Rights Act is Alabama's gift"*: Ibid.

272 *"a textbook example of"*: Ibid.

273 *"a fox filing a"*: Ibid.

273 *"Texas is under assault"*: Quoted in "GOP Presidential Debate," Fox News Channel, Jan. 16, 2012.

273 *"Rather than heed this"*: Brief of Former Government Officials as Amici Curiae in Support of Petitioner, *Shelby County v. Holder*.

273 *"Far from raising constitutional"*: Brief of Dick Thornburgh, Drew S. Days, John R. Dunne, et al. as Amici Curiae in Support of Respondents, *Shelby County v. Holder*.

274 *"Those Justices recognized that"*: Oral Argument, *Shelby County v. Holder*. Includes statements of Rein, Sotomayor, Verrilli, Roberts, Kennedy, Scalia, and Kagan.

277 *"dramatized the need for"*: Quoted in Berman, "John Lewis's Long Fight for Voting Rights."

277 *"a valid effectuation of"*: *South Carolina v. Katzenbach*.

278 *"One hour ago"*: Quoted in Maria Recio, "Supreme Court Reviews Whether Parts of 1965 Voting Rights Act Are Out of Date," McClatchy Newspapers, Feb. 27, 2013.

278 *"That night was unbelievable"*: Quoted in Berman, "John Lewis's Long Fight for Voting Rights."

279 *"We enforced unjust laws"*: Ibid.

279 *"Whites won't vote for"*: Quoted in Mary Orndorff Troyan, "Minority Districts at Issue in Case," *Montgomery Advertiser*, March 3, 2013.

279 *"Although our nation has"*: Remarks by Eric Holder, Selma, Ala., March 3, 2013, www .justice.gov/opa/speech/attorney-general-eric-holder-speaks-edmund-pettus-bridge -crossing-jubilee.

280 *"examples of progress more"*: Opinion Announcement, Part 1, June 25, 2013, *Shelby County v. Holder*.

281 *"The Court points to"*: Opinion Announcement, Part 2, *Shelby County v. Holder*.

281 *"In the Court's view"*: *Shelby County v. Holder* (Ginsburg dissenting).

282 *"This decision restores an"*: Quoted in Bill Mears and Greg Botelho, " 'Outrageous' or Overdue?: Court Strikes Down Part of Historic Voting Rights Law," CNN.com, June 26, 2013, www.cnn.com/2013/06/25/politics/scotus-voting-rights/.

282 *"Eric Holder can no"*: Greg Abbott, Twitter post, June 25, 2013, 8:02 a.m, twitter.com /gregabbott_tx/status/349543005931311104.

282 *"The Supreme Court did"*: Abigail Thernstrom, "A Vindication of the Voting Rights Act," *Wall Street Journal*, June 26, 2013.

282 *"This decision represents a"*: Remarks by Attorney General Eric Holder, "The Supreme Court Decision on the Voting Rights Act," Federal News Service, June 25, 2013.

282 *"I might not be"*: Quoted in President Barack Obama and President Sall of the Republic of Senegal Hold a Joint Press Conference, Political Transcript Wire, June 27, 2013.

282 *"I know Dr. Martin"*: Quoted in Sebastian Kitchen, "Lawmaker: Martin Luther King 'Turning Over in His Grave,'" *Montgomery Advertiser*, June 26, 2013.

282 *"Disappointed isn't even the word"*: Quoted in Bob Johnson and Jay Reeves, "Ala. Leaders Pleased by Voting Rights Ruling," Associated Press, June 25, 2013.

283 *"I'm shocked, dismayed, disappointed"*: Quoted in Rebecca Elliott, "Rep. John Lewis: Supreme Court Ruling 'a Dagger,'" Politico, June 25, 2013, www.politico.com/story /2013/06/john-lewis-voting-rights-act-supreme-court-ruling-93339.html#ixzz3KPQ gTyJq.

283 *"These men never stood"*: Quoted in Ari Berman, "What the Supreme Court Doesn't Understand About the Voting Rights Act," TheNation.com, June 25, 2013, www.thenation .com/blog/174973/what-supreme-court-doesnt-understand-about-voting-rights-act.

283 *"History did not end"*: *Shelby County v. Holder*.

283 *"the unfounded belief that"*: Brief for the Honorable Congressman John Lewis as Amicus Curiae, *Shelby County v. Holder*.

284 *"a 'fundamental principle of' "*: *Shelby County v. Holder*.

284 *"Shelby County is the"*: James Blacksher and Lani Guinier, "Free at Last: Rejecting Equal Sovereignty and Restoring the Constitutional Right to Vote," *Harvard Law & Policy Review*, vol. 8, 2014.

284 *"relief from a great"*: *Giles v. Harris*, 189 U.S. 475 (1903).

284 *"Perhaps no statute"*: Brief of Reps. F. James Sensenbrenner, John Conyers, Steve Chabot, Jerrold Nadler, Melvin L. Watt, and Robert C. Scott as Amici Curiae in Support of Respondents, *Shelby County v. Holder*.

285 *"This Court's expansive reading"*: Brief for John Lewis, *Shelby County v. Holder*.

10. AFTER SHELBY

288 *"Now we can go"*: Quoted in Gary D. Robertson, "NC Senator: Voter ID Bill Moving Ahead with Ruling," Associated Press, June 26, 2013.

290 *"We / don't need"*: Quoted in "Greensboro Students Protest NC Voter Legislation | North Carolina A&T Bennett College," YouTube, Apr. 24, 2013, www.youtube.com /watch?v=KFBNWJATZXo&list=UUeBaVCo1Abl6J-g5E1x080w.

290 *"We call this restoring"*: Quoted in Laura Leslie, "Tillis: Fraud 'Not the Primary Reason' for Voter ID Push," WRAL.com, March 16, 2013, www.wral.com/tillis-actual-voter

-fraud-not-the-primary-reason-for-voter-id-push-/12231514/#mIptaxLzEkW5g Qqi.99.

291 *"North Carolina has the"*: Quoted in "The Crucifixion of Voting Rights," YouTube, Apr. 12, 2013, www.youtube.com/watch?v=LSJIJ_xTaBw&list=UUeBaVCo1Abl6J -g5E1x080w.

291 *"Dr. King said that"*: Quoted in "Voter ID-Day: Students Protest as Voter ID Bill Passes the House," YouTube, Apr. 26, 2013, www.youtube.com/watch?v=Sasy_L5cLUg&list =UUeBaVCo1Abl6J-g5E1x080w.

291 *"What type of legacy"*: Ibid.

291 *"Ain't gonna let no"*: Ibid.

291 VOTER ID TAKES CLOSER: Rob Christensen, "Voter ID One Step Closer to Become State Law," *News & Observer*, Apr. 24, 2013.

292 *"The legislature is filled"*: Rob Christensen, "'The North Carolina Way' Takes a Sharp Right Turn," *News & Observer*, July 27, 2013.

292 *"Voter ID is the"*: Quoted in "Civil Disobedience Leads to Arrests at NC General Assembly," YouTube, May 3, 2013, www.youtube.com/watch?v=GyIgUz4hgn4&list =UUeBaVCo1Abl6J-g5E1x080w.

292 *"peaceful pray-in"*: Quoted in Ari Berman, "North Carolina's Moral Mondays," *Nation*, Aug. 5–12, 2013.

292 *"It's a whole new"*: Quoted in "Civil Disobedience Leads to Arrests at NC General Assembly," YouTube.

292 *"I was never more"*: Ibid.

292 *"Why We Are Here"*: Quoted in "The Story of Moral Mondays, the North Carolina NAACP and Building the Forward Together Movement," North Carolina NAACP, Jan. 2014.

293 *"It really caught on"*: Quoted in Berman, "North Carolina's Moral Mondays."

293 *"Rosanell, you don't have"*: Quoted in Ed Pilkington, "Woman Who Faced Jim Crow Takes On North Carolina's Powers over Voting Rights," *Guardian*, Sept. 25, 2014.

294 *"I'm ninety-two years old"*: Quoted in "Rosanell Eaton Speech," YouTube, June 25, 2013, www.youtube.com/watch?v=gWtfibuL_tg.

294 *"I just received a"*: Josh Stein's Facebook page, July 22, 2013, m.facebook.com/story.php ?story_fbid=10200895286880231&id=1106786207.

295 *"The first week of"*: Quoted in "New Voting Restrictions in NC: Sen. Stein Questions Sen. Rucho at Committee Hearing," Story of America, YouTube, July 24, 2013, www .youtube.com/watch?v=0w-yCkXXy8A. Includes exchange between Stein and Rucho.

296 *"Justice Robert's pen"*: Quoted in Michael Tomsic, "Sen. Rucho Stands by Controversial Tweet," WFAE 90.7, Dec. 16, 2013, http://wfae.org/post/sen-rucho-stands-controversial -tweet.

296 *"It was designed to"*: Quoted in "New Voting Restrictions in NC: Sen. Stein Questions Sen. Rucho at Committee Hearing."

296 *"It got abused"*: Quoted in "Sen. Bob Rucho Interviewed by Annabel Park," part 2, Story of America, YouTube, June 30, 2013, www.youtube.com/watch?v=Iy3IBz-vZmY.

297 *"Why are you making"*: Quoted in "Sen. Josh Stein Debates Voting Restrictions in North Carolina," Story of America, YouTube, July 30, 2013, www.youtube.com/watch ?v=iMZgQZwVgCM&index=91&list=UUFPJI_tQ37yfocaG6kV6CMA.

297 *"Today we witnessed the"*: Quoted in "6 Arrested in Voting Rights Sit-in—NC Speaker's Office Occupied," Story of America, YouTube, July 25, 2013, www.youtube.com/watch ?v=SUo_NvTpUsA&list=UUFPJI_tQ37yfocaG6kV6CMA.

297 *"I want you to"*: Quoted in North Carolina General Assembly, House, Audio Archives, July 25, 2013, www.ncleg.net/DocumentSites/HouseDocuments/2013–2014%20Session /Audio%20Archives/2013/07-25-2013.mp3.

298 *"deliberative, responsible and interactive"*: Quoted in Gary D. Robertson, "NC House Republicans Lay Out Voter ID Bill Process," Associated Press, March 6, 2013.

298 *"It was the most"*: North Carolina NAACP v. McCrory, 1:13CV861, Transcript of the Preliminary Injunction Motion Hearing, July 7–10, 2014.

298 *"I have been trying"*: Rick Hasen, "Thoughts on the Road Ahead in North Carolina," Election Law Blog, Aug. 12, 2013, electionlawblog.org/?p=54296.

299 *"This is the Department's"*: Remarks by Eric Holder, National Urban League, Philadelphia, July 25, 2013, www.justice.gov/opa/speech/attorney-general-eric-holder-delivers-remarks-national-urban-league-annual-conference.

299 *"Just because you haven't"*: Gov. Pat McCrory, "Why I Signed the Voter ID/Election Reform Bill," News & Observer, Aug. 12, 2013.

299 *"There is plenty of"*: Quoted in Michael Biesecker, "McCrory Not Familiar with All of Bill He's to Sign," Associated Press, July 27, 2013.

299 *"I want to know"*: Quoted in "Original Draft of SNCC Chairman John Lewis' Speech to the March," Aug. 28, 1963, www.crmvet.org/info/mowjl.htm.

299 *"I gave a little"*: Quoted in "John Lewis at March on Washington: 'I'm Not Going to Stand By and Let the Supreme Court Take the Right to Vote Away,'" Think Progress, Aug. 24, 2013, thinkprogress.org/justice/2013/08/24/2523101/john-lewis-march-washington-going-stand-let-supreme-court-vote/.

300 *"I stand here to"*: Remarks by Eric Holder, Washington, D.C., Aug. 30, 2013, www.justice.gov/opa/speech/remarks-prepared-delivery-attorney-general-eric-holder-lawsuit-against-state-north.

300 WELCOME TO NORTH CAROLINA: Quoted in Ari Berman, "North Carolina's Moral Monday Movement Kicks Off 2014 with a Massive Rally in Raleigh," TheNation.com, Feb. 8, 2014, www.thenation.com/blog/178291/north-carolinas-moral-monday-movement-kicks-2014-massive-rally-raleigh.

300 *"The John Lewis Voting"*: Quoted in Ari Berman, "A New Strategy for Voting Rights," Nation, July 22–29, 2013.

301 *"I don't think it's"*: Quoted in Ari Berman, "Election Reform Should Be a Top Priority for the New Congress," TheNation.com, Jan. 23, 2013, www.thenation.com/blog/172385/election-reform-should-be-top-priority-new-congress.

301 *"The Voting Rights Act"*: Quoted in Ari Berman, "Rep. John Lewis: 'The Voting Rights Act Is Needed Now like Never Before,'" TheNation.com, July 17, 2013, www.thenation.com/blog/175336/rep-john-lewis-voting-rights-act-needed-now-never.

301 *"I think our state"*: "Cochran Statement on U.S. Supreme Court Ruling on the Voting Rights Act," June 25, 2013, www.cochran.senate.gov/public/index.cfm/2013/6/cochran-statement-on-u-s-supreme-court-ruling-on-the-voting-rights-act.

301 *"There is no evidence"*: U.S. Congress. House. Committee on the Judiciary, Subcommittee on the Constitution, Voting Rights Act After the Supreme Court's Decision in Shelby County, 113th Cong., 1st sess., 2013.

301–302 *"The decision in Shelby"*: U.S. Congress. Senate. Committee on the Judiciary, The Voting Rights Amendment Act, S. 1945: Updating the Voting Rights Act in Response to Shelby County v. Holder, 113th Cong., 2nd sess., 2014.

302 *"I was devastated"*: North Carolina NAACP v. McCrory, Transcript of the Preliminary Injunction Motion Hearing. Includes statements of Coleman, O'Connor, Eaton, Meza, Russ, Peters, Bowers, Strach, and Coates.

305 *"A preliminary injunction is"*: North Carolina NAACP v. McCrory, 1:13CV861 (M.D. N.C. 2014).

305 *"no record of registration"*: Quoted in Ari Berman, "Hundreds of Voters Are Disenfranchised by North Carolina's New Voting Restrictions," TheNation.com, Sept. 10, 2014, www.thenation.com/blog/181566/hundreds-voters-are-disenfranchised-north-carolinas-new-voting-restrictions.

306 *"While black voters make"*: "Be Prepared: Hundreds of Voters Lost Their Votes in 2014 Primary Due to New Election Rules," Democracy North Carolina, Sept. 10, 2014, www.democracy-nc.org/downloads/DisenfrancVotersPrim2014.pdf.

306 *"Why doesn't North Carolina"*: Quoted in Ari Berman, "Voting Rights Victory in North Carolina," TheNation.com, Oct. 1, 2014, http://www.thenation.com/blog/181831 /voting-rights-victory-north-carolina.

306 *"these measures likely would"*: *North Carolina v. League of Women Voters of North Carolina*, 574 U. S. ____ (2014) (Ginsburg dissenting).

306 *"Because I've earned it"*: Elizabeth Gholar, Oral Videotaped Deposition, *Veasey v. Perry*, 2:13-CV-00193 (S.D. TX 2014).

307 *"Voting is a right"*: Ibid.

307 *"I felt terrible"*: Quoted in Trial Transcript, *Veasey v. Perry*. Includes statements of Carrier, Westfall, and Smith.

308 *"The Court holds that"*: *Veasey v. Perry*, 2:13-CV-00193 (S.D. TX 2014).

309 *"Even after the Voting Rights Act"*: Quoted in Ari Berman, "Voter Suppression Backfires in Texas and Wisconsin," TheNation.com, Oct. 10, 2014, www.thenation.com/blog /181942/voter-suppression-backfires-texas-and-wisconsin.

309 *"now widely regarded as"*: Quoted in John Schwartz, "Judge in Landmark Case Disavows Support for Voter ID," *New York Times*, Oct. 15, 2013.

309 *"The impact of the"*: Quoted in Jess Bravin, "Voter-ID Laws Worry Jurist," *Wall Street Journal*, Oct. 17, 2013.

310 *"It can no longer"*: Eric H. Holder, Jr., "A Breakthrough in the Discussion Around Voting Restrictions," Huffington Post, Oct. 10, 2014, www.huffingtonpost.com/eric-h -holder-jr/gao-voting-restriction-report_b_5965014.html.

310 *"substantially disturbs the election"*: *Veasey v. Perry*, No. 14-41127 (5th Cir. 2014).

310 *"The greatest threat to"*: *Veasey v. Perry*, 574 U. S. ____ (2014) (Ginsburg dissenting).

310 *"It is a major"*: Quoted in Adam Liptak, "Supreme Court Allows Texas to Use Strict Voter ID Law in Coming Election," *New York Times*, Oct. 18, 2014.

311 *"When the voter ID"*: Quoted in Dana Liebelson, "Texans Slam Voter ID Law: 'Now That It's Happened to Me, I'm Devastated,'" Huffington Post, Nov. 7, 2014, www .huffingtonpost.com/2014/11/07/texas-voter-id_n_6117742.html?&ncid=tweet lnkushpmg000.000.16.

312 *"All I want to"*: Quoted in Ari Berman, "Did Voting Restrictions Determine the Outcomes of Key Midterm Races?," TheNation.com, Nov. 6, 2014, www.thenation.com /blog/188697/how-new-voting-restrictions-impacted-2014-election.

312 *"The last time I"*: Quoted in Deon Roberts, "Turnout: NC Sets Record for Midterm Election; Mecklenburg Lines Long," *Charlotte Observer*, Nov. 5, 2014.

313 *"Let us not forget"*: Quoted in "NC Voting Rights: What Is the Status Quo?," YouTube, July 8, 2014, www.youtube.com/watch?v=BAWtx0Xcng4&list=UUeBaVCo1Abl6J -g5E1x080w.

AUTHOR INTERVIEWS

Debo Adegbile, WilmerHale
Archie Allen, Voter Education Project (VEP)
Joaquin Avila, Mexican American Legal Defense Fund (MALDEF)
William Barber II, North Carolina NAACP
James Blacksher, civil rights lawyer
Dan Blue, Jr., North Carolina Senate (NC-14)
Edward Blum, Project on Fair Representation
Julian Bond, SNCC
David Bositis, Joint Center for Political and Economic Studies
Richard Bourne, Department of Justice, Civil Rights Division
G. K. Butterfield, member of Congress (NC-1)
Ramsey Clark, U.S. attorney general, 1967–1969
James Clyburn, member of Congress (SC-6)
Gerry Cohen, special counsel, North Carolina General Assembly
Chuck Cooper, Department of Justice, 1981–1988
Drew Days III, assistant attorney general for civil rights, 1977–1980
John Dean, Department of Justice, 1969–1970
Armand Derfner, civil rights lawyer
Judith Browne Dianis, Advancement Project
Frank Dunbaugh, Department of Justice, Civil Rights Division
John Dunne, assistant attorney general for civil rights, 1989–1992
Rosanell Eaton, North Carolina NAACP
George Evans, mayor of Selma, Ala.
Bruce Fein, Department of Justice, 1981–1982
Luis Fraga, University of Washington
Charles Fried, U.S. solicitor general, 1985–1989
Carl Gabel, Department of Justice, Civil Rights Division
David Garrow, University of Pittsburgh Law School
Jose Garza, MALDEF

Nathan Glazer, Harvard University
Howard Glickstein, Department of Justice, Civil Rights Division
Lisa Graves, Center for Media and Democracy
Lani Guinier, Harvard Law School
Edward Hailes, Advancement Project
Paul Hancock, Department of Justice, Civil Rights Division
Rick Hasen, University of California–Irvine Law School
Gerry Hebert, Department of Justice, Civil Rights Division
Dale Ho, ACLU Voting Rights Project
David Hunter, Department of Justice, Civil Rights Division
Luci Baines Johnson
Gerald Jones, Department of Justice, Civil Rights Division
Vernon Jordan, VEP
Al Kauffman, MALDEF
Robert Kengle, Department of Justice, Civil Rights Division
Randall Kennedy, Harvard Law School
George Korbel, MALDEF
Natasha Korgaonkar, NAACP Legal Defense Fund
Morgan Kousser, California Institute of Technology
Bernard Lafayette, SNCC
Brian Landsberg, Department of Justice, Civil Rights Division
John Lewis, member of Congress (GA-5)
Elliott Lichtman, civil rights lawyer
Ian Haney Lopez, University of California–Berkeley Law School
David Marblestone, Department of Justice, Civil Rights Division
Charles Mauldin, civil rights activist, Selma, Ala.
Thomas McCain, civil rights activist, Edgefield, S.C.
Laughlin McDonald, ACLU Voting Rights Project
Larry Menefee, civil rights lawyer
Ernest Montgomery, city councilman, Calera, Ala.
Heather Moss, Department of Justice, Civil Rights Division
Timothy Mullis, U.S. Civil Service Commission
Cherie Murdoch, VEP
Laura Murphy, ACLU
Victory Navasky, Columbia University School of Journalism
Ralph Neas, Leadership Conference on Civil Rights
Silas Norman, SNCC
Nina Perales, MALDEF
Stephen Pollak, assistant attorney general for civil rights, 1967–1969
Mark Posner, Department of Justice, Civil Rights Division
Donna Pressley, U.S. Civil Service Commission
William Quigley, civil rights lawyer
George Rayborn, Department of Justice, Civil Rights Division
William Bradford Reynolds, assistant attorney general for civil rights, 1981–1988
Joe Rich, Department of Justice, Civil Rights Division
David Richards, civil rights lawyer
Allison Riggs, Southern Coalition for Social Justice
Rolando Rios, Southwest Voter Registration Project
John Rosenberg, Department of Justice, Civil Rights Division
Alexander Ross, Department of Justice, Civil Rights Division
Hank Sanders, Alabama Senate (AL-23)
James Sensenbrenner, member of Congress (WI-5)
Terri Sewell, member of Congress (AL-7)

Karl Shurtliff, Department of Justice, Civil Rights Division
Derick Smith, North Carolina A&T
Paul Smith, Jenner & Block
Brad Snyder, University of Wisconsin
Willie Steen, Florida voter
Josh Stein, North Carolina Senate (NC-16)
Rob Stephens, North Carolina NAACP
Edward Still, civil rights lawyer
Tyler Swanson, North Carolina A&T
Steven Teles, Johns Hopkins University
Jeffrey Toobin, *The New Yorker*
Jim Turner, Department of Justice, Civil Rights Division
Patricia Villareal, Jones Day
Joanne Walker, VEP
Mel Watt, former member of Congress (NC-12)
Barry Weinberg, Department of Justice, Civil Rights Division
Wendy Weiser, Brennan Center for Justice
Jeff Wice, Sandler Rieff
Leslie Winner, Z. Smith Reynolds Foundation
Art Wolf, Department of Justice, Civil Rights Division
Andrew Young, former member of Congress (GA-5)
Ben Zelenko, counsel, House Judiciary Committee
Bob Zellner, SNCC

ACKNOWLEDGMENTS

So many people helped make this book a reality.

Thank you to Ben Wyskida for initially urging me to write about voting rights, to Eric Bates for publishing my first article on the subject for *Rolling Stone*, and to my agent, Nick Ellison, for encouraging me to pursue this topic as a book.

It was a thrill to work with FSG again. Thank you to Eric Chinski for his brilliant editing and insight from beginning to end, to Peng Shepherd for her attention to every detail, and to Lottchen Shivers for spreading the word far and wide.

Thank you to my wonderful friends and colleagues at the Nation Institute and *The Nation* for their longtime support, especially Taya Kitman, Katrina vanden Heuvel, Roane Carey, Richard Kim, Peter Rothberg, and Caitlin Graf.

Thank you to Eyal Press for his invaluable feedback on every stage of this process, from the proposal to the final copy, and to Zachary Newkirk for his tireless research support.

Thank you to the more than one hundred people who agreed to be interviewed for the book, especially Congressman John Lewis. A special thanks to those interview subjects who shared their rich archival material, particularly Jim Turner, Stephen Pollak, and Ralph Neas.

Thank you to Allen Fisher at the LBJ Library, Kayin Shabazz and Courtney Chartier at the Robert Woodruff Library, Elaine Hall at the King Library, and Christina Jones at the National Archives for assisting with my research.

I learned so much from the work of the voting rights historians Steven Lawson, Morgan Kousser, David Garrow, Peyton McCrary, and Gary May.

This book would not have been possible without the support of Bill Moyers, Karen Kimball, Cristobal Alex, Vik Malhotra, Allison Barlow, Angela Kahres, and Karen Narasaki.

Thank you to my parents, Warren and Harriet, and my sister, Ali, for their unconditional love and encouragement.

My wife, Meredith Blake, is my best friend and most trusted copy editor. She always makes sure to dot my i's and cross my t's.

Our daughter, Nora, was born days before I handed in my book manuscript. She is my inspiration to create a better world.

This book is dedicated to my Grandpa Joe, who passed away days after I finished the final manuscript. I wish he could have read the book.

INDEX